"Loyd Allen has done all parents and youth workers a real service. . . . There are a lot of books available about drugs but most deal with the subject either from the viewpoint of street work and counseling or anecdotally. Dr. Allen has given us definitive and well-documented technical information along with some compelling arguments as Christians.

"I would recommend this book highly to parents of young people, but especially to youth workers and parents whose children are involved in some way in the drug scene. I am recommending it to all of our staff in *Youth for Christ.*"

Jay Kesler,
President, *Youth for Christ*

Loyd V. Allen, Jr.

DRUG ABUSE

What Can We Do?

Other good Regal reading:
Alcoholism: The Way Back to Reality by Claire Costales with Jo Berry
Christian Maturity Manual by David Wilkerson
How to Be Fit and Free by Rick Kasper

The foreign language publishing of all Regal books is under the direction of GLINT. GLINT provides financial and technical help for the adaptation, translation and publishing of books in more than 85 languages for millions of people worldwide.
For more information write: GLINT, P.O. Box 6688, Ventura, California 93006.

Scripture quotations in this publication are from the following versions:
NASB, New American Standard Bible. © The Lockman Foundation 1960, 1962, 1963, 1968, 1971, 1972, 1973, 1975. Used by permission;
NIV, New International Version, Holy Bible. Copyright © 1978 by New York International Bible Society. Used by permission.
KJV, Authorized *King James Version.*

Published by Regal Books
A Division of G/L Publications
Ventura, California 93006
Printed in U.S.A.

Library of Congress Catalog Card No. 79-92950
ISBN 0-8307-0744-1

Contents

PREFACE

What Is the Problem?

Drug abuse is not new to society—people have abused drugs for thousands of years and the effects of this abuse are evident in their society. Whether he uses cannabis (marijuana) and opium—naturally occurring drug substances—or the newer synthetic chemicals—PCP and toluene—man seems intent on destroying the body and mind his Creator gave him.

Too many times, parents are suddenly confronted with a situation where their teenager—or younger child—is involved in drug use. These parents have very little knowledge or information about the drugs and their effects on their young people. In other situations parents, in trying to teach their children about drugs, often make statements that are incorrect. Their teenagers know they are incorrect or they find out later. This presents a barrier between the parent and the child because, from the teenager's point of view, "If they were wrong about what they told me about drugs, are they wrong about other things they have taught me?" or, "They are so far behind the times that what they are telling me just doesn't apply to my generation." Often the end result of this is that the teenager will get his drug education from other teenagers, drug pushers, underground newspapers and magazines, or other unreliable sources of information.

As a professor of pharmacy and Director of the Drug Analysis Laboratory at the University of Oklahoma Health Sciences Center, I frequently encounter drug abuse victims as well as their families and friends. The drug problem is *not* decreasing. It is the purpose of this book to provide people everywhere—parents and teenagers—with factual information concerning drugs, their use and abuse, and what we can do to aid those who are involved in abusing drugs. In addition I will attempt to point out what I feel is at the root of the drug problem and what we must do in order to help those we love who are involved in drugs. I feel that we can deal with the drug problem most effectively in a Christian atmosphere and in Christian love.

INTRODUCTION

Why Is It a Problem?

Drugs are substances which by their nature have an effect on the mind or the body or both. There are thousands of drug substances available today. Many of these are safely used in life-threatening situations to restore health to individuals. Many are used to enable us to lead more comfortable, more productive lives when minor ailments cause us discomfort.

The proper use of drugs is good. God has provided us with drugs so that we can maintain or regain a state of health and well-being and enjoy the world He has created for us. Drugs are one of the means by which God heals. The most nearly perfect mechanism is a human body functioning normally. Whenever this mechanism becomes injured or diseased, proper medical care and drug therapy can result in restoration to health.

As it is with most good things, however, mankind tends to abuse and misuse that which was originally intended for our benefit. The misuse and abuse of drug substances has been a problem for thousands of years, and it is a problem of increasing magnitude here in the United States.

SOCIETY CONTRIBUTES TO DRUG ABUSE

Our society is becoming more and more "drug oriented." One doesn't have to listen to radio or watch television very long before he is confronted with commercials for drugs to cure or treat various illnesses and disorders—aspirin for headaches, liniments for sore muscles, sleeping aids for insomnia. In addition, in a dramatic program whenever the star becomes confronted with a stressful situation he immediately pours himself a drink of alcohol. What message is TV transmitting to both children and adults across America? *Whenever you are physcially ill or have a problem (social or otherwise), drugs will help you make it through.* How much exposure to these false teachings can we allow before they start affecting all of our lives? Because our society is becoming more drug oriented, people are using more and more drugs without understanding the consequences.

Whenever the topic of drug abuse is brought up, people immediately think of youth and the drug problem. In reality, the drug problem with adults is just as great if not greater than the youth drug problem. Alcohol consumption is at an all-time high among adults. Tobacco use is extensive. Abuse of legally prescribed drugs is increasing in magnitude. For example, the use of the minor tranquilizers (Valium, Librium) is increasing at an alarming rate. These are legally prescribed drugs that are being grossly abused. Housewives and businessmen are consuming tranquilizers, mood elevators, sedatives, stimulants, and other drugs just to cope with life on a day-to-day basis. How can these individuals set themselves up as moral judges for society? Drug abuse is drug abuse, whether it is among the youth or among the adult population.

Why has every society been cursed with the problem of drug abuse over the years? Why can the problem not be solved?

Before we answer these questions let's look at some of the reasons sociologists, psychologists, political leaders, etc., give for drug abuse.

WHY IS THERE DRUG ABUSE?

Drugs Are Used as an Escape

Many people use drugs to escape problems they encounter every day. By using drugs as a mechanism of avoiding the necessity of tackling daily problems they attempt to lead a "carefree" life.

One of the dangers here is that the problems do not go away. They are still there when the effects of the drug wear off. The drug abuser not only loses his ability to handle his daily problems, but a small problem becomes magnified to gigantic proportions to that person. People who use this method of escape usually will not mature emotionally and psychologically as well as those who handle their problems with their full mental and emotional faculties.

Drugs Are Used as a Form of Protest

When the relationship between a parent and teenager is strained, the young person often indulges in some form of activity aimed at hurting the parent because of his frustrations. By becoming involved in the use of drugs the young person is "getting back" at one of the authority figures with which he does not agree. Being disciplined, whether by parents or some other unit of society (teachers, law enforcers, government, etc.), is a difficult thing to accept, especially in today's world where individual freedom is played up so much. An important point to make concerning freedom, however, is that every free society is free only because of certain limitations imposed upon its members. Also, the use of drugs as a form of protest eventually hurts the user more than the authority he is protesting against.

Drugs Are Used to Relieve Boredom and Frustration

Many individuals are bored and frustrated with their everyday lives. Mechanization and modern-day conveniences have resulted in more free time than ever before. If spare time is not filled with something constructive or meaningful, people may react in a destructive way, such as the housewife who tries to relieve the loneliness and boredom of her day with alcohol. Sometimes they may turn to pacifiers, such as television. When they realize that their lives are not as exciting and dramatic as those portrayed in the programs, they then feel frustrated that they don't measure up to the "ideal" they see on television; sometimes this "ideal" is portrayed even in commercials.

Some people turn to drugs because they have no one for whom they are responsible or nothing worthwhile to live for. They wander from one source of diversion or entertainment to another in hopes of filling the void in their lives. When they eventually turn to drugs these individuals find an exciting alternative—for a few hours. However, after the effects wear off their situation has not changed and they then repeat the drug experience until they are caught up in it.

Some Use Drugs to Experience "Happiness"

What kind of happiness can come from drug use? None! There is only a temporary "high," which some interpret as happiness. Repeated experiences of this type often result in dependence on drugs. Solomon says, "Happy is the man that findeth wisdom, and the man that getteth understanding" (Prov. 3:13, *KJV*). Abusing drugs is not wise and will not bring happiness.

Many Abuse Drugs to Be One of the Crowd

Acceptance by our peers is important to all of us. To be accepted, loved and appreciated is vital to fulfilling the ideals we have for ourselves, but these qualities are not obtained easily and cheaply.

Many will participate in an activity the group is involved in so that they will feel a part of that group, thereby fooling themselves that they are appreciated and loved. Real acceptance, love and appreciation come by being a friend to others, not merely by participating in a group activity.

Participation in sin is more comfortable to the sinner if others are involved. Group beer busts and pot parties are more acceptable than drinking alone or smoking pot alone. Oftentimes much pressure is put on teenagers to be one of the crowd, as if to say, "Everyone is doing it so it must be okay." Anyone not participating in these activities is often called a coward when, in reality, it takes much more courage, determination and strength to say no than it does to go along with the crowd. It is the "coward" who says yes to the crowd; a strong individual says no.

Threat to Emotional Maturity

A special hazard for young users of drugs has to do with the process of maturing. During the teenage years, the physical body is developing and the young person is involved in adjusting to physical, emotional, and psychological changes in his or her life. It is important that he has control of all his thinking faculties so that he can properly handle the daily problems he faces. If he does not learn how to cope with problems as a teenager, he will not be able to cope with them as an adult.

In other words, emotional and psychological maturity comes with tackling our problems every day with full control of our mind and body. If we try to escape our problems through drug use, the problems do not go away and we lose a valuable learning experience. If this is repeated too often, we never learn to cope with the pressures and problems of everyday life. This further complicates the remainder of our lives—job, family relations, social life. As we grow, we need to seek realistic solutions to our daily problems.

Drug Abusers Need to Be Aware of God's Love

All of the reasons for drug abuse I have named are superficial in nature and do not get down to the root of the problem. I believe people abuse and misuse drugs because they do not have a personal relationship with our God.

If we have a close, day-to-day relationship with the person of Jesus Christ we will not feel imprisoned by our circumstances. He promised us that we need not be concerned about the needs and problems of everyday life because "your heavenly Father knoweth that ye have need of all . . . things" (Matt. 6:32, *KJV*). If we are walking in the Holy Spirit we will not need to seek relief from boredom and frustration through chemical alternatives. Everyone has a need for God. He is waiting to help you. Instead of trying to fill your life with worldly desires; turn your life over to Christ and experience the peace, love and joy that only Christ can give.

WHO ARE THE DRUG ABUSERS?

Many drug users are not immature, irresponsible, disadvantaged, immoral, alienated, rebellious, or emotionally ill. Also, many drug users consider the drug effects as pleasurable and continue to use drugs because they want to, not because the drug makes them. Psychological dependence often results when the drug fills a need the person has, or is a people substitute. Individuals will not usually cease their drug use until they find something they can substitute which they interpret to be better.

Not all drug users are at the same level of involvement in their patterns of use. Distinction should be made between the different types of users.

Different Types of Users

The experimenter is an individual who tries

a drug only a few times, often because of curiosity or peer pressure; he does not plan to continue the use of the drug.

The moderate user or *social group user* uses drugs with some degree of regularity, every weekend, or two to three times weekly. However, drugs have not become the most important things in his life.

The chronic user regularly uses drugs and he is drug dependent. Drugs, their use or acquisition, have assumed a central role in this individual's life-style. The chronic user seems to exist for the use of the drug and spends much time in acquiring it and using it.

While it is not correct to say that everyone who experiments with drugs will become either a moderate or chronic user, it is important to know that the chronic user usually began by experimenting with drugs. Also, the individual with the psychological and emotional makeup that leads to experimenting with some of the milder drugs, is the same type of an individual who often will progress on to the stronger or more dangerous types of drugs.

Not every person who uses marijuana will graduate into heroin use; however, often the type of person who starts "playing around" with marijuana will also start "playing around" with heroin and other drugs. The safest thing to do is to not become involved in any type of drug experimentation.

Different Types of Drug Dependence

There are different types of drug dependence that can occur in an individual: psychological drug dependence (habituation) is the psychological or mental desire to repeat the use of a drug intermittently or continuously because of emotional needs; *physical or physiological drug dependence* (addiction) is the actual physical dependence upon the use of a drug—the body actually needs the drug for the individual to function.

A person who becomes addicted to drugs is faced with two problems: (1) developing a tolerance, and (2) withdrawal.

When a drug abuser develops a tolerance it means that his body requires an increasing amount of the drug in order for him to experience the desired effects. Therefore, the addict needs to take larger and larger doses. Tolerance can be due to several physiological factors involving the metabolism and excretion of a drug; but the net result is that the drug is in the body for a shorter period of time and exerts a smaller effect in the person.

Withdrawal is the result of discontinued use. If the user does not get the next dose of his drug within a certain period of time, his body revolts and numerous physical symptoms occur. These vary from drug to drug but often include severe cramping, nausea, vomiting, diarrhea, chills, profuse sweating, muscle cramping, the feeling that tiny bugs are crawling under the skin, and in some cases, death. The onset of withdrawal symptoms varies as well as the duration of their effects. These symptoms are usually relieved by administering another dose of the drug. If the drug is not administered, then the user goes "cold turkey," he begins the process of getting off the drug without medical assistance. Withdrawal can be alleviated in some cases under medical supervision so that the individual can be brought back to normal with less discomfort.

Danger from the Pushers

Another problem often encountered in drug abuse is summed up in the phrase, "What you buy is not necessarily what you get!" Whenever a person buys a drug from a pusher there are no guarantees as to the composition of the material he purchases. Examples of this are plentiful.

One of the more popular sources of information concerning this is the Pacific Information Service on Street Drugs. During one investigation, this organization came up with the following summary.

1. Of over 500 samples sold as amphetamine, less than 40 percent actually contained the labeled drug.
2. Only two-thirds of the drugs sold as cocaine actually were cocaine.
3. Of over 150 samples sold as pure THC, none contained the pure drug.
4. Only about one-sixth of the samples sold as psilocybin or mescaline actually contained either substance.

It should be emphasized over and over that the primary interest of the drug pusher is money. He doesn't really care about you or what you do as long as he gets his money for the drugs he sells. The latest information on drug analyses on street samples shows that over 50 percent of the samples analyzed contained materials other than the alleged drug.

The following chapters will give you a general overview of some of the various drugs in wide use in our nation. We haven't included them all because there are many, and the evil genius of mankind is discovering and creating more drugs and more ways to make money by destroying the youth of the world through drug abuse. "Be self-controlled and alert. Your enemy the devil prowls around like a roaring lion looking for someone to devour" (1 Pet. 5:8, *NIV*).

In the last chapter I have some suggestions for what you can do to help alleviate the drug problem. No one is immune, we are all affected by drug abuse, if not personally or within our own families, we are affected because of the tremendous amount of tax money that is spent each year as a direct result of drug abuse. We have a social, economic, moral and spiritual obligation to fight drug abuse.

Chapter One

Alcohol

The number one dangerous drug in the United States is alcohol. Alcohol is classified as a drug because: (1) it is mood altering; (2) it depresses the central nervous system; and (3) it can induce psychological and physical dependence.

An estimated 100 million persons in the United States consume alcoholic beverages. About nine million of these are addicted, they are alcoholics. Approximately 10 percent of the adult population must, at some time in their lives, seek professional counseling as a direct result of alcohol-related problems. Over one-third of all arrests and suicides, over one-half of all homicides, and more than 25,000 traffic deaths annually are alcohol-related.

Unlike some of the other natural and chemical drugs this book discusses, alcohol is not a new problem. The first mention of alcohol in the Bible is in Genesis 9:21: "When [Noah] drank some . . . wine, he became drunk" (*NIV*).

Alcohol is classified as both a food and a drug. As a food it has calories but no nutritional value. In medicine it is a very effective antiseptic.

There are several misconceptions about alcohol. Some of these misconceptions are: alcohol is a stimulant (it isn't; it is a depressant); alcohol is a food (no nutritional value); it aids digestion; it relieves fatigue; it is harmless. None of these notions is true.

HOW DOES ALCOHOL AFFECT THE HUMAN BODY?

When you take a drink about 20 percent of the alcohol is absorbed directly through your stomach; it does not have to be digested. Your bloodstream rapidly distributes it throughout your body, including your brain. The alcohol acts directly on your brain, causing a decrease in brain activity—thought process, memory, muscle control, speech, etc. The remaining 80 percent of alcohol is processed a little slower, being absorbed throughyour small intestine.

There are several immediate effects you will feel or your body will experience after you drink. You will breathe faster (when you drink a large amount of alcohol you will breathe slower and suffer a slight hormonal imbalance). Your skin will feel warm because your blood vessels will dilate, and your basal temperature will be lowered. You will have to urinate more frequently and sexual ability will decrease. Because alcohol depresses the higher brain centers, the lower brain centers take control resulting in more primitive actions—the embarrassing part of overindulging.

Continuing to drink over a long period of

time can result in heart disease, cirrhosis of the liver, chronic gastritis, muscle tremors, among a few disorders. When a pregnant woman drinks to excess it can result in a characteristic pattern of birth defects, known as the fetal alcohol syndrome. The defects include abnormalities in behavior, in the face and head, and in the limbs and nervous system.

WHY DO PEOPLE DRINK?

The primary reason people drink, of course, is social. In many circles it is considered impolite not to serve some form of liquor in your home and at meals. Liquor is provided at most social gatherings, business functions and luncheons, and nearly every event is preceded by a cocktail hour. Young people begin drinking because it is available and accepted in their homes, or as a result of peer pressure.

Psychologists say that people abuse alcohol because they believe that liquor will heighten their self-esteem, abolish tension and anxiety, dispel the threat of danger, or banish self-recrimination or guilt. They drink in a search for pleasure or to summon courage to do something they believe is wrong.

Some people are able to consume greater quantities of alcohol than others without displaying any obvious effects. However, their bodies still suffer the damage from alcohol abuse. The scientific stages of intoxication are determined by the amount of alcohol concentration in the bloodstream: (1) .05 percent concentration results in a dulling of the capacity for self-criticism; (2) 0.1 percent constitutes a legal drunk; (3) .15 percent concentration causes interference with motor and sensory control; (4) 0.3 percent results in stupor, anesthetic sleep; (5) 0.4 percent causes coma; (6) 0.6 percent, paralysis of the central nervous system and death.

Taking a cold shower, breathing pure oxygen or drinking black coffee do not aid in sobering up; alcohol takes a specific time to be metabolized and cannot be speeded up by these processes.

WHAT DOES THE BIBLE SAY ABOUT STRONG DRINK?

King Solomon, in his proverbs, said a great deal about drinking wine: "Who has woe? Who has sorrow? Who has contentions? Who has complaining? Who has wounds without cause? Who has redness of eyes? Those who linger long over wine, those who go to taste mixed wine. Do not look on the wine when it is red, when it sparkles in the cup, when it goes down smoothly; at the last it bites like a serpent, and stings like a viper. Your eyes will see strange things, and your mind will utter perverse things. And you will be like one who lies down in the middle of the sea, or like one who lies down on the top of a mast. 'They struck me, but I did not become ill; they beat me, but I did not know it. When shall I awake? I will seek another drink'" (Prov. 23:29-35, *NASB*).

"Wine is a mocker, strong drink a brawler, and whoever is intoxicated by it is not wise" (20:1, *NASB*). "Do not give . . . your ways to that which destroys kings. It is not for kings, O Lemuel, it is not for kings to drink wine, or for rulers to desire strong drink. Lest they drink and forget what is decreed, and pervert the rights of all the afflicted. Give strong drink to him who is perishing, and wine to him whose life is bitter. Let him drink and forget his poverty, and remember his trouble no more" (31:3-7, *NASB*).

Isaiah also advised against alcohol abuse: "Woe to those who rise early in the morning that they may pursue strong drink; who stay up late in the evening that wine may inflame them! And their banquets are accompanied by lyre and harp, by tambourine and flute, and by wine; but they do not pay attention to the deeds of the Lord, nor do they consider the work of His hands" (Isa. 5:11,12, *NASB*).

These are just a few of the verses in the Old Testament that warn against the danger of alcohol. Not so much is given in the New Testament—Paul in Ephesians 5:18 exhorts the Christians to "not get drunk with wine, for that is dissipation, but be filled with the Spirit" (*NASB*). What should be the Christian's stand on alcohol? What about Bible wines? Didn't Jesus drink wine? Didn't Paul suggest that Timothy "use a little wine for the sake of your stomach and your frequent ailments" (1 Tim. 5:23, *NASB*)?

WHAT ABOUT BIBLE WINES?

The Bible refers to wine as *poisonous* and *destructive* (see Deut. 32:33; Prov. 23:31,32), but also as a *blessing, comfort,* and *necessity of life* (see Gen. 27:28; Deut. 11:14; Ps. 104:14,15; Joel 3:18); and as the cause of *intoxication, violence* (see Prov. 4:17), *woe* and *sorrow* (see Prov. 23:29,30), and as a *betrayer* (see Hab. 2:5). But wine was also presented at the altar as an *offer-*

ing to God (see Num. 18:12; Neh. 10:37); it is the symbol of spiritual blessing (see Isa. 55:1), but also the symbol of *punishment*, of eternal ruin (see Rev. 14:10; 16:19). Above all, wine is the symbol of the *blood of atonement* (see Matt. 26:26-28; Mark 14:22-24).

Do these blessings and curses refer to the same substance? If Jesus drank wine, and we are to pattern our lives after His, should we not also drink wine? To shed some light on this question let's look at some literary, historical, scientific, archeological and biblical evidence.

The Old Testament was written in the Hebrew language. Several different Hebrew words were used to describe beverages, whether from grapes or other sources. Some of the most common are:

yayin—a general term that means the juice of the grape—fermented or unfermented—usually translated as wine. This word is mentioned about 141 times in the Old Testament (see Deut. 32:33; Prov. 23:30; Ps. 104:15; Hab. 2:5, for example).

tirosh—*must* or fresh grape juice, just squeezed out (see Gen. 27:28; Deut. 11:14, for example).

shakar—usually translated "strong drink"; refers to juice obtained from dates and other fruits (grapes usually excluded) and certain grains, either in fermented or unfermented state; appears 23 times (see Lev. 10:9; Num. 6:3; Deut. 20:6; 1 Sam. 1:15, for example); the context usually uses this word in connection with "wine and strong drink," or, as in Proverbs 20:1, "Wine is a mocker, *strong drink* is raging" (*KJV*), or in Isaiah 28:7 as "strong drink" (*KJV*).

Other words used for wine less frequently in the Old Testament are: *khemer, ahsis, soveh, mesek.*

When these Hebrew manuscripts were translated into Greek, the Greek term *oinos* was used, which closely approximated the term *yayin.* The New Testament, written in Greek, contained the term *oinos* to designate the beverages during this later time period. The problem that has arisen is that these terms were translated into Latin *vinum* and English *wine.*

The term "wine" appears throughout many translations of the Bible, as the Greek manuscripts were used in their translation. The net result is that "wine" has different meanings in Scripture. Wine refers to various beverages: sweet as well as strong; fermented as well as unfermented; intoxicating as well as nonintoxicating.

Another word used in Acts 2:13 is *glūkos,* translated as "new wine."

Two outstanding passages that are often used when Jesus is connected with wine are the wedding at Cana (see John 2:1-11) and the Last Supper (see Matt. 26:26-30). Did Jesus drink fermented wine on these two occasions?

First, there is no indication that Jesus drank any of the water-turned-to-wine Himself at the wedding feast, even if it was unfermented. Second, since *oinos* refers to wine as fresh-squeezed from the grape as well as fermented wine, who's to say which the miracle wine was—grape juice or wine? All the Scripture tells us is that it was "good wine." Third, Jesus performed the miracle not for the purpose of keeping the whole town in a drunken stupor, but to begin

His ministry (see John 2:4).

The other example often used where Jesus is said to have drunk wine is the Last Supper. First, Jesus said that "I will not drink of this fruit of the vine from now on until that day when I drink it new with you in My Father's kingdom" (Matt. 26:29, *NASB*), still no indication that He drank any out of the cup. However, the second and most important consideration here is not whether Jesus drank the wine, but what were the requirements of the Passover Feast. Before the death angel visited Egypt on the night when all the firstborn died, the Israelites were told that for "seven days shall there be no leaven found in your houses . . . You shall not eat anything leavened" (Exod. 12:19,20, *NASB*). This applied not only to the bread which they were to eat at the Passover meal, but also to any leaven in any food. Since leaven and fermentation are achieved by the same process, it is highly unlikely that Jesus served fermented wine to His disciples at the Last Supper.

HOW COULD FERMENTATION BE AVOIDED?

If unfermented wine was a possibility, how did the ancients preserve fruit juice year round without refrigeration, freezing or canning?

Fermentation will normally occur under the following conditions: (1) proper concentration of sugar; (2) presence of yeast or other fermenting agent; (3) suitable temperature; and (4) no material(s) present to hinder fermentation.

Fermentation will *not* take place if (1) a sufficient amount of water is removed, leaving a thick syrup; (2) the (grape) juice is filtered and yeast cells are removed; (3) the temperature is less than approximately 45 degrees or greater than 75 degrees; (4) sulfur, oil of mustard or certain other materials are introduced to the juice.

The ancients did possess the knowledge and ability to preserve grape juice—fresh, sweet and unfermented—throughout the entire year. At least four methods are known to have been used: (1) boiling; (2) filtering; (3) settling; (4) fumigating.

In the first method the fresh juice was boiled until a thick syrup formed. This thick liquid was called *sapa* or *defrutum*, depending on the final concentration. In this state, fermentation could not occur because of the high sugar concentration (similar to a syrup). Today the same principle is applied in preserving certain drugs (cough syrup).

When the family got ready to drink the thick juice, the housewife added water to it and served it. The amount of water she added depended on the thickness of the syrup and the time of year. Aristotle mentions "scraping" wine from containers; Columella speaks of "boiling" wines; Pliny describes wines as being of the consistency of "honey."

The second method, filtering, resulted in removing the yeast that might be present on the skins of the grapes, preventing fermentation. Simple filtration, through sand or other materials, was used then and is still a technique used today to purify liquids. Pliny and Horace both mention preparing wines percolated by the filter and rendered in accordance with nature.

The third method of avoiding fermentation, settling, consisted of placing the fresh juice in a clean container and placing it in a cool place—cave, river, creek or a hole in the ground. After the residue—with the yeast cells in it—settled, the juice was carefully poured off into new or clean containers, leaving the residue at the bottom of the old container. This clean juice could then be stored for a longer period of time.

The fourth method, fumigation, consisted of stopping fermentation by means of introducing sulfur-containing materials—fumes of sulfur, egg yolks or other materials—to the juice. When it was time to drink the juice it was filtered to remove the material.

THE CHRISTIAN'S RESPONSIBILITY

In this chapter on alcohol we have seen that the Scriptures discuss the use of wine. We know that even one drink is excessive for many people—they are alcoholics. But for the most of us, alcohol will never be a problem. So what is our position as Christians towards the non-Christian world and towards our brothers in Christ? Paul, in 1 Corinthians 8:8,9, tells us that "food does not bring us near to God; we are no worse if we do not eat, and no better if we do. Be careful, however, that the exercise of your freedom does not become a stumbling block to the weak" (*NIV*); and again in Galatians 5:13: "You, my brothers, were called to be free. But do not use your freedom to indulge the sinful nature; rather, serve one another in love. The entire law is summed up in a single command: 'Love your neighbor as yourself' " (*NIV*).

Most of the non-Christian world expects a Christian not to drink. Therefore, drinking alcoholic beverages can ruin a Christian witness.

In respect to your brothers and sisters in Christ, consider the new Christian—the babe in Christ, and remember Jesus' words to His disciples: "If anyone causes one of these little ones who believe in me to sin, it would be better for him to have a large millstone hung around his neck and to be drowned in the depths of the sea" (Matt. 18:6, *NIV*).

Chapter Two

Tobacco

"Warning: The Surgeon General Has Determined That Cigarette Smoking Is Dangerous to Your Health." The research in the 1960s into the effects of cigarette smoking resulted in this warning being required on all cigarette packages and advertising. The frightening statistics concerning the physical damage to smokers indicate that millions will die prematurely from lung cancer and heart attacks, as well as other diseases.

However, cigarette smoking is still the most widespread recreational drug abuse in the United States—about a quarter of the country's population, according to the Department of Health.

WHAT IS TOBACCO?

Tobacco is a plant native to North and South America. It is related to the potato, pepper, tomato and the eggplant. The plant grows from small seeds (about 350,000 seeds per ounce) and one plant can yield 1,000,000 seeds. It has broad leaves and a large mature plant can have a leaf surface area of about 25 square feet. The tobacco leaf is picked, dried, cured, stemmed, aged, cased, blended, cut, formed, and packaged.

Columbus found tobacco in use by native American Indians. It was also used by the Aztecs of Mexico and the Incas of Peru. It was smoked in cigars and pipes, chewed and used as snuff. Tobacco was introduced in Europe and elsewhere. Sir Walter Raleigh popularized its use in England. It was used by the well-to-do and fashion dictated its use—if the king used it, other royalty used it also.

Tobacco was grown as a money crop beginning in the 1600s in Virginia and from there its cultivation spread so that today it is found in at least 18 states.

There are basically four types of tobacco: (1) bright or flue-cured, used for cigarettes; (2) burley or light air-cured, used for cigarettes, pipe tobacco and snuff; (3) fire-cured, used for snuff and twistchewing tobacco; (4) dark, air-cured or sun-cured, used for plug chewing tobacco.

Regular size cigarettes are about 70 millimeters in length; *long* cigarettes about 80 millimeters long; *king* size about 85 millimeters, and the newer lengths are 100 millimeters and 120 millimeters, or almost twice the length of the earlier cigarettes.

Why do people start smoking? Several reasons are given: "My parents smoked and I picked up the habit"; "They help my nerves, a kind of a pacifier"; "I feel grown up, it looks cool"; "I like the taste and smell."

Many smokers are victims of "Madison Avenue techniques." In 1977, $779 million were spent on promotion and advertising. Advertisers sell products, in some instances, by finding the consumers' weaknesses and playing on them. Such weaknesses as body consciousness, hostility, shyness, rebellion, awkwardness, and social ineptness are used by the promoters who show that people who smoke are strong, outdoor-type men. Cowboys, jet pilots, professional workers, auto racers, scuba divers, and parachutists are shown smoking and enjoying it. Men easily identify with these images, so they are led to feel that smoking results in these desirable self-images.

Advertisers reach the female population by portraying sexually attractive young women—often in bathing suits or other revealing apparel, independent professional-type women, and sportswomen.

However they are reached and begin smoking, tobacco addicts soon discover they are hooked and have difficulty quitting, even when they want to.

WHAT IS NICOTINE AND HOW DOES IT AFFECT THE BODY?

Nicotine is a poisonous, oily liquid, used widely as an insecticide. Large doses will lead a person to convulsions and death from respiratory failure. Small amounts in smoke are readily absorbed into the bloodstream from the mouth, lungs and stomach (swallowed saliva). Cigarette smoke, in addition to nicotine, includes gases (carbon monoxide, carbon dioxide), particles and tar.

Nicotine and cigarette smoke are physiologically addictive and adversely affect just about every function, every system in your body in many ways. Obvious effects include: nausea—due to a direct effect on the brain; dizziness—due to a direct effect on the vestibular apparatus in the ear; blurred vision—due to decreased blood flow to the eyes; coughing; hoarseness; sore throat; stuffy nose; nasal discharge; irritability. You can develop tolerance to all of these effects to your central nervous system and your respiratory system.

You do not develop a tolerance to the increase in your heart rate and blood pressure. Neither do you develop a tolerance for the deposits of tar in the lungs. It is now a proven fact that smoking cigarettes over a long period of time causes chronic bronchitis, pneumonia, lung cancer, emphysema, coronary heart disease and lung cancer. In fact, if you smoke habitually, you shorten your life by an average of five and one-half minutes for each cigarette you smoke. Nicotine decreases your appetite and also decreases the contractility of the stomach, resulting in stagnation of food. It decreases the blood flow through the stomach and the secretions of mucous which usually serve to soothe and protect the lining of the stomach. In the kidneys, nicotine decreases the rate of formation of urine.

However, if you now smoke, don't feel that all is lost. By quitting the habit there is still hope.

BREAKING THE SMOKING HABIT

More and more people have succeeded in quitting what has been described as one of the most difficult habits to break. *What are some of the immediate benefits of quitting smoking?* (1)

You will have better "wind" for athletic events—or for just walking up a flight of stairs; (2) you will have an all-around healthier "feeling"; (3) food tastes better; (4) flowers, perfumes, etc., smell better; (5) yellow stains on your teeth and fingers will disappear; (6) no more ashes on the floor, furniture, clothes and no more burned upholstery, carpets, clothing (cigarettes are the leading cause of fatal home fires); (7) you will have more money to spend in other ways (at one pack a day you spend over $200 a year on cigarettes); (8) you will be calmer, less nervous. It is true that initially you will be nervous, but this does not last very long. (9) You will smell better and will be readily accepted in any surroundings and by more people; (10) you will feel a sense of conquest because you succeeded in doing something that is really hard.

These immediate benefits of not smoking are attractive, but *the long-term benefits are critical.* (1) Your chances of becoming a victim of heart disease, lung cancer and respiratory disease decrease; (2) you will have fewer absences from work and school due to illnesses associated with smoking; (3) you can lead a busier, more energetic life during your thirties, forties, fifties—and even longer; (4) you will no longer be a slave to a habit that does not enhance your image as a whole person or as a Christian.

Many classes, seminars and books are available to help you quit smoking. Some of the aids they all recommend are the following:

1. Throw away the cigarettes
2. Avoid prolonged association with smokers
3. Keep busy
4. Substitute something else, e.g. chewing gum

5. Do not fall into the trap of "tapering off"; just quit
6. You must want to quit.

What does smoking or not smoking mean to you as a Christian? First, God will *not* love you more if you quit smoking. God's love for you is not dependent upon what you do or don't do. "I am convinced that neither death nor life, neither angels nor demons, neither the present nor the future, nor any powers, neither height nor depth, nor anything else in all creation, will be able to separate us from the love of God that is in Christ Jesus our Lord" (Rom. 8:38,39, *NIV*). That "anything else" includes smoking.

Second, since your body is the temple of the Holy Spirit (see 1 Cor. 6:19) you have an obligation to your Creator to care for it and keep it healthy.

Third, Paul admonishes us as Christians not to put a "stumbling block or obstacle in [our] brother's way" (Rom. 14:13, *NIV*). Even though you may smoke for many years without it seemingly affecting *your* body, you may influence someone else to begin smoking whose health would be damaged by cigarettes—and more than likely he or she could be a person who is very dear to you.

Chapter Three

Marijuana

"Marijuana makes me unable to operate normally—for instance, drive a car or operate a machine."

"It slows me down quite a bit and I lost my initiative when I started to use marijuana."

"I got in quite a bit of trouble while I was high on marijuana; stole to get money to party and to buy marijuana; got involved in gang fights and was arrested twice for rape."

"Under the influence of marijuana, I broke into a church and robbed the collection box."

"You smoke a stick of marijuana in the morning, get lazy on the job and get fired. In my case it led to fixing with heroin."

"Marijuana makes me too generous; I gave away everything I had including money. I would buy drinks for everybody in the bar."

"After starting marijuana, I started doing all sorts of things different. I lost interest in school and sports and was a disappointment to my teachers and my parents. I finally dropped out of school. Before long I started using heroin."

"I did about 15 drugstore robberies for narcotics. My partner and I used to get high on marijuana first."

"It makes me weak, passive, and paranoid, but I don't get into trouble . . . I just want to be left alone where I don't think people are spying on me."

"If I'm in a bad mood it makes me a lot worse. I got out of jail once and my mother was mad at me so I smoked a couple of joints; instead of calming me down, it made me violent."

"I thought I was better at music and typing in high school but it wasn't so . . . I flunked out."

"It made my throat raw and I had hallucinations—I kept trying to brush a spider off my shoulder; I'd see bugs and things like that after only one cigarette. I lost my equilibrium and could not stand up."

"Marijuana causes distortions. Once I hit a fireplug which I thought was a long way off and once I jumped a curb on the freeway and wrecked my car which I never would have done if I hadn't been high."

These are just a few personal descriptions of how marijuana affects the users. Marijuana is the third most widespread recreational drug used in the United States (alcohol and tobacco are first and second) with an estimated 16 million users.

In 1978 a national drug-abuse survey concluded that one in nine high school seniors was smoking pot on a daily or near-daily basis; that pot smoking is now common among junior high students; that pot smoking among 8- to 12-year-olds is increasing.

MARIJUANA OR CANNABIS

Marijuana comes from the plant *cannabis sativa.*

There are about 100 different varieties of Cannabis sativa described around the world. It grows well in temperate and tropical regions and is an adaptive plant. *Cannabis* means "hemp," *sativa* means "planted," and the third descriptive term usually refers to the country of origin—for example, *Americana* for America and *Indica* for India.

Cannabis is an annual plant that reproduces each year from seed. Certain varieties of the hemp type of cannabis can grow at a rate of up to 3.5 inches per day and reach a height of 20 feet. The stalk may be up to 4 inches in diameter and is solidly anchored to the ground. It grows and spreads like a wild weed and thrives in different types of soils. It is attacked by very few insects and survives weather changes well. It possesses a characteristic odor similar to fresh hemp rope when it is growing in fields. This odor is particularly prominent among the flowering tops of female plants.

Cannabis grows wild throughout various regions of the United States—the central plains, midwest, and the east. It is not as prevalent in the western mountainous regions.

Although we are familiar with the terms *cannabis, marijuana* (marihuana) and *hemp* that refer to the plant and plant parts of Cannabis sativa, there are many other terms, depending on what part of the world you are in, that refer to the plant itself, the flowering tops, the leaves, or the resinous material of the plant.

The chief psychoactive component in cannabis is the substance *delta-9-tetrahydrocannabinol*, or THC. The concentration of THC in the plants is dependent upon various genetic and environmental factors. The method of preparation of the different portions of the plants, the process of extraction, storage and exposure to air, moisture, light and heat also determine the ultimate concentration of THC. The THC content is higher in the bracts, flowers and leaves, and lower in the stems, seeds and roots. THC is unstable and starts degrading as soon as marijuana is harvested.

For convenience, cannabis is placed into two categories, based on the THC content. There is the fiber-type of cannabis, usually with a THC content of less than 0.2 percent, and a drug-type of cannabis, with a THC content reaching 5 percent. In 1975, most marijuana grown in the U.S. was of the fiber type with a low level of THC, usually less than 0.1 percent. However, the Department of Health, Education and Welfare reports that by 1979 samples as high as 5 percent THC were common. Countries growing the drug-type cannabis include Mexico, Thailand, Panama, Columbia, India, and Africa.

It is not uncommon for the marijuana sold in the United States to be diluted or "cut" with other materials—alfalfa, lawn clippings, or oregano. Of the cannabis confiscated by the Federal Bureau of Narcotics and Dangerous Drugs in 1970, over 12 percent did not contain any intoxicating material, just the diluting material.

WHAT IS THE HISTORY OF MARIJUANA?

Marijuana is not new as a drug of abuse. Its recorded use dates back almost 4,000 years when an emperor-pharmacist in China, Shen Nung, advocated its use as an all-purpose medication and as a sedative. However, cannabis was not used extensively in China as a psychoactive substance. From China, the use of cannabis spread to India and neighboring Asian countries.

In India, the use of cannabis was originally limited to the priests for the performance of religious rituals in the temples. Banghu (cannabis) was referred to as a sacred grass in the *Atharva Veda*, a religious book. It was also referred to by several synonyms that describe its mind-altering properties. The use of cannabis then spread to the common class of people where it was used as an intoxicant. The early Hindus proclaimed the use of cannabis in the treatment of catarrh, leprosy, fever, and for creating energy and stimulating the mind. Additional uses by the Hindus and the Muslims included the treatment of constipation, dandruff, hemorrhoids, obesity, asthma, urinary tract infections, loss of appetite, inflammation, and cough. It is felt by some that the introspective, meditative aspect of the yogi culture is due in part, to the influence of this drug.

The use of cannabis spread to surrounding countries—Assyria, Persia, and the Middle East. It appears that the Egyptians and Hebrews knew nothing of cannabis as it is not mentioned in the hieroglyphic texts or in Old Testament Scriptures. The Egyptian tombs have revealed no cloth made of hemp.

In the Middle East cannabis met little cultural opposition since the Muslim religion forbids the use of alcohol but is not specific concerning other intoxicants such as cannabis.

Cannabis was introduced into Egypt as hashish in the thirteenth century, according to the historian, Magrizy. The common people followed the lead of the wealthy and sought intoxication by the use of cannabis extracts. Cannabis became known throughout Egypt as the grass of the poor. The introduction and widespread use and acceptance of hashish in Egypt precedes and parallels the beginning of a long period of economic, social, moral, and cultural decay under the Mamelouk dynasties (1250-1517).

In Egypt, during the fourteenth century, the emir ordered all cannabis plants uprooted and destroyed. He also condemned some cannabis users to have their teeth extracted; other offenders were jailed. The social use of cannabis was too ingrained in the society and these measures were ineffective. In 1800 when Napoleon conquered Egypt he was astonished at the extent of cannabis use and observed the general stagnation of the people. He related the stagnant society to their use of cannabis and forbade its use any longer. The decree failed, as did many others before and after. To this day, cannabis is a widely abused drug among the Muslim population.

Historically, societies in which cannabis has become socially accepted tend to become degraded socially, economically and politically. Many political leaders, past and present, are aware that the universal use of social intoxicants is not conducive to a thriving, energetic, ambitious society.

Marijuana and the United States

Hemp was widely cultivated as a fiber crop in

the United States by early American settlers. It was used in making ropes but was not used as a mind-altering drug at that time. It is felt by many that the reason it was not used by the early settlers is that the life-style of the marijuana user is incompatible with the hardy, robust life led by these people during the early, formative years of our nation. Cannabis, as a mind-altering drug, was introduced into the United States from Mexico around 1910. Mexican farmers began smuggling it across the border and its use was primarily limited to the poor black and Mexican workers in Texas and Louisiana. A few years later, New Orleans became the primary port of entry for cannabis and it made its way up the Mississippi River and from there to the larger cities. The drug was available in most larger cities by 1930 but was mainly used by jazz musicians and minority groups.

The Federal Bureau of Narcotics became concerned with the danger that cannabis intoxication might bring to the individual and society. The bureau proposed the Marijuana Tax Act of 1937 that made illegal the cultivation, possession, or distribution of the drug. The bureau was concerned with the potential abuse of the more potent forms of cannabis (hashish), that were used in the East and were associated with many negative effects in the individual and in society. According to their point of view, how could hashish be forbidden if marijuana was accepted? If one considers other social intoxicants, the unimpeded use of the milder form often results in the introduction of the stronger forms. For example, many people who start drinking beer and wine progress to the distilled spirits; and the user of opium to heroin. It does not take any imagination to see the extent of the problems associated with these in our society.

After the passage of the Marijuana Tax Act, the next significant event concerning cannabis occurred in New York City. Because of an extensive problem with marijuana use in Harlem, Mayor LaGuardia requested the New York Academy of Medicine to conduct a scientific and sociological investigation into marijuana usage. The results of the report were released in the early 1940s. But the nation was involved with World War II; therefore, the marijuana issue subsided. During the war, hemp was cultivated commercially in some countries to provide rope for the armed forces.

When the post-war generations entered high school and college, the marijuana debate began again on a wider scale. As time passed, the ideals of church, family, and country did not inspire and motivate young adults and young people as they did in the past. Many were discouraged with a materialistic society. Most of their basic needs—food, clothing, and shelter—were abundantly provided for them and they sought to demonstrate the futility of their basic ideals. There were ill feelings with the Vietnam war, a consumer society, and economic and social inequalities. The use of cannabis became a means of rebellion, a pastime, and a sign of independence. Open support for the use of cannabis came when professor Timothy O'Leary and poet Alan Ginsberg proclaimed the "harmless" nature of the drug. It was used openly by musicians at rock concerts, which had an influence on their enthusiastic followers. Cannabis use has steadily increased in the United States to the point where many individuals use it either socially—several times a week—or regularly—several times a day.

Marijuana and Other Countries

The U.S. is not alone in facing the cannabis problem. Cannabis preparations are still widely used in the Muslim countries, in spite of restrictive legislation, including Iran, North Africa, Syria, Lebanon, and Turkey. In addition, cannabis abuse is found in the U.S.S.R., Afghanistan, Israel, Egypt, Tunisia, Algeria and Morocco. Cannabis smoking is prevalent from Tanzania to Mozambique, in Liberia, the Congo, and from Rhodesia to Zambia. Many smoke the cannabis in calabash pipes made of clay, or use it in water pipes.

Cannabis has been cultivated in Europe and in England since the Christian era. It has been used as a source of fiber for ropes and clothing but it was not used for its psychoactive properties until the middle of the twentieth century. It was used as a mind-altering drug by a significant section of the European population in the 1950s. This is attributed to long working hours and the depressed social environment during the post-World War II years as many of the people were involved in industrial and construction work. Later, the younger generation became interested in cannabis as a new experience, partially due to the erosion of traditional religious values, the erosion of family and home life, and a general permissive attitude. The use of cannabis is most prevalent today in Great Britain among high school and university students.

During the '60s, cannabis extracts became widely used among young people of college age in the large cities of Western Europe, especially Sweden and Denmark. Cannabis use is not as pronounced in France, Germany, Spain and Italy. The U.S.S.R. evidently has a problem with cannabis; however, they don't admit it publicly. Many individuals feel that whatever happens in the U.S. will be an important factor in what happens in many other parts of the world.

Government Attention to Marijuana

The Indian Hemp Drug Commission (1893-1894) was the first appointed commission to receive the charge to evaluate the physical, mental, and moral effects of cannabis intoxication on the people of India. The commission's work was based on the testimonials of 1193 "witnesses." These included 335 physicians as well as people right down the economic scale to illiterate peasants. The witnesses were asked to respond to seven questions. The answers made up the evidence for the commission. The medical witnesses gave opposing and conflicting views within their own group which led the commissioners to conclude that it was impossible to obtain accurate records and statistics or reliable information.

To further confuse their work, the secretary of state, when giving the charge to this commission, warned that prohibition of marijuana might represent an "unjustifiable interference and that repressive laws might be impossible to enforce." Cannabis had an accepted place in the social and cultural life of India and was regarded as a holy plant. Therefore, the commission was warned that any report that conflicted with the cultural traditions of India was not desired.

The commission was in an impossible situation and, as a result, gave cannabis the benefit of a doubt and, in essence, discarded the case against the drug. Many American writers today continue to quote the scientifically unjustified conclusions of the Indian Hemp Commission and claim that the findings were "impartial," relevant to the United States today and the most authoritative available.

The LaGuardia Report (1940-1941) was presented to the New York Academy of Medicine in 1938. The subjects in this study were prison inmates, some users and some nonusers in different experimental groups. The crude plant or alcoholic extracts were used but the concentration of the active ingredients could not be measured. Some of the test results revealed (1) impaired mental and motor performance, (2) the development of tolerance to the drug, (3) tachycardia and conjunctival congestion and (4) the fact that cannabis produces its effect more rapidly when it is smoked than when it is ingested orally.

There were several problems associated with this report. One is that there were no dose-response curves correlating the quantity of the drug or active component to the actual physical or psychological effect. In addition, there are contradictory statements in the report that are misleading. The results of this report and the conclusions contained therein apply only to the relatively inactive cannabis preparations in use in New York City in the early 1940s.

Egyptian President Nasser appointed a

scholarly committee to study the effects of hashish use on the Egyptian population. This ongoing study has been under way since 1957 at the National Center for Social and Criminological Research in Cairo. The findings of these standardized experiments, performed by trained psychologists, have been published.

Their results reveal that a significant fraction of young adult Egyptian males use hashish. These users are more neglected by their parents and are more "anxious." They tend to develop a psychological dependence upon the drug and have great difficulty in discontinuing its use. They exhibit an impairment of memory, randomized ideas, and difficulty in concentration. They also exhibit poor work performance—both in quality and in quantity—and are slow learners. This was perhaps one of the most comprehensive studies on cannabis but it has been largely ignored by the President's Commission Report on Marijuana in the United States.

The Chopra Studies (1969) were conducted over a period of 30 years by Chopra, an Indian pharmacologist and physician. These studies contain questionable methodology and are difficult to evaluate. However, much can be learned by reading the results of his work. The cannabis preparations utilized were obviously more potent than those used in the LaGuardia studies, as the responses of the subjects were quite different. A summary of Chopra's studies could be stated as follows: the typical cannabis (ganja) abuser is emaciated, thin, and lacks general vitality; bronchial irritation and chronic laryngitis is common among excessive smokers of cannabis; Chopra also states that occasional and moderate use of cannabis does not affect physical health, however, he does not define moderate use. Chopra goes further to state that he does not feel that cannabis abuse leads to violent crime but, instead, to physical and mental deterioration with eventual social effects.

The National Commission on Marijuana and Drug Abuse was established by the Congress of the United States in 1970. The purpose of the commission was to study and investigate the causes of drug abuse and their significance. The first report was published in 1972. The most recent (at the writing of this book) conference on marijuana abuse was the National Institute of Drug Abuse which met in March 1979 in Virginia.

In July 1978 the International Symposium on Marijuana held in Reims, France presented evidence collected by some 50 researchers from 14 countries. Their study included the effects of marijuana on reproduction, lungs, cellular metabolism and the brain. Their evidence shows that pot smokers may be unwittingly damaging their brains, and decreasing their chances of conceiving and producing completely healthy offspring.

THE EFFECTS OF MARIJUANA

Marijuana produces a multitude of effects in its subjects. These have been described historically by many individuals. Over its nearly 4,000-year history, the drug has been used for the treatment of many disorders—pain, insomnia, overweight, underweight, constipation, diarrhea, hemorrhoids, dandruff, urinary tract infections, cough, bronchitis, asthma, dysentery, and others. Even today, marijuana advocates continue to extol its supposed beneficial effects.

Marijuana can be introduced into the body by various means. Formerly, it was taken orally in the form of an extract, prepared as a beverage or candy. Today it is inhaled in the form of smoke. It is approximately three times as potent when it is smoked as when it is ingested orally and the individual will start experiencing an effect in about 15 minutes; the effects will last from two to four hours. Many individuals experience nothing the first time they use marijuana, due either to inexperience or the lack of THC in the preparation.

The effects on the user depend upon many factors: the amount of THC present, the dose of the drug, route of administration, rapidity of smoking and depth of inhalation if smoked, the experience of the user, mood of the user and the environment in which the drug is ingested.

The deeper the person inhales and the longer he holds the smoke in his lungs, the greater will be the effect of the drug. As a user becomes more experienced in the use of marijuana, he can more easily adjust his response by altering these variables. His mood and his expectations concerning the experience affect his response to the drug. One who is in a more passive and expectant frame of mind will tend to obtain a greater effect from the drug than one who is agitated, with many thought processes occurring. An environment of dim lights, music and, oftentimes, flashing lights lends itself to a greater effect than a cold sterile environment of a well-lighted, properly arranged room. Undoubtedly there are other factors influencing response, such as preexisting mental conditions, emotional disorders, and concurrent usage of other drugs.

To others, the marijuana user in the early stages of intoxication may appear animated with rapid, loud talking and bursts of laughter. In the later stages, he may be sleepy or stuporous. His pupils are usually dilated; he has an odor similar to burnt rope on his clothing or breath; he may have remnants of marijuana, either loose or in partially smoked joints, in his clothing or pockets. Unless he is under the influence of the drug, it is oftentimes difficult to detect a user.

Normally the effects of marijuana include a rapid heart rate, redness of the eyes, dryness of the mouth and throat, nausea, vomiting, dizziness, increased appetite, an altered state of consciousness, illusions or hallucinations, mood alterations, and disturbed perceptions regarding a distortion of the senses of time and distance. The latter two are especially common and are part of the reason individuals under the influence of marijuana should not drive.

The more potent forms of cannabis, such as hashish or charas, when ingested in large doses, can produce panic states, fear of death, illusions, dual personality, impulsive behavior, toxic psychosis, the speaking of random ideas, and hearing and visual hallucinations. These effects are not common in the U.S. due to the fact that the cannabis preparations used here are less potent. They do occur, however, in other countries where more potent forms are prevalent.

What Happens with Long-Term Use of Marijuana?

With moderate usage (social usage) over a

prolonged period of time the marijuana user tends to develop the following characteristics:

1. He becomes indolent and nonproductive in society.
2. He shows neglect of personal hygiene and does not care for himself properly.
3. He loses interest in vocational tasks and recreational pursuits.
4. His intellectual functions, his learning and memory ability, become impaired.

For the most part, these individuals are not aware these changes have occurred in their lives and are very hesitant to admit it. It is quite possible that it is in this area that some of the very real dangers of marijuana lie. What type of society will result when marijuana is used throughout the society as a social intoxicant?

How Does Marijuana Affect Performance and Learning?

THC has an affinity for fatty tissue. Two specific areas in the body with high fat content are the brain and the sex organs. Marijuana's 10 cannabinoids are soluble in fat and are attracted to the body's fatty organs. It can take from five to eight days for only one-half of the THC in a single marijuana cigarette to clear from the fatty portions of the body.

The effect of marijuana on the brain results in impairment of mental processes—learning, mood, memory, speech, etc. One scientist's study over a period of several years indicated that marijuana users displayed poorer performance in five psychological functions: (1) speed of psychomotor performance; (2) estimation of distance; (3) estimation of time; (4) immediate memory for digits and designs; and (5) visual-motor coordination.

The December, 1979 issue of *Reader's Digest* told about one tall, handsome teenager who complained about problems he was having in concentration and memory. He said he felt "bummed out all the time." An electroencephalogram (EEG) revealed he had brain impairment. In fact, his brain-wave readings were typical of those of a 6- to 8-year-old. A chronic (daily or near-daily) pot smoker, his doctor advised the young man to give up marijuana for two months. At the end of that time his EEG was better but not yet normal. After another two months his report was "within normal limits for his age."

The doctor made further study and experimentation with 43 "typical" teenagers. After smoking marijuana for four months all 43 tested out as being "markedly immature" and indicated diffuse brain impairment.

Other reports indicate that short-term memory may be impaired for several years, or even permanently, after a five-year period of smoking marijuana.

Does Marijuana Affect Chromosomes and Reproduction?

The most terrifying results of marijuana abuse are beginning to show up in the testing of its effect on sex and the reproductive organs.

For example, as little as a billionth of a gram of THC affects the hypothalmus—a small lump of tissue in the center of the brain that is connected to the pituitary gland. The pituitary regulates endocrine functions and the hormones controlling sex and reproduction.

It has now been revealed that young women who smoke marijuana undergo menstrual cycle changes that could affect the nourishment of a growing embryo. Also the women have a decrease in prolactin, a hormone important in milk production. It has been proven that THC accumulates in the ovaries, as well as other organs.

Not only does marijuana adversely affect the reproductive systems of women but evidence is increasing that men may also suffer from marijuana abuse. Animal experiments indicate that THC can reduce the sperm count and cause a greater number of abnormally shaped sperm.

Dr. Gabriel Nahas, of Columbia University College of Physicians and Surgeons, warns, "Today's pot smoker may not only be damaging his own mind and body, but may be playing genetic roulette and casting a shadow across children and grandchildren yet unborn."

Does Marijuana Affect Driving?

The smoking of marijuana has a detrimental effect on driving skills and performance. And this effect is even greater when the user is driving under stress as compared to driving under normal circumstances.

In 1975, the Boston University Traffic Accident Research Team surveyed 267 drivers that were considered "most responsible" for fatal accidents. Of the 267 drivers, 16 percent had been smoking marijuana prior to the fatal accident. A California study indicated that 16 percent of 1,792 drivers who were arrested as the result of accidents, had sufficient THC in their blood to constitute marijuana intoxication. Fewer than half of those arrested agreed to give a blood sample, so 16 percent is a conservative estimate.

The effects of marijuana on driving are predicted to be even more dramatic under the following situations: (1) the user *drives at night*, which is usually more stressful than daytime driving; (2) *alcohol is taken* in combination with marijuana; (3) *larger doses* of marijuana are taken just before driving; (4) he drives at *high speeds* which may depend on sharper reactions and decision-making. Since performance of the user is still unknown under these situations, study indicates that driving under the influence of marijuana should be avoided as much as should driving under the influence of alcohol.

Marijuana has been implicated in automobile accidents several times. One such occasion was when a 19-year-old male was killed when his car collided head-on into a truck while he was attempting to pass another automobile. Inspection of the car revealed packets of marijuana, and a high level of THC was found in the youth's blood and urine. Other investigators have estimated that marijuana use increases the risk of being involved in fatal accidents three and one-half times.

How Does Marijuana Affect Pilots?

Ten certified pilots participated in one research study. During their operation of a flight simulator, all 10 pilots showed a significant decrease in flying performance 30 minutes after smoking active marijuana. They experienced the greatest difficulty in short-term memory and in their sense of time. They often forgot where they were in a given flight sequence and had difficulty remembering how long they had been in a given flight sequence. The pilots also experienced alterations in concentration and attending behavior; for example, they would concentrate on one variable at the expense of other variables. Upon realizing what had occurred, they over-controlled or over-compensated in order to make the adjustment. They also exhibited a complete loss of orientation at times with respect to navigational fix.

What Effect Does Marijuana Have on Breathing?

Smoking marijuana definitely has an effect upon a person's ability to exchange air in his lungs. He suffers approximately a 10 percent decrease in his ability to force out air from his lungs, to breathe in fresh air, and in the amount of oxygen diffused into his blood. There appears to be a significant correlation between the quantity smoked and the degree of functional impairment. Some of these changes appear to be somewhat irreversible.

Additional study on lung function has been reported, especially relating to the carcinogenic compounds contained in marijuana. Two studies in one journal reported that when human lung explants were exposed to fresh marijuana smoke and tobacco smoke, there were alterations in DNA and chromosomal complement. It was suggested that this change may be indicative of an early state preceding malignancy.

Another earlier report states that there is a significantly higher concentration of some carcinogenic compounds in marijuana as compared to tobacco. The concentration of benzopyrene, a potent carcinogen, is almost double that contained in tobacco. This, coupled with the fact that marijuana smokers inhale deeply and hold the smoke in their lungs longer, leads many to feel that there is a greater hazard of cancer with a marijuana smoker as compared to a tobacco smoker.

How Does Marijuana Affect the Eyes?

There are numerous reports concerning the effect of marijuana on the eyes. Some of these are conflicting in nature. For example, there was a discussion of the decrease in intraocular pressure induced by marijuana and the observation that upon chronic use, there was a resultant increase in intraocular pressure (glaucoma). Another report revealed a 20 percent decrease in intraocular pressure with no tolerance after 60 days usage.

Another publication reports numerous cases of paralysis of one of the muscles controlling the eye. The authors attribute this effect possibly to the observation that higher levels of marijuana constituents persist in the spinal fluid and brain tissue for a longer time than in any other organ tissue.

How Does Marijuana Affect the Cardiovascular System?

There have been numerous articles concerning the blood and the heart, and marijuana. A reduction in blood platelets was reported in animal as well as in human blood. The effects of marijuana on the heart have been described as an elevation in heart rate and pulse rate. One study showed that tolerance develops to this effect. Impaired circulatory responses to standing, exercise, and other tests suggest sympathetic insufficiency, or an inability of the body to maintain adequate blood pressure to assure that blood reaches all parts of the body in sufficient quantity. These investigators also reported a marked weight gain related to fluid retention and plasma volume expansion.

WHAT DOES RECENT RESEARCH ON MARIJUANA REVEAL?

The active ingredient in marijuana, THC, was not isolated until 1965 at the Laboratory of National Products of the Hebrew University in Jerusalem by two investigators. The isolation of this substance gave researchers the material and the impetus to perform more scientifically valid investigations on marijuana. One of the major problems with the research to this point was the fact that the potency of the marijuana which was used in the studies had not been determined, as the active ingredient had not yet been isolated. However, during the past 15 years there has been a great deal of research on the effects of marijuana. For example, physicians who have observed marijuana users over a long period of time are now convinced that the drug does produce psychological and physical dependence, whereas it was not thought so before. These physicians have watched many young people go through the effects of withdrawal after long-time use—anxiety, sleeplessness, sweating, lack of appetite, nausea, and general malaise.

One physician reported on the effects marijuana had on a boy who began smoking pot when he was in the ninth grade. A good student, baseball player, gifted artist and very dynamic, after about a year of heavy marijuana use he lost interest in everything except getting high on pot. He was expelled from school, left home and wandered for months until his father found him and placed him in a psychiatric institution. The hospital discharged him after six months. Ten years later the boy was still wandering aimlessly with nothing to look forward to, unable to make any contribution to anyone or anything.

ARE THERE ANY POSITIVE USES OF THC?

Scientific pharmacological and medical investigations are underway in the areas of the ophthalmic effects of marijuana, pulmonary and preanesthetic effects, effects on mental functioning, antiemetic effects in cancer, antitumor effects, anticonvulsant effects, and the pharmacological effects of the synthetic cannabinoids.

For ophthalmic effects, *intraocular pressure reduction* is now an accepted effect of some of the newer synthetic cannabinoids. When a safe, long-acting, topically applied ophthalmic preparation is developed that does not result in tolerance, it may become a useful marketed medication.

As an antiasthmatic agent, patients seem to respond to aerosolized THC and selected synthetic cannabinoids. Smoking marijuana does not appear to be an effective method of asthma treatment because it is so irritating.

Additional studies are underway to investigate the safety of long-term administration of these drugs and their bronchial and systemic effects.

In treating cancer patients it is still too soon to determine whether THC can assume a role in the treatment of nausea and vomiting in patients undergoing cancer chemotherapy. In these patients the usual antiemetics are not very effective and newer agents are being investigated and welcomed.

Animal data concerning the *anticonvulsant activities of marijuana* and its derivatives are encouraging, but there is not much recent work on this effect in humans, and the finding that THC is also a convulsant in some animals makes any conclusion premature at this time.

In many conditions, experiments involving marijuana are ambiguous and the results are not thoroughly proven. Among these are the use of THC as a hypnotic, chemotherapeutic agent, as an antidepressant, analgesic, preanesthetic agent, and in the treatment of alcoholism. Certain of these therapeutic indications appear to be more likely to result in a marketed cannabinoid analogue product than others.

One should not expect to see a commercially available cannabinoid for medical use in the very near future because of the time required for the approval process of a new drug. If a product is marketed it will more than likely need to follow certain requirements that most drugs follow: it must produce primary therapeutic effects and minimal side effects; it must be stable for storage and easily formulated into dosage forms.

Some of the undesirable side effects of marijuana need to be minimized or eliminated altogether. These include nausea, psychological effects, gastrointestinal effects and cardiovascular effects. THC is a relatively unstable compound and newer chemically related compounds with greater physicochemical stability will need to be developed prior to marketing. Some of the newer cannabinoid derivatives are more water soluble, resulting in more reliable absorption from the gastrointestinal tract and making injectable dosage forms more convenient.

Marijuana, per se, will probably never be used extensively medically because its preparations contain many constituents with undesirable side effects. If a cannabinoid is marketed in the future it will probably be a synthetic analogue, tailored to produce a specific effect, and without the psychological actions of present-day marijuana dosage forms.

Slang Terms for Marijuana

Acapulco Gold
Baby
Bale
Bhang
Broccoli
Canadian Black
Dagga
Duby
Fu
Fumo d'Angola
Frifa
Friffo
Gage
Gangster
Giggle Weed
Golden Leaf
Grass
Green
Grefa
Greta
Gunga
Gungeon
Haircut
Hay
Hemp
Herb
Indian Hay
Indian Hemp
Intsaga
Intsangu
Jive
Juanita
Kief
Kif
Kilter
Light Stuff
Loco
Locoweed
MJ
Macon
Maconha
Mary Jane
Mexican Brown
Mexican Green
Mezz
Mor a Griefa
Mota
Mu
Muta
Panamanian Red
Pot
Red Dirt Marijuana
Roaches
Rope
Rose Maria
Sativa
Scissors
Superpot
Sweet Lucy
Tea
Texas Tea
Twist
Weed
Yesca

Slang Terms for Marijuana Cigarettes

Ace
Jay Smoke
Joint
Number
Panatella
Reefer
Roach
Root
Stick
Toke Up
Torch

Slang Terms for Hashish

Black Gunion
Black Hash
Black Russian
Charas
Hash
Smack
Smash

Chapter Four

Phencyclidine — Angel Dust

The story of angel dust, *phencyclidine* (PCP), began over 20 years ago when a number of new anesthetic compounds were being developed. PCP, and many of the others developed, were being investigated as general anesthetics that were nontoxic, nonflammable, and produced few side effects. Early animal studies demonstrated that this drug could be a very effective anesthetic. So in 1957, investigators began testing the drug on humans.

A drug company received the patent for the drug in 1963 and began marketing it under the trade name of *Sernyl*. It was generally an effective anesthetic but was found to produce some unpleasant side effects in patients as they came out from under the anesthesia. In early 1965, the drug company requested that further usage for humans be discontinued.

Since PCP was found to be an effective and satisfactory anesthetic agent for certain animals, it was marketed for this use in 1967 under the name of *Sernylan.*

There are at least 30 similar drugs to PCP, some of which have already appeared on the illicit market. One of these is TCP, and it appears to be acceptable by PCP users. Its effects are similar to PCP but it seems to be more active, or stronger.

If PCP is poorly or incompletely synthesized, a contaminant appears in the product. This contaminant has been identified as *1-piperidinocyclohexane carbonitrile* (PCC). PCC, an unstable compound, is an intermediate product in one method of PCP synthesis. PCC degrades to several products, one of which is *piperidine,* which has a strong fish-like odor. PCC is psychoactive and can produce undesirable effects, including nausea, vertigo, "the crazys," abdominal cramps, bloody vomiting, diarrhea and coma. The presence of a fish odor in PCP generally denotes a bad batch and the user will usually experience undesirable effects.

PCP ABUSE

PCP abuse was first reported in the Haight-Ashbury district in San Francisco in 1967. The drug was being marketed as the *PeaCePill* at that time. The effects the users experienced were evidently not desirable. So the use of the drug was reported to have ceased by early 1968. However, by the summer of that same year, a drug called *hog* appeared in New York City. This drug was analyzed to be PCP.

During this time period, the effects of the drug were not considered to be choice by users. So by 1969, it was often mislabeled and sold as something else, especially as a psychedelic drug (LSD, THC).

The abuse of angel dust has increased during the '70s to the point that about half of all street samples submitted for analysis (anonymous testing) contain varying percentages of PCP. The intentional or unintentional use of PCP has resulted in an increased number of patients being treated for unexplained psychosis, dystonic reactions, status epilepticus or coma at emergency rooms of our nation's hospitals.

Ten years ago, PCP had a negative reputation among drug users; however, now there is a new generation of users and the drug no longer carries that reputation. Authorities estimate that PCP accounts for up to 25 percent of psychedelic drug abuse. PCP is available on the street either plain or in combination with other drugs such as amphetamines, cocaine, mescaline, LSD, or marijuana.

The manufacture of PCP is a very lucrative business; it is manufactured in illicit laboratories called "pig outfits," hidden away like moonshine stills. The investment of about $500 in chemicals will yield about $50,000 on the street. The primary illicit production centers appear to include Washington, D.C., Detroit, Los Angeles, and San Francisco.

How Is PCP Used?

PCP, in the dry form, is a white granular powder, soluble in both water and alcohol. It is relatively stable, both in the crystalline form and in solution.

PCP can be injected, sniffed, taken orally, or smoked. When it is taken orally, the powder is commonly sprinkled on leaves or other material, and chewed. When it is smoked, the powder is sprinkled on parsley (angel dust) or other material (such as marijuana) and smoked directly. Formerly, the drug was dissolved in acetone or ether and the user soaked the desired smoking material in this solution; however, this practice has largely been replaced by sprinkling the dry powder on the leaves.

The quantity of PCP used for making the "joints" varies from about 170 milligrams for a "heavy joint" to about 80 milligrams for a "good joint," and about 40 milligrams for a "street joint." This is referring to the street quality PCP which has normally been mixed with some diluent. There is a lot of variation in the preparation of these cigarettes and this, coupled with the fact that there is a great deal of variation in actual drug content of PCP powder, makes it difficult to predetermine the strength of a dose that is going to be used—it could be negligible or very large. Very often PCP is prepared in gelatin capsules and sold. The capsules may contain PCP, PCP in combination with THC, or PCP in combination with other drugs.

What Are the Overall Effects?

The effects of PCP are dependent upon several variables, including the dose, the experience of the user, social setting, other drug involvement, personality traits, and the route of administration. Most experienced smokers use inhalation of the smoke as the most reliable method of titrating the effect they desire. A chronic user will feel the effects of one PCP joint usually within two to five minutes. These effects will peak in about 15 to 30 minutes during which time the user is "dusted" or "loaded" and is usually noncommunicative. This high feeling often continues for four to six hours and then develops into a state of mild depression, irritability, feelings of isolation and sometimes paranoia. Usually 24 to 48 hours are required for a user to return to normal.

The physical effects of PCP, *in usual doses* of 5 to 10 milligrams, include increased blood pressure, increased breathing, vertical, horizontal, and rotary involuntary movements of the eye, drooping eyelids, flushing of the face, sweating, analgesia, sleepiness, loss of muscle coordination, double vision, dizziness, occasional nausea and vomiting, a general uneasy feeling, a grimacing appearance on the face, and increased deep tendon reflexes. The patient may or may not be able to communicate.

The psychological effects of PCP include disturbances in body image, loss of personality, anxiety, fear, restlessness or excitement, feelings of weightlessness, distortion of the senses, visual or hearing "hallucinations," feelings of apathy, indifference, emotional and social isolation, emptiness, despair, a preoccupation with death, difficulty in thinking or concentrating, impairment of learning and memory functions, impairment of the senses, and regressive behavior.

Moderate dose effects may be experienced by inhaling (smoking) or sniffing 10 to 20 milligrams of PCP. The onset usually occurs rapidly and the duration of acute symptoms (coma) is usually one-half to one hour. The patient may be in a coma or a stupor, his eyes may be open with drooping eyelids, he may have involuntary vertical, horizontal, or rotary movements of the eyes, and his pupils' response to light may be normal or sluggish. He may make purposeless and repetitive movements, shiver, make jerking movements in his arms and legs. He has rigid muscles, grimacing of the face, and he vomits and drools. Patients will usually become communicative and ambulatory within an hour but still manifest symptoms of the "low dose" state.

The high dose effects may be experienced by oral dosages of 100 milligrams or more of PCP. The onset of action is usually about 45 minutes and a duration of the acute symptoms of about 6 to 12 hours. At least two to four days are required for the subject to return to normal. The patient is usually comatose, responding only to painful stimuli, has a decreased pulse rate, increased blood pressure, a normal or sluggish light reflex. His eyes will be closed and will exhibit the involuntary vertical, horizontal, and rotary movements. The user will make purposeless movements, his muscles may be rigid, he may have seizures, or vomit and drool. Also characteristic of high dose intoxication is a long recovery phase with alternating periods of sleep and waking, misperception, disorientation, "hallucinations" and the low dose state symptoms.

PCP is metabolized in the body by the liver and is excreted via the urine. These metabolites apparently do not contribute to the activity of PCP. The metabolism of certain other drugs is enhanced by pretreatment with PCP and tolerance to the effects of PCP may develop with regular usage. Cross-tolerance between PCP and other drugs has not been reported.

Primary Danger of PCP

Numerous deaths attributable to PCP have been reported. These deaths occurred because of PCP's pronounced behavioral toxicity—the inability of a person under the influence of PCP to remove himself from a dangerous situation. Angel dust abusers die because if there is a fire they cannot mobilize their bodies and escape; if they fall in thestreet they cannot get up and flee an oncoming car; if they fall in water they cannot swim because they have no control over their muscles.

PROFILE OF AN ANGEL DUST USER

It appears that PCP induces a relatively neutral state when smoked and users feel detached from all feeling when on the drug. They speak of a "buzz" in place of feeling "high" or a sense of well-being. To them, a feeling of nothing is preferable to experiencing their own feelings.

It is possible that an individual attempting to escape negative feelings about himself may become an angel dust user, rather than the person who is bored or who feels good about herself or himself.

It also appears that PCP creates a strong psychological dependence. Although users don't feel good about using the drug, it is difficult to cease using the drug. A profile of PCP users is illustrated in the following table.[1]

Average Age		19
Sex:	Male	73%
	Female	27%
Race:	Caucasian	89%
	Other	11%

Marital Status	
Single	77%
Married	13%
Separated	6%
Divorced	4%
Highest Grade Completed:	
1 Year College	5%
12th Grade	25%
11th Grade	19%
10th Grade	10%
Less than 10th Grade	6%
G.E.D.	2%
Not Known	33%

	Yes	**No**	**?**
Previously jailed or imprisoned	83%	14%	3%
Previous psychiatric treatment	35%	61%	4%
Presently on probation	57%	39%	4%
Pending criminal proceedings	49%	49%	2%
Current medical problems	18%	78%	4%
Presently employed	31%	66%	3%
Presently enrolled in school	25%	61%	14%
Considers PCP a problem	77%	19%	4%

Self-image as evaluated by counselor: Good 7%; Poor 58%; Neutral 12%; Unknown 23%

There are evidently at least two reasons why individuals stop using PCP: (1) the lack of money and (2) the realization of what PCP is doing to them. Tolerance develops to the effects of the drug and the cost can become prohibitive. When users become aware that their reflexes and thinking have dulled and that they cannot do what they want to do much of the time, many of them will stop using the drug.

No antidote for PCP has been conclusively demonstrated to be effective. Some drugs have been used with inconclusive results. The usual antidotes do not seem to work well with PCP intoxication.

FUTURE OF ANGEL DUST

Since the first draft of this book, PCP abuse has become even more widespread. Reasons for this include the fact that it is relatively inexpensive, widely available, easily manufactured, and there is an attitude among users of "so what if you say it is harmful . . . I don't believe you."

The U.S. Senate is attempting to come to grips with the problem but this will take time. According to the National Institute of Drug Abuse (Drug Abuse Warning Network—DAWN) there were 124 deaths and 5,742 hospital emergency room admissions in 800 hospitals participating in the DAWN program in 1978. This results in a projection throughout the United States of 310 deaths due to PCP and 14, 400 hospital emergency room admissions.

Slang Terms For Phencyclidine

Angel Dust	*Crystal Joints*
Angel Mist	*Cyclones*
Animal Tranquilizer	*DOA*
Cadillac	*Dust*
CJ	*Dust of Angels*
Crystal	*Elephant Tranquilizer*

Erth
Flying Saucers
Goon
Hog
Horse Tranks
Killer Weed
KJ
Magic Mist
Mist
Monkey Tranquilizer
Peace
Peace Pill
Peace Weed
Rocket fuel
Scuffle
Sheets
Snorts
Soma
Stardust
Supergrass
Superweed
Surfer
TAC
TIC
Wack
Wobble

Note

1. *Clinical Toxicology*, 1976, vol. 9. Issue 4, pp. 593-600. Arthur Bolter, Alan Hemiger, Gale Martin, Moira Fry.

Chapter Five

LSD and Other Hallucinogenic Drugs

A hallucinogenic drug produces changes in sensation, thinking, self-awareness and emotion. Also, depending on the dosage and the setting, it can cause changes in time and space perception, illusions, hallucinations, and delusions. These effects can occur at the time the drug is taken, but the effects of some hallucinogenic drugs recur days, weeks or months after the last dose. These flashbacks may be spontaneous or they may be precipitated by some physical or emotional stress.

The users usually sit or recline quietly in a dream or trance-like state. They may become fearful and experience a degree of terror which makes them attempt to escape from the group. Their senses of sight, hearing, touch, body-image and time are distorted. Their mood and behavior are affected, depending upon the emotional and environmental condition of the user. It is unlikely that persons using hallucinogens will do so in school, at work, or at home where they might be observed. Usually, these drugs are taken in a group situation under special conditions designed to enhance their effect.

WHAT IS LSD?

Joe, a 19-year-old college dropout, lives in San Francisco. He has been periodically using LSD for the past three years. When he takes acid his blood pressure and body temperature increase, his pupils dilate, his hands and feet shake; he has cold, sweaty palms, a flushed face and a wet mouth. He shivers, has goose bumps and chills, breathes irregularly and is nauseated. He also suffers a loss of appetite. "I experience two opposite feelings at the same time. I feel happy and sad, I laugh and cry, I am tense and relaxed—you know! I see illusions, lose track of time and misinterpret my senses. Sometimes I have a good trip, sometimes a bad one. I don't know why I use acid, I don't understand it."

Lysergic acid diethylamide, LSD, was first developed in 1938 from one of the ergot alkaloids. Ergot is a fungus that grows as a rust on rye—a common grain plant. LSD is so potent that one ounce is enough to provide 300,000 doses. It is generally taken by mouth on a sugar cube, cracker or cookie; sometimes the user licks it off a postage stamp or other object. The effects of one dose of LSD generally last about eight to ten hours.

There are several mental and physical dangers to a user of LSD. These include:

1. *Panic*—LSD is a long-acting drug. The user cannot stop the drug's action and he panics and fears he is losing his mind.

2. *Flashbacks*—A repetition of the drug experience may occur days, weeks or months after the last dose. Such stimulation as light, sound, odor, or another drug such as marijuana may trigger a flashback.
3. *Paranoia*—an LSD user may suffer paranoia for as long as 72 hours after the drug effect wears off. He becomes suspicious of everyone, feeling that someone is out to harm him.
4. *Accidental death*—LSD victims sometimes leap out of windows or off cliffs because they believe they can fly. The floating feeling the drug induces deceives them. They also believe they are capable of superhuman actions such as stopping a train or a truck by jumping in front of it.
5. *Birth defects*—Some researchers have described birth defects in new babies born to mothers who had used LSD.

MESCALINE—"PEYOTE"

Peyote use was introduced to the Indians of Arizona, New Mexico and Texas during the nineteenth century by native tribes from Mexico. The drug, from the peyote cactus, began to be used in religious-magical rites of various tribes and soon the users formed organized cults. By the beginning of the twentieth century the white man was making attempts to put an end to the use of peyote. Knowing the strong laws that protect freedom of religion, proponents of the drug joined together to form a church—"Mescal Bean Eaters" in 1906, the "Union Church" by 1909.

When the Bureau of Indian Affairs tried to induce Congress to enact anti-peyote legislation in 1918, the Indian tribes formed the "Native American Church of the United States," on October 10, 1918 in Oklahoma. By 1955 peyotism had spread into Canada and the church became the "Native American Church of North America." Their current membership numbers about 225,000. All attempts to prohibit the Indians' religious use of peyote have been unsuccessful.

The active component of peyote, *mescaline,* was isolated in 1896 and successfully synthesized in 1919. At the time of the Spanish conquest peyote was already in use by Indian tribes from Central America to the southern United States to relieve fatigue and hunger, and to treat various diseases. Not only are the peyote buttons used as a drug—chewed for some time to release the active mescaline—they are also worn as amulets to protect the wearer against danger. The drug also was, and still is, used in group setting to induce a trance-like state necessary for some tribal dances.

The physical effects of mescaline are much the same as for other hallucinogenic drugs—dilated pupils, increased blood pressure and body temperature. The psychological effects depend, to a large degree, on the psychological makeup of the user (his personality, mood, and expectations) and the environment in which the drug is used. Mescaline impairs the ability to perform complex tasks, impairs memory and the ability to solve problems. It also causes an alteration in vision and visual perceptions, and produces illusions or false-hallucinations.

Although peyote was used medicinally in the late 1800s as a respiratory stimulant, cardiac tonic, and as a depressant, there is no accepted medical use for it today.

PSILOCYBIN—"SACRED MUSHROOM"

"At first I just felt lightheaded—a little dizzy, and my stomach hurt. Then I was nauseated and got weak. My muscles ached and my hands and legs felt heavy. I felt anxious and tense," explained Jean, a freshman at a Southwestern university. She was describing how it felt the first time she tried the "sacred mushroom." She went on, "Then for about a half hour my vision became blurred. Colors were all brighter than usual and I was tracing [experiencing long visual afterimages]. I kept yawning; I was sweating and my eyes watered. I couldn't think very fast or concentrate. I didn't feel like I was in my body and I couldn't control my muscles." Jean went on to explain that she began to see weird things, deep in color. She lost her visual perspective and felt euphoric and stimulated. After about an hour and a half she said, "I could understand my mind better, and I felt my body and mind senses at a higher level." After about two hours the effects began to disappear. Five hours after she took the drug Jean was nearly back to normal.

Psilocybin is from the mushroom, *Psilocybe mexicana.* Its effects are similar to those of LSD and peyote. The "sacred mushroom" has been used for centuries by Indian cultures of Mexico and Central America—as far back as 1500 B.C. The first recorded use was during the coronation feast for Montezuma in about 1502. As Christianity was introduced into the New World, the use of psilocybin was discouraged; however, the drug is still prevalent today.

Somewhere between LSD and mescaline in potency, psilocybin acts on the user very much like the other drugs. Their effectiveness again depends on the user—his environment, personality, mood, preparation, expectations, and his tolerance. The primary danger of the sacred mushroom lies in its psychological effects—increased anxiety, panic, mood changes, depressive or paranoid reactions, disorientation and lack of ability to distinguish between reality and fantasy. A person under the influence of psilocybin can be treated by the "talk-down" method, in a quiet, secure, nonthreatening environment by an experienced therapist.

OTHER HALLUCINOGENIC DRUGS

DOM or "STP"—Serenity, Tranquillity, Peace

This chemically produced psychedelic drug is about 100 times more potent than mescaline but about 30 to 50 times less potent than LSD. STP produces just about the same physiological effects as the other drugs do. Psychological effects include multiple images, vibration of objects, visual hallucinations, distorted shapes; objects appear lighter, colors more vivid, bodies distorted. Time slows, contrasts increase, hearing increases, the user has difficulty controlling his thoughts and laughs uncontrollably.

The user develops a tolerance to STP quite rapidly. When consumed the action of the drug lasts from 16-24 hours.

MDA or "Love Drug"

First synthesized in the 1930s, MDA possesses some stimulant properties and appetite suppressant properties. When under the influence of MDA a person has dilated pupils, increased rate of breathing, rigid neck and jaw muscles, and grinds his teeth. Psychological effects include an intensification of feelings and self-insight, three-dimensional music, amnesia, erratic behavior and delirium.

The drug may be in liquid or powder form, usually in a capsule or tablet. It can be taken by mouth, "snorted" in the nose or injected intravenously. The ordinary street dose is from 100 to 150 milligrams per dose. It is often mixed with other drugs—amphetamines, cocaine, LSD and atropine.

Catha Edulis—Kat (Khat)

Also called gat, gúat, chat, tshat, tshott, Abyssinian tea, djimma, miraa, mira, cafta, and bushman's tea, kat (*Catha edulis*) is a native alkaloid grown in Ethiopia since prehistoric times and used by Arabs since the fourteenth century. It is related to amphetamine and is said to produce excitation and release from the need to sleep. The tree grows wild in Africa today but it is cultivated in two main centers, Harrar in Abyssinia and Meru in Kenya.

The drug is usually taken by chewing branchlets or leaves until all the juice is extracted. It can also be mixed with honey and eaten as a paste or sprinkled on food as a powder. It usually is used in social gatherings for its euphoriant effect, but it can cause hallucinations and agitated psychosis. It also is used to alleviate the sensation of hunger and fatigue. Currently, a large amount of the drug is consumed in Africa and the Middle East.

Bufotenine

Bufotenine comes from the plant, *Piptadenia peregrina*, and from a South American toad. Its actions are like those of LSD. The plant was used to prepare a snuff, *cohoba*, which supposedly rendered warriors fearless and insensitive to pain. The use of this hallucinatory snuff has been described as early as 1496 during the second voyage of Columbus.

Caapi—"Vine of Death"

Caapi, also called ayahuasca, pilde, and wild rue, comes from a South American jungle vine, *Banistericopsis caapi*, also called the "vine of death." It contains harmine and produces frenzy, visions, psychoeroticism and sleep.

Cohaba

Also called *niopo* or *parica*, cohaba comes from a Central American mimosa, the *Acacia niopo*, and other sources. It contains bufotenin and other materials and is used as snuff or as an enema. Cohoba produces a burning mouth, purple face, vomiting, drunkenness, gaiety, and colored visions.

Harmine

Harmine, also called *banisterine*, *yageine*, and *telepathine*, comes from many plants, including *Peganum harmala*. It is a psychic sedative and has been used by several tribes in South America. An intravenous dose of 70 to 100 milligrams or an oral dose of 300 to 400 milligrams will produce effects that persist for about six hours. Physically, there is a loss of feelings in the hands and feet, a feeling of pressure in the head and chest with nausea, vomiting and a general uneasy feeling. The mental effects include visual images and dreamlike sequences.

Ibogaine

Extracted from the root of an African plant, *Tabermanthe iboga*, this mild preparation, ibogaine, is said to relieve fatigue. There are no modern studies on this drug, but it has sufficient use in the United States to be considered a dangerous drug.

Myristicin

Myristicin comes from nutmeg and produces bizarre central nervous system symptoms. Taken in powdered form, orally, or by sniffing a 10-gram dose can produce mild euphoria accompanied by lightheadedness and central nervous system stimulation. Often fear and tension are also experienced. A quantity greater than 10 grams will produce a rapid heartbeat, thirst, anxiety, and sometimes panic.

Morning Glory Seeds

When taken alone in a quiet place, morning glory seeds can produce visual hallucinations and sleep. They have been used by the Aztec Indians. They are also called *ololuiqui* and *bador*. Their ready availability has contributed to their misuse by teenagers and adults who experience the hallucinogenic effect by ingesting the seeds.

Mexican Bindweed

From the *Rivea corymbosa*, also called the Mexican bindweed, "flower of the virgin," can produce effects similar to morning glory seeds.

Yagé

Yagé comes from *Haemadictyon amazonia*;

it contains harmine. Yagé first stimulates then depresses the user, causing drowsy hallucinations. (See caapi.)

Jimsonweed

The jimsonweed, *Datura stramonium*, is an uncultivated plant found throughout the United States. It contains the belladonna alkaloids, atropine and scopolamine. The seeds appear during the fall and contain approximately .4 percent belladonna alkaloids.

With large doses, the jimson seed effects include fever, rapid heart rate, increased blood pressure, dilation of the pupils, dry mouth and nose, nausea, vomiting, retention of urine, and dry, flushed skin. Mental effects include visual and auditory hallucinations, irritability, restlessness, disorientation, and amnesia. Coma and death have occurred from jimson seed poisoning.

Atropine

The atropine and related alkaloids (atropine, hyoscyamine, and scopolamine), are derived from the flowering plants *Datura stramonium* and *Atropa belladonna*. Commonly called deadly nightshade, henbane, mandrake, thornapple, and jimsonweed, this group is among the oldest of the hallucinogenics. In medieval Europe they were associated with mass hysteria, visions, dances, euphoria, excitement, or depression. Scopolamine (nightshade family) has been used as a truth serum; atropine has been used in large doses in the treatment of schizophrenia and gastrointestinal disorders and to dilate the pupils of the eye.

Areca—Betel Nut

Betel nut stimulates and produces a sense of well-being. It produces red saliva and stains the teeth when it is chewed with lime. It is a widely used euphoriant in Southeast Asia.

Kava

Kava is prepared from the roots of *Piper-methysticum* in the South Pacific. It is also called ken, kava-kava, and ava. It contains a resin, *kawain,* which produces gentle stimulation, followed by depression.

The preparing and drinking of kava is intimately bound to the social and religious practices of South Pacific natives. The roots are cleaned, debarked, then cut into small pieces so they can be chewed, but not swallowed. The active ingredients are *dihydrokawain* and *dihydromethystian*. Kava, in large doses, can produce staggering and sleepiness. Chronically used, kava can produce mental weakness and result in skin eruptions.

Soma

Soma is a traditional Vedic ritual potion. It is thought to be the juice of the vine, *Sarcostemma acidum*, of East India. The extract is personified and worshiped as a god. Its name was adapted in Huxley's *Brave New World* for a panacea. The pressed juice of the plant has been fermented into a wine which purportedly gives courage, health, long life, visions of paradise, and a feeling of immortality.

It has been speculated that the psychological techniques of yoga became more popular after soma became less available.

Virola Bark

Ingestion of the resin of the *virola bark* can cause hallucinogenic activity. This resin has been used by the Indian tribes in Columbia. Although there are many species of virola, the one with the greatest activity is *Virola theiodora.* Virola resins for oral administration may be prepared alone or may be mixed with dried filtrate of ashes of other plants. This bark appears as a sticky, dark reddish-brown gummy material which has been shown to contain tryptamine and other indolic hallucinogens. Also called parica and yagee.

Asarone

Asarone, *Acorus calamus,* is a plant known in Asia, Europe, and North America for its medicinal properties. It is also known as flag root, rat root, and sweet calamel. Indians in Canada used it for fatigue, as an analgesic, antiasthmatic, a drug for oral hygiene and for the relief of a hangover. It has been shown to have similar effects to LSD. The active principals in Acorus calamus are asarone and beta-asarone. Another source of asarone is the wild carrot fruit collected in Central Asia.

Safrole

Safrole is the principal component of oil of sassafras, Brazilian sassafras oil, and oil of *Illicium paviflorum.* It is also a minor component of cinnamon leaf oil, California laurel oil, American wormseed oil, camphor oil, and nutmeg. Safrole was a commonly used flavoring agent in the United States for beverage root beer and of course was present in sassafras tea. Safrole is similar in structure to myristicin and asarone. Safrole produces euphoria in small doses and hallucinogenic experiences in large doses. Safrole is no longer used in foods because of the possibilities of carcinogenic properties.

Vinho de Jurumena

A narcotic beverage prepared from the seeds of *Mimosa hostilis*, called Vinho de Jurumena, is used by the Pancaru Indians of Brazil. It is a hallucinogen and is used by the Indians in religious ceremonies and magical rites.

Iochroma Fuchsioides

Iochroma fuchsioides, a relatively new hallucinogen, grows in southern Columbia and has recently come into use in the northern Andes. In the 1940s, the leaves were crushed and taken in water by medicine men as a narcotic. In the early 1970s, reports were received of its use in childbirth and of its effects on the mind. The fresh bark from the tree, the stems, and the leaves are boiled in water to make a tea. The user will usually experience hallucinogenic effects for about a three-hour period. The drug is also called little bell tree, hummingbird flower, and other names.

Asthmador

Asthmador has some hallucinogenic properties and contains scopolamine and atropine. The most common source formerly was Asthmador cigarettes, which were purchased at a drug store and smoked. They could also be ingested in the form of a slurry consisting of the contents of the cigarettes suspended in a sweet liquid, such as hot chocolate or a cola beverage. The effects included a slowing of the heart rate, runny nose, salivation, sweating, and abdominal distress.

Banana Peel

In the late 1960s, banana peel smoking became popular. Analysis of baked banana skins has not revealed the presence of *bufotenin* or *dimethyltryptamine.* No hallucinogenic effects have been demonstrated in controlled experiments. There have been some mild autonomic effects reported which were secondarily given psychologic elaboration and experienced as a high. However, this was probably a placebo reaction. It has been postulated that the banana smoking craze was a put-on by the hippie community in an effort to tempt a politician to place his name on something as ludicrous as an Anti-Banana Act. By the 1970s, banana smoking had drifted into obscurity.

Slang Terms for Hallucinogens

Drug	Slang Terms
Asarone	*Calamus root, Sweet root Sweet Cinnamon, Sweet Cane*
Asthmador	*Asthmador cigarettes*
Ayahuasca	*Jungle drug*
Banana Peel	*Banana*
Belladonna	*Horror Drug*
Bufotenine	*Mappine Ch'an Su*
Diethyltryptamine	*DET*
Dimethyltryptamine	*DMT*
Dipropyltryptamine	*DPT*
Harmaline	*Passion flower, May-pop Apricot vine*
Hyoscamine	*Mandrake*

Drug	**Slang Terms**
Ibogaine	*Ibogaine*
Khat	*Kat*
Lobeline	*Indian tobacco, Bladder pod Wild tobacco*
Lysergic Acid Diethylamide	*Acid, Baby Wood Rose, Big "D", California sunshine, Crackers, "D", Grape parfait, Hawaiian Wood Rose, Lysergic acid, Mind detergent, Owsley's acid, Pellets, The ticket, Purple barrels, Purple ozoline, The beast, The chief, The cube, The ghost, The hawk, Twenty-five, "25", Yellow dimples*
Mescaline	*Button, Button cactus, chief, Coral beans, Dumpling cactus, Mesc, Mescal, Mescal beans, Peyote, Peyotl, Red beans, San Pedro cactus*
4-methy 1-2, 5-dimethoxyamphetamine	*DOM, STP*
Methyldioxyamphetamine	*Love drug, MDA*
Morning Glory Seeds	*Blueheaven, Flying saucers, Heavenly blue, Pearly gates*
Myristicin	*Nutmeg, Mace, Elemicin*
Peyote	*Bad seed, Button, Moon, Peyotl, Topi*
Scopolamine	*Mandrake*
Stramonium preparations mixed with carbonated beverages	*Mud*

Chapter Six

Stimulants

Susan is a freshman in a private school. She and three of her girlfriends have started using uppers. The girls feel that they need the pills to "help us keep alert when we're studying." Susan says that uppers also "decrease my appetite, give me energy, wake me up and make me feel like doing things. I have more confidence when I take uppers." When asked about any bad effects from the drugs, Susan admitted that even though they helped her to concentrate and work harder they also made her "talk too much and move around too much. I can't sit still. I'm jittery and have to do something."

"Uppers" is a slang expression referring to chemical stimulants. Stimulants are drugs that increase the activity of the central nervous system. The active chemical component of many stimulants is *amphetamine*.

AMPHETAMINES

Amphetamine was first synthesized in 1887.

Forty years later, the therapeutic possibilities were investigated; a patent was issued for the drug in 1932. The drug was used in the Benzedrine Inhaler to aid dilating the nasal and bronchial passages. During the 1930s, many other benefits were discovered and in 1937 amphetamine became available as a tablet to treat narcolepsy, a disease producing an uncontrollable urge to sleep.

As clinical use continued, amphetamine's effects as an appetite suppressant and a stimulant became known. During World War II in Japan, large quantities of the drug were used to counteract battle fatigue, maintain alertness, and help workers achieve high production quotas imposed by the war.

After the war, large quantities of the drug became available without prescription and the number of heavy users of amphetamines increased so rapidly that medical problems from its use developed. From 1948 to 1955, legal controls were enacted with the result of greatly reducing the amphetamine abuse problem in later years. Further controls were enacted in the 1970s by the federal government.

Therapeutic Effects of Stimulants

Probably the most widespread use of stimulants is in nasal decongestants. Public attention has been directed to the possible harmful effects of nasal decongestants in recent years; however, if this medication is used as directed and for short periods of time—three or four days—they are relatively safe. If used longer a condition known as *rebound congestion* can occur. These nose sprays contain chemical analogues of the amphetamines that produce the desired decongestion without the undesirable effects associated with the amphetamines. After the topical effect of the applied drug has worn off, the tissues in the nose swell back to their previous size or to a slightly larger size than they were originally. In order to allay the discomfort, usually another dose of of the nose spray is used. This then results in greater congestion and sets up a repetitious cycle. Consequently, many people become "hooked" on nose sprays. This is one reason why many physicians and pharmacists recommend orally administered nasal decongestants rather than nose sprays. If nose sprays are used, they should be used only for short periods of time.

Stimulants are also used to treat hyperkinetic syndrome in children. Hyperkinetic syndrome is manifested by impulsive, hyperactive behavior. Children thus affected usually have an unusually short attention span. Administering amphetamines to such children has a paradoxical effect; the medication acts as a tranquilizer, increasing attention span and decreasing hyperactive behavior. This use is currently being reevaluated, however.

Amphetamines have been used in weight loss programs; however, weight loss will usually only occur for about four weeks in one who is using amphetamines. The user develops a tolerance to the appetite suppressant effect of the drug in this time period, making possible a desire to increase the amount that should be taken.

Other therapeutic effects of stimulants include the control of hemorrhage, decrease in the absorption rates of local anesthetics, treatment of hypotension and shock, treatment of cardiac failure and allergic disorders, pupillary dilation, and in the treatment of narcolepsy, depressant drug poisoning, pyschogenic disorders, alcoholism and fatigue.

Amphetamine Abuse

Amphetamine abusers come from all walks of life—businessmen, housewives, students, truck drivers, multiple drug abusers, and others. They take the stimulants by mouth in the form of capsules, tablets or liquid. Some abusers inhale the drug, snort it in their noses or inject it. The subjective effects depend on the user, the environment, the dose of the drug and the route of administration.

When a person is on amphetamines his pupils may be dilated, he has bad breath, his mouth and nose will be dry, so he frequently licks his lips; he is usually irritable, argumentative and nervous, and may be chain-smoking. He will go for long periods without sleeping or eating; he is excessively active and has difficulty sitting still. His heart rate and blood pressure increase; he breathes rapidly. He may suffer from headaches, confusion, apprehension, delirium, fatigue, dizziness, and painful and difficult urination.

Abusers take amphetamines to stay awake, keep alert, elevate their mood, increase their initiative, give them confidence, stimulate motor and speech activity and their physical performance, and to increase their concentration.

There are at least three categories into which amphetamine users fit:

1. Intermittent low-dose users—These people

occasionally take between 5 and 20 milligrams orally to allay fatigue, elevate their mood while doing unpleasant tasks, produce prolonged wakefulness, help recover from a hangover, or to get "high." These individuals may be any age and usually have little interest in amphetamine use as a lifestyle.

2. Sustained low-dose use—These individuals usually obtain the amphetamines from their physicians for weight control, but take them three to four times daily for the stimulation and euphoria produced by the drug. A strong psychological dependence may be produced by the drug. If the individual does not get the next dose, depression sets in that is "cured" by another dose of the drug. Consequently, this is a habit that is very difficult to break.
3. High dose-use—Several times the usual dose, especially of methamphetamine, is called "speeding.." Speeding involves using as much as 500 to 1,000 milligrams intravenously every two to three hours over acouple of days. Immediately after the injection there is a "flash" or a "rush" described as an intense feeling of pleasure. After coming down, the individual usually sleeps for one or two days followed by a state of depression that usually lasts for two to three weeks.

Effects of Amphetamine Abuse

People who use stimulants for a long period of time suffer chronic effects from their intoxication. These include marked weight loss, irritability, dental caries, multiple vitamin deficiencies, instability, dermatitis (occasional), and psychotic reactions with vivid hallucinations which can hasten the onset of incipient schizophrenia.

A person who takes amphetamines in large doses achieves the therapeutic results he is looking for, but he also finds that he must contend with irritability, insomnia, confusion, assaultiveness, anxiety, hallucinations, panic states, suicidal or homicidal tendencies in mentally ill patients, palpitations, arrhythmias, profuse sweating, dry mouth, metallic taste, nausea, vomiting, diarrhea, and abdominal cramping.

There are a number of medical complications for the person who injects methamphetamine intravenously, not only from the drug itself but from the injection techniques. These include complications resulting from injecting drug contaminants, undissolved particles, or using nonsterile injection techniques. Serum hepatitis is a very real possibility from using dirty equipment. In addition, the individual may inject live fungus or bacteria into the bloodstream, resulting in tetanus, syphilis, malaria, septic pulmonary emboli, endocarditis, or peripheral obstruction of the arteries.

Adverse physical and psychological reactions to high-dose intravenous injections of methamphetamine (speeding) include:

1. Anxiety reactions—The individual becomes fearful, trembles, and worries about his physical well-being.
2. Amphetamine psychosis—The individual misinterprets the actions of others, hallucinates, and becomes unrealistically suspicious.
3. Exhaustion syndrome—The individual ex-

periences an intense feeling of fatigue and the need to sleep.

4. Prolonged depression.
5. Prolonged hallucinosis—The individual continues to hallucinate after the drug has been metabolized.

   Additional effects include skin lesions, abscesses, respiratory problems, acute gastrointestinal distress, and abdominal cramps.

Although amphetamines are not addicting—unless large doses are taken—psychological dependence is quite common. As a matter of fact, abrupt withdrawal after chronic use of amphetamines can result in a deep and suicidal depression, prolonged sleep and fatigue. Generally, physicians will bring about withdrawal slowly in a controlled environment.

COCAINE

Cocaine—*Erythroxylon coca*—is emerging as one of the most popular drugs in our society, particularly among the rich class of people. It is often called the "rich man's speed."

The cocaine story began 3,000 years ago according to Inca records found in Peru and Bolivia. Coca leaves were given as a reward for special services performed; it was a drug used mostly by the ruling class. The conquistadores gave the Indians coca leaves to chew as it gave them the stamina to work in the silver mines. Coca is still used in this way.

The Indians working the mines chew the leaves, sprinkled with a little bit of lime. For them, the chewing of "cocada" has become a way of life in the cold, thin air of the 3-kilometer-high atmosphere where there is a scarcity of food. The coca plant grows in the foothills but it is consumed in the mountains. It is said that miners who come down to the plains to work give up their coca habit.

Cocaineis a substance derived from the leaves of the coca bush (*Erythroxylon coca*) grown in Peru and Bolivia. It is chemically related to the belladonna alkaloids and is used in medicine because of its ability to block nerve conduction in humans.

Medical History of Cocaine

In the late 1800s there were a number of "celeries"—patent medicines that claimed to be good for what were vaguely described as "nervous disorders." These patent medicines were available under the names of *Paynes Celery Compound; Celery Bitters; Celery-Vesce; Celery Crackers; Celerena; Celery-Cola; Celery Malt Compound.* The ingredients usually consisted of celery extract, hops, coca (from which cocaine is obtained), and about 21 percent alcohol.

Prolonged use leads to loss of appetite, weight loss, insomnia, nausea, anxiety reactions, digestive disorders, changes in mental and moral qualities, oversuspiciousness, skin abscesses, occasional convulsions, hallucinations, and paranoid thinking. Cocaine is a powerful vasoconstrictor of small blood vessels; this accounts for ulceration of the nasal septum when cocaine has been "snorted" over a long-time period. Cocaine can be injected or inhaled.

An overdose of cocaine results in the user having pallor of the face, dizziness, nausea, pulse failure, cyanosis, tremors, convulsions, delirium, and some hallucinations. Death is due either to cardiovascular collapse or respiratory failure.

The development of tolerance and the occurrence of withdrawal to cocaine is doubtful, however; there is an intense psychological desire to repeat the experience that leads to chronic cocaine use. It does produce psychological dependence. Getting off the drug for a chronic cocaine user generally involves removal of the drug, treatment of the ensuing depression that often results, and altering the person's life-style and attitudes.

Today, about the only medical use for cocaine is that it is a very effective anesthetic for the eye.

Some medical scientists purportedly are developing a chewing gum containing cocaine to give the population of the United States the same "benefits" as the Andean Indians have in South America. This could result in serious consequences.

Cocaine users think of the drug as a safe "recreational" drug. However, the *Journal of the American Medical Association* reports that more than half of all narcotic overdose deaths also involve cocaine; and in one investigation, of 68 cocaine-associated deaths, 24 were found to have resulted directly from the toxic effects of cocaine.

Patterns of Cocaine Abuse

At least four patterns of cocaine abuse can be identified:

1. Cokehead—One who uses only cocaine, often as many as dozens of injections daily,

to maintain the intoxicated state. This is very expensive as cocaine sells for about $1,000 per ounce.

2. Multiple drug user—One who uses cocaine when it is available and other drugs when it isn't.
3. Cocaine-heroin combination—One who uses this combination is often called a "speedball artist." This combination is used so the jitteriness or excitement caused by cocaine is offset by the depressant effect of heroin.
4. In connection with Methadone maintenance—Methadone will prevent the high due to heroin, but not the high due to cocaine, amphetamines, or sedatives. Therefore, many abusers on methadone maintenance to treat heroin addiction will resort to the use of cocaine for their "highs."

Slang Terms for Stimulants

Drug	Commercial Names	Slang Terms
Amphetamine (includes dextroamphetamine, levoamphetamine and amphetamine)	*Benzedrine, Biphetamine, Delcobese, Bexedrine, Eskatrol, Fetamin, Obetan, Obetrol, Obotan*	*Beans, Bennies, Black beauties, Bombido, Brown and Clears, Browns, Cartwheels, Chalk, Chicken powder, Christmas tree, Coast to Coast, CoPilots, Crank, Crossroads, Crystal, DAS, Dexies, Diet pills, Eyeopeners, Footballs,*

Drug	Commercial Names	Slang Terms
		Forwards, Hearts, Jolly babies, LA Turnabout, Leapers, Lidpoppers, Lidproppers, Oranges, Peaches, Pep pills, Roses, Sparkle Plenties, Speed, Splash, Splivins, Thrusters, Truckdrivers, Ups, Wake-ups, West Coast Turnabouts, Whites
Benzephetamine	*Didrex*	*Bennies*
Chlorphentermine	*Pre-Sate*	
Diethylpropion	*Tenuate, Tepanil*	
Fenfluramine	*Pondimin*	
Hydroxyamphetamine	*Paredrine*	
Mazindol	*Sanorex*	
Mephentermine	*Wyamine*	
Methamphetamine	*Desoxyn, Efroxine, Methedrine, Norodin, Syndrox*	*Bombita, Chicken powder, Crank, Crystal, Desoxyephedrine, Meth, Speed, Splash*
Methylphenidate	*Ritalin*	
Phendimetrazine	*Bacarate, Plegine, Statobex*	
Phenmetrazine	*Preludin*	*Sweeties*
Phentermine	*Adipex-P, Fastin, Ionamin, PreSate, Wilpo*	

Slang Terms for Cocaine

Bernice	*Corrine*	*Her*
Bernie's Flake	*Dream*	*Him*
Boy	*Dust*	*Joy Powder*
Burese	*Flake*	*Lady Snow*
C	*Girl*	*Snow*
Charlie	*Gold Dust*	*Star Dust*
Coke	*Heaven dust*	*White Stuff*
Corine		

Slang Terms for Cocaine and Heroin

Speedball	*Stardust*

Chapter Seven

Sedatives and Depressants

Sedatives and depressants are drugs that are used for medical purposes to relax or depress the central nervous system.

The oldest member of the depressant group is *chloral hydrate*. It was first prepared in 1832 and used in practice in 1869. It was a popular drug until the barbiturates were introduced into medicine. Recently, however, chloral hydrate's popularity has increased.

Barbital, the first hypnotic barbiturate, was introduced into medicine in 1903 under the name of *Veronal*. Following this came phenobarbital in 1912 and since that time, more than 2,500 barbiturates have been synthesized. About a dozen or so barbiturates are still widely used in medicine today.

The first attempt to give a depressant intravenously was made in 1665. The first real manuscript on this topic was published in 1875 involving the use of chloral hydrate, but this drug was not suitable for use in this manner. The longer-acting barbiturates were also slow to induce an effect; therefore, it was not until the introduction of the ultrashort-acting barbiturates (1935) that intravenous administration of depressants became widely accepted in the area of anesthesia during surgery.

MEDICAL BARBITURATES

The primary medical uses today for barbiturates depend on the type of barbiturate used. There are basically four types: (1) ultrashort-acting, including thiopental, (2) short-acting, including pentobarbital and secobarbital, (3) intermediate-acting, including amobarbital, and (4) long-acting, including phenobarbital.

The ultrashort-acting barbiturates are used as anesthetics. The short-acting barbiturates are used as sedatives, for sleep, and for rapid epileptic seizure control. The intermediate-acting barbiturates are used as daytime sedatives and the long-acting barbiturates are used for control of epilepsy, as daytime sedatives, and in the treatment of sedative-hypnotic withdrawal.

Effects of the Barbiturates

In normal doses barbiturates depress the action of the nerves, skeletal muscles and heart muscle. This results in a slowing of the heart rate, breathing rate, and a lowering of the blood pressure. In larger doses, the effects resemble drunkenness due to alcohol. Intoxication symptoms include sluggishness, difficulty in thinking, slow speech, poor memory, faulty judgment, irritability, laughing or crying, narrow attention range, untidy habits, hostile and paranoid ideas and suicidal tendencies.

People who begin abusing depressants are often people who have difficulty sleeping or are unable to deal with anxiety. Several years ago mostly adults were abusing depressant drugs; however, now they are being consumed more and more frequently by teenagers and preteenagers as a fad drug. Symptoms of sedative-depressant abuse are similar to the symptoms of alcohol intoxication—staggering or stumbling, falling asleep, drowsiness, disorientation and a lack of interest in school, work or activities.

A person who has overdosed on depressants may become comatose; he will have a depressed breathing rate, diminished reflexes, low body temperature, low blood pressure, and constricted pupils.

Dangers Associated with Barbiturate Abuse

Sometimes a user of depressants does not intend to abuse the drug. He may take a barbiturate for sleep, become confused and wake up later not remembering whether or not he had taken the medication. Therefore he repeats the dose. This can happen several times until a lethal dose has been taken. Effects from using depressants for sleep include drowsiness, hangover, headache, overt excitement and altered motor performance. These symptoms may last for several hours after waking.

Intentional abusers—"barb freaks"—are those who want to get a "rush" from barbiturates. This is achieved only by intravenous injections. Barbiturate capsules are dissolved in water and injected. The rush is described as an intensely pleasurable, warm and drowsy feeling occurring immediately after injection.

Regardless of the intent, barbiturates do produce addiction in chronic users. There are three types of toxicity associated with barbiturate use:

1. Suicide—the intentional ingestion of large amounts of barbiturates.
2. Automatism—becoming confused about whether or not he had taken the sleeping medication and then repeating the dose.
3. Synergism—taking barbiturates, or other depressants, with alcohol, resulting in an enhanced effect of the two drugs occasionally resulting in death.

Barbiturate withdrawal should be accomplished only with medical supervision as it is a dangerous procedure. During the first 12 to 16 hours a person who is withdrawing from depressant addiction is restless and anxious. He suffers with tremors, weakness, abdominal cramping, nausea, vomiting and low blood pressure fainting. During the second or third day these symptoms usually peak with short-acting barbiturates and meprobamate. At this time convulsions may occur.

Long-acting barbiturates and chlordiazepoxide usually peak at about seven or eight days. Usually the symptoms are over about the eighth day, after a period of prolonged sleep. Because deaths due to withdrawal of depressants have been reported, a better method of tapering off includes using selected alternative drugs.

VALIUM

The nation's number one prescribed drug—

more than 60 million prescriptions written in 1978—is Valium (*diazepam*). *Diazepam* is a non-barbiturate and a potentially addicting drug. The U.S. Senate is currently investigating the implementation of stronger controls on this drug.

METHAQUALONE

Methaqualone is a non-barbiturate sedative-hypnotic. Abusers use this drug in large doses, 300 to 600 milligrams, often with wine. Some get a high feeling by fighting off the urge to sleep. Much larger doses may be needed as tolerance develops.

Methaqualone tablets found on the street are usually legally manufactured drugs obtained by using forged prescriptions, robbing pharmacies, or by other means. Its adverse effects include headaches, hangover, menstrual disturbances, tongue changes, dryness of the mouth, cracking at the corners of the mouth, nosebleed, depersonalization, dizziness, skin eruptions, numbness, pain in the extremities, diarrhea and anorexia.

Methaqualone does cause physical dependence or addiction with chronic use.

Slang Terms for Depressants

Depressant	Commercial Names	Slang Terms
Amobarbital	*Amytal*	*Blue angels, Bluebirds, Blue bullets, Blue devils, Blue dolls, Blue heaven, Blues, Blue tips*

Depressant	Commercial Names	Slang Terms
Amobarbital and Secobarbital	*Tuinal*	*Double trouble, Gorilla pills, Rainbows, Red and blues, T-Birds, Toolies, Tootsies, Trees, Tuies*
Aprobarbital	*Alurate, A.P.B.*	
Barbiturates		*Barbs, Candy, Courage pills, Dolls, Down, Downers, Floaters, GB, Goofballs, Goofers, Gorilla pills, Idiot pills, Peanuts, Phenos, Pink ladies, Purple hearts, Sleeping pills, Sleepers, Softballs, Stumblers*
Barbiturate and Amphetamine	*Dexamyl*	*Christmas trees, Greenies, In-Betweens*
Butalbital in Combination	*Fiorinal*	
Carbromal	*Carbrital*	
Chloral Betaine	*Beta-Chlor*	*Chlorals, Corals,*
Chloral Hydrate	*Noctec, Somnos, AquaChloral, Felsules, Kessodrate*	*Joy juice, Knock-out drops, Mickey, Mickey Finn, Peter*
Chlordiazepox ide	*Librium, Sk-Lygen*	*Black and Greens, Green and Whites*
Clonazepam	*Clonopin*	
Clorazepate	*Tranxene, Azene*	
Diazepam	*Valium*	
Ethchlorvynol	*Placidyl*	

Depressant	**Commercial Names**	**Slang Terms**
Ethinamate	*Valmid*	
Flurazepam	*Dalmane*	
Glutethimide	*Doriden*	*CB, CD, Cibas*
Lorazepam	*Ativan*	
Mephobarbital	*Mebaral*	
Meprobamate	*Equanil, Kessobamate, Miltown, Sk-bamate*	
Methaqualone	*Optimil, Parest, Quaalude, Somnafac, Sopor*	*Mandrakes, Ludes, Soapers, Quacks*
Metharbital	*Gemonil*	
Methohexital	*Brevital*	
Methyprylon	*Noludar*	
Oxazepam	*Serax*	
Pentobarbital	*Nembutal*	*Nebbies, Nembies, Nemish, Nemmies, Nimby, Yellow bullets, Yellow dolls, Yellow jackets, Yellows*
Phenobarbital	*Luminal, Eskabarb Sk-Phenobarbital*	*Purple hearts*
Prazepam	*Verstran*	
Secobarbital	*Seconal*	*F-40's, Mexican reds, M & M's, Pinks, R.D.'s, Redbirds, Red bullets, Red devils, Red dolls, Red lillies, Reds, Seccies, Seccy, Seggies, Seggy*
Sodium Butabarbital	*Buticaps, Butisol, Sodium*	
Sodium Diethylbarbiturate, Sodium Isobutylallylbarbiturate, and Sodium Phenylethylbarbiturate	*Plexonal*	

Depressant	Commercial Names	Slang Terms
Sodium Thio-pental	*Pentothal*	
Thiamylal Sodium	*Surital*	

Chapter Eight

Opium and Other Narcotics

Cindy works at a large hospital in a major northeastern city. She was caught and convicted of diverting morphine, an opium derivative, from the hospital for her personal use, and of falsifying the hospital's narcotic records.

"I got started a couple of years ago blowing pot and then got onto M," Cindy said. "We use a lot of it at the hospital and I would empty the drug vials, put in salt water, and take the M home. When I shot up I didn't feel pain, I got drowsy and couldn't think straight or concentrate. My arms and legs felt heavy, I felt warm, my mouth was dry and I breathed real slow. I used to like it but I don't anymore. Now I wish I hadn't ever started the stuff. I'm all messed up still now."

WHAT IS A NARCOTIC?

Narcotic is a general term used to describe

drugs that induce a state of *narcosis* or sleep. Narcotics may be natural or synthesized and are employed primarily for the relief of pain. The use of these drugs in medicine is potentially dangerous because all *opiates* (narcotics) are addicting, that is, they induce physiological dependence.

One of the oldest, most widely-used narcotic is *opium.* Opium is obtained from the milky exudate of the incised unripe seed capsules of the poppy plant, *Papaver somniferum,* native to Asia Minor. The milky juice is dried in the air and forms a brownish, gummy mass. This material is further dried and powdered to make powdered opium.

Early records reveal that opium, as well as other drugs (such as hemlock), were used in medicine. The earliest mention of the poppy in history is in the Sumerian language of non-Semitic people from the uplands of Central Asia. These people settled in the land of Mesopotamia about 5000 B.C. As the culture and influence of this people spread throughout the Near and Far East, so did the use of the opium poppy. By the tenth century A.D., the opium poppy was brought to China.

When large numbers of Chinese people immigrated into the United States to work on construction projects of that time, they brought the poppy and addiction to opium smoking with them. Opium smoking, a social pastime in China, became a part of the American culture. By the end of the nineteenth century, several patent medicines containing opium were on the market (*Dr. Barton's Brown Mixture, Dover's Powders,* etc.).

Drugs are still available that contain opium

derivatives; however for the most part they must be obtained through a prescription. Some opium derivatives which were at one time or still are used in medicines include: *laudanum*—a tincture of opium containing 10 percent opium; *paregoric*—a camphorated tincture of opium containing, in each four-milliliter dose, 16 milligrams of opium or 1.6 milligrams of morphine; and *codein*. Codeine, in some states, is still available without a prescription in cough syrups; in other countries in painkillers. Abusers will visit several drug stores until they have an adequate quantity of cough syrups and then they will take them orally. The effects are similar to those of morphine.

Morphine

Opium powder contains about 10 percent morphine and about 0.5 percent codeine (in addition to *thebaine, papaverine, noscapine* and other alkaloids). Morphine, at one time, was widely used as a painkiller. The first large-scale morphine addiction problem in the United States occurred during the Civil War. Because of its extensive use, coupled with poor medical facilities, a large population of ex-soldiers became morphine addicts, so much so, that morphine addiction was known as Soldier's Disease.

By the turn of the century the dangers of morphine addiction became apparent to members of the medical profession and they began exercising restraints on the prescribing of opiates.

In 1914, Congress passed the Harrison Narcotic Act which sought to control narcotic and drug abuse. Over the next 40 years, the heroin problem became confined to urban ghettos and was invisible to most Americans. By the 1960s, however, heroin use became visible again in the general community when the phenomenon spread from the urban ghetto to the middle-class suburbs. The problem later reached epidemic proportions and federal measures were undertaken to educate the public, liberalize treatment opportunities and strengthen drug traffic control.

The therapeutic uses of morphine include such things as relief of pain, suppression of cough, and relief of diarrhea.

In addition to analgesia, or pain relief, morphine—the prototype of narcotics—affects the user in several ways. He becomes drowsy, he experiences mood changes, euphoria and mental cloudiness—the inability to concentrate. His arms and legs feel heavy, his body is overly warm, his mouth is dry and he has difficulty in urinating. His respiration and cough reflex are depressed, and there is a decrease in the secretions and motility of the gastrointestinal tract; the vessels of his skin are dilated.

The morphine user also may suffer nausea, vomiting, dizziness, restlessness, a general uneasy feeling, and constipation.

Heroin

"Right after I hit up I go high, real high—for a few minutes and then I feel real relaxed and don't worry about nothing." Bret lives in New York City. He has snorted and mainlined heroin for the past six months. He continues, "I don't think about nothing, don't eat . . . don't think . . . just go on the nod . . ."

Of all the narcotics, the one with the greatest addiction potential is heroin. "Heroin" is from the German word *heroisch*, which means large or powerful. It is made from morphine, but is more potent.

The drug is smuggled into the United States through well-organized criminal channels. It is a very lucrative business—one kilogram of 80 percent pure heroin, for example, costing the importer from $5,000 to $7,000 can eventually yield a profit of at least $250,000.

Almost any white powder is used to "cut" heroin—starch, lactose, quinine, etc. The user generally takes the drug by injecting it into his body. However, he may also smoke it or take it by "snorting" it: he places the dry powder on a piece of paper (or other material) then draws the powder into his nostrils by a sharp, quick sniff. Heroin is quickly absorbed through the nasal membranes.

During the summer of 1980, the Associated Press carried a story stating that the flow of heroin into the United States from the poppy fields in Iran, Pakistan and Afghanistan is rapidly increasing. The "Persian" heroin is extraordinarily pure: 92 percent in one sample, compared to as low as two to four percent in heroin from other countries. The article also stated that reports indicate that smoking heroin is on the increase. Authorities and doctors are concerned that the practice will spread among young Americans who have already smoked marijuana but dislike injections.

The new heroin addict is younger—about 24, better-educated and white. He/she is likely to be more naive about street and drug life.

The person who uses heroin initially experiences an intense high which lasts for a few minutes. This is accompanied by an easing of tension, easing of fears and relief from worry. The high feeling is followed by a period of inactivity bordering on a stupor—called being "on the nod." The user's brain decreases its activity and he has a decrease in both hunger and thirst.

This intense "high," which drug users first experience and which they continue to seek, generally lessens over a period of time in the heroin addict. But the addict finds he must continue to take the drug in order to feel "normal"; if he doesn't take the drug, then he begins to suffer withdrawal symptoms. Since it costs from $75 to $200 dollars per day to support a heroin habit, addicts often must turn to crime and prostitution to get the money to buy the drug.

In addition to the harmful effects of the drug on the user, and the threat to society because of the addict's criminal activities, there are other dangers associated with heroin abuse. Addicts usually prepare their own injections and maintain their own equipment. This equipment often is shared between users. It is seldom kept sterile, so it becomes contaminated. Heroin addicts commonly transmit infections, abscesses, hepatitis, septicemia and endocarditis to one another.

As if all these negative effects weren't enough, there is still another one. A pregnant woman who is a heroin addict affects her unborn child. The baby also becomes addicted to the drug as the mother takes it. At birth, the child is suddenly shut off from its supply of the drugs which it has been receiving from its mother's blood. Within hours, it will suffer withdrawal symptoms.

NARCOTIC WITHDRAWAL

Withdrawal is the reaction of the body to the lack of a drug to which it has become accustomed. These withdrawal symptoms usually begin about 18 to 24 hours after the last dose of the drug. Some physical symptoms begin to manifest themselves about eight to 12 hours after the last dose. These symptoms include tearing, runny nose, yawning and sweating. More severe effects will then become manifest and will peak after about 48 to 72 hours.

The addict in withdrawal will have dilated pupils, loss of appetite, gooseflesh, restlessness, irritability, and muscle tremor. As the syndrome approaches peak intensity the patient experiences increased irritability, insomnia, marked loss of appetite, violent yawning, severe sneezing, tearing, pronounced weakness, depression, vomiting, intestinal spasms, diarrhea, waves of gooseflesh, abdominal pain and cramps, muscle spasms and kicking movements, increased breathing rate, weight loss and dehydration. Characteristics of this state include an increase in heart rate and blood pressure, chills alternating with flushing and excessive sweating. Without treatment, withdrawal lasts from seven to 10 days but it is not known how long it takes to regain physiological equilibrium.

Methadone, a drug with similar properties to morphine, is often used in the management of narcotics addiction. Methadone also induces dependence similar to morphine and other narcotics, but withdrawal develops more slowly and is less intense, however, it is more prolonged.

One technique used in treating narcotics addicts is called "detoxification treatment." Methadone is taken as a substitute narcotic drug in decreasing doses until the addict reaches a drug-free state. Detoxification treatment uses methadone for 21 days. "Maintenance treatment," another technique in treating addicts, involves using methadone in conjunction with medical and social services for a period in excess of 21 days as an oral substitute for heroin or other morphine-like drugs. An eventual drug-free state is the treatment goal.

Slang Terms for Narcotics

Narcotic	Commercial Name	Slang Term
Alphaprodine	*Nisentil*	
Camphorated Opium Tincture		*Blue velvet, PG, PO*
Codeine		*Schoolboy*
Dihydrocodeine in Combination	*Synalgos*	
Fentanyl	*Sublimaze*	
Fentanyl & Droperidol	*Innovar*	
Heroin		*Caballo, Chiva, Dogie, Doojee, Duji, Dust, Good H, "H", Hard Stuff, Harry, Henry, Horse, Joy Powder, Pure, Scag, Scat, Smack, Tecata, White Lady, White Stuff*
Hydrocodone in Combination	*Hycodan*	
Hydromorphone	*Dilaudid*	

Narcotic	Commercial Name	Slang Term
Levorphanol	*LevoDromoran*	
Meperidine	*Demerol*	*Diane*
Methadone	*Dolophine*	*Doll, Dollies, Fizzies*
Morphine		*M, Mary, Microdots, Miss Emma, Mojo, Morph, Whitestuff*
Opium		*Black, Black Stuff, Hop, Tar, Yen shee*
Opium Alkaloids	*Pantopon*	
Opium Tincture (Laudanum)		
Oxycodone in Combination	*Percodan*	
Oxymorphone	*Numorphan*	
Paregoric		*PG*
Pentazocine	*Talwin*	
Propoxyphene	*Darvon, SK-65*	

Chapter Nine

Volatile Inhalants

Jimmy is a junior high school dropout who currently works in a service station. He dropped out because he started sniffing glue and lost interest in his studies. According to Jimmy: "I sniff glue, gas, whatever is around. When I get glue, I get high and dreamy, kind of drunk, you know. I get shaky, sleepy, and can't tell where I am sometimes. I see things and sleep hard sometimes."

A service station isn't the best place for a fellow like Jimmy to work. He also sniffs gas. "I get gassed by putting some on a rag and breathing deep. I get a bad taste in my mouth and feel kind of sick, lightheaded; things start moving, spinning, floating, and I'm being pulled like a magnet. I can't eat; sometimes I drool; I get sleepy, feel weak, forget who I am; shapes and colors look different; can't tell how close or far things are away. I get high [euphoric]. I get afraid sometimes and feel guilty and lonely. I wish I didn't do it. I can't seem to stop. I just keep doing it."

Since ancient times people have breathed vapors to allay pain. The ancient Hebrews breathed burning spices and early Greeks breathed cold vapors coming from clefts of rocks. Early drugs used as anesthetics included mandragora (belladonna alkaloids), alcohol, marijuana and opium. Priestly discovered the first inhalation anesthetic, nitrous oxide (laughing gas), in 1776. Its use as an anesthetic for surgical operations was suggested as early as 1799, but it wasn't implemented until 1844.

A dentist, Horace Wells, attended a demonstration of laughing gas—a form of entertainment. He saw the potential for using the gas in his dental practice and tried it the next day. However, it wasn't until the 1860s that the gas was accepted in dentistry. Meanwhile the public demonstrations and administrations went on as a form of public entertainment.

In 1818 Faraday reported on the analgesic effects of ether, but it took several years for it to be accepted in medical practice; but ether parties, or "jags" were held by several medical students. The search for other anesthetics was soon underway. In 1831 chloroform was discovered. While medical men were trying to validate the use of various inhalants for surgery, drug abusers were already discovering their intoxicating effects.

In the 1960s, reports of glue sniffing were received from Tucson, Arizona, Pueblo, Colorado and other western cities. Glue sniffers were kids between the ages of 8 and 18 years who were probably model airplane builders.

INHALANTS USED TO ALTER STATE OF CONSCIOUSNESS

A wide variety of industrial solvents, anesthetics, and other chemicals produce intoxication. They can usually be divided into three groups:

1. Solvents—toluene, xylene, benzene, naphtha, hexane, acetone, trichloroethylene, carbon tetrachloride, paint thinner, gasoline, cleaning fluids, nail polish remover, cigarette lighter fluid, and others (found in model airplane glue and plastic cement).
2. Anesthetics—chloroform, ether, nitrous oxide.
3. Aerosols—chlorinated and fluorinated hydrocarbons used as propellants in many household and commercial sprays.

Inhalant abusers drench a rag with liquid or the glue, or place the chemical in a bag, then inhale the fumes. In using an aerosol, the user breathes in directly from the can or sprays the contents in a bag and inhales. Gases such as *nitrous oxide*, laughing gas, can be inhaled directly.

One who has been inhaling a volatile substance generally has the odor of the substance on his breath and clothes. He will have excessive nasal secretions and watery eyes, poor muscle control, drowsiness or unconsciousness. He will have an increased preference for being with a group rather than being alone. He will also pick his nose a lot. Plastic or paper bags or rags, containing dry plastic cement or other solvent, will be found at home or in a locker at school or at work.

"Sniffers" are usually between 8 and 18 years

of age, male, frequently from impoverished, deprived families with broken or chaotic homes. However, recently children from middle class homes have become involved in sniffing glue.

EFFECTS OF INHALING VOLATILE SUBSTANCES

A person who inhales volatile drugs can develop a tolerance to their effects. He can be both physically and mentally damaged by them. For example, inhaling carbon tetrachloride causes irreversible kidney and liver damage; gasoline and naphtha create heart complications and bone marrow depression; chloroform causes liver damage. Breathing a large concentration of laughing gas, produces hypoxia which may lead to coma and irreversible damage to the central nervous system.

Small canisters of laughing gas can be easily purchased in "novelty shops" or "head shops." Five or six canisters and an adapter cost from $10 to $15.

"Discorama" (*butyl nitrite*), a room deodorizer causes the formation of methemoglobin in the blood, making it very difficult for the blood to carry oxygen to the brain.

Mentally, inhaling volatile drugs induces a state of intoxication in which judgment and motor functioning are impaired, resulting in accidents, suffocations, etc.

Volatile inhalants do not appear to be addicting; however, there does seem to be a strong psychological desire to repeat their use.

TREATING INTOXICATED USERS

Because acute intoxication from volatile inhalants is of fairly short duration, people under their influence rarely are treated during their intoxicated state. Treatment usually is along the same principles as that for psychedelic drug intoxication—removal of threatening stimuli, protecting the user and those around him from potential hostile outbursts, and creating a supportive setting with observation.

A deterrent to the use of volatile inhalants may be used. Such a deterrent, that will cause nausea and vomiting when inhaled, is synthetic oil of mustard. This deterrent is frequently added to model airplane glue.

Decreasing the use of inhalants includes: (1) making the substances harder to acquire by limiting their availability in stores and in homes; (2) educating young people as to their potential dangers; and (3) giving psychological and spiritual aid to those who are currently using inhalants or who live in an environment where "sniffing" may become a problem because of their home situations or as a result of exposure to common usage.

Slang terms that refer to amyl nitrite inhalants are: snappers, poppers andpearls. Butyl nitrite is referred to as locker room, rush, hardware, bolt, oz and Satan's scent.

Chapter Ten

What Can We Do to Alleviate the Problem?

Now that we know the nature of the problem, what can we do about it? Since drug abuse is a complex problem, the prevention also appears to be complex, so various approaches need to be utilized. These approaches should be made from the standpoint of (1) education, (2) legislation, and (3) substitution.

Education for Adults As Well As Young People

Although there is currently a great deal of publicity through schools, television, etc., about the danger of drug abuse, there doesn't seem to be much that can actually provoke a decision to not experiment in drugs. Schools should provide instruction to adults, as well as youth, that is accurate and not oversimplified. Drug education needs to begin at the elementary level, since this is where many young people are contacted by pushers. If their parents are well informed through educational programs then the children will have stronger guidelines for resisting experimentation in drugs.

But education cannot be limited to schools. Churches need to get involved in drug abuse education. There seems to be an abundance of lesson material, films, records, etc., that can be used in Sunday School and youth meetings about teenage sex, self-esteem, discipline, and parental relationships, but I have found very little concerning drug abuse—except some on alcohol. Responsible religious leaders and educators need to prepare materials that can be used in the churches to help combat drug abuse.

Of course, the most effective place for educating young people to the dangers of drug abuse is in the home. Parents need to approach drug abuse as they do anything that could be dangerous for their children. They also need to set examples for their families to follow.

One factor that might make some impact on the drug problem is for parents to eliminate the double standard they have established in their homes. By this I mean the attitude that "alcohol and tobacco are okay for adults, but you kids keep away from beer and pot." Everyone needs to live and be judged by the same standard.

A second factor that could help alleviate the drug problem is for parents to stop exposing their children to the fallacy that the stresses of everyday life require chemical relief. Respect for drugs should be instilled at an early age.

Parents are responsible for the proper development of the family through their modeling and teaching. A group of high school students participated in a survey about parent relationships. They listed characteristics they felt parents ought to possess; these included love, caring, concern, trust, closeness, sharing, willingness to listen, warmth, cooperation, doing things together, mutual respect, and relating well to children as well as other adults. Regarding discipline they said that family discipline should be reasonable—not overly permissive or restrictive; they felt discipline should be such that they would have to solve their own problems; that parents should allow or suggest activities that foster responsibility; that there should be open discussion and that parents should keep "tabs" on them.

These students also compiled a list of suggestions for parents. These suggestions were as follows:

1. Be parents, not buddies
2. Accept parental responsibilities
3. Stop spoiling kids and trying to buy happiness
4. Stay home once in awhile
5. Listen
6. Look to the real, meaningful things of life
7. Cut down on drinking, smoking and pill-popping
8. Ease up on social, academic, and other pressures and love your kids
9. Help your kids with problems, when they need it
10. Become educated about drugs and know the signs of drug misuse.

Children usually adopt family patterns during their growing-up years. Parents are charged with the responsibility of drug education through life education. Parental example has a powerful impact on children, as most parents know by experience. What we transmit to our children about drugs is, in essence, what we transmit to them about life.

Legislation to Alleviate Drug Abuse

Most states have laws regulating the use and sale of drugs and prohibiting the sale and use of illegal drugs. The problem is, for whatever the reason, that these existing laws are not always enforced. Parents, religious leaders, and educators can do much to see that law enforcement agencies act to enforce the laws, particularly those against the drug pushers.

Stiffer penalties should be imposed on drug suppliers. Mandatory hospitalization for addicts could be enacted. Early detection and treatment could improve the mental health of drug users. Improvement of environmental living conditions would also help. Any legislation that would reduce the unimpeded drug traffic should be initiated and enforced.

Substitutes for Drug Abuse

It is important that we, as a nation, decide which is more important: to provide alternatives to drug abuse or to continue to cope with increased job absenteeism because of drugs, rising hospital charges, high costs to taxpayers as a result of drugs, increased welfare and crime, and thousands of wasted lives.

Alternatives to drug abuse must be realistic, meaningful, attainable, offer active participation and involvement and a feeling of commitment, and must contribute to an individual's identity and independence. There are many alternatives already available that meet these requirements.

Vocational skill development provides a person with training for working with his hands and mind in learning a trade. These skills should be taught beginning in junior high school (carpentry, welding, printing, ceramics, leathercraft, vocal and instrumental music, cooking, and wood, metal, and plastic machining) and continuing through high school (cosmetology, office machines, cooking, vocal and instrumental music, computer programming, plumbing, electronics, stenography, auto mechanics, electrical repair, and small appliance repair). These skills provide a person with a sense of pride in his work, a sense of accomplishment, personal satisfaction, and a sense of contribution.

Self-reliance development aids an individual in gaining some control over his environment. A chronic drug abuser is often mechanically incompetent and dependent upon others, which leads to frustration. Providing training to help develop basic mechanical skills will help foster some degree of independence and self-reliance.

Activities that encourage creativity will lead an individual to realize a degree of accomplishment, pride in his work, and personal satisfaction. Creative experiences can take the form of sketching, painting, sculpting, weaving, pottery making, gardening, composing, singing, acting, playing a musical instrument, cooking, writing, etc. These activities can be learned and encouraged in the home, at school, civic centers and churches.

Personal awareness is involved with developing oneself physically, mentally, and socially. Physical activities develop physical and sensory awareness, strength and muscle coordination. Such activities include athletics, outdoor work, hiking, camping, etc. Mental (psychological) awareness is determining why you do what you do and becoming aware of the feelings of others. Interpersonal awareness is involved with ascertaining the effect of your behavior on others. These latter activities are usually conducted by trained counselors. Enhancing interpersonal relations is an aid in preventing loneliness and is concerned with understanding people, sharing with people, respecting them and gaining personal respect.

Intellectual exercises include creative games and puzzles, training in concentration and in memory, exploring ethics, value systems, nature of reality, imagination, and even constructive daydreaming.

The most important alternative to drug use is that of a *spiritual experience.* For a spiritual experience to be effective, it must (1) be personal, applicable to everyday life and grow stronger every day, (2) produce discernible, positive attitudes towards self, life, others, (3) recognize God and acceptance of Jesus Christ as Lord and Saviour, and (4) answer the questions of self-fulfillment and the ultimate purpose of life.

It is often easy to sit back and say, "Well the drug problem is a national problem; let the government handle it." Or, "The schools should take the full responsibility for educating our young people in drug use and abuse." Or even, "If the churches would be more socially concerned they could make an impact on our drug-minded society." But alleviating drug abuse is up to you—especially if you are a Christian. Paul exhorted Timothy to "set an example . . . in speech, in life, in love, in faith and in purity" (1 Tim. 4:12, *NIV*). "For God did not give us a spirit of timidity, but a spirit of power, of love and of self-discipline" (2 Tim. 1:7, *NIV*).

A vital part of witnessing in our daily lives is to exercise self-control and discipline. The decision not to use drugs is a continuing one and reflects the self-control and discipline characteristic of a strong Christian. Peter tells us that "for this very reason, make every effort to add to your faith goodness; and to goodness, knowledge; and to knowledge, self-control; and to self-control, perseverance; and to perseverance, godliness; and to godliness, brotherly kindness; and to brotherly kindness, love. For if you possess these qualities in increasing measure, they will keep you from being ineffective and unproductive in your knowledge of our Lord Jesus Christ" (2 Pet. 1:5-8, *NIV*).

The most important thing that can happen to an individual while he is on this earth is to come to the saving knowledge and acceptance of Jesus Christ as his personal Saviour. The most important thing that you can do for someone else is to lead him to Jesus Christ. We are witnesses every day, either in a positive way or a negative way.

We as Christians are commanded to live our lives in such a way that we will not keep any person from receiving Jesus Christ as his personal Saviour. "Make up your mind not to put any stumbling block or obstacle in your brother's way" (Rom. 14:13, *NIV*). "It is better not to eat meat or drink wine or to do anything else that will cause your brother to fall" (Rom. 14:21, *NIV*).

Most people are aware of what it is to be a stumbling block in an active manner. That is, they are aware that if they commit an act that prevents another person from accepting Christ they are a stumbling block. However, there is also the possibility of being a passive stumbling block, a "silent Christian" or a person who does not live his Christianity. A passive stumbling block is one who does not take advantage of an opportunity to witness whenever it is presented to him. Being a Christian is a serious matter and involves serious responsibilities. "Each of us will give an account of himself to God" (Rom. 14:12, *NIV*). A Christian ought to go to great pains never to approve or to appear to approve of alcohol or drug abuse, or to lend his influence to it in any way, shape or form.

Glossary

Commonly Used Terms in the Drug Culture

A-bomb. *A mixture of marijuana and heroin smoked in a cigarette*
ace. *An older term for a marijuana cigarette*
acid head. *A heavy user of LSD, also acid freak*
acid test. *A party at which LSD has been added to the punch*
a.d. *Drug addict*
amys. *Amyl nitrite, also called pearls and snappers*
apple. *A non-addict*
are you anywhere? *Do you smoke marijuana?*
artillery. *Equipment for injecting drugs*
babo. *Nalline—a drug used to treat narcotic overdoses*
backtrack. *To withdraw the plunger of a syringe before injecting drugs to make sure the needle is in the proper position*
backwards. *Tranquilizers to counter the effects of uppers and LSD*
bad trip. *A panic reaction after taking a hallucinogen*
bag. *A container of drugs*
bagman. *A drug supplier*
bale. *A pound of marijuana*
bam. *Amphetamine tablet or injection*
bang. *An injection of narcotics*
bank bandits. *Barbiturates*
bar. *A solid block of marijuana stuck together with syrup or honey*
barb freak. *Intravenous barbiturate user*
B-bombs. *Benzedrine Inhalers*
been had. *Arrested or cheated out of something*
belly habit. *Opium addiction*
belongs. *On the habit*
bent. *High or intoxicated*
big John. *The police*

big man. *High level narcotics dealer*
bindle. *A small quantity or packet of narcotics*
bit. *Time served in jail*
biz. *Equipment for injecting drugs*
black and white. *A patrol car*
blanks. *Poor quality merchandise*
blast. *To smoke a marijuana cigarette*
blasted. *Under the influence of drugs*
blow. *To smoke a marijuana cigarette*
blow a stick. *To smoke a marijuana cigarette*
blow Charlie or blow snow. *Sniff cocaine*
blow horse. *Sniff heroin*
blow your cool. *To lose self-control*
blow your mind. *To become high*
blue cheer. *A combination of LSD and methamphetamine dyed blue*
blue velvet. *Paregoric and an antihistamine*
bogue. *Sickness from withdrawal of drugs*
bolsa. *A bag of heroin*
bomb. *High potency heroin*
bombed out. *High or intoxicated on drugs*
boxed. *In jail; high or intoxicated on drugs*
brain ticklers. *Barbiturates or amphetamines*
bread. *Money*
brick. *Kilogram of marijuana in compressed brick form*
bring down. *To clear the mind or bring back from a drug experience*
brown. *Mexican heroin*
bull. *A federal narcotics agent; a police officer*
bum bend. *A psychotic or panic reaction*
bum kicks. *Troubled; worried; depressed*
bummer. *A bad experience or a bad trip on acid or marijuana*
bundle. *A package of bags of heroin*
bunk habit. *Lying around where others are smoking opium to inhale the fumes*
burn artist. *A drug peddler noted for cheating others*
burned. *To receive phony narcotics*
burned out. *Sclerotic blood vessels from too many injections*
burning. *Smoking marijuana*
bust. *An arrest*
buy. *A purchase of drugs*
buzz. *Feeling at the onset of a marijuana high*
buzz on. *To feel good*

C & H. *Cocaine and heroin mixed*
C & M. *Cocaine and morphine mixed*
cadet. *A new addict*
can. *An ounce of morphine*
candy man. *A pusher of drugs*
cap. *A container of drugs*
carry. *To have drugs on the person; to carry drugs*
cashing a script. *Getting forged or bogus prescription orders dispensed*
catch up. *Withdrawal process*
champ. *Drug abuser who won't reveal his supplier*
charged up. *Under the influence of drugs*
chasing the bag. *Hustling for heroin; addicted*
chasing the dragon. *An oriental method of ingesting heroin*
chillum. *A clay pipe used for smoking ganja in India*
Chinese cure. *A method of withdrawing from heroin; the drug is mixed with a tonic in decreasing amounts daily until just tonic is taken*
chipping. *Taking small amounts of drugs on an irregular basis*
chippy. *An abuser taking small, irregular amounts of drugs*
cleared up. *To withdraw from drugs*
coasting. *Under the influence of drugs*
cocktail. *A regular cigarette with marijuana inserted into the end which is to be lit*
cokie. *A cocaine addict*
cold. *Tough deal*
cold turkey. *Sudden drug withdrawal*
collar. *An arrest*
come down. *To lose the effects of a drug*
connect. *Make a drug purchase*
connection. *A drug supplier*
contact. *A drug supplier*
contact high. *Becoming high merely by interacting with one who is high*
cook. *To heat a mixture of heroin and water to dissolve the heroin*
cook up a pill. *To prepare opium for smoking*
cop. *To purchase drugs*
cop out. *To alibi, confess*
cope. *To function although intoxicated*
cottons. *Cotton saturated with narcotic solution to strain foreign matter when drawing solution up into a*

hypodermic syringe or eyedropper

crash. *Fall asleep while using drugs; come down hard and fast from a high or a trip*

crater. *A hole in the flesh caused by repeated injections of drugs in the same spot*

creep. *An addict who begs drugs rather than engaging in activities to get the money to purchase them*

croaker. *A doctor who illegally prescribes drugs for money*

crutch. *A container for a hypodermic needle*

cubes. *LSD on sugar cubes*

cura. *A shot of heroin*

cut. *To adulterate a narcotic; to dilute*

dabble. *To take small amounts of drugs on an irregular basis*

dawamesk. *A mixture of cannabis, sugar, orange juice, cinnamon, cloves, cardamom, nutmeg, musk, pistachios, and pine kernels made into a green, aromatic cake; eaten in North Africa*

dealer. *Drug supplier, peddler*

deck. *A small packet of narcotics*

deal. *To peddle in narcotics*

depressants. *Sedatives; drugs which cause depression of the central nervous system*

dime bag. *A $10 purchase of narcotics*

dirty. *To be in possession of drugs*

domino. *To purchase drugs*

dope. *Any narcotic*

dope fiend. *A drug addict*

doper. *An addict*

doup. *To smoke a joint or take an injection of heroin*

downers. *Sedatives*

dragged. *Frightened after using marijuana*

dried out. *Detoxified or off of a drug*

drop. *To swallow*

dropped. *Arrested*

dummy. *Counterfeit heroin*

dusting. *Mixing heroin in a marijuana cigarette; mixing PCP in a marijuana cigarette*

dynamite. *Cocaine and heroin taken together; undiluted or high quality heroin*

electric Kool-Ade. *Punch containing LSD*

explorers club. *A group of acid heads*

factory. *Equipment for injecting drugs; a location where illicit drugs are processed*

falling out. *Dozing off while under the influence of a drug*
fatty. *A thickly rolled marijuana cigarette*
fine stuff. *Narcotics of unusually good quality*
fink. *Informer; phony*
fit. *Equipment for injection by the hypodermic route*
fix. *To inject drugs*
flaky. *Addicted to cocaine*
flash. *Euphoric reaction; a sudden strong reaction to a drug (flush)*
flashing. *Glue sniffing*
flea powder. *Poor quality narcotics*
flip out. *A temporary or chronic psychotic reaction to a drug*
floating. *Under the influence of drugs*
flunky. *An addict who takes large risks in acquiring money for drugs*
flying. *In a state of drug intoxication*
frantic. *Nervous; jittery; in need of a fix*
freak out. *Have a bad trip*
freak up. *To act in a bizarre, grotesque way*
freaking freely. *Spontaneous, random, LSD-induced behavior*
freaky. *Bizarre, abnormal behavior induced by drugs*
fresh and sweet. *Out of jail*
Frisco speedball. *A mixture of heroin, cocaine, and LSD-25*
front. *Putting up a false display of respectability*
full moon. *A large peyote chunk comprising the top of the cactus, resembling a full moon*
fuzz. *The police*
gammon. *One microgram*
gaping. *Experiencing opiate withdrawal symptoms*
garbage. *Poor quality merchandise*
garbage head. *An individual who takes any kind of drug*
gassing. *Sniffing gasoline fumes*
gate keeper. *One who initiates another into the use of LSD*
gear. *Drugs in general*
gee-head. *A paregoric abuser*
geetis. *Money*
geezer. *A narcotic injection*
get off. *To inject heroin*
get on. *To take drugs for the first time*
getting on. *Smoking marijuana*

gimmicks. *The equipment for injecting drugs*
glad rag. *A piece of cloth that is saturated with a substance to be inhaled*
globetrotter. *An addict who travels around an area in order to select the best heroin*
glow. *High, drugged euphoria*
gluey. *A glue sniffer*
goblet of jam. *A confection containing cannabis (marijuana)*
going down. *Going well*
going high. *A continuing state of intoxication*
goods. *Narcotics or other drugs*
good sick. *Nausea and vomiting associated with heroin injection. It is not considered unpleasant*
good stuff. *High quality heroin*
goofing. *Under the influence of barbiturates*
go up. *To get intoxicated*
gow. *Opium*
gow head. *An opium user*
gram. *Gram of heroin, approximately 10 capsules*
grasshopper. *Marijuana user*
gravy. *Mixture of blood and heroin which is heated because it has coagulated*
greasy junky. *A lazy addict who begs drugs rather than engaging in drug-hustling activities*
groovers. *Teenagers who use drugs*
grooving. *Being intoxicated on drugs*
groovy. *The high experience of a drug effect*
ground control. *Caretaker in an LSD session*
gun. *Hypodermic syringe*
guru. *Companion on a trip who has tripped before*
habit. *Dependent on drugs*
H-caps. *Heroin in gelatin capsules*
half load. *15 packages or bags of heroin*
hallucinogen. *A substance which alters perception and produces illusions and/or hallucinations*
hand-to-hand. *Delivery of narcotics person to person*
hang up. *A personal problem*
hang tough. *Phrase used for encouraging an addict going through withdrawal*
hard stuff. *Narcotics, usually heroin*
hassle. *Annoyances or efforts required to obtain drugs*
head. *One who is involved with drugs to the extent that the drug has become an important part of his life*
heat. *The police*

heavy drugs. *Hard narcotics*
heavy stuff. *Heroin, cocaine, morphine, etc.*
heeled. *Possessing drugs*
high. *Under the influence of drugs*
hip, hep. *To understand*
hit. *Drag off a marijuana cigarette; to make a purchase of drugs*
hitting up. *Injecting drugs*
hocus. *A narcotic solution ready for injection*
hold. *To have drugs for sale*
holding. *Possessing narcotics*
hookah. *A pipe for smoking marijuana which bubbles the smoke through water*
hooked. *Addicted*
hop dog. *An opium addict*
hop head. *Narcotic addict*
hopped up. *Under the influence of drugs*
horning. *Sniffing narcotics by nose*
horror drug. *Any preparation containing belladonna alkaloids*
hot. *Wanted by the police*
hot shot. *A fatal dose*
hubbly bubbly. *See hookah*
hustling. *Obtaining money for drugs by criminal means; prostitution*
hype. *To inject by needle*
ice cream habit. *A small, irregular drug habit*
idiot pills. *Barbiturate or other sedative pills*
inhalers. *Volatile substances inhaled for their intoxicant effects*
in transit. *On an LSD trip*
jab. *To ambush someone*
jacked up. *To be interrogated or arrested*
jag. *Prolonged stimulation by a drug*
jammed up. *An overdose*
Jefferson airplane. *A holder for the butt of a marijuana cigarette made by splitting a match into a Y shape*
jive sticks. *Marijuana cigarettes*
job. *To inject drugs*
joint. *Syringe and needle; marijuana cigarette; opium smokers' den*
jolt. *An injection of narcotics*
jones. *Dependence on a drug; a habit*
joy-pop. *To inject small amounts of drugs irregularly*
juice. *Liquor*

juice head. *One who drinks liquor*
junk. *Narcotics*
junkie. *A narcotic addict*
key. *A kilogram*
kick. *To abandon a drug habit*
kickback. *To return to taking drugs*
kick cold turkey. *To withdraw from drugs abruptly*
kick the habit. *To go through withdrawal*
kicking. *Withdrawal process*
kicks. *The initial rush of a drug's effect*
kicksticks. *Marijuana cigarettes; joints*
kilo. *2.2 pounds*
King Kong pills. *Barbiturates or other sedatives*
kit. *Equipment for injecting drugs*
layout. *The equipment for injecting drugs*
legal high. *Substances that are not prohibited by law and can be obtained without a prescription*
lemonade. *Blank*
lid. *A container of drugs*
line. *To inject a drug into the vein*
lit up. *Under the influence of drugs*
load. *25 to 30 packets of heroin ready for delivery*
loaded. *Under the influence of heroin or marijuana*
lush. *A heavy drinker*
M. *Morphine*
mace. *A common spice mixed with hot water to produce stimulation*
machinery. *Equipment for injecting drugs*
made. *Being exposed for what you really are*
mainline. *To inject drugs directly into a vein*
mainliner. *One who injects drugs directly into the vein*
mainstash. *Home*
majoon. *A jam containing marijuana (also majoun)*
make. *To purchase drugs; to detect someone*
make a buy. *To purchase drugs*
make a meet. *To purchase drugs; to leave*
make it. *To achieve something; to get a high*
man, the. *Police*
manicure. *To prepare marijuana for use in cigarettes by cleaning it*
match box. *Small container of marijuana*
meet. *To buy drugs*
mind trippers. *Young people, 17 to 22 years old, who use drugs for self-therapy*
mojo. *Narcotics*

monkey. *A drug habit where physical dependence is present*
morning shot. *Wake-up*
mother. *The drug peddler*
mud. *Stramonium preparations mixed with carbonated beverages*
muggles. *Marijuana cigarettes*
mule. *A person who transports narcotics, not necessarily a peddler*
multihabituation. *Dependence on more than one drug*
nab. *An arresting officer*
nail. *A hypodermic needle*
narc. *A narcotics officer*
needle. *Hypodermic syringe with needle*
nickel bag. *A $5 purchase of drugs*
no-art. *Psychedelic art*
nod. *A drowsy, sleepy state usually associated with heroin use*
number. *Marijuana cigarette*
O.D. *Overdose; death*
off. *Withdraw from drugs*
on. *Using drugs*
on a trip. *Under the influence of LSD or other hallucinogens*
on the needle. *Injecting narcotics*
on the nod. *Under the influence of drugs, usually heroin*
on the street. *Out of jail*
outfit. *Equipment for injection by the hypodermic route: syringe, needle, spoon, safety pin, razor, etc.*
overjolt. *Overdose*
paddy. *A Caucasian*
panatella. *A bigger, fatter than normal, marijuana cigarette*
panic. *A scarcity of drugs usually caused by the arrest of a big peddler*
paper. *Paper of heroin (bindle) or a prescription for narcotics*
partying. *Enjoying heroin sociably*
pass. *A transfer of drugs*
peddler. *One who sells drugs*
picked up. *Having smoked up*
piece. *Container of drugs*
pill freak. *Pill head*
pill head. *A heavy user of pills—either depressant or stimulant*

pillows. *Heat-sealed polyethylene bags containing drugs*
pilly. *Pill head*
pin. *A marijuana cigarette*
pit. *The main vein leading to the heart*
place. *The setting of an LSD trip*
plant. *A cache of narcotics*
poison. *Heroin*
poison people. *Heroin addicts*
poke. *A puff of a marijuana cigarette*
pop. *To inject a drug; to take a drug orally*
poppers. *Small vials containing amyl nitrite*
popping. *Injecting drugs immediately under the skin*
pothead. *A marijuana smoker*
potlikker. *A tea brewed from marijuana waste*
potsville. *Using pot*
psyching. *Insane*
pure. *Pure heroin, prior to adulteration*
push. *To peddle drugs*
pusher. *One who sells narcotics*
quill. *A folded matchbook cover from which narcotics are sniffed through the nose*
rap. *To talk*
rapping. *Talking*
rat fink. *Informer for police*
reader. *A prescription*
reader with tail. *A forged prescription*
reefer. *Marijuana cigarette*
ripped. *Intoxicated by drugs*
roaches. *Librium capsules; butts of marijuana cigarettes*
roach holder. *A thin-pronged instrument, often decorated, for holding a roach; a roach pick*
root. *A marijuana cigarette*
rope. *Marijuana*
roust. *An interrogation or arrest*
ruler. *A judge*
run. *A period of addiction*
rush. *Initial onset of euphoria and physical well-being immediately after a drug is injected*
salt shot. *An injection of saline or salt water*
sam. *Federal narcotics agents*
scars. *Traces left by needle marks*
scene. *Social patterns or areas of drug use*
schmecker. *A heroin user*
scoff. *To take narcotics daily*
scoop. *A folded matchbook cover; to sniff cocaine or*

heroin through a matchbook cover that has been folded

score. *To purchase drugs*

scratch. *Being an addict*

script. *A prescription*

script writer. *Sympathetic physician; one who forges prescription orders*

scrubwoman's kick. *Naphtha, a cleaning fluid*

seed. *Roach, the butt of a marijuana cigarette*

seeds. *Marijuana seeds*

set up. *To entrap a user by informing officers of a sale*

sharps. *Needles*

shirt. *A quantity of drugs*

shlook. *A puff of a marijuana cigarette; poke; toke, toak*

shoot up. *To inject drugs*

shooting gallery. *A place where an injection of narcotics can be bought, but which does not permit loitering*

shooting gravy. *Injecting a warmed-up mixture of blood and drugs*

short. *Automobile*

short con. *A petty confidence game*

short count. *The supplier shorting the pusher an amount of drugs*

short go. *A short weight*

short sled. *Automobile; vehicle*

shot. *An injection of narcotics*

shying. *Cooking opium and preparing it for injection*

sick. *Suffering withdrawal symptoms*

sickie. *A college student using drugs*

siva. *The god of the Hindu worship who brought marijuana to mankind*

sizzle. *Narcotics carried on a person*

skin. *Cigarette paper for rolling marijuana cigarettes*

skin pop. *Injection into the skin; just under the surface of the skin*

skinning. *Skinpopping*

slammed. *In jail*

sleepwalker. *A heroin addict*

smack. *Heroin*

smashed. *Intoxicated on drugs*

sniffing. *Using narcotics by sniffing*

snop. *Marijuana*

snort. *To inhale marijuana or cocaine through the nose*

snowbird. *A cocaine user*

source. *Supplier of drugs*

spaced. *Intoxicated on hallucinogens*
speedball. *Heroin and cocaine mixture for injection*
spike. *Needle*
split. *To run away; to leave*
spoon. *A quantity of heroin theoretically measured in a teaspoon, usually between one and two grams*
square. *One who does not know what is happening; one who does not use drugs*
stash. *A cache of narcotics*
steamboat. *Inhaling the smoke from the butt of a marijuana cigarette stuck in the side of an empty toilet paper roll; the hand closes one end of the roll and the mouth is closed over the other end*
stick. *A marijuana cigarette*
sting. *To rob or defraud*
stoned. *Under the influence of drugs*
stool. *Informer for police*
straight. *A person holding, or under the influence of narcotics; also, a person not using drugs; a non-marijuana cigarette*
street, on the. *To be using drugs*
strung out. *Using drugs*
stuff. *Narcotics; usually heroin*
sugar. *Powdered narcotics*
system, the. *An addict's tolerance*
swingman. *A drug supplier*
tab. *Tablet*
tabs. *Capsules containing LSD-25*
take off. *To get high*
tall. *High or intoxicated*
tar beach. *A roof used for sleeping by drug users*
taste. *A small sample of a narcotic*
tea head. *A marijuana smoker*
tea pad. *A place where marijuana is used*
third eye. *The inward looking eye*
thoroughbred. *A high-type hustler who sells pure narcotics*
throwing rocks. *Committing a crime*
thumb. *A fat marijuana cigarette*
toke up. *A light marijuana cigarette; to light a marijuana cigarette (toake up)*
toke pipes. *Short-stemmed pipes in which marijuana is smoked*
tools. *Equipment for injecting drugs*
top. *A brand of flavored papers for rolling marijuana*

cigarettes
torch. *A marijuana cigarette*
torn up. *Intoxicated by a drug*
tossed. *Searched for drugs*
toss out. *To fake withdrawal symptoms to obtain narcotics from a doctor*
tracked up. *Numerous injection marks along a vein*
tracks. *Needle scars*
trap. *A hiding place for drugs*
travel agent. *LSD supplier*
trip. *An LSD adventure*
trip, tripping. *Being high on hallucinogens, particularly LSD*
turkey. *A capsule purported to be a narcotic but filled with a non-narcotic substance*
turkey trots. *Marks and scars from using a hypodermic needle*
turned on. *Under the influence of drugs; involved and excited*
turned out. *Being introduced to drugs*
turning people on. *To give others drugs; to excite and interest them*
twisted. *Suffering from withdrawal symptoms*
tying up. *Using a tourniquet to prepare to inject drugs*
uncle. *A federal narcotics agent*
up. *Intoxicated*
upper. *An amphetamine or other stimulant*
uptight. *Worried, defensive, paranoid*
user. *One who uses narcotics*
vendelor. *A pusher*
violated. *Arrested for a parole violation*
vol. *volunteer*
voyager. *A person under the influence of LSD-25*
wad. *A piece of cloth saturated with a material to be inhaled*
wake-up. *The addict's first injection in the morning*
wallbanger. *Someone intoxicated and uncoordinated on downers*
washed up. *Withdrawn from drugs*
wasted. *Heavily under the influence of drugs*
weed-head. *Marijuana user*
weeding out. *Smoking marijuana*
weekend habit. *A small, irregular drug habit*
wheel. *A car*
whiskers. *Federal narcotics agents*

wig. *The mind*
wig out. *An abrupt change in the mood*
wings. *The first mainline shot.*
works. *The equipment for injecting drugs*
zig zag. *A brand of flavored cigarette papers used for rolling marijuana cigarettes*
zonk. *Under the influence of drugs*

DRUGS
ALCOHOL
& SEX

PATRICIA J. BUSH, PH.D.

RICHARD MAREK PUBLISHERS
NEW YORK

Library of Congress Cataloging in Publication Data

Bush, Patricia J
Drugs, alcohol, and sex.

"How you can help or harm your sex life with alcohol, prescribed and over-the-counter medicines, and recreational drugs; includes aphrodisiacs, the pill, marijuana, uppers, downers, psychedelics, hormones, antihypertensives, steroids, volatile inhalants, and feminine hygiene products."
Includes index.
1. Generative organs—Drug effects. 2. Drugs—Physiological effects. 3. Alcohol—Physiological effect.
I. Title. [DNLM: 1. Psychotropic drugs—Pharmacodynamics—Popular works. 2. Sex behavior—Drug effects—Popular works. 3. Alcohol, Ethyl—Pharmacodynamics—Popular works. WM270 B978d]
RM380.B87 613.9'5 80-15481
ISBN 0-399-90080-2

PRINTED IN THE UNITED STATES OF AMERICA

To My Parents Who Urged Me to "Look It Up"

CONTENTS

Part V. Sex Through Chemistry in the Present and the Future

Appendixes

PREFACE

If you're running five miles a day, you're watching your cholesterol and sugar, your blood pressure's low, your heart rate is down, you never take anything stronger than aspirin, you've switched from Scotch to Perrier water or soda and white wine, if you don't need megavitamins because your diet is lo-cal, additive free, and balanced; if you get high on love and nature, and you're even smugger about your sex life since you found out that each occasion of sexual intercourse burns up about two hundred calories, this book is *not* for you.

This book is for mere humans, those of us who know we should get more exercise and quit smoking and quit the junk foods and stop doing drugs and find less stressful jobs and, for heaven's sakes, start taking care of ourselves. But we don't seem to get around to it, or we start and then stop because we hurt, or we think we're too old, or we don't have time, or we simply lack the resolve. Some of us are bewildered and turned off. "Is nothing safe?" we moan. Sugar and overweight are bad we were told, so we drank diet soda and put first cyclamates and then saccharin in our coffee and tea. Now (surprise!) we're informed that these chemicals cause cancer. We were told that a high protein diet was good, so we ate lots of eggs and red meat. Then we learned that eggs and meat contain cholesterol, and that lots of cholesterol may lead to something called atherosclerosis, which predisposes to clogged arteries and an early demise. This goes for cheese, butter, and whole milk, too, all foods that we used to think made good little eaters grow into big strong handsome adults. And bacon. And liverwurst. And smoked meats. All relegated to the outcast category "carcinogenic." Red food dye—no more red M & M's. Worry about whether it's in lipstick, and how much we've swallowed over the years. And hair spray—glad to give that up—and bug spray—we need it—and salt—everything tastes lousy without it—and so it goes.

Smoking. That's a good one. How to be sophisticated, cool, and sexy, right? Humphrey Bogart in slouch hat and trench coat—his face momentarily lighted up as he cups his hands against the wind and—inhales. Duke Wayne on the range—cigarette dangling, eyes squinting as he scans the horizon and—inhales. A gorgeous couple at a—do you remember?—nightclub. He leans romantically over the table, eyes fixed on her décolletage and flicks his lighter. She smiles into his eyes, reaches for his hand and—inhales. Yes, you've come a long way, baby, and then they told you: lung cancer, emphysema, bronchitis, stroke, low birth-weight babies. Ouch.

For many of us, it's too late. Our mothers bottle-fed us and fed us baby food with salt in it, and we've been sitting on our behinds ever since, stuffing potato chips, and damn it, we're already sick, or feel like we're about to be. And we still have the stressful jobs, and the big mortgages, and we don't know how to change from our A type personalities into the more restful, nonachieving B types. And who wants to anyway? And the bottom line of all this is—we're a little bit worried and that's the unkindest cut of all, because we're told that too much worrying will make us sick, and that makes us worry even more.

So most of us are taking medicines prescribed by our doctors, medicines that we're increasingly suspicious of, and most of us are buying over the counter from our druggist what our TV insists helps us with our upset stomachs, our headaches, our insomnia, our coughs, our hemorrhoids. In one survey of the persons living in a large city, two-thirds of those interviewed said they had taken one or more medicines in the preceding two-day period.

Despite all that, most of us would like to believe that our sex life is as good as the next fellow's, even though the next fellow may be one of those clear-eyed, smug and sweaty runners held together with organic foods. We're willing to concede to the health freaks that they're probably going to live longer than we are, but we're not willing to concede that they're necessarily living better or having more fun. We certainly don't want to concede to them that their sex lives are better than ours. In fact, some of us believe that some of the things we're doing—the alcohol, the drugs, and the medicines—are making our sex lives better.

For many, particularly young people, sex and drugs go together. And not just some of the time, but all of the time. For example, one twenty-six-year-old woman, in responding to a questionnaire about the effect of drugs on her sexual desire and response, said, "I've been using drugs and having sex about the same length of time. In fact, I can't imagine one without the other."

For the martini set, alcohol may be as much of an accompaniment to sex as drugs are for the young. Tens of thousands of women rely on liquor to relax them enough to enjoy sexual relations. Indeed, the classic romantic setting involves candlelight, soft music—and wine.

The relationship of sex to medicines, whether prescribed or purchased over the counter without a prescription, is a mystery to most people. And no wonder. There are over 10,000 prescription drugs, and altogether about 200,000 different drugs on the American market when all the different brands of over-the-counter drugs are included. Many of these drugs, both prescribed and nonprescribed, affect sexual function. Many of them affect the sexual function of some, but not all, of the people who take them. When prescribed drugs do affect sexual function, most of them interfere with it, rather than help it.

This book is for those who want to know what drugs, alcohol, and medicines can do to their sex lives, so they can talk to their physicians about what's happening to them and make better choices. It's for those who drink, those who smoke, those who "do" drugs, and those who do the combinations, that is, mix drugs and alcohol or drugs and drugs. The purpose is to demystify the confusion surrounding prescription drugs, so that you'll know which ones are most likely to affect you sexually and how you may be affected. You'll also find out about aphrodisiacs, whether there really are any, and whether sex is better or worse or simply unaffected by alcohol and drugs that are taken recreationally. These include nicotine and caffeine, drugs that are so common they're not usually thought of as drugs at all. For all of these, the mechanisms of action are explained so that you can understand why as well as what is happening. A discussion of drugs used deliberately to alter sexual function and sex appeal is also included. Some of them are prescribed by doctors, and others are taken deliberately by persons who wish to alter their appearance or other characteristics, such as the way they smell.

Much of the information in this book has been obtained from scientific literature and medical journals, but some has been obtained directly from persons who filled in a questionnaire.

THE QUESTIONNAIRE

If you want to know how people feel and think they respond sexually after they've taken a recreational drug or had a few drinks, you won't find very much in medical textbooks or scientific journals. Scientists haven't been very interested in the subject; there hasn't been much money available for sex and drug research; and it is very hard to find volunteers who are into sex and drugs and are willing to be interviewed, or to take part in experiments, especially if they use drugs that are illegal, or that are legal but have been obtained on the illegal drug market. Most drugs used recreationally have been acquired on the illegal market, and users are often reluctant to admit to any but their closest and most trusted friends that they use drugs, let alone to establishment authority-figure scientists.

Even the most scientific investigations are open to criticism when the subject is sex. The now highly respected Kinsey Reports on human sexuality were subjected to considerable criticism when they first appeared. It was charged that the persons interviewed in the surveys, who provided the material for the books, must have represented an unusual and biased sample of Americans. Many did not believe that an average person would have been willing to discuss his or her sex life so openly with a stranger who came round to the door with a survey. Those who compared their own sex lives with those in the reports and found them different were especially critical and refused to believe that the reports could possibly be representative of the experience of normal people.

The work of Masters and Johnson and the Hite Report were subsequently subjected to similar kinds of criticism and charged with opportunism and appealing to prurient interests. Some believed that the emphasis on sexual fulfillment was contributing to a "me first" ideology and a breakdown in the moral fiber of America, and that the books projected an average that was not an average but an extreme, corrupting those who tried to become like those persons described in the books. Others believed that the representativeness of the people in the sex surveys was open to question, but that the surveys had performed an immeasurable service by bringing the subject out of the closet and by telling people not only that it was okay to be sexual, but that human sexuality was a marvelous gift that was meant to be enjoyed by all. Sex makes people feel good. It's fun. It's free. It can be the warmest, most caring expression of human contact. It can be enjoyed into old age. Therefore, the more everyone knows about it the better. That is precisely the spirit of this book, a spirit that seeks to shed, not all light, but as much light as possible.

Obviously, it was impossible to obtain a list of all the people who had engaged in sexual activity while under the influence of a drug in order to obtain a random sample and perform a representative survey. Therefore, the next best thing was to prepare a questionnaire. Persons known to the author—medical students, friends, college students—were asked to take copies of the questionnaire, which inquired into the effect of alcohol and recreational drugs on sexual desire and function, and either fill one out themselves or pass them on to persons whom they knew had had some alcohol or drug experience. The questionnaire was entirely anonymous, and each copy was accompanied by an addressed, stamped envelope. The questionnaire was also distributed at an annual meeting of the American Pharmaceutical Association. Further information was obtained by placing advertisements in the Personal column of the classified section of such newspapers as *The Village Voice*, *High Times*, and *The Berkeley Barb*, asking readers to send for a copy of the confidential questionnaire. Finally, some of the individuals living in a community of ex-drug addicts volunteered to fill in copies of the questionnaire. Over 250 copies were completed.

I am grateful to every person who took the time to fill in a questionnaire, a copy of which appears in Appendix A. As much information as I could find was abstracted from the scientific literature and included in the book, but that alone would have been insufficient and even of questionable validity. Experiments carried out in laboratories do not necessarily represent the experience of persons in their natural surroundings. Much of sex and the effect of alcohol and drugs is psychological. What one gains in the laboratory by the measurement of physiological responses with scientific instruments is surely lost in terms of the quality of subjective response, and in terms of the effect of milieu on response.

In addition to information obtained from scientific measurements with electronic devices, people want to know how others felt, what their experience was, did drugs make things better or worse, and, if so, in what ways; what were the circumstances? For complete information, laboratory experimentation is not enough. An analogy may make the point. If you were going to a new restaurant, you would be unlikely to accept the word of a scientist who told you about nutritional value, food temperature, aroma, calories, and the age and sex of the customers after they had eaten the meal. You would be much more likely to trust the subjective opinion of a friend who had eaten at the restaurant, whom you believed shared your views of eating pleasures, and who could convey the total experience of dining, and not just a recital of the menu or its prices. You would like to have the subjective experience of your friend, even if he were fooling himself regarding some of his experience, for the perception of people's experience is also real and valuable.

The information obtained from the questionnaires is not a valid representation of the physiological sexual response of individuals to drugs. It is the subjective perceptions of those who were asked to fill in the questionnaire and were willing to do it. Others may have entirely different perceptions. That makes the experiences of those who filled in a questionnaire no less valuable.

Many people drink, and many people smoke marijuana, so it was very easy to find subjects who were willing to report on their experiences while drinking or smoking marijuana. Other recreational drugs, such as methaqualone (Quaaludes), amphetamines, heroin, PCP, or amyl nitrite, are not used as frequently or by as many persons, so it was harder to find people to fill in the questionnaire in these categories, and those who did may be less representative of the average experience than those who reported the effects of alcohol and marijuana on sexual function.

WHAT ABOUT TERMS?

There's a problem with the words "drugs" and "medicines." Medicines that are used for illness are often called drugs and, in this book, the distinction should be clear from the context. Drugs that are used recreationally or for nonmedical purposes, such as marijuana, cocaine, or LSD, will always be called drugs.

For legal drugs, the generic name (the name assigned by the federal government) is given in small letters; brand names (the name given by drug manufacturers) starts with a capital letter. If there is more than one brand name, the most common appears in the text.

When each drug category is introduced, a table will list the generic name and the associated brand names as well as the brand names of combination drugs.

WARNING

Nothing in this book should be interpreted as a recommendation to an individual to stop taking a drug that he has been prescribed, to start taking any prescribed or over-the-counter medicine, or to use recreational drugs. The material contained herein is for information only. Many recreational drugs are illegal, and many are illegal and harmful. *Caveat emptor.*

A THANK YOU

I wish to express my appreciation to those friends and strangers who filled in questionnaires and passed them along to others, who pointed me in the direction of appropriate articles and books, and who provided general support and encouragement. A special thank you is due the members of my family for their patience and interest and to the following who advised, read, and typed: Joan Veal, Denise Rivera, and Carol Jones.

Patricia J. Bush, Ph.D.
Washington, D.C.
1980

PART I

AN OVERVIEW

1

WHAT THIS BOOK IS ABOUT

Without sex, life indeed would be a flat and colorless affair. Sex accounts for our being here in the first place; it gives us our first and most prominent identities; and it provides us with an almost constant source of pleasure—and sometimes worry and pain. Through the greater part of our lives, most of us are concerned about how attractive we are, usually meaning how attractive we are to the opposite sex. Through most of our lives, we're concerned about our sexual feelings, responses, and performances. We worry about the size of our penises, our vaginas, and our breasts. We worry about whether we've too much hair in some places and not enough in others. We worry about body odors. We worry about our ability to have orgasms and our ability to help our partners have them. We worry about whether we're normal or average. As we grow older, we worry about our sex appeal and the threatened loss of our ability to function sexually. As a nation, we spend millions of dollars annually on perfumes, clothes, books, magazines, psychiatrists, psychologists, marriage counselors, doctors, operations, sex therapists, mechanical devices, vitamins, and drugs, all in a conscious effort to become more sexually appealing.

Almost everyone would love to find a pill or potion that would make sex even more exciting, that would make the object of our desire find us irresistible, that would make men into inexhaustible lovers and guarantee women multiple orgasms. Imagine a pill that would raise us to new heights of sensate experience, that could guarantee that nobody had it better than we did. What wouldn't most of us give for that?

The search for a drug, or a food or drink, that would increase sexual desire and improve performance has been going on since man first began recording his activities and presumably before that. Early writings, particularly from India and North African countries, list over a thousand different plant and animal substances that have been endowed with aphrodisiac properties.[1] The idea that many of these, such as cabbage roots soaked in goat's milk, grilled red mullet, or honey and pigeon's blood, could affect sexual desire seems ridiculous, if not positively disgusting, these days.

The search for a true aphrodisiac that would work for everyone has proved as elusive as the ancient alchemist's search for a way to turn baser metals into gold. When aphrodisiacs have "worked," their success has rarely been attributable to their pharmacological* properties, but to the human body's ability to fool itself by responding to the *belief* that a substance is an aphrodisiac.

People of all ages past puberty, in many cultures, have tried to find aphrodisiacs. Men in particular have deeply resented and have actively fought against the threatened loss of sexual potency that comes with advancing age and have looked for a drug to maintain their sexual vigor. Historically, women have been more concerned about infertility and have looked for a substance to help them become pregnant. In many cultures, to be barren has been the ultimate failure for a woman, and in some, such as Iran, even today, it is grounds for divorce. The Shah of Iran divorced his wife Soraya because she had failed to produce an heir, leading some to comment that his subsequent exile was poetic justice.

Only in recent times, with the advent of the birth control pill, have drugs been taken to prevent pregnancy.

Occasionally substances have also been sought that were capable of decreasing sexual desire (anti- or anaphrodisiacs). In the past, antiaphrodisiacs were sometimes given to adolescent boys to decrease their sex drives. Antiaphrodisiacs have also been used by celibate monks, priests, and shamans, and they have been used as a sort of chemical chastity belt for women whose husbands were absent for extended periods of time. Rumors sometimes occur of antiaphrodisiacs being put into food or water to "control" the population. The most common rumor, widely believed by boarding-school boys and servicemen, is that saltpeter (sodium nitrate) is put into their food so they will forget about sex and concentrate on studying or fighting. More recently, antiaphrodisiacs have been given to hypersexed men who have

*A substance that is pharmacologically active has a chemical structure that causes a change in the body.

committed sex-related crimes, such as rape and pederasty, and to mentally defective persons, both men and women, who engage in embarrassing public sexual activity such as masturbation. The search for an antiaphrodisiac has been much more successful than the search for an aphrodisiac. As we shall see, many drugs, however not saltpeter, have antiaphrodisiac properties.

Almost all mind-altering drugs have been associated with sexual activity, and the use of such drugs to enhance sexual experiences is apparently more common now than at any time in history. In the past, in some cultures, plants such as peyote and "magic mushrooms" containing mind-affecting (psychoactive) drugs were associated with sex in religious ceremonies, even though few religions sanctioned the pursuit of sexual pleasure for its own sake.[2]

There is no doubt that sex is a major life—and economic—force. We don't need the most often cited works, whether Freud, Kinsey, Masters and Johnson, or Hite, to remind us. One look at what the crowd around the airport magazine rack is reading is enough. No longer is sex a matter of blushes and pretended ignorance. People are not only enjoying sex more openly, but if they have sexual problems, they think they should be able to have them corrected. Although most often correction involves a psychological method and sometimes surgery, it may also involve drugs.

If drugs can be used medically, i.e., prescribed by doctors, to correct sexual problems, few people would deny them to anyone. However, when drugs are used in relationship to sex for nonmedical reasons, it becomes evident that there are still some very strong antipleasure values around, and that many people strongly disapprove of using a drug for no other reason than to increase sexual desire or pleasure.

Drugs are used medically to treat sexual problems, and, despite the disapproval of many, nonmedically to increase and decrease sexual desire, and to expand or modify the actual sexual experience, sometimes through changing states of consciousness to increase pleasure and excitement. Other uses are to maintain sexual vigor diminished by advancing age; to change the body chemistry so that people are more or less fertile; and simply to make people more physically appealing. In all of these instances, drugs are used intentionally to affect sexual processes, whether they are taken by individuals on their own or have been prescribed by physicians.

The unintended effects of drugs on sexual function is something different. Nobody wants to be given a drug for a medical problem that also turns out to interfere with his or her sex life, particularly without having some inkling ahead of time that it might occur. People want to know not only whether a particular drug could cause a problem with sexual functioning, but also exactly what the problem is, how severe it will be, how likely it will be to happen, how long it will last, and if the damage might be permanent. They also want to know if there are alternative forms of therapy that might decrease the chance of such adverse effects. Some persons might decide they would rather put up with the illness and its consequences, or take a reduced chance for its cure, than risk any loss of sexual desire or ability to perform. People should have that choice, but they rarely do.

Why aren't people better informed? Why are they left in ignorance about a situation that's so important to them? And is there anything they can do about it? The problem seems to stem from several factors: ignorance and embarrassment on the part of physicians and patients, and the complexity of the sexual response which is not only highly variable among individuals, but is made more complex by the addition of drugs. Not only is the subject of drugs and sex embarrassing to talk about, it is also difficult to talk about.

WHY DON'T DOCTORS TELL?

In many cases, doctors who prescribe drugs don't know much about human sexuality. Until recently, it was a subject ignored in medical schools. Unless a doctor has taken a special course, or has done a lot of reading on the subject on his own, he's probably quite ignorant about even normal sexual functioning, let alone sexual problems or the problems that may be caused by drugs. Of course some doctors do specialize in sexual problems, or are in specialties such as urology or obstetrics and gynecology where sexual problems are more likely to come up. Most frequently, though, drugs are prescribed for illnesses by general or family practitioners, or doctors specializing in internal medicine or surgery. Even when these doctors are knowledgeable about sex, few have received the kind of training that allows them to feel comfortable when talking to patients about it.

And then there's ignorance of the drugs themselves. It is almost impossible for doctors to be fully informed on all the drugs they are prescribing. There are over 10,000 different prescription drugs on the market, and the average drug is only on the market for five years. Keeping up with the way they work, their side effects, and how often the side effects occur is a full-time job in itself. In the area of sex and drugs, the relationships are especially complicated. There are almost no drugs that produce the same effect on sexual function in every person every time. This means that even if he or she is aware of a potential problem, the doctor simply can't say, "Drug X is going to make you impotent," or "Drug Y is going to keep you from having orgasms."

Moreover, most of the drugs that can cause any kind of sexual problem do so only in a minority of patients. If a doctor were extraordinarily knowledgeable about the research done on a particular drug, the best he or she could usually do would be to tell you that, for example, 10 percent of patients who took the drug had some kind of a problem. The doctor may not be able to tell you exactly how long the problem will last, but should be able to tell you whether the problem is likely to be permanent, and whether normal sexual functioning will return when the drug is discontinued.

Because doctors are aware of the effect of the mind on sexual functioning, they are often reluctant to suggest that a problem may occur. They know that the power of suggestion is very strong, particularly in sexual behavior, and they recognize that, if they tell their patients a sexual problem may occur after use of a drug, the very suggestion may actually create the problem. So some doctors, even when they know the drug they have prescribed may have an adverse side effect on sexual functioning, prefer not to mention it to their patients, optimistically believing that the patients will tell them if they have problems. For example, at a seminar on sexual problems observed by doctors in family practice, the following conversation was reported in a medical journal:

> Dr. Fisher: I have had men with sexual problems secondary to a drug reaction. Most commonly in my practice any hypertensive drug, as we all know, may be the cause of impotence in a hypertensive patient.
>
> Even though I know they are taking a drug which will cause impotence, I never forewarn them about that. I prefer to let them come to see me about it. Then as they are walking out the door, they will mention something to the effect that their sex life is not as good as it used to be and wonder if blood pressure changes their sexual drive. I tell them to wait a second and we go through that.
>
> Dr. Fink: That is a good point about not forewarning them that they may become impotent, because if they have any small grain of hysteria they will become impotent in compliance with your suggestion.[3]

These doctors did not discuss those men who don't have "any small grain of hysteria," but nevertheless may be too shy, inhibited, or intimidated to bring up sexual matters.

To their credit, some physicians do recognize their patients' reluctance to discuss sexual matters, and not only do they question their own patients, but they advise other doctors to ask patients specific questions about sexual functioning whenever a drug has been prescribed that has any possibility of causing a sexual problem. These doctors believe that sexual problems caused by drugs may be much more frequent than is thought and that doctors have mistakenly inferred that drug-connected sexual problems are rare because of the reluctance of patients to talk about sexual matters.

Even though a doctor may know that a certain drug often causes a problem and isn't afraid that talking about it to the patient will make it happen, the doctor simply may believe that sexual problems aren't very serious, and that the benefits of the prescribed drug are far more important. Moreover, the doctor may believe that he or she is the one to weigh the relative benefits of the drug against its potential adverse effects on the patient, without the patient having any say in the decision.

Embarrassment is not confined to patients. Many doctors find it embarrassing to talk about sexual matters to their patients. We often forget that doctors are people too, and not only are they ill-prepared in their training to deal with sexual matters, but they share the same moral beliefs, inhibitions, and social restraints that pervade the rest of society. Although patients are likely to be more ignorant and embarrassed than their doctors, the combination of an even moderately embarrassed physician and a shy patient almost guarantees that the subject of sex will never arise between them. Unless they are specifically asked, most patients are reluctant to tell their doctors they are experiencing a sexual problem, or that their sexual performance or activity has changed after they have taken a medicine. Patients often suffer in silence, believing that the problem is somehow their fault or that it results from their illness or is related to their age. Not only do these patients suffer—often needlessly—but their sexual partners, their wives, husbands, boyfriends, or girlfriends suffer as well. An unfortunate result of the reluctance to speak of sexual matters, while at the same time finding any interference with their sex lives intolerable, is that some patients simply stop taking a drug that is important for their physical or mental health. This is especially unfortunate when it is possible to correct the problem by reducing the dosage of the drug, or by prescribing another drug equally useful in treating the medical problem without an adverse effect on the patient's sexual functioning.

In addition to embarrassment, patients are reticent about sex because they don't understand very much about their bodies and how they work, and they don't know the right words to use. Doctors use many medical terms that are unfamiliar to most of us. Medical terms make explanations more precise and clinical, which seems to relieve some of the embarrassment between doctors and their patients, but it also means that patients don't always understand what they're told. It also means that patients don't talk about sex to their doctors because they may know only slang or street words, and they have learned there is an unwritten rule against using them when talking to health professionals.

HOW DOES THE BODY DO IT?

Because the purpose of this book is to provide you with some information about the effects of all kinds of drugs and alcohol on sexual functioning, and to help you talk to your doctor about drugs and sex, it is important for you to understand normal or average sexual responses, what causes them, and how they are measured. This sort of knowledge should make it easier to understand how drugs can change sexual responses for better or for worse, why some kinds of drugs are more likely to cause sexual problems than others, and why the same drug can affect one person and not another. This information should also make it easier for you to ask your doctor about the possibility that a drug about to be prescribed will cause a problem with sexual function, and after you have taken a drug and have found you are having a problem or change in your sexual function, to bring it to your doctor's attention. To understand the sexual response, it helps to understand how the body is organized.

The body is usually described in terms of various sytems, such as the circulatory system, which includes the heart and blood vessels; the musculoskeletal system, which includes the bones and muscles; the pulmonary system, which includes the lungs and air passages; the gastrointestinal system, which includes the stomach and other pathways for food and waste products; the nervous system, which includes the brain, spinal cord, and the nerves; the reproductive system, which includes the external and internal sex organs; and the endocrine system, which includes various glands and the hormones they produce that are responsible for growth and sexual development. There is some overlap between the reproductive and the endocrine systems, because some of the sex organs, such as the testes in men and the ovaries in women, produce hormones. All of these systems work together by a complex system of chemical messengers called neurotransmitters. Unfortunately for ease of understanding, the sexual response is a combination of all these systems working together to affect the entire mind and body instead of a single system affecting only the genital area. This means that almost anything capable of affecting any one of these systems can affect the sexual response.

The sexual response is usually considered to have two phases. In the first, the arousal (libidinous) phase, the nervous system causes some constriction of blood vessels in the genital area which results in the erection of the penis in the male and the swelling of the clitoris and surrounding genital area, along with lubrication of the vagina, in the female. This tumescence leading to erection is a reflex phenomenon over which there is very little voluntary control, which simply means that erections cannot be demanded at will.[4] Arousal may be caused directly by touch and stroking, and indirectly by sounds, sights, smells, tastes, touch, the conscious imagination, and unconsciously in association with dreams.

Although the erect penis becomes rigid, it is not because of bones or muscles. Erections are entirely due to the blood that is pumped into the penis and held there. The system is rather like that of plants. When a leaf needs water it hangs and droops. When you give it a drink the water flows into the leaf and it springs erect. Unlike leaves, however, the valves that hold the blood in the penis can relax very quickly, returning the penis to its usual flaccid state.

The second phase is the orgasmic phase. When the sexual stimulation becomes very intense, a message is sent from a reflex center in the spinal cord which stimulates the muscles in the genital area, and results in ejaculation in men and pelvic area muscle contractions in women.

In men, after these phases, the blood usually leaves the area and the penis goes limp again. The situation is not so simple in women. Some women are capable of having several orgasms with only brief time periods between each one.

Although sexual problems may exist in either of the two phases for either sex, it is more common to find problems in the arousal phase in men and in the orgasmic phase in women. Men may suffer from decreased or absent sexual desire and either of two kinds of impotence. One kind of impotence is failure to have or sustain an erection, and the other is failure to ejaculate. Sometimes men attain an erection, but ejaculate almost immediately—a condition called premature ejaculation. Men do not have to have an ejaculation to achieve an orgasm. This experience occurs most often in preadolescence. Men may fail to have an orgasm, either with or without an ejaculation. Men may also suffer from a painful problem called priapism in which the penis fails to return to its normal flaccid state after an erection. This problem can lead to permanent damage of the tissues in the penis.

Women also suffer from diminished or absent sexual desire and failure to achieve orgasms. Both men and women may be infertile, and both may also complain of being oversexed (hypersexuality). Hypersexuality often makes an individual uncomfortable, or causes embarrassment. It can make a person feel like masturbating all the time, and can cause men to have spontaneous erections. Hypersexuality may lead some people into committing antisocial acts, such as indecent exposure, or an aggressive sexual crime, such as rape.

So far, most of the efforts to correct sexual problems have concentrated on the male's failure to have or maintain an erection. This is because of the necessity for the man to have an erect penis for sexual intercourse and the association of male sexual activity with aggression, virility, and masculinity. In contrast, femininity is not associated with sexual desire or the ability to have orgasms, but with gentleness and passivity. Only recently have experts begun to recognize the full complexity of the sexual response in both men and women and to be concerned with sexual problems in women as well as men.

HOW DRUGS CAUSE PROBLEMS

Because of the involvement of almost all of the body's systems, it is not surprising that many different drugs, as well as alcohol, can affect sexual response. Although not everything is understood about how the sexual response works, it is possible to predict what classes of drugs are most likely to have a deleterious effect, and this is usually borne out in practice, at least for some drugs in each class. We know that an adequate blood supply is needed for the first phase of the sexual response, and that smooth muscles must be able to contract in the second phase. We also know that the phases are controlled by the nervous system. Therefore, drugs that interfere with the blood supply or that interfere with the ability of muscles to contract, particularly smooth muscles over which there is no voluntary control, are more likely to adversely affect the sexual response. However, the most important group of drugs affecting the sexual response is that which includes drugs that affect the mind, such as tranquilizers, drugs that fight against depression, and drugs capable of causing hallucinations.

Mind-affecting drugs seem to work by interfering with the chemical messengers in the brain and along the nerve pathways. In some instances, mind-affecting drugs increase sexual desire by dampening centers in the brain that are responsible for control and therefore inhibitions. Sometimes the pathways aren't working properly because of illness, and the mind-affecting drugs can correct the situation. Drugs capable of causing hallucinations change perceptions of time and space, sounds, and odors, so that the experience of sexual activity is changed.

The drugs that are most often thought of in terms of sex are the male and female hormones. Both men and women have both male and female hormones, but in different amounts. Although the relationship of these hormones to sexual characteristics and the reproductive cycle is quite well understood, their relationship to the sexual response is more uncertain. For example, testosterone is a hormone produced by the testes that makes men virile, aggressive, and sexually active. Production of testosterone begins at puberty, increases into the twenties, and then very gradually decreases as men age. The decrease is so gradual that impotence can rarely be attributed to lack of testosterone. Where impotence occurs, the problem is usually in the man's mind or may be caused by a drug he is taking. Testosterone alone is not responsible for erections, which occur from infancy even before puberty when production of the hormone begins. However, adult men can have erections after removal of both testes. Despite the lack of clear evidence that the decline in sexual activity as men age is related to testosterone, they are often given it or other similar male hormones to maintain or increase sexual potency.

Women also produce testosterone and other male hormones. Too much male hormone may cause enlargement of the clitoris and secondary male characteristics such as facial hair and deepening of the voice. However, an adequate amount of testosterone is necessary for women to respond sexually.

DRUG CLASSES

In addition to the classification of drugs by the kind of action they have on the body, they are also classified by federal law. There are drugs that anyone can buy over the counter without a prescription, drugs that may only be sold by the prescription of a licensed practitioner, usually a physician, and drugs such as heroin and marijuana that are illegal. Many of the drugs whose sale is restricted by law to prescription only are also sold "on the street" in the illegal market. Among drugs in this group are amphetamines, barbiturates, tranquilizers, and cocaine. These, along with drugs in the totally prohibited group, are mind-affecting drugs that alter perceptions and psychic states. They are called drugs of abuse when they are not used for medical purposes as prescribed by physicians, but are taken recreationally or solely for the change in feelings they produce. The Drug Enforcement Administration of the United States Department of Justice lists 157 different drugs in this category.[5]

Alcohol is a rather special case. In a sense it's an over-the-counter drug because it's sold without a prescription. But it's much more powerful in its ability to alter feeling states than other legal nonprescription drugs.

The use and abuse of recreational drugs and combinations of recreational drugs and alcohol have increased rapidly in the past fifteen years, and have become increasingly more common among teenagers. Along with the increase has come increased sexual activity. It isn't possible to say that drugs and alcohol cause greater sexual activity, but they may make it easier to happen by decreasing inhibitions. Because recreational drugs and alcohol alter feelings and perceptions, they alter the sexual response as well, thus permitting a greater variety of sexual experiences than can be had without them.

PART II

APHRODISIACS

PROBLEMS IN SEX?

Complete Control For The Over Eager Male
STA-POWER SPRAY
Now You Can Go On and On and On

Does early climax stop many exciting moments of sexual intercourse? This is a common problem that Sta-Power will help you with. Sta-Power Spray contains benzocaine and is three times stronger than our cream. It is a safe, proven, scientific compound that can be sprayed directly on the penis without the knowledge of your partner. It will help you delay your climax in order to coincide with that of your partner. You will feel and appreciate the improvement the very first time that you use it.

STA-POWER SPRAY $6.95

For A Better Erection That Will Astound You And Delight Your Partner
ERECTION PILLS
Results Are Immediate and Long Lasting

Don't leave her unsatisfied. Erection Pills can make even the limpest of men powerful. Give her what she's craving. Be the big man you always wanted to be. This preparation is a must for those of you who are having difficulties in obtaining and maintaining a fulfilling erection. Instant action guaranteed. Your money back if not completely satisfied.

ERECTION PILLS $6.95

Not Getting It Up Lately?
STA-POWER PILLS
For A Terrific Rise — Erection Supreme

Has a stimulating power. Ideal for a balling hot time. Will enable you to go on and on and on. What more can we say than is already said by the name of this fine preparation. Effects will last for hours. Also ideal for turning her on. This pill will do everything we say it will or your money will be immediately refunded. This pill can be mixed in any type of drink.

STA-POWER PILLS $5.95

Do You Need Help?
INSTANT ERECTION CREAM
Create a New Dimension of Sexual Delight

Instant Erection Oil is scientifically formulated to help you get an instant erection when rubbed on the head of the penis. It is skillfully compounded into a sensuous true fruit flavored oil base. When rubbed briskly onto the head and shaft of the penis, it causes a flow of blood to rush into the penis, giving you an instant erection. Not only should it give an instant erection, it should cause the penis to get harder and larger for a prolonged period of time. Like the Instant Erection Cream, this new and amazing product is for men who have tried everything else and have no luck. No longer need you let the best of joys that life has to offer pass you by. With this fantastic product you too can now stand up and be counted. You owe it to yourself to try some today.

CREAM $6.95

Guaranteed To Make Her Hot
IMITATION SPANISH FLY & GINSENG
Do You Measure Up? You Can.
Unbelievable in Their Effect.

Ginseng is a plant which is chiefly grown in the Far East, especially in China. The Chinese have used it as an aphrodisiac for over 1,000 years. Ginseng has recently been introduced into the United States and is very popular. Legendary writings say Ginseng is highly effective in awakening and producing sexual desires in men and women alike. We have added our imitation Spanish Fly to the Ginseng to make it work faster and longer. We have also made it easier and more pleasant to take now, in a capsule. We are making it available to you, the public, at a price you can afford. If you need Ginseng you cannot afford to be without it. Ginseng is sometimes called "The Turn-On Root". To quote S. Steingold" . . . if you think you have been turned on before you ain't seen nothing yet". Try our Ginseng with Spanish Fly Capsules and find out what he means. Can be emptied and mixed into any drink.

24 TABLETS $8.95

POTENT PHARMACEUTICAL PRODUCTS, INC. P-278
P.O. Box 535 Cooper Station New York, N.Y. 10003

Reprinted by permission of Potent Pharmaceutical Products, Inc.

2
WHY APHRODISIACS WORK—SOMETIMES

Ads similar to the one on the opposite page appear in the leading men's "sexploitation" magazines. They all tout products that the copy says will cure sex problems. The claims for the pills, capsules, powders, creams, and sprays are enticing. The ads say the products can "help you delay your climax in order to coincide with that of your partner," "make even the limpest of men powerful," "enable you to go on and on and on," "cause the penis to get harder and larger for a prolonged period of time," and "awake and produce sexual desires in men and women alike." While the ads vary somewhat in their products and their promises, they all share two characteristics. The advertised products are expensive, ranging from about six to nine dollars, and at the top of the ad, in big black letters, you can hardly miss reading the word PLACEBO.

PLACEBO SEX AIDS. How can those be FANTASTIC or WHAT EVERY MAN NEEDS? Who would be so foolish as to pay nine dollars for something advertised as a placebo? One must presume that many people do respond to these ads, otherwise the product manufacturers wouldn't find it worthwhile to pay the considerable cost of printing them. Several explanations come to mind. The world may be full of practical jokers who buy these products as birthday gifts for their aging golf buddies, or as silly presents for about-to-be bridegrooms. *Or* it just may be possible that the purchasers know something that the Federal Trade Commission with its truth-in-advertising laws doesn't know, and that these products can do what they claim they can do. *Or,* it's possible that an awful lot of people don't know what the word means, and in their heart of hearts they don't believe the products will work, but their longing for sexual delights and the ability to act out visions from their fantasy worlds lead them to send in their money anyway. As a gamble, it may not seem very good, but if there is even the slimmest chance of a payoff, the rewards must seem very great and, in this sense, not so very different from many other gambles.

The word placebo comes from a Latin verb meaning "to please." A placebo is a fake medicine—usually a tablet or a capsule that contains nothing but sugar or an injection that contains nothing but a salt solution. Therefore, it's plain that something advertised as a Fantastic Placebo Sex Aid is really being advertised as a Fantastic Fake Sex Aid

Strange as it may seem, fake medicines and fake sex aids can work Just as in *Peter Pan,* when the audience indicates it believes in fairies, thereby reviving Tinker Bell, a dying sexual ardor can be revived by the belief that a pill is a potent aphrodisiac. Indeed, placebos probably "work" better for sex problems than in any other area of human concern, because of the predominant part the mind plays in sexual desire and performance.

When they are given by doctors to treat illnesses, placebos can be very powerful "medicines." An appreciation of the power of placebos and the placebo effect can help one understand not only why people have believed in aphrodisiacs for so many years, and indeed, why they "work," but why the response to drugs that are supposed to affect a person's sexual desire and performance is so varied and unpredictable. An understanding of the placebo effect may also convince you why it is not possible to evaluate a drug's pharmacological effect on sexual function without properly designed "double-blind" studies.

THE PLACEBO EFFECT

Doctors don't give sugar pills or salt solutions for sex problems or any other kind of problem very often. Until sulfa drugs became available in the thirties and antibiotics in the forties, most drugs might as well have been sugar pills. This is still true of many drugs that people buy over the counter to treat their health problems. Doctors don't give plain sugar pills because patients get angry if they find out, and because doctors can't predict when and how well they'll work, or which patients they'll work on. Moreover, in this scientific era, a doctor is expected to find out what's really wrong and to prescribe a drug that's specifically formulated to treat the problem. A doctor charging patients for sugar pills would be considered a bit of a quack. Thus, you're unlikely to find doctors handing out frank placebo sex aids to treat impotence or frigidity or any other sex problem. Because doctors don't prescribe sugar pills, it doesn't mean they aren't aware of the placebo effect. Today, the placebo effect is receiving very serious attention from medical scholars, and the meaning has been extended far beyond the sugar pill. A placebo effect is ". . . any effect attributed to a pill, potion, or procedure, but not to its pharmacodynamic or specific properties."[1] This definition has generally been expanded to mean any effect that is associated with the color or size of the medication, or the environment, including the personality of the doctor, in which the medicine is given or taken. What this really amounts to is that a drug can have an effect because the patient expects it to, and this expectation can be increased or decreased by all sorts of factors that don't have anything to do with the chemical properties of the drug.

The expectations of a drug's effect can be surprisingly strong. Some persons have been withdrawn from experiments because they have had dangerously violent reactions to totally inert pills. In some other cases, the usual effect of a drug has been completely reversed. The reversal has been demonstrated many times in the laboratory, with subjects reporting they felt stimulated by sedatives after they were told they had been given stimulants, and the reverse situation, in which actual stimulants sedated persons who believed the drug they had taken was a sedative.

Not all cases occur in the lab. A few years ago, a commanding officer of one of the United States Navy's nuclear submarines was having a great deal of trouble sleeping, because of his heavy responsibilities and the constant interruptions when he finally did get to sleep. Finally, in desperation, he raided the medical locker for some sleeping pills. When he got back from his cruise, he was telling a doctor friend about the terrific pills he had found. "One pill and I slept like a baby," he said. "Nice," said the doctor, "what were they?" "Don't remember," said the captain. "I'll get them and show you." "Hey," said the doctor, "those aren't sleeping pills; they're amphetamines, uppers, wakey-wakey pills, stimulants, goofballs." "But," said the captain, "it says right on the label they're for insomnia." "Take another look," said the doctor. "Don't they teach you guys to read? It says 'contraindicated' in insomnia." "Oh," said the captain, "now I suppose they aren't going to work anymore."

The captain was right. Once he failed to have the strong need for sleeping pills and lost the belief that his pills were for sleeping, they would never again work for him as sleeping medication.

If belief is so strong that it can completely reverse the usual activity of one of our strongest drugs, it is not very surprising that even a small amount of belief about a "placebo sex aid" can increase the eroticism level and get the juices of desire flowing.

The placebo effect has been described as the mind fooling the body. Berton Roueché, author of many popular books and articles about medicine, wrote in *The New Yorker* in 1960 that the placebo works because of the "infinite capacity of the human mind for self-deception." The mind certainly exerts very strong control over the body. An expectation of harm or threat can mobilize the body into a fight or flight stance; the adrenaline fairly pours through the body; the heart rate increases; the breathing rate increases. The fear that one is about to make a fool of oneself produces the well-known phenomenon of stage fright with its attendant sweaty palms, faintness, and heart palpitations. We know now that people can will themselves into control over body processes once believed to be totally a matter for the unconscious mind. For example, people are learning to raise and lower their blood pressures and body temperatures and control their heart rates by means of a process known as biofeedback. In biofeedback, people are hooked up to machines that record their body processes. When the individual is successful, for example, in lowering his blood pressure, the machine lets him know it. Apparently, the pleasure he feels at pleasing even a machine is a reward that reinforces whatever steps the body took to lower the blood pressure, and with practice, he can will his body into taking action that results in a more healthful state.

The placebo effect in healing works because it triggers specific biochemical processes in the body. It translates the will to live and to be well into specific actions. Totally inert substances have "cured" fever, headache, coughs, colds, insomnia, angina (heart muscle pains), postoperative pain, and even warts. They have affected processes such as blood cell counts, gastric juice secretions, pupil dilation, blood pressure, and respiratory rates.[2] It is now believed that thought processes and beliefs in therapy can help the body fight even diseases like cancer by mobilizing the body's natural immunological system.

There is a great deal of exciting research going on right now with respect to alleviation of pain and endorphins, which are naturally occurring substances in the body. It has long been known that placebos work especially well in controlling pain. It appears that the body's expectation of help promised by taking what is believed to be a legitimate medicine triggers the release of endorphins, which are chemically similar to the strong opiates, morphine and heroin.

If placebos can trigger the release of narcoticlike substances, they may also stimulate the release of chemicals that take part in other body processes and affect the sexual response.

Doctors have believed for years that the proper attitude can work miracles in some people, and attitudes of hopelessness and giving up can literally kill. In African and Caribbean societies, people have died when they have become convinced that another, more powerful person has put a curse on them from which there is no escape. Thus, we can see that the placebo effect can be not only extremely powerful, but a force for harm.

Quacks heal—sometimes. Fake drugs cure—sometimes, and humbuggery survives, all because of the placebo effect. Apparently, if people have strong beliefs almost anything is possible. The lack of faith in physicians and their ability to cure some diseases, such as cancer, has driven some people to faith healers and placebo drugs like laetrile. Despite a vigorous search, no reputable medical research institution has been able to find any ingredient in laetrile that the body could use to fight disease. So-called cures probably have not been effected by the drug, but result from the body's expectation of help that laetrile has offered.[3]

It is important that the doctor, as well as his patient, have faith in the therapy to mobilize the placebo effect. The doctor's belief and attitude are a strong message to the patient. If the doctor is, in effect, sending out signals saying, "I can help you—my medicine will help you—you're going to get better—I know what I'm doing—your hope and faith are not misplaced," the placebo effect has its greatest chance to work and help the patient mobilize his own defenses. Doctors do not believe in fake medicine and therefore rarely give actual placebos, but they do take advantage of the placebo effect. Moreover, research into the effects of medicines is carefully controlled by a research design called the "double-blind" so that the placebo effect will not fool doctors into thinking that a drug has real pharmacological activity.

Doctors and other health-care specialists employ the therapeutic assistance of the placebo effect by demonstrating an interest in the patient's welfare, trying to reduce the patient's anxiety, and offering assurances of help. Because the placebo effect can be so important in healing, many of these anxiety-reducing efforts have been routinized in hospitals. For example, it is commonplace for an anesthesiologist to visit a patient the night before surgery to tell him about the anesthesia procedures that will be used, to answer any questions, and to reduce concerns. The anesthesiologist does this because research has shown that a patient who is less anxious before surgery recovers faster afterward.

Amazingly, the effect on postoperative recovery rates of reducing anxiety can be transferred to others. When doctors or others reduce the anxiety levels of mothers before their children's surgery, the benefit is somehow transferred to the children, who recover faster from their operations.[4]

Doctors used to think that some people were more likely than others to benefit from the placebo effect, but now they believe that every person can respond under the right circumstances. On the average, about 30 percent of persons will respond in a given situation, but it wouldn't necessarily be the same people in a different situation. Doctors do know that response is greatest when they are trying to help someone recover from a problem in which mind and body interaction is very important, such as psychological problems, pain, ulcers, rashes, asthma, insomnia, indigestion, hypertension, and heart rate irregularities.

Because sexual function is about 95 percent mental, and 5 percent physical, the placebo effect is, in fact, the most successful therapy currently employed to treat sexual problems. Sex therapists rarely use drugs to treat impotence or premature ejaculation or lack of orgasm, or any other sex problems. Sex therapists convince their patients that they are experts who can help. Then they plan a treatment in which the patient learns to give up his or her anxieties and to control his or her own body.

The lack of drugs that a doctor can use to treat sex problems is one of the reasons that most doctors aren't trained to treat them or feel very comfortable doing it. Doctors are trained to diagnose problems and then to treat them, usually with drugs which in scientifically controlled studies have been demonstrated to work. Many doctors also use the prescription as a signal to the patient that it's time for him to get up and leave the office, and as a symbol to the patient that he's being taken care of by an expert. Doctors are reluctant to use actual placebo drugs such as the ones in the advertisement at the beginning of the chapter, and they know that there are very few legal drugs that can help. The psychological counseling, which is the most successful treatment, takes a long time, and most doctors are not qualified to undertake it.

There may be more hope in the future for people with sex problems. Holistic medicine, which recognizes the importance of the mind to the body's function, is gaining attention in the medical community. There are now serious scientific evaluations of approaches to medicine where the patient becomes involved in his or her therapy. In holistic medicine, the patient is not merely a passive receiver of the miracles of science, but works actively with the therapists to mobilize all of his or her defenses for treatment. Sometimes this results in a total change in the patient's life-style. Approaches such as biofeedback and holistic medicine are receiving serious attention for treatment of such problems as high blood pressure and even cancer. If patient involvement can work for these illnesses, their potential to help with sex problems seems very great.

For doctors to believe that a drug is efficacious, it must have been proven in a "double-blind" study. Although scientists are supposed to be skeptical, often they are biased in favor of finding a successful new drug or medical procedure. If they do find a new drug that works, they can publish articles about it, receive acclaim from their fellow researchers, perhaps be rewarded with a bonus or a promotion, and generally benefit. If they prove that a new drug or medical procedure doesn't work, that may have done the public a better service, but only rate a yawn in the scientific or popular press. The double-blind study guards against a researcher misperceiving that a drug works because he is biased in favor of finding that it does so. The double-blind study also guards against scientists interpreting a placebo as having a real or pharmacological effect.

It is important to understand how a double-blind study is designed and why, to understand that it isn't possible to believe that a drug is an aphrodisiac or can help with sex problems solely on the basis of a friend's telling you he or she tried it and it worked.

Suppose you sent off for one of the Placebo Sex Aids, perhaps the "Instant Erection Cream," and you wanted to know if it would actually work. As subjects you would have to get several, perhaps twenty, male friends to help you, preferably of the same age, and another to be the research assistant. You could write your friends' names on pieces of paper and put them into a hat. Then, so you wouldn't know who got which, the research assistant would draw the names out of a hat and alternately assign them to one of two groups. The research assistant would give Group One the "Instant Erection Cream," and Group Two would get a cream that looked exactly like it, but one that contained only inactive substances. Next, you would have to make certain that you told all the subjects the same story, and gave them all the same directions. For example, they might be told that they have been given erection cream, and that over the next month, whenever they desired to have an erection, they should rub a teaspoon of the cream, no more and no less, into the head of the penis for one minute, no more and no less, using a counterclockwise motion. They should then record the date and time and estimate how many seconds it took them to achieve an erection, and whether the penis swelled to a large, smaller, or average size, and how long the erection lasted. During the study month, neither you nor the subjects would know which persons got the "Instant Erection Cream," and which got the imitation control cream. Both you and the subjects have been, in effect, "blinded." At the end of the month, the data would be compared and the code broken to see if those subjects who got the "Instant Erection Cream" took significantly longer to achieve erections, and if their erections seemed to be bigger and to last longer than those of the subjects who got the mixture you made. Because you know about the placebo effect, you would not be surprised to find that many of the men who used the control substance reported that it worked. The question is, did the control cream you made work as well as the cream you sent away for? If there were no significant statistical differences in the two study groups, you would conclude that there is no reason to believe that the "Instant Erection Cream" worked any better than an inert substance, and that any effect attributed to it was, in fact, a placebo effect.

Of course, there could be many variations of this experiment. The two creams could be compared with rubbing and using no cream at all, the subjects' age and the "laboratory conditions" could be varied, the size of the erection could be measured electronically, and so on, but what must always occur for the study to be scientific, is that neither the subjects nor the evaluators must know which subjects got the treatment, and which got the control substances. Without this condition and a study in which subjects are assigned randomly to treatment and control groups, you can't really evaluate the merit of claims such as the following:

Your cousin Sally got a vitamin enriched cream and by careful attention to application and massage, increased her bust a whole bra-cup size.

Your roommate's older brother who had the clap and then couldn't get it up, cured his impotence by taking vitamin E every morning.

Your barber tried for six years to get his wife pregnant, but she became pregnant within three weeks of the day they both started eating oysters every night before retiring.

The steroids that are in the meat of male animals can make you more virile.

Fish eggs are potent aphrodisiacs.

Men who take male hormones can produce children until they are eighty-five or older.

Women who take oral contraceptives are more (or less) sexy than others.

Drug X is (or isn't) a sexual stimulant or depressant.

In other words, all claims may be viewed with suspicion until subjected to rigorous testing. But you cry, "I can't carry out these double-blind or any other kind of study. How am I to know?" The best advice is to use or take nothing on your own that might cause you or anyone else harm. Frankly fake aphrodisiac placebos are okay if they fit this criterion, and if you know just why a fake can seem to work. "Catch-22" here, of course, is that if you know why the placebos work, and you know you're taking one, it probably won't work.

Clearly, rigorous testing is very difficult and expensive, and there are all sorts of factors that are theoretically possible to test for, but that time and money exclude. What if someone says, "Hey, I used 'Instant Erection Cream and I used a clockwise motion and got a fantastic erection." Or "I used 'Instant Erection Cream' in a hot sauna bath and it really worked." Without including clockwise and sauna baths in your research design, you can only say, "There's no theoretical reason why it should work better than a placebo cream. In my experiment, which didn't include clockwise and sauna baths, but did include thus and so, it didn't work better than a placebo."

Moreover, when statistical tests are used to suggest that one product is better than another, conclusions are based on probability and not on certainty. Scientists who do the testing say something like, "There is a five in one hundred chance or less that there is no difference between the product we tested and the placebo product." As we know, even five in one hundred long shots sometimes cross the finish line first. To try to prove that a drug really is any different from a placebo, the experiment must be repeated. The more often it is repeated under different circumstances and using different subjects, the more certain we can be that we know the truth about the pharmacological activity of a product.

The lack of properly designed experiments is one of the reasons that myths about substances having aphrodisiacal properties are so enduring. Even in the face of scientific evidence, people who want badly enough for something to be true will tend to believe what they perceive is in their interest to believe. Moreover, many people are suspicious of scientific evidence. Scientists have been wrong before. And scientists haven't done much research in the area of the relationships between drugs and sex.

So old myths about drugs and sexual function die hard; new ones abound; and some people make money off others' hopes that a drug can open the gate of a sexual garden of delights.

3

THE SEARCH FOR APHRODISIACS*

The consensus among today's scientists is that no true aphrodisiac exists.[1] They claim all perceived aphrodisiac activity attributed to drugs in the past has been entirely due to the placebo effect, or to misinterpreting physical responses as sexual responses.

For example, Spanish fly, believed to be the most potent of aphrodisiacs. It's potent, all right. It's a killer. Spanish fly is a ground-up beetle, cantharides, also called Mylabris. Its scientific name is *Lytta vesicatoria,* and it's found in southern Europe, especially Spain. When eaten, it causes ulcers throughout the intestinal tract and dysentery, and it irritates the bladder and the urethra. The misinterpretation of the irritation of the urethra as sexual desire is why this highly dangerous substance is believed to be an aphrodisiac. The powdered beetles, whose active ingredient is cantharidine, is reputed to have been slipped into the soup of Louis XV by no less than Madame de Pompadour herself. Louis is believed to have misinterpreted his urinary tract irritation as a powerful lust for the lady. Others have not been so lucky when feeding the Spanish beetles to the objects of their desire. No less than the Marquis de Sade was jailed for slipping it to a prostitute.[2] As

---

*Much of the information in this chapter is from Alan Hull Walton, *Stimulants for Love: A Quest for Virility* (London: Tandem Books, 1966); and John Davenport, *Aphrodisiacs and Love Stimulants,* ed. by Alan Hull Walton (New York: Lyle Stuart, 1966). Other helpful sources were John Allegro, *The Sacred Mushroom and the Cross* (New York: Doubleday, 1970); H. E. Wedeck, *Love Potions Through the Ages* (New York: Philosophical Library, 1963); and especially *The High Times Encyclopedia of Recreational Drugs* (New York: Stonehill, 1978).

recently as 1954, the manager of a wholesale chemist in London mixed Spanish fly into some coconut sherbet and gave it to two young girls who became violently ill and died very shortly thereafter.[3]

With Spanish fly, the words "I'm dying of love for you" have more than literary meaning. Despite its dangers, cantharides was used extensively in Europe before the twentieth century where it graced tables hidden in candies, cookies, cakes, and biscuits. Nicholas Venette, a French physician, has recounted a tale of the dangerous effects of Spanish fly:

> . . . Spanish Flies have so powerful an effect upon the bladder and the genital organs of both sexes, that if only two or three grains are taken, such an inflammation arises that one becomes immediately ill. A proof of this was experienced by one of my friends a few years ago, and fortunately he lives to tell the tale. His rival, in despair at seeing him marry his mistress, advised her to put cantharides into a pâté composed of pears, and to give it to her husband on the wedding night. When the night came, the husband embraced his wife so much that she began to suffer exhaustion; but these delights quickly changed to misfortune; for the poor man began to experience the effects of inflammation by midnight, had the greatest difficulty in urinating, and saw a discharge of blood from his member. Fear augmented the illness, and he fainted more than once. Considerable care had to be taken of him until his health was restored. . . .[4]

The cousin of the Spanish fly is the Russian fly. The Russian cantharis beetle shares the misattribution of aphrodisiac qualities with Spanish fly and also its dangers. Similarly, the Russian fly causes severe abdominal pains, fetid breath, vomiting, bloody diarrhea, priapism, and delirium which may precede death.[2]

Dangerous, uncertain in effect, cantharides is definitely *not* an aphrodisiac that is all right to use because it "at least does no harm." Not surprisingly, cantharides or any combination of drugs containing it has not passed the Food and Drug Administration's requirement that a drug be both safe and efficacious before it is approved.

Frank Gawin, a physician writing in the *Journal of Sex Research,*[1] has suggested that the reason the medical community claims there are no true aphrodisiacs is because they define aphrodisiac too narrowly. Aphrodisiac has generally meant a substance that increases sexual drive or libido. Most modern scientists are concerned with sexual frequency, performance, and drive, if they are concerned at all. So they, being objective employers of the scientific method, try to find the answers to questions like, "After you took drug X, how many times did you have sexual intercourse, or an erection, or an orgasm, or an ejaculation?" If they can measure these activities under controlled laboratory conditions with instruments, so much the better. These objective methods haven't turned up much in the way of help. Many drugs interfere, but not many help. Gawin argues, however, that the definition of an aphrodisiac and the scientific inquiries have been too narrowly focused. He argues that the definition of aphrodisiac should be broadened to include the "subjective pleasure experienced in sexual activity." The meaning of aphrodisiac should not be restricted to a substance increasing sexual drive or libido, but should be extended to include substances that increase the pleasure and expand the experience of sexual intercourse. A redefinition would open up new avenues of research into substances that nonscientific persons are telling us increase their pleasure or provide pleasurable variations in their perceptions of sexual experience. If sex is for more than procreation, and most of us believe it is, why not focus on pleasure as well as physical responses that may be measured and counted? The search for a pleasure-enhancing or expanding aphrodisiac may be no less scientific than experiments that compare the reported experiences of persons given the substance in question with those given placebos under double-blind experimental conditions. An aphrodisiac response may then come to include an effect of a pharmacological substance on the subjective pleasure of sexual experience, independent of any effect at all on what is commonly considered libido or sexual drive.

As Dr. Gawin has noted,[1] the prevailing view in the medical community is that all pleasure-enhancing effects of drugs on sex are "mere" placebo effects. The results of this judgment have been that no valid double-blind studies have actually been carried out to evaluate the aphrodisiac effects of drugs that have commonly been used to modify the sexual experience. This amounts to a scientific judgment without scientific evidence, a situation that is insupportable in view of the fact that research into the placebo effects of drugs on pain and disease is a popular and common area of scientific inquiry. Scientists, it seems, as well as others, may be "blinded" by an outdated morality.

Meanwhile, now as ever, people aren't standing around waiting for the scientific community to get around to redefining aphrodisiac or performing double-blind experiments. They're experimenting themselves.

APHRODISIACS IN ANCIENT EUROPE

One of the earliest (and certainly authoritative) mentions of an aphrodisiac is in the Bible's book of Genesis:

. . . And Reuben went in the days of wheat harvest, and found mandrakes in the field, and brought them unto his mother, Leah. Then Rachel said to Leah, Give me, I pray thee, of thy son's mandrakes.

And Jacob came out of the field in the evening, and Leah went out to meet him, and said, Thou must come in unto me; for surely I have hired thee with my son's mandrakes. And he lay with her that night.

And God hearkened unto Leah, and she conceived, and bare Jacob, the fifth son. . . .

The mandrake, officially *Mandragora officinarum,* a root in the potato family, was in ancient times what ginseng is today. Mandrake, as ginseng is now, was believed to have a wide range of beneficial uses, healing powers, and protection against debilitation in old age, but most especially, mandrake was used for fertility and aphrodisia.

In early times, when there was little understanding of physiology or disease processes, and no understanding of the scientific basis of therapeutics, medicine was a matter of trial and error, myth and magic, and people often believed that a plant that resembled a part of a person was a medicine that should be used to treat the particular part that the plant resembled. For heart problems, heart-shaped plants were used, and so on. The most desirable of all plants were roots that resembled sexual organs, such as the mandrake, the "manlikeness," which made it a natural for love potions, as a cure for female sterility, and to increase the chance that conception would take place during an individual act of sexual intercourse.

There were very strange beliefs about the mandrake root. One of these related to hangings. There was a European superstition that when a person was hanged, the ejaculate or urine that fell to the earth under the body caused mandrakes to grow under the gallows. Thus, if a man were hanged, the root would look like a man, and if a woman were hanged, it would resemble the female form. There were other folktales about digging up the root. One held that the proper way to remove the root from the earth was to tie a dog to it who would then pull it from the earth. When the plant was pulled out, it was supposed to shriek like a person in pain. In Shakespeare's *Romeo and Juliet,* Act IV, Scene 3, we find: And shrieks like mandrakes, torn out of the earth, / That living mortals, hearing them, run mad.

The purple-flowered mandrake plant is found chiefly in Mediterranean countries which accounts for it being mentioned most often in Greek and Roman literature. The Greeks believed it was used by the goddess, Aphrodite, and referred to her as Mandragoritis. Pliny the Elder remarked on the resemblance of the root to male genitalia and its purported ability to secure the love of females. The sorceress, Circe, was associated with it in Homer's *Odyssey* where it was called Circe's plant.

The fertility qualities of mandrake are mentioned in John Donne's "Song," a poem that is learned by, but that makes little sense to, school children

> . . .Go and catch a falling starre,
> Get with child a mandrake roote . . .

Although mandrake does seem to have some hallucinogenic qualities, and it may still be used in some Greek and Italian folk remedies, its ability to ensnare the heart of another must be attributed more to the wine in which it was soaked and the omnipresent placebo effect than to magical chemical qualities.

A plant mentioned by ancient Greek and Roman writers of erotica more frequently than mandrake is satyrion; however, no one is certain what satyrion is. The educated guesses assign it to the orchid family. Again, it was the testeslike shape of the roots that captured the fancy of early lovers and love-potion makers. Absolutely marvelous sexual feats were attributed to these testicular tubers, especially when they were tossed off in a libation of goat's milk. On one occasion, satyrion is credited with sustaining seventy, successful, successive instances of coitus. The Greek mythological hero, Hercules, is reported to have deflowered all fifty of the daughters of his (overly) generous host, Thespius, who plied him with a decoction of satyrion. Similarly, Proculus, assisted by the erectile liquid, dispatched the maidenheads of one hundred women over a period of fifteen days. Encouraged by stories such as these, it is understandable why satyrion was imbibed by old men to rekindle their flagging sexual abilities.

> . . . Behold the Satyrion root, is it not formed like the male privy parts? No one can deny this. Accordingly, magic discovered it and revealed that it can restore a man's virility and passion. . . .[5]

Indeed, the remarkable satyrion was described as being so strong that it aroused sexual response when it was merely held in the hand.

Beliefs in the aphrodisiac and fertility-enhancing qualities of roots, herbs, insects, fruits and spices, and more esoteric substances, such as the fleshy excrescence from the head of a newborn foal, were not limited to uneducated peasants or confined to mythology. References to love potions are found, not only in novels, but in the writings of the leading historians of the times, and in medical literature. For example, Pliny in his *Natural History* gives advice about using lettuce to cool off the intense lust incurred by satyrion, and Dioscorides, an army physician of the first century A.D., discusses aphrodisiacs such as mandrake, satyrion, and "boy-cabbages." Xenocrates, a Greek physician writing in the same century, recommended drinking the sap of mallow trees as a surefire love stimulant.

Nevertheless, despite frequent references to them, there is little hard information that would enable one to reproduce the mixtures. The actual recipes of love potions, philters, and aphrodisiacal mixtures were closely guarded secrets. Clearly, there has always been an enormous market for sex adjuncts, and those who held the secret of a preparation purported to be a successful aphrodisiac must have enjoyed a considerable monetary income, as well as a certain cachet accorded to a possessor of highly sought after secrets. Most certainly, there was an element of risk involved in the chemistry of aphrodisia as well. Not only Spanish fly, but many ingredients of aphrodisiacs were potentially dangerous, and have been cited as causing insanity and even death. The wise old crone or aging courtesan who sold a concoction that caused harm was at considerable risk of harm to herself. Among the more dangerous ingredients were plants or extracts of plants, many of which are in use today, albeit not for aphrodisiac purposes. Deadly nightshade or beautiful lady *(Atropa belladonna)*, henbane, jimson weed, foxglove—even their names have a ring of antiquity, intrigue, and danger that is not associated with the drugs turned out by contemporary pharmaceutical manufacturers.

The number and variety of aphrodisiacs found in early writings are mind boggling. Sometimes a substance that was considered to be an aphrodisiac at one time and place was believed to have the opposite effect at another. Here is a brief list of some of the substances purported to be aphrodisiacs in Rome in the first, second, and third centuries A.D.:

spices: cumin, dill, aniseed, celery seed, capers, thyme, ginger, basil, oregano, pepper, caraway, sesame, mustard, garlic
vegetables: shallots, artichokes, beans, asparagus, turnips, truffles, parsnips, leeks, beets, cabbage, chicory, cucumber, radishes, lettuce
fish: red mullet, tuna, sea bream, octopus, mussels, sea urchin, oysters, cuttlefish, squid, crayfish, ray
eggs
honey
bird organs
insects
genitalia of almost any kind of animal
milk of an ass mixed with bat blood

Gold, frankincense, myrrh, wine, fruits, vegetables, spices, fish, meats, nutritious, disgusting, harmless, harmful, you name it. Almost anything that is possible to eat or apply has been used by someone at some time to affect the love process. In few areas of human endeavor have men and women proved themselves to be more imaginative or more gullible. Even today, there is a serious threat to the rhinoceros population of the world because of the Oriental conviction that the phallic-symbol horn of the animal is a powerful aphrodisiac.

APHRODISIACS IN THE EAST

The elaborate and varied use of aphrodisiac substances was certainly not confined to Europe. Indeed, the erotic literature of the Middle and Far East was considerably more civilized in its serious and often beautiful and caring approach to sexual relationships. No sly jokes, tricks, or vulgarity here. Drugs, ointments, foods, incense, all are considered in a total milieu intended to provide the greatest sensual pleasure. Ancient Hindu literature is replete with every imaginable guide to sexual techniques and to male and female characteristics, as well as love potions. Neither the Hindu nor the Arab literature is prurient or lascivious, but treats its subjects almost reverently as it covers such sexual subjects as harlotry, transvestism, homosexuality, lesbianism, courtship, adultery, physical criteria, passion, love drugs, and foods. For example, the well-known *Kama Sutra* of Vatsyayana of the fourth century A.D. lists not only foods and drugs to stimulate sexual ardor, but carefully outlines thirteen kissing methods.

To the Indian, Kama (love pleasure) was essential to virtue and fortune, and plants and foods were to be used appropriately to help attain it.

In the *Kama Sutra* we find:

> . . . When a person fails to obtain the object of his desires by any of the ways previously related, he should then have recourse to other ways of attracting others to himself.
>
> Now, good looks, qualities, youth, and liberality are the chief and most natural means of making a person agreeable in the eyes of others. But in the absence of these a man or a woman must have resort to artificial means, or to art, and the following are some recipes that may be found useful:
>
> (a) An ointment made of the tabernamontana coronaria, the costus speciosus or arabicus, and the flacourtia cataphracta can be used as an unguent of adornment.
>
> (b) If a fine powder is made of the above plants, and applied to the wick of a lamp, which is made to burn with the oil of blue vitriol, the black

pigment or lamp black produced therefrom, when applied to the eyelashes, has the effect of making a person look lovely. . . .[6]

The Indians were especially fond of aphrodisiac foods, especially fish, milk, garlic, onions, honey, beans, and a rancid butter known as ghee. Mixtures, including honey, licorice, pepper, mangoes, and thorn apple were recommended to be applied directly to the "lingam" or "yoni," which are the Indian words for the male and female genitalia respectively. One recipe advises that a man drink milk with sugar, which has been boiled up with a ram's or goat's testicle, to obtain sexual vigor.

The *Kama Sutra* ends one section with the following advice, some of which sounds pretty sensible over 1500 years later:

> . . . The means of producing love and sexual vigour should be learnt from the science of medicine, from the Vedas, from those who are learned in the arts of magic, and from confidential relatives. No means should be tried which are doubtful in their effects, which are likely to cause injury to the body, which involve the death of animals, and which bring us into contact with impure things. Such means should only be used as are holy, acknowledged to be good, and approved of by Brahmans, and friends. . . .[7]

The Perfumed Garden written by Nefzawi about A.D. 1400 is probably the best-known Arabic amatory work and it contains a great many references to aphrodisiacs. It was the annotated manuscript of the translation of this book that so shocked Lady Burton, when she found it after the death of her husband, Sir Richard Burton, that she summarily dispatched it into the fire. Nefzawi cations the readers of *The Perfumed Garden* that in order to maintain full sexual vigor, it is important to be healthy, free of care, and very well nourished. Although fifteenth-century ideas of nutrition may not be scientifically based, his advice is sound. Sexual pleasure does depend on good health and may be damaged by medication. Nefzawi especially recommends almonds, honey, and pine tree grains, this to be taken before going to bed by those feeling they are too weak for intercourse. Alternatives are onion seed and honey, cubeb pepper, cardamom grains, boiled green peas and onions mixed with cinnamon, ginger, and cardamom, which "create for the consumer amorous passion and strength for coitus."[8]

The Perfumed Garden offers specific remedies for specific problems:

> . . . Men whose impotence is due either to the corruption of their sperm owing to their cold nature, or to maladies of the organs, or to discharges or to their excessive promptness in ejaculation, can be cured. They should

eat stimulant pastry, containing honey, ginger, pyrether, syrup of vinegar, hellebore, garlic, cinnamon, nutmeg, cardamoms, sparrow's tongues, Chinese cinnamon, long pepper, and other spices. They will be cured by using them. . . .

The author of *The Perfumed Garden* dealt with the problem of premature ejaculation as well as two types of impotence, one caused by inertia or insensitivity, the other by weakness or general feebleness. The cure for premature ejaculation was stated to be nutmeg and incense mixed with honey. For the second kind of impotence, honey was again prescribed, but to be mixed with various seeds or common spices such as ginger, cinnamon, and cardamom. For the first kind of impotence, the following were to be pounded together, and mixed in a broth: cinnamon, cloves, a root called galanga, cachou (not a sneeze but an Indian vegetable mixture), nutmeg, cubebs, sparrowwort, pepper, thistle, cardamom, pyrether, laurel seed, and gilly flowers. As much of this broth was to be drunk as possible, every morning and evening. Water was also to be taken before and after the broth. Also one was advised that when the mixture was taken with honey, the best possible results were obtained.

Egg yolks or egg yolks and onions were very strongly recommended to increase the intensity of intercourse. Other ingredients that might be taken with eggs to produce sexual energy were asparagus, fat, butter, and the usual honey and spices. Camel's milk and chick-peas were also on the list of sexual gourmet treats.

A whole chapter of *The Perfumed Garden* gives advice on increasing the size of the penis. One recommendation is to rub honey and ginger into it, another involves hot pitch, and still another suggests the application and drinking of an oil in which an ass's penis has been soaked.

One of the early fathers of pharmacy, Avicenna, an eleventh-century Arab physician-philosopher, also gave advice on increasing sexual pleasure and the size of the penis. Male sexual pleasure, according to Avicenna, could be enhanced by chewing, but not swallowing, cubebs or ginger and pepper with honey, and then applying the saliva mixture to the end half of the organ. For size he recommended "rubbing in hot fats and oils after friction with a rough cloth, and the pouring of different sorts of milk over it, mostly sheep's milk; and by the subsequent application of a pitch-plaster . . ."[9]

Avicenna also recognized the adverse effects of the abuse of alcohol and sexual excitants on sexual capacities.

The Moroccans and Persians also used honey and spices as aphrodisiacs, the Moroccans sometimes adding Spanish fly, while the Persians liked quinine and pills containing ground-up precious jewels or pastilles containing marijuana. Flagellation and cold showers and baths were also recommended in the Eastern world.

Arabian books dealt extensively with the art of prolonging intercourse as well as sexual stimulants and treatments of premature ejaculation. The secret of prolongation was attributed to the ability to avoid muscle tension while keeping the brain occupied. This was accomplished by eating, chewing, drinking, or smoking during intercourse. One might imagine that a modern-day equivalent would be watching the late show on television during coition.

Although hallucinogens did not seem to take a major place in early erotic recipes for sexual satisfaction, they were used if the following translation of an Arabian poem is an indication:

> The member of Abdu'l Haylukh remained
> In erection for thirty days sustained
> By smoking hashish
> Abdu'l Hayjeh deflowered in one night
> Eighty virgins in a rigid rite
> After smoking hashish[2]

In *The Arabian Nights,* Sir Richard Burton mentions the use of a mixture of opium along with the usual honey and spices and also a small lizard to "thicken the seed" so that pregnancy would be more likely to occur. The Indians also used bhang, a drink whose principal ingredient is the hemp (cannabis or marijuana) plant, as an aphrodisiac.

The major Hindu work, the *Ananga-Ranga* (Hindu Act of Love), by Kalyanamalla is similar to the *Kama Sutra* and *The Perfumed Garden* in its approach to sexual relationships. About 130 recipes are given for thirty-seven different subjects such as "hastening the paroxysm of the woman, delaying the orgasm of the man, enlarging the lingam, narrowing and contracting the yoni, removing body hair, perfuming the yoni, causing pregnancy, limiting the number of children, for enlarging the breasts, for raising and hardening pendulous breasts, for causing a pleasant smell to the breath, for reducing others to submission, for winning love and friendship, and for enabling a woman to attract and preserve her husband's love."[10]

It is remarkable how the concerns of men and women have altered so little over the centuries, and what little advance modern scientific man has made toward their resolution. Why, one might suppose that those early sexual sages had been retained as advertising consultants to hype the drug and cosmetic industry's pills, potions, lotions, perfumes, dipilatories, deodorants (breath, feet, armpit, crotch), pre-, during-, and after-shave, and hair dyes. Although many of the recipes can only be viewed as ludicrous, the worries, longings, and fears to which they appealed were exactly the same as those of contemporary society. Moreover, much of the advice—to be clean, to eat well, to be healthy, to be kind, to be considerate, to be loving, to enjoy sexual relations—is as sound today as it was those hundreds of years ago. Unfortunately, there is little reason to believe that the ingredients in the recipes had any specific pharmacological effect on sexual function. However, many of the ingredients are a mystery, for the recipes referred to mixtures, the components of which are unknown, or there is uncertainty because of difficulty in translations.

Not surprisingly, as they were native plants, opium and Indian hemp were used as aphrodisiacs in the Orient. On the other hand, a contrary opinion was handed down by the Indian Hemp Drugs Commission of 1894, which declared that cannabis had no aphrodisiac properties whatsoever. The commission noted that it had quite the opposite purpose for Indian ascetics, who used it to destroy their sexual appetites. Nevertheless, once taken, there is considerable evidence that even the minor hallucinogenic drugs, such as marijuana, may alter sexual perceptions and experiences in pleasurable ways.

One of the most remarkable stories of sex and hallucinogenic drugs was recounted by Marco Polo. In the eleventh century, in Afghanistan, there was a unique erotic-religious sect called the Assassins, led by a powerful man called Hasan i Sabbah, the Old Man of the Mountain. Hasan i Sabbah maintained his power by terror through the use of "double agents," particularly against Moslems and Christians. His followers infiltrated themselves into the households, businesses, and military staffs of powerful people, where they performed their designated tasks with devoted loyalty. When and if Hasan so decreed, and at his signal, often many years after the agent had obtained a position of trust, the agent's employer would be found dead with a flame dagger, the trademark of the Assassins, in his throat.

The story goes that the followers of Hasan were recruited by revealing to them a glimpse of what they could expect in the hereafter, if they were only true to Hasan. Under the influence of hashish, the resinous part of the cannabis plant, the prospective agents were ushered into a "Garden of Delights," where they spent an enchanted erotic evening with what they believed were the supernatural houris (dancing girls) promised in Mohammed's view of heaven. Because it seems unlikely that hashish alone could fool men into believing they were actually in heaven, some writers have suggested that other drugs, such as henbane,* might have been used in addition to hashish.[11] Probably, however, one should not underestimate what people will believe with or without drugs. It seems quite reasonable that the con was possible, given the year and the great desire of men to have not only an afterlife, but one filled with sexual gratification. It is not hard to find greater cons or con artists in history, even ones that have resulted in the deaths of hundreds of persons. Murder and other crimes have been committed by cooperative believers who did not have the excuse that they were influenced by drugs that altered their perceptions of reality. Moreover, men in our own century have described the experience of coitus under the influence of marijuana as a perception of the lady as glowing or covered with jewels or flowers, or a peak experience of total ecstasy in which the whole universe was one's own body.[12] Surely, then, it does not strain credulity that a "Garden of Delights," offered by a powerful man, would seduce the loyalty of many eager believers whose perceptions were modified by hallucinogenic drugs.

The Encyclopedia of Sexual Knowledge, published in 1934 in London, comments on the use of opium as an aphrodisiac in China:

> . . . It is impossible to write about China without thinking of drugs and opium dens, though today these evils are perhaps more prevalent in the white countries than in China. However, opium has been used in China as a sexual stimulant to a greater extent than anywhere else. Its effects have been tested and reliably recorded. Opium smoking induces strange sexual fantasies which are associated with a sense of voluptuous pleasure, and for a time it also produces erection, though after continual use, this effect ceases and, indeed, continued opium smoking eventually leads to total impotence. In women, too, opium smoking intensifies the sexual instinct to a considerable extent. . . .

An anonymous French surgeon observed the dose-related effects of opium as used by the Chinese.

> . . . When moderate doses are taken (i.e., ten to twelve pipes) any suggesion of erotic excitement in the individual, whether by direct contact or merely by mental image, immediately produces an erection. Despite this, however, the penile nerves, especially those of the glans, become anaesthetized, with the result that orgasm and emission are considerably

---

*Henbane is a plant in the Solanaceae family containing scopolamine or hyoscine, which is a central nervous system depressant. It can produce drowsiness, euphoria, relief of fear, and amnesia. Small amounts of scopolamine are found in some sleeping pills.

> retarded. A similar effect is produced in the female (vulval, vaginal, and rectal nerves being anaesthetized). The rectal and vaginal constrictor muscles become relaxed. Under this condition pederasty has been practised more easily, and without pain, despite an obvious anatomical disproportion. More than fifteen to twenty pipes do not produce this stimulation and its accompaniments; and after twenty-five pipes the erections also cease, becoming weaker and weaker with each additional pipe smoked. Hardened opium smokers are said to present genital signs of their habit; slack penis, shrunken glans, with a degree of hardness, and a pale mucous surface; the scrotum shrivels, and the testes eventually atrophy. . . .[13]

Although opium was used by the Chinese in association with sexual activity, it was not the drug of choice for virility or sexual problems. Here, nutrition was the first line of defense. Only when a varied, wholesome diet failed were medicines to be taken. The Chinese recognized the disabling effects of stress and sorrow as well as excesses in eating and drinking that could diminish sexual appetites and capabilities. If early Orientals had to choose between a food or drug that made them capable of vigorous sexual intercourse and one that changed the perception of it, they would surely have chosen the former. They well knew that without the ability, a modified perception, however ecstatic, is of questionable value.

Bird nest soup was a favorite sexual strength-building food, one that probably was restricted to the Mandarin class because of its great expense. In addition to its rarity and high cost, qualities that are almost guaranteed to induce a positive placebo effect, the soup, made from seaweed nests held together with fish, contains a high percentage of phosphorus, a mineral needed for good health. The poor man got his phosphorus from *nuoc-man*, a kind of rotten fish oil flavored with garlic and pimento.

Some early European writers had a difficult time sorting out the differences between the effects of a little opium, a great deal or chronic use of opium, and their own moral biases. For example, a certain Dr. Acosta, a sixteenth-century physician living in Spain, wrote a book on drugs from the East Indies.[14] Dr. Acosta found it a contradiction that opium, a drug he knew caused impotence in those addicted to it, could enhance sexual experiences. ". . . all the learned physicians of our rank tell me that it caused impotence in men, and soon became incapable to perform . . . but so many people use this for fleshly lust they cannot all be deceived. . . ." Dr. Acosta's explanation for his observation that opium was "the most common and ordinary remedy used by the vile children of Venus" was people's imaginations:

> . . . the imagination of common folk is so powerful that it can transform impotence into potency, and they commonly imploy it to increase their carnal pleasures . . . the imagination is so great a stimulus to lascivious pleasures, and this is superior to the ejaculatory virtue, the latter obeys the first. . . . And because the imaginative virtue is so powerful, it dominates the explosive one forcing into testicles the genital seed, and the greater the imagination the more rapid the emission of the seed. And as those who take Amfiam (Opium) have lost control, they actually complete this venereal act much later. And because many females do not give away the seed that quickly, and when the man is also slow she completes the act of Venus much later, the act of conception ends exactly at the same time, and taking of Amfiam is here a help. . . .[14]

If the good Dr. Acosta only could have known, he was surely one of the first authors to write about the extraordinary power of the placebo effect.

In relative importance, the Indian hemp plant, *Cannabis indica,** was to the Hindus who eschewed alcohol as opium was to the Chinese, although each drug was certainly known to the other culture. The Indians use the hemp plant in three products.[15] Bhang, similar to alcohol, is not used primarily for its effect on sexual function, but to produce a sense of well-being, stimulate the appetite, relieve stress, and sometimes, paradoxically, to reduce hunger.

Ganja contains some of the resin of the plant along with the leaves and flowering tops, so it's more potent than bhang, and would be similar to a mixture of the hashish and marijuana usually available on the American market.

Charas is the resin of the cannabis so it's what we know as hashish or hash, and is five to six times stronger, ounce for ounce, as bhang. Bhang, ganja, and charas all produce the same pharmacological effects. It's a matter of how much, how fast, and the mode of ingestion. Ganja and charas are smoked, while bhang shows up in food and drink, or is chewed. Bhang is especially popular on festival days. Sometimes, large pots of it are placed in the center of the village for public consumption, while in urban centers, bhang ice cream cools off and livens up social occasions.

Bhang, ganja, and charas have been used for centuries in India to modify sexual experiences, but like marijuana and hashish in the United States, their primary use is to bring about peace, tranquillity, and mellowness or euphoria on social occasions. There is no evidence

---

**Cannabis indica* is almost identical to *Cannabis sativa,* the marijuana of the Western world.

that any hemp product is an aphrodisiac in the sense of driving people to sexual acts or excitement.

Cannabis ingestion, in the form of bhang, was associated with sexual activity in the formal ceremonies of Tantric Yoga, practiced first in India thirteen centuries ago. Tantric Yoga, whose goal is attainment of the "greatest nirvana" (liberation), requires its initiates to break the usual religious taboos under rigidly controlled conditions. Thus, what is normally sinful, eating meat, drinking wine, and even incest, are employed in conjunction with marijuana, to transcend desire. Tantric Yoga is thus a risky and radical shortcut to attaining freedom from the desire for pleasure-producing agents. The initiate is placed at risk of embracing pleasure instead of becoming freed from its constraints.[16]

The Tantric ceremony involves the deliberate use of taboo substances, marijuana and sex Yoga. Initiates begin the long ceremony with meditation, followed by ritual cleansing. After this there are more prayers and ablutions, all carried out in a most rigid and formal manner in which every gesture and word is prescribed. Once at the temple, or other place of worship, the initiate marks off a triangular seat and worships by invoking the name of Kamarupa, a goddess in mythology who was dismembered, and whose yoni, falling to earth, landed on what is now the Kamarupa shrine. By sitting on the triangle in the correct position facing the correct direction, and invoking the mantra, the Kamarupa's sexual energy is supposed to be channeled to the initiate. The next step in the ritual is to consecrate and drink bhang, usually in the form of a flavored milk drink. Then more ritual cleansings and prayers are performed as the initiate begins to get high and to feel the "godhead" within him. Only as a divine human is he fit to take part in the second part of the ceremony.[16]

In the second part, a circle of men and women is formed around the initiate, and as each taboo object of the initiation is purified with ritual prayer, it is eaten or drunk by each. Thus, on top of the marijuana, wine is drunk. The ritual copulation is performed after purification of the female partner. During the actual sex act, the initiate recites a verse, and finally ejaculates while saying, "OM, with light and ether as my two hands, I, exulting one, relying on the ladle, I, who take *dharma* and non-*dharma* as sacrificial ingredients, offer [this oblation] lovingly into the fire. . . ." According to Aldrich, the Hindu ceremony requires the male to abandon his sperm, while the Buddhists instruct him to retain it. In either case, the intercourse is prolonged as long as possible while Sanskrit is recited to "build up the tremendous sexual energy thereby generated until the couple is surrounded with a golden fiery aura, a much-prolonged and not genitally-specific coming, a sense of divine unity. Sparks shower for hours in this cosmic dance, the brain melts away, and liberation—*mahanirvana*—is experienced."[16]

In the Tantric ceremony, which is intended to enable the initiates to feel divinity within themselves, marijuana serves as a disinhibitor, but also heightens and intensifies sensations, while affecting the sense of time and space. Large oral doses of marijuana are hallucinogenic, and when the full effect of the bhang is felt, about an hour and a half into the ceremony at the time of sexual intercourse, the combination of the temple setting, made optimal with incense, flowers and lamps, and the concentration demanded by the earlier portion of the ceremony must interact to assure an ecstatic experience which the participant may truly attribute to a divine presence within him.[16]

Tantric Yoga may be secretly but is not officially practiced today. Its ceremonial use of marijuana was based on an even earlier religious use. The oldest religion for which there are complete records is that of the Vedas, two hundred years B.C. Vedic ceremonies required the ingestion of a drink called soma which is believed by some historians to have contained the hallucinogenic mushroom, *Amanita muscaria*. Thus, in Tantric ceremony, the earlier tradition of combining a hallucinogen with religion is combined with a Hindu practice of drinking poison as a divine act and drug Yoga which has a long and honorable tradition in India, despite the admonitions of contemporary swamis that their followers should forgo drugs. [16]

While early Arabs and Orientals were tripping on opium and cannabis, early Westerners were more likely to be using cocaine, "magic mushrooms," peyote, or, like Europeans, one of the hallucinogenic plants in the Solanaceae family. Mandrake is a Solanaceae, as are henbane, belladonna, and the nightshade.

APHRODISIACS IN THE NEW WORLD

Erythroxylon coca, "coke," cocaine, along with peyote and *Pscilocybe mexicana* (the magic mushroom), were the aphrodisiacs of the Americas. Especially cocaine. Like opium and cannabis, cocaine's primary use was not for its sexual effects. Indeed, there are no drugs capable pharmacologically of altering the sexual response that were used *primarily* for this purpose in either the ancient or the new world. However, there are a number of substances used only for their aphrodisiac properties that are entirely pharmacologically inactive, and whose efficacy is entirely attributable to the placebo effect.

Cocaine is a stimulant that prolongs the time to orgasm and ejaculation, and heightens sensory awareness during sexual activity.

Just as it is currently fashionable among the wealthy in the United States, so it was over 3,000 years ago in Peru and Bolivia.[17] According to their records, the Inca royalty had their own "toot" parties over 3,000 years ago. At that time, the leaves of the coca plant were the property of the Inca rulers who dispensed them as special rewards to those with whom they were especially pleased. Along came the Spanish conquistadores who, as the ruling class, continued to control the distribution of cocaine but dispensed it, not as a special reward, but as wages for labor. The Spanish were no fools. They were in the tin and silver mining business in Peru and Bolivia, and they quickly discovered that the Indians would work long hours with little food if they were chewing coca leaves. Although historians generally credit first, Inca royalty, then, the Spanish with being able to control the distribution of coca leaves, it seems more likely that they had as much success in maintaining exclusivity, as the federal government's Drug Enforcement Administration has of controlling marijuana distribution in the United States. The coca plant was wild and indigenous, and it must have been there for the picking for those Indians who wanted to chew it, despite the claim of ownership by the ruling class of the time.

The Western world is a veritable hothouse of hallucinogenic plants. In addition to *Cannabis sativa* and *Erythroxylon coca,* more than one hundred plants native to the American continents have hallucinogenic properties. Most of these are flowering plants, and the rest are some kind of fungi.

Because of the ability of hallucinogenic plants to modify perceptions and distort reality, their early users endowed them with other-worldly or divine properties. Sometimes they were used in association with the black arts, witchcraft and sorcery, but most often in religious practices. No plant is more firmly fixed in religion than peyote, which even today is the legal sacrament of the North American Church, to which about a third of North American Indians belong.

Peyote *(Lophophora williamsii),* a gray-green cactus, is found among the arid sand and rocks of Mexico just south of the Rio Grande. The tops of the briefly blooming, barely three-inch-high plant, when sliced off and dried, are the grooved "buttons" containing the potent alkaloid, mescaline.

There is remarkably little recorded mention of peyote in association with sex. In fact, according to De Ropp,[18] peyote is associated with abstinence from sexual intercourse. Before the Indians go out to gather the sacred cactus in the fall, they prepare themselves for their holy mission by fasting and forgoing sexual activities for several weeks.

Divinity was already in the cactus when the Spanish arrived in Mexico. It was known as "the flesh of the gods." Despite the Catholic

Church's attempt to substitute its sacramental wafer, representing the flesh of Christ, and to repress peyote, the Indians continued to prefer the bitter nauseating buttons which provided them with a remarkable visual interpretation of the hereafter. As peyote religion spread into North America, the missionaries tried hard to stamp it out, although there is no evidence that it ever produced debauchery. Indeed, its adherents generally subscribed to chastity and sober industrious living, and the peyote ceremonies are characterized by solemnity, prayer, and meditation.

De Ropp has described the peyote worship among a group of North American Indians:

> Among the Kiowa Indians the rite of peyote eating generally takes place on a Saturday night. The men sit quietly on the carefully swept earth, forming themselves into a circle about a flickering campfire. All bow their heads in prayer, then, taking the mescal buttons from the jar in which they are stored, the leader of the ceremony hands four buttons to each man. One of these, freed from the tufts of hair that cover it, is put into the mouth and thoroughly softened, ejected into the palm of the hand, rolled into a bolus, and swallowed. In this way as many as twelve buttons may be taken at intervals between sundown and 3 A.M. with the accompaniment of occasional prayers and rites. Throughout the ceremony the campfire is kept burning brightly and attendants maintain a continual beating of drums. The Indians remain seated from sundown to noon of the following day. As the effect wears off they get up and go about their work without experiencing unpleasant aftereffects. On the following day, purely for ritual reasons, they abstain from using any salt with their food.[18]

Almost all of the earliest scientific work on hallucinogens was done on mescaline, after news of its properties spread to Europe in the late nineteenth century, and mescaline was isolated in 1896. Not only were scientists interested in its properties, but anthropologists, artists, and intellectuals were exploring its hallucinatory effects as well. None other than Havelock Ellis, who pioneered in studies of human sexual behavior, decided to give it a try himself. Although he left a vivid account of the kaleidoscopic visions induced by the drug, for example, "I would see thick, glorious fields of jewels, solitary or clustered, sometimes brilliant and sparkling, sometimes with a dull rich glow. . . ." Ellis did not mention any sexual feelings associated with the drug. After his own experience, Ellis used many of his friends as peyote guinea pigs, and there are numerous detailed accounts of the strange and beautiful visions induced by peyote and its active ingredient, mescaline, but none convey even a hint that the drug has aphrodisiac properties. Apparently, experimenting with peyote and other hallucinogens while engaging in sexual activities was a product of the sixties, a generation that was not held to rigid social or religious rules, and that tried almost everything with everything.

The hallucinogenic mushrooms, *Psilocybe* and *Amanita muscaria*, are a different story. A Spanish priest in the seventeenth century referred to persons who ate mushrooms as those who "saw visions, feel a faintness of heart, and are provoked to lust."

The phallic shape of the mushroom alone was almost enough to guarantee that early man would associate it with fertility and incorporate it into religious practices. The shape, along with the remarkable ability of some mushrooms to produce strange and wonderful visions, assured its place in primitive ceremonies as a window into the hereafter. The mysterious soma of the Vedas, the early Tantric ceremonies, the European bacchanalian cult, are believed by many historians to have been based on *Amanita muscaria*, the fly agaric mushroom. Mushroom-shaped stones over a foot high and dating to 1500 B.C. have been found in Guatemala and southeastern Mexico, suggesting religious ceremonial use of mushrooms. There is documentation of ritualistic mushroom-eating during the coronation of Montezuma II in Mexico in 1503. At least one historian has suggested that man developed his concept of divinity after eating mushrooms while foraging for food, and that all modern religions have sprung out of cults that used a hallucinogenic plant product to attain a vision of other worlds, or the longed-for life after death. The linguist and Dead Sea Scroll scholar, John Allegro, has argued that Christ and his disciples were "enlightened" by eating *Amanita muscaria*.[19]

Amanita muscaria, commonly called fly agaric because an abstract of it was once used to kill flies, grows in the United States around the Great Lakes, in New England, the Rockies, and the Pacific Northwest, usually in birch and evergreen forests. The active ingredients are probably muscinol and ibotenic acid. The mushrooms are eaten fresh or dried, and they are also smoked in the dried form. They are extremely toxic and dangerous. The first effect is drowsiness, a feeling of numbness in the legs, loss of coordination, and possibly nausea. Next come the dreamy hallucinations, especially Alice-in-Wonderland-size distortions, which are followed by a euphoric stage during which energy and physical strength are perceived to increase. This energizing stage is the one that may result in, or is felt as, sexual activity.

A bacchanalian orgy has been described as follows:

> Eating the god (mushroom) made it possible to induce and to some extent control an experience which was fundamental to fertility philosophy. The

> repeated bouts of drug-stimulated excitement were in the nature of violent and unnaturally prolonged sexual orgasms, whether or not they resulted in erection and ejaculation on the part of the men or spasmodic vaginal contractions by the women.[19]

With or without sex, with the end of the amanita mushroom trip comes a deep depression and sleep.

Psilocybe and *Stropharia* are the "magic mushrooms" of native Americans. The active ingredients, psilocybin and psilocin, were not identified until 1958. The chemical structure of these alkaloids is similar to other hallucinogens such as LSD and bufotenine, as well as serotonin, a naturally occurring transmitter of messages along the nerve pathways in the body. Serotonin plays a major part in sexual function.

The mushroom ceremony, also known as *agape* (love feast), is not a wild Indian sex party, but a communal way to resolve social problems in the tribe. At night, in a private place, mushroom songs are chanted by a leader while the participants, who have abstained from food and sex, eat raw mushrooms. The hallucinations that occur during the resulting "trip" are interpreted as answers to the particular problems or questions that have brought the group together. Eventually, everyone goes to sleep, and in the morning, they share breakfast.

The magic mushroom begins to take effect about fifteen minutes after it is eaten, and the peak effect is within sixty to ninety minutes. It takes from five to six hours for the trip to end. With two to four mushrooms, one becomes relaxed, emotionally detached, dreamy, and euphoric. With more mushrooms, strong time and space distortions are accompanied by audio and visual imagery. People may have a sense of traveling through time and space or the sense of observing oneself in another place.

Both peyote and magic mushrooms were given by the Yaqui Indian, Don Juan, to Carlos Castaneda, who reported his experiences in three books. To Don Juan peyote, "mescalito," is a teacher and the mushroom is an ally or helper. By eating these plants a "man of knowledge" may cast off the limitations of earthly beliefs and expectations, attain access to supernatural worlds, power and wisdom. Don Juan also taught that the drugs can be extremely hazardous for those who are weak and do not have expert guidance. Noticeably lacking in the Castaneda books are references to these drugs in association with sexual activity. Only a species of *Datura,* the jimson weed, Don Juan's "little smoke," the third drug used by Don Juan in his apprenticeship training, is mentioned in association with sex, and that is only in passing.

Don Juan mentions that, "In a diluted form it is good for all the matters of manhood, old people who have lost their vigor, or young men who are seeking adventures, or even women who want passion. . . . The weed is used only for power. The man who wants his vigor back, the young people who seek to endure fatigue and hunger, the man who wants to kill another man, a woman who wants to be in heat—they all desire power. And the weed will give it to them!"[20]

Over twenty species of *Datura* have hallucinogenic properties. The nightshade family, the Solanaceae, also includes potatoes and tobacco in addition to the more toxic members, belladonna, henbane, and mandrake. With these drugs, a trip is perceived as exactly that. Even a paste made of jimson weed, belladonna, or henbane, when rubbed into the skin, particularly the mucous membranes, can produce illusions of flying and sexually frenetic dreams. With such remarkable properties, no wonder the nightshades long ago formed the favorite chemistry of sorcery and witchcraft, as well as the basis for native ceremonial magic.

Among the active ingredients are the alkaloids, scopolamine, hyoscyamine (or hyoscine), and atropine. These drugs are used in modern medicine as well. Scopolamine has the most mind-bending properties, and has been used as a truth serum, as "twilight sleep" during childbirth, and at present in very small doses in nonprescription sleeping pills. The plants containing these alkaloids are very potent, and the history of these drugs is replete with reports of deaths, both deliberate and accidental.

Reported Dioscorides of *Datura,* "The root being drunk with wine has the power to arouse not unpleasant fantasies. But two drams being drunk makes a man beside himself for three days and four being drunk kill him."

If you weren't done in directly by the drug there was, nevertheless, a risk. Throughout the Middle Ages in Europe, the effects produced by hallucinogenic plants were associated with the Devil. Indeed, another name for belladonna besides "beautiful lady" is "devil's weed" or "sorcerer's herb." Persons who took part in ceremonies were considered (with the strongest encouragement of the Church) to be witches or wizards and to be the Devil's agents. The outcome of many of the witch-hunts provided entertainment for the community. Usually the culprits were tortured until they confessed and then they were burned alive in the public square.

In one sad sixteenth-century case, the teenage daughter of a local Bavarian minister was enticed into a midnight ceremony by her boyfriend. Part of the secret ritual involved preparing with suitable incantations a drink which all the participants imbibed. Apparently the mixture was a potent disinhibitor, for the normally modest miss abandoned her clothing and submitted to being anointed with "witches' salve." Soon she was experiencing the full hallucinatory effects of *Datura,* replete with flying, soaring over mountains and frenzied sexual feelings. The poor girl was convinced she had truly been possessed by the Devil, and in a most costly stroke of honesty, confessed to her shocked father. The loyal member of the cloth saw his duty, and summarily handed her over to the authorities who arrested the rest of the midnight revelers and dispatched the lot—albeit prayerfully and after a suitable amount of torture—into a public bonfire.

The witches' salve applied to the hapless girl most assuredly contained belladonna and probably henbane. A thirteenth-century bishop informs us that henbane was always in brews intended to conjure up demons, and another historian has made a logical case that the chief ingredients in witches' brews were belladonna, *Datura,* henbane, and mandrake, and sometimes opium and marijuana, all dissolved in bat's blood or oil, and sometimes even human fat. The hallucinations, sexual excesses, and wild wide-eyed appearance of the participants in such ceremonies were convincing evidence that they had had intercourse with the Devil. The stories of such drug induced orgies and possessions led to hysterical witch-hunts and outrages in the name of Christianity that were anything but Christian.

Two kinds of *Datura* are native to the Western Hemisphere. *Datura stramonium* and *Datura inoxia* (or *D. meteloides)* grow in the Middle Atlantic states and the Southwest. The name, jimson weed, arose after some *D. stramonium* was accidentally added to the salad of soldiers stationed in Jamestown, Virginia, in 1676. Other common names for the American variety are locoweed, stinkweed, and devil's weed. *Datura* is more likely to be called thorn apple in Europe.

D. inoxia is the most commonly used hallucinogen of American and Mexican Indian tribes. According to *The High Times Encyclopedia of Recreational Drugs,*[20] the Navajo, Paiute, Zuni, and Tarahumara tribes drink a mixture *(toloache)* of Datura seeds, roots, and leaves during a *rite de passage,* in divination rituals, and to commune with the dead. The Aztecs are more likely to use a species called *Torna loca* (maddening plant). Tree Daturas are used in South America for many shamanistic purposes, interpreting visions, diagnosing illness, catching thieves, and predicting the future. Ecuadorian Indians give it to their children to quiet them down, a practice paralleling the contemporary use of amphetamines to calm hyperactive children in the United States.

In India, whores gave Datura seeds to their patrons, and criminals used them surreptitiously to render their victims unconscious. It was believed that those who used Datura could foresee the future and discover buried treasure. Datura was widely held to be an aphrodisiac; but it has also been used to lessen sexual excitement in cases of nymphomania. Along with other drugs, preparations made from it were used to lure girls into prostitution. Insanity and death have been caused by eating the plant, affecting children particularly, yet certain American Indians used an infusion of the seeds to quiet unruly children![20]

There are several other hallucinogenic mixtures that have been used by South American Indians. In Brazil, *caapi,* along the Amazon, *ayahuasca,* and along the base of the Andes, *yage,* are made from *Banisteriopsis caapi* and *Banisteriopsis inebrians,* which are woody vines. Although the drugs are believed to assure the love of wives, their main use is as the basis of a religion. The Indians believe that during their "trips," they actually become the fantastic color hallucinations they have of animals and birds. The drugs are also used to predict the future, and to produce energy, power, and freedom and to obtain self-knowing.

Bufotenine, an alkaloid found in toad skin and some plants, has been used in mixtures with other hallucinogens. Bufotenine has a chemical structure similar to serotonin, which plays a part in hallucination, as well as sex chemistry, in the body.

Bufotenine is a hallucinogenic alkaloid that pops up in many diverse places. Although it is usually referred to as a substance found in toad skin, it is also in the hallucinogenic mushroom, *Amanita muscaria,* a tree, a vine, rabbit lungs, and even human urine. Bufotenine is not a strong hallucinogen, so it has usually been used in mixtures with other more potent ingredients. Its mild reactions probably contributed to its early popularity as an aphrodisiac. In general, when people want to enter into sexual activity, they don't want to be totally out of it, but merely to have their inhibitions decreased and their perceptions and responses modified. Thus, mild hallucinogens, such as this drug and marijuana, are more popular for use with sex.

Bufotenine is one of the ingredients used in European witches' brews along with the hallucinogenic members of the Solanaceae family, datura, henbane, belladonna, and mandrake. One might speculate that fairy tales which had a toad changed into a prince were based upon the hallucinogenic and thus magical properties of the toad alkaloid.

In the New World, bufotenine was a component of *Cohoba,* a Haitian snuff, introduced to the Europeans by Columbus in 1496, who noted that the Indians sniffed a "dust" that made them "become like drunken men."[20] *Cohoba* is made from the seeds of a tree of the mimosa family. However, the seeds are not always used as snuff. The Mura Indians soak the seeds in water and then give it to themselves in an enema. The enemas are used by the Muras to enliven ceremonies which last eight days and are associated with every sort of debauchery, according to one author who describes the effects as follows:

> His eyes started from his head, his mouth contracted, his limbs trembled. It was fearful to see him. He was obliged to sit down or he would have fallen. He was drunk, but only about five minutes; he was thus gayer.[18]

One cannot imagine from this description that the recipient of the enema would have made a particularly attractive or competent sexual partner.

There are many more hallucinogenic plants than have been mentioned here. Ibogaine, an alkaloid of *Iboga* which grows in the Congo and Gabon, is a powerful cocainelike stimulant in low doses and a hallucinogen at high doses. Yohimbine from West Africa is a mild hallucinogen which is made into a drink, a snuff, and a smoking mixture. Kavakava, a ceremonial drink in the Polynesian Islands, is prepared by having the village virgins chew roots of the plant *Piper methysticum* and then soaking them in water. The effects of kavakava vary from mild stimulation to full-blown visions. Whether these are of the village virgins is uncertain.

Nutmeg and mace. San Pedro, a Peruvian cactus. Sweet flag, a marsh plant found in Europe, Asia, and North America. Donaña, a cactus growing in the southwestern states. Mescal bean. The list of hallucinogenic plants is extensive. However, few mind-bending plants are specifically associated with sexual activity. Yohimbine is one of the exceptions. It is often referred to as an aphrodisiac, is sold in the United States in "sensuous herb" teas and smoking mixtures, and is the toasting drink of some contemporary California marriage ceremonies.[20]

Certainly, more plant drugs have been taken in association with religious practices than with sexual activity. Where sex and religion have come together, as with the Tantrists, it is likely that drugs have played a part. Astrology, mysticism, yoga, paganism, fortune-telling, divination, witchcraft, magical healing, all have been associated with psychoactive drugs which have been smoked, drunk, rubbed in, chewed, sipped, sniffed, eaten, smelled, and infused. Historically, mind-bending drugs have been used in rites and ceremonies according to rigid social rules that governed all aspects of who, where, how, and how often. But they were also used by rule-breaking adolescents.

Many persons would probably agree that psychoactive drugs would make a young person of today "shameless, presumptuous, lewd, tottering, wicked, vile, brutal and brazen . . . impudent, vain, proud, debauched, vicious and promiscuous, a libertine who exhausts himself by a life devoted to pleasure."[21] However, this quote was not used to describe a sybaritic, contemporary, long-haired pot-smoker, but a sixteenth-century Aztec youth who ate magic mushrooms.

The social and ritual use of plant drugs was almost stamped out in the Western world by a modern society that apparently approved only of alcohol and administered both social and legal punishment to those who used hallucinogenic plants. However, with the social experiments of the fifties, the beat generation, hippies, flower children, there came a renewed interest in psychoactive plants—an interest that continues today. The present experimentation is not bound by the rigid social rules of primitive cultures, and so many natural drugs once restricted to formal religious rites are now used solely for the physical and psychological changes they produce, including those associated with sex.

PART III

PRESCRIBED AND OVER-THE-COUNTER MEDICINES

4

PRESCRIBED DRUGS: HOW THEY CAN HURT YOUR SEX LIFE

Many medicines that are prescribed by doctors can interfere with sexual desire and performance. Most problems with sexual function, however, are caused by mental illness or cultural and social factors that cause psychological inhibitions. Very rarely is a drug prescribed that improves sexual function.

Keep in mind that there's a lot more to be learned about how drugs work and especially how they relate to sexual function. Nothing that you read in this chapter or the rest of this book should cause you to stop taking a drug that's been prescribed for you by your doctor. However, if you think you're having a drug-related problem, and there isn't any mention of it here, don't let that be a reason for not telling your doctor about it. If, when you tell your doctor you think you have a drug-induced sexual problem, he doesn't take it seriously, doesn't explain what's going on, seems embarrassed, or doesn't seem to know much about it, and isn't willing to go into it further or to refer you to someone who does understand it, then you might want to consider changing doctors. You might also want to consider telling your doctor ahead of time that you don't like surprises, and that you prefer to be forewarned if there's any possibility that a drug he's prescribing for you could interfere with your sex life.

If it does happen, *don't panic. Remember that the situation is almost never permanent*, and that in most cases, sexual function will return to normal by a simple adjustment of the dosage or by switching to a different drug in the same class with the same kind of therapeutic action.

Remember, too, if you are very sick, you won't be very interested in sex anyway. So sometimes, even though your sexual function may be somewhat decreased by a drug, you may feel so much better overall than you did without it, that on balance there is an improvement. Again, discuss it with your doctor. You have a right to be informed and to participate in decisions that affect your body. A good doctor will welcome your questions, and will answer them to the best of his ability.

If, when you do ask your doctor a question about the way a drug affects your sex life, the answers sound equivocal, it may not be his fault. Drugs and sex may well be the most indefinite area in medicine. Sexual response is so much an individual matter that the sexual response to a drug seems to be individual too. In many instances, a drug will only affect a small percentage of patients who take it. Moreover, not all of those affected will have the same experience. The drug may cause one man to lose his sexual desire, another to fail to sustain an erection, and another to fail to ejaculate any semen, while having no effect on women at all.

Most of what follows is about the effects of drugs on the sexual functioning of men. That doesn't mean that the drugs can't or don't affect women, but only that not much is known about how they affect women.

What are these prescribed drugs that can lead to sex problems? We know that, although all of the body's systems participate in the total sex response, drugs with certain kinds of actions are more likely to affect sexual functioning than do others. These are the mind-affecting drugs, and drugs that affect the muscles and blood circulation. Often these drugs work by interfering with the chemical messengers in the nervous system.

In the first group considered are the drugs that most directly affect the muscles. They include the anticholinergics (a fancy name meaning drugs that block one of the chemical messengers, acetylcholine, at the nerve endings), and levodopa, a drug used to treat a disease that causes muscle tremors. The second group contains the antihypertensives, which are drugs used to lower blood pressure.

The mind-affecting drugs are in the third group. They include the antianxiety agents (minor tranquilizers such as Valium); the antidepressants (drugs used to elevate the mood), and the antipsychotics or major tranquilizers, which are used to treat mental illnesses. The fourth group is reserved for a few miscellaneous drugs that have affected sexual function, but don't fit into the above categories. If you want to know about a specific drug, consult the index at the end of the book.

All of the drugs in a category are listed at the beginning of each section. On the left are all the brand names beginning with capital letters; in the center are all the generic names. In general, if there are more brand than generic names listed, the exclusive right for one manufacturer to produce a drug in the category has expired, and the price you pay is likely to be lower if the generic drug name is written on the prescription instead of the brand name. Why add insult to injury by paying more for drugs that may interfere with your sexual function?

DRUGS THAT AFFECT MUSCLES

Most often, muscle-affecting drugs are used to relax muscle spasms. The problem here is that drugs aren't very selective. Suppose you want to relieve stomach cramps. A drug that will do that will also affect other involuntary muscles in the body, some of which are important for normal sexual response. The drugs work at the nerve endings where the chemicals act as messengers telling the muscles to relax and contract, and they interfere with the chemicals in the brain or spinal cord where messages originate. Those drugs that work at the nerve endings, usually anticholinergics, are more likely to inhibit the sexual response, while those acting centrally may stimulate it.

ANTICHOLINERGICS

Brand Name	*Generic Name*	*Component in*
	atropine	
	belladonna	Butibel
Homapin Novatrin	homatropine	Hycodan Probilagol
Banthine	methantheline	
Pamine	methscopolamine	
Eumydrin	methylatropine	
Piptal	pipenzolate	
Probanthine	propantheline	

Anticholinergics can produce impotence and interfere with ejaculations. One of them, methantheline (Banthine), has produced impotence in almost every man who has taken it.[1]

A large number of different drugs are in the anticholinergic group, and some of them are among the oldest drugs known. They may be obtained from plants of the potato family or made synthetically. *Atropa belladonna*, the deadly nightshade, *Hyoscyamus niger* or henbane, and

Datura stramonium, jimson weed or thorn apple, are all in this group. These plants have been used as hallucinogens and as aphrodisiacs.

The alkaloids extracted from these plants are commonly used to decrease secretions in the nose and air passages and to relieve spasms in the stomach and the rest of the digestive tract. They may also be found in preparations that treat menstrual cramps. When you have your pupils dilated for an eye examination, your ophthalmologist has probably used an anticholinergic.

Atropine is the number one drug among the anticholinergics. This is how it works. There are receptors widely spread throughout body systems. When acetylcholine is released at some of these receptors, there is stimulation, and when it is released at others, there is relaxation. Anticholinergics cause the opposite to happen. For instance, acetylcholine causes smooth muscle, such as that needed for contractions during orgasm, to contract. At the same time, it has a sedating effect in the brain. When anticholinergics such as atropine come along, they block the receptors and thus keep the acetylcholine from working. The effects are to relax smooth muscles and, in large doses, to stimulate the brain.

Small doses of atropine have little effect on the central nervous system, but in large doses atropine causes excitation, restlessness, and talkativeness, a condition called "belladonna jag." With toxic doses, delirium, stupor, and coma result.

Atropine and the related anticholinergics are deceptive. The brain and heart stimulation, and dilation of blood vessels on the surface of the body which gives a warming feeling, may trick an individual into feeling sexually aroused. But, as with alcohol, the effect on performance is negative. The smooth involuntary muscles that are needed to concentrate blood in the genital area, and for the ejaculatory and orgasmic phases, simply can't work very well when an anticholinergic drug is preventing the chemical messengers from telling the muscles to contract.

It is highly unlikely that any American could get through life without having taken an anticholinergic. Because they decrease nasal secretions and have relaxing properties, anticholinergics are found in many combination cough and cold and sleep-aid preparations that may be purchased over the counter without a prescription. More about these over-the-counter drugs may be found in Chapter 8.

Theoretically, all of the drugs in this group should inhibit erections and possibly interfere with ejaculations, at least in high doses. When they are used to treat ulcers and to relax muscle spasms in the urinary and gastrointestinal systems, they may harm sexual function, but in cold and sleep remedies, the doses are probably too small to do any damage to sexual function.

ANTIHYPERTENSIVES

Probably more people experience an adverse effect on their sex lives from taking an antihypertensive than from any other kind of drug. This is because there are so many antihypertensives (as you can see in the table below), so many antihypertensives affect sexual function, and so many people suffer from hypertension.

ANTIHYPERTENSIVES

Brand Name	*Generic name*	*Component in*
Rau-Tab Rautensin Rauwiloid	alseroxylon	Rauvera
Naturetin	bendroflumethiazide	Rauzide
Exna Aquatag	benzthiazide	
Bethanidine	bethanidine	
Diuril	chlorothiazide	Diupres
Hygroton	chlorthalidone	Regroton
Catapres	clonidine	
Aquex	clopamide	
Anhydron	cyclothiazide	
Harmonyl	deserpidine	
Lasix	furosemide	
Ismelin	guanethidine	Esimil
Apresoline Lopress	hydralazine	
Esidrix Hydrodiuril Oretic Thiuretic	hydrochlorothiazide	Aldactazide Butizide Aldoril Dyazide Hydropres

Brand Name	*Generic name*	*Component in*
Saluron	hydroflumethiazide	Salutensin
Inversine	mecamylamine	
Enduron Aquatensin	methyclothiazide	
Aldomet	methyldopa	Aldoril Aldoclor
Lopressor	metoprolol	
Eutonyl	pargyline	
Dibenzyline	phenoxybenzamine	
Renese	polythiazide	
Minipres	prazosin	
Inderal	proprandol	
Raudixin Raupena Rauserpa Rauserfia Rautina	rauwolfia serpentina	Rauzide
Moderil	rescinnamide	
Rau-sed Reserpoid Sandril Serpasil Sertina SK-Reserpine Vio-Serpine	reserpine	Butiserpazide Diupres Hydropres Metatensin Naquival Regroton Renese R
Aldactone	spironolactone	Aldactazide
Dyrenium	triamterene	Dyazide
Metahydrin Naqua	trichlormethiazide	Metatensin Naquival

Approximately one in five Americans has hypertension. Although the name implies it, hypertension does not mean "very tense." It refers to high blood pressure. Antihypertensive drugs do not cure hypertension. They lower the blood pressure so that it causes limited damage to the body, but once you have hypertension, and you stop taking your antihypertensive drugs, your blood pressure will rise. If you have had drugs prescribed for hypertension you will probably need them for the rest of your life. Only a few persons successfully lower their blood pressure by losing weight and changing their diets.

Unfortunately, patients frequently stop taking their antihypertensives because they think the treatment is worse than the disease. Those with high blood pressure often don't have any symptoms, so they're very annoyed to find they're taking drugs that actually make them feel worse or that interfere with their sex lives. Indeed, more men stop taking their blood pressure medicine because they think it has damaged their sexual abilities than for any other reason. But if hypertension is not treated, it leads to stroke, kidney damage, heart problems, eye damage, and a reduced life expectancy.

Weight loss, a low salt diet, and a simple diuretic drug that increases the production of urine may lower the blood pressure to normal limits. Diuretics increase the body's output of urine and sodium which tends to relax the blood vessel walls and thus lower the pressure in the vessels. All the drugs in the table on pp. 73–74 with "thiazide" at the end of their generic names are diuretics. If you are taking a thiazide diuretic, you are hardly alone. There are about 13.5 million new (not including refills) prescriptions written for the thiazide diuretics each year.

Diuretics, such as a very commonly prescribed one, hydrochlorothiazide (Hydrodiuril), do not affect sexual function in most persons, but the likelihood increases as people age, and more older than younger people have hypertension. A third of older men with severe hypertension who are taking a diuretic have problems with impotence, and one in seven has difficulty with ejaculation.[2]

You may believe that older men have problems anyway. They certainly don't behave like twenty-year-olds, but they're far from being sexually dead. Kinsey found that 95 percent of sixty-year-olds are still sexually active. If men are slowing down by this age, that's all the more reason not to compound the problem with drugs that slow them down too.

When a simple diuretic drug, together with a low salt diet, does not keep the blood pressure where it ought to be, the doctor will begin adding other drugs that can relax blood vessel walls or reduce the activity of the sympathetic nervous system.

We know how important the action of blood vessels is during the arousal phase of the sexual response. This knowledge, along with knowledge about the sympathetic nervous system's role in managing the orgasmic phase, tells us that an individual is almost certain to have sexual difficulties when he's taking these drugs. Sometimes, a person is taking a diuretic and the other two kinds of drugs at the same time. Obviously, the risk of having his sexual function disturbed is much greater than if he were taking only one drug.

As usual, and experts can't always tell you why, some drugs that are similar chemically are more likely to cause sex problems than others. As you have seen in the table listing the antihypertensives, there are a lot of individual and combination drugs for your doctor to choose from. The variety may make the choice more difficult for the doctor, but it can work to your advantage. If you find that you're having problems with erections or ejaculations after taking some of these drugs, and you tell your doctor about it, a switch to a drug that will treat the blood pressure problem and spare the adverse effects on your sex life may be possible.

There are also diuretics that do not have "thiazide" at the end of their names but that can also damage sexual functioning. Among these are chlorthalidone (Hygroton), furosemide (Lasix), spironolactone (Aldactone), and triamterene (Dyrenium).

These drugs also reduce the volume of fluid and salt in the body and body tissues by increasing the volume of urine produced and relaxing the walls of the blood vessels. Two of them, triamterene and spironolactone, are better at leaving the potassium salt in the body and eliminating only the sodium salt than are the others. All of these diuretics can cause impotence, but spironolactone has another unpleasant side effect as well.

Not only can spironolactone (Aldactone) cause impotence, but it can also cause gynecomastia, the condition where the glands in men's breasts become tender and enlarged.[3,4] Apparently this unwelcome side effect occurs because the drug is a steroid similar in chemical structure to the sex hormones. At high enough doses, virtually all men will have breast enlargement, first on one side, and then on both sides. The lumps go away when the drug is stopped.

Because it is a steroid, spironolactone may cause menstrual cycle irregularities in women too.

Drugs that work best to reduce the blood pressure act directly on the sympathetic nervous system. The more selective they are, the better. Some drugs affect the sympathetic nervous system but they also affect the parasympathetic nervous system and the brain and cause depression. The best high blood pressure fighter would relax only the tiny blood vessels in the arterial blood vessel system,* and leave the rest of

*The arterial system carries the bright red oxygenated blood out from the lungs to the rest of the body. The venous system carries wastes and brings the blood back to the lungs for oxygen.

the body system, including the parts needed for sexual activity, alone.

The plant *Rauwolfia serpentina* and the alkaloids extracted from it are the kind of antihypertensives that affect the sympathetic nervous system, but they cross into the brain to cause mental depression and depress sexual activity.

Rauwolfia serpentina (Raudixin, Rauzide, and others—see table) is a large climbing or twining shrub found in tropical regions and in India. The first part of the name comes from the German botanist-physician who found it, Dr. Rauwolf. The shrub's root which contains the active ingredients looks like a snake, hence the name, serpentina. *Rauwolfia serpentina* has been used since the early 1930's to treat hypertension, but in its native countries it had been used much earlier to treat a variety of ills, including snake bite and mental disorders.

The active ingredients, the alkaloids, were extracted from the plant in the early 1950s. They include reserpine (Serpasil and others—see table), alseroxylon (Rauwiloid, Rautensin, and others), deserpidine (Harmonyl), and rescinnamide (Moderil).

Although these drugs have different chemical structures, they all can cause mental depression. Many physicians don't prescribe them for this reason, recognizing that many patients are depressed enough just by discovering they have hypertension.

Rauwolfia serpentina and its alkaloids do away with the sexual desire of about half of the patients who take them.[5,6,7] Men on these drugs also may have problems with erections. This situation can turn into an unpleasant impasse because erection problems depress patients too.

Although thousands of people are taking drugs for hypertension, doctors are beginning to use drugs that are more selective, and that don't enter the brain to depress the central nervous system. Unfortunately, many of them still interfere with sexual function.

Guanethidine (Ismelin), bethanidine, methyldopa (Aldomet), and hydralazine (Apresoline, Lopress) block the action of the nerves to relax the smooth muscles of the arterial blood system which, in turn, lowers the blood pressure. They do not cross the blood-brain barrier so they don't cause depression, which is a good thing, but they still can wreak havoc on a patient's sex life.

Guanethidine (Ismelin): Men who take this drug have a six in ten chance of having difficulty or total failure with ejaculation.[2,5,7–9]. Libido is depressed less frequently, but over half the patients have problems with impotence.[2,8,9]

This drug, and another called bethanidine, are the worst antihypertensives in terms of their side effects on male sexual performance. In one group of patients, twenty-six of the twenty-eight patients who took guanethidine complained of the symptoms it produced as shown in the following table.[8]

EFFECTS OF GUANETHIDINE ON 28 MEN	
Decreased libido	8
Decreased potency	11
Ejaculation problems	9
No ejaculation	11

In a recent survey of doctors across the nation, performed by the Heart, Lung, and Blood Institute, 72 percent of the doctors said they give guanethidine to their male patients with hypertension even though they know it causes impotence.[10]

Some doctors believe the sexual function of all men will be affected by guanethidine if the dose is high enough. However, because there is a very large number of antihypertensive drugs available, it is probable a doctor can prescribe one that is much less likely to affect sexual function than this one.

If you are given this drug and problems with ejaculation occur, rest assured they're temporary. One guanethidine user with ejaculation problems merely stopped using the drug for a few days each month before his wife's ovulation time, and succeeded in getting her pregnant.[11]

Bethanidine: This drug works in a similar fashion to that of guanethidine in the sympathetic nervous system. Both drugs interfere with a chemical messenger to relax blood vessel walls which, in turn, also blocks the messengers responsible for sexual response.

Two-thirds of patients taking bethanidine are impotent, and over two-fifths do not have ejaculations.[2]

Methyldopa (Aldomet): About one-fourth of men taking this drug will have decreased sexual desire.[5,6,8,12] Up to one-half have problems attaining and maintaining an erection,[5,6,12] and sometimes they are totally impotent.[5,12–14] A smaller proportion, from 10 to 25 percent, experience delay with ejaculation;[5,7,8,12,14] sometimes there is a decreased amount of semen and sometimes there is no ejaculation at all.[5]

In one group of twenty-seven men who were taking methyldopa, eleven of them had side effects severe enough to cause their doctor to switch them to a different drug. Here is a table showing the sort of side effects they had, and how many men had them.[8]

EFFECTS OF METHYLDOPA ON 27 MEN

Decreased libido	4
Decreased potency	10
Ejaculation problems	2
No ejaculation	3

Fortunately, all of these patients returned to normal a few days after they stopped taking methyldopa.

Methyldopa affects women too. Up to 25 percent of hypertensive women given this drug begin to produce breast milk even though they haven't had a child, and about one in fifteen has her menstrual cycle disturbed.[15]

One of the drugs that is usually used to treat depression also lowers blood pressure. That sounds like a good combination of effects because hypertension often causes depression. However, pargyline (Eutonyl) is not very selective, and it is one of the worst offenders when it comes to causing impotence and interfering with ejaculation. Many men can't ejaculate at all after taking this one.[16]

Clonidine (Catapres) is another blood-pressure-lowering drug that exerts some sedative action in the brain and thus may cause a decrease in libido.[17] In two studies, about one in twelve patients became impotent when taking clonidine,[6,18] but in another study almost a fourth of the men taking Catapres became impotent.[19] On the other hand, some patients who have problems with erections on other antihypertensive drugs have no trouble after switching to this one.[17]

Prazosin (Minipres) is an antihypertensive drug that seems to cause few problems with sexual function.

Propanolol (Inderal) and metoprolol (Lopressor) are among the newest, but already among the most widely used drugs for high blood pressure. So far there isn't any evidence that they affect sexual function very much. Only about two patients in one hundred complain of having decreased libido, so patients who are impotent on other drugs may be all right on these two. Propanolol and metoprolol are more selective about where they work in the body than some of the other antihypertensives. They block the action of chemical messengers at certain kinds of receptors in the sympathetic nervous system. That's why, if you're taking one of them, you might hear your doctor say the words, "beta-adrenergic blocking agent." The meaning to you is a drug that is less likely than most others to interfere with libido and potency.

Finding the right blood-pressure drug or combination can be a complicated problem, and depends on many factors other than the sexual. Some drugs can't be used because you have other health problems that would be exacerbated by the drug's action. If this is the case, your doctor can tell you about it. Don't make a discussion of the damaging effects of an antihypertensive drug on your sex life a topic with yourself, your neighbor, or your spouse alone. What can they do? Do yourself a favor. Tell the doctor. The two of you can then decide what to do about it.

MINOR TRANQUILIZERS

Brand Name	*Generic Name*	*Component in*
Tranxene	chlorazepate	
Librium Libritabs SK-Lygen	chlordiazepoxide	Librax Menrium
Valium	diazepam	
Dalmane	flurazepam	
Atarax Vistaril	hydroxyzine	Ataraxoid Cartrax Enarax
Verstran	lorazepam	Vistrax
Equanil Miltown	meprobamate	Bamadex Deprol Milpath Milprem Miltrate PMB-400
Serax	oxazepam	
Ativan	prazepam	
Sparine	promazine	

The minor tranquilizers relieve anxiety. One of them, diazepam (Valium), is the most frequently prescribed drug in the United States, and another one, chlordiazepoxide (Librium), usually appears among the top ten to fifteen drugs prescribed in a given year. Because of their action on the central nervous system, Valium and Librium and other drugs in this category are prescribed for persons who are nervous, who are under stress, or who exhibit symptoms of anxiety. Flurazepam (Dalmane) is usually reserved for people who can't get to sleep. No one completely understands how these drugs work.

After taking minor tranquilizers, a few people have discovered that they have decreased sexual desire. The decrease in libido is believed to result indirectly from the psychological depression sometimes caused by tranquilizers.[20]

There is only one case reported in the medical literature of a minor tranquilizer, chlordiazepoxide (Librium) causing a serious sexual problem. A forty-one-year-old married college lecturer was given a large dose of Librium to treat his psychological feelings of inadequacy, dependence, and claustrophobia. He told his physician that Librium caused him to have difficulty with ejaculation. The difficulty prolonged the duration of his sexual intercourse, and sometimes he couldn't ejaculate at all. When he stopped taking the drug, his difficulty with ejaculation disappeared, and he returned to normal.[21]

The patent has recently expired on Librium, and it is now marketed under several other names, including its generic name, chlordiazepoxide.

Considering that millions of persons take minor tranquilizers and there is only one reported case of them causing a problem with sexual function, you certainly shouldn't be concerned that they might affect yours. Indeed, their ability to reduce anxiety and stress may make sexual relations so much more relaxed and pleasurable for you that you are more likely to interpret your feelings as increased sexual desire. On the other hand, you can't enjoy sex very much if you're so tranquilized you're asleep.

ANTIDEPRESSANTS

There are three kinds of drugs used to treat depression and make people feel happier. One group is known as the monoamine oxidase inhibitors (MAOIs) and another is known as the tricyclic antidepressants. Although these two groups differ in chemical structure, and exert their antidepressant effects at different sites in the body, each of them can cause problems with sexual function. As usual, there are not nearly as many studies of the effects of these drugs on female as on male sexual function.

The third kind, lithium, is different from either the MAOI group or the tricyclics. Lithium is used to treat a kind of depression whose symptoms include loss of appetite, sleeplessness, loss of interest in usual daily activities, and loss of libido. Thus, if lithium works the way it's supposed to, if it succeeds in treating depression, it should, by definition, facilitate the return of libido to its normal level.

However, lithium may actually cause impotence in some men. In a study carried out at the Institute of Psychiatry in Prague, two of twenty-three male patients being treated with lithium found they were unable to have erections. In a follow-up study to investigate the phenomenon, one-fifth of the patients became impotent after taking lithium. When the impotent patients were switched to placebos, their ability to achieve erections returned, but the problem reappeared after they were put back on lithium therapy.[22] This kind of study, if carried out properly so that neither the patients nor the doctors know who received the active drugs and who received the placebos, can produce the strongest sort of evidence supporting a side effect caused by a specific drug. However, study results are always suspect when the number of patients in the study is as small as it was in the case of this study, and when it has not been repeated with similar results.

MONOAMINE OXIDASE INHIBITOR (MAOI) ANTIDEPRESSANTS

Brand Name	*Generic Name*
Marplan	isocarboxazid
Actomol	mebanazine
Niamid	nialamide
Eutonyl	pargyline
Nardil	phenelzine
Parnate	tranylcypromine

The monoamine oxidase inhibitors (MAOI) are tranquilizers that may cause delay of ejaculation and impotence.[23–26] One of them, pargyline (Eutonyl), has caused total failure of ejaculation.[16] The mechanism of action of the MAOIs is not well understood. They are believed to regulate and normalize body chemistry so that factors causing depression are removed.[27] They are also used to treat the symptoms of anxiety such as sleeplessness and rapid heartbeats. Some of these drugs have more of an antianxiety effect than others.

Among the MAOIs, there are some, Parnate, Actomol, and Nardil, that may also cause erectile impotence, according to reports in medical journals. Actomol and Eutonyl may cause a delay and even failure of ejaculation.[28,29] Paradoxically, there are also reports of some of these drugs causing an increase in libido and on some occasions hypersexuality.

In one instance, in a private medical experiment, six normal men volunteered to take Parnate. After one week of taking the drug they were interviewed about their sexual function. Of the six, three of the men reported changes in their sexual response. One of the men became impotent, a temporary effect that returned to normal when he began taking less of it. One of the three said he had an increase in his sex drive, and the third said he was so stimulated by the drug that he was embarrassed by an increase in the number of uncontrollable erections.[29]

In the same experiment, another male patient who was depressed to the extent he was unable to work but was functioning well sexually was given Actomol. The drug relieved his mental disorder so that he was able to return to work, but it caused him to have difficulty in attaining an erection and depressed his libido.[29]

In one of the few reports of a drug affecting female sexual response, an adverse effect of Nardil was found by accident. Seven patients, three men and four women, were given Nardil to treat narcolepsy, a relatively rare illness that causes extreme sleepiness. However, after taking the drug, all three of the men reported they were awake, but had problems in achieving an erection. Two of the four women said they couldn't achieve orgasms anymore.[28]

TRICYCLIC ANTIDEPRESSANTS

Brand Name	*Generic Name*	*Component in*
Elavil Endep	amitriptyline	Etrafon Triavil
Norpramin Pertofrane	desipramine	
Imavate Janamine Presamine SK-Pramine Tofranil	imipramine	
Aventyl Pamelor	nortriptyline	
Triptil Vivactil	protriptyline	

There are many more reports of the effects of the tricyclic antidepressants on libido and sexual performance than there are of the

M.A.O.I.s.[27,29–34] Apparently, the tricyclics alter the nerve-hormone chemistry in the central nervous system in the same way as do anticholinergics, and this change, in turn, affects the chemical messengers at the nerve endings. As was noted with the M.A.O.I.s, when this interference occurs, sexual function, and particularly the orgasmic phase, may be disturbed.

Imipramine is one of the oldest and most common tricyclic antidepressants in use, which may account in part for the larger number of reports about its side effects than there are for the rest of the drugs in this group.[27,29,33] In one study, imipramine was given to 107 men and 198 women, of whom a third had depression, and the rest other mental problems. Imipramine depressed the sexual functioning in 6 percent of the patients, and stimulated it in about 2 percent. The stimulation was believed by the physician running the study to be a secondary effect following from the improvement in mood that is the primary effect of the drug.[27]

In another study, six normal men were given imipramine. After one week the drug affected the sexual function of three of the men. One man experienced a decrease in his sexual drive that eventually led to impotence. A second could not achieve an erection, and a third had a decrease in his libido.[29]

Certain cases reported in medical journals indicate the effects experienced by some patients after taking imipramine.

Case 1. A fifty-one-year-old army sergeant had a mild stroke. During the following year he made an excellent physical recovery, but found that he was crying frequently, that he had difficulty concentrating, and that he frequently lost his temper. He talked to his physician about "the damage" that he believed the stroke had done to his mind. He was given imipramine to treat his mental problems and, within two weeks, he was impotent, which had never happened before. By the third week of taking the drug, he was totally incapable of sexual intercourse. The problem appeared to be related more to his failure to achieve and maintain an erection than it did to a failure to achieve ejaculation. His doctors decreased his dosage of imipramine and his sexual potency returned to normal.[34]

Case 2. A forty-four-year-old man suffering from depression and symptoms of anxiety was given imipramine. After taking the medication, he said his erection was flaccid, and that it took him at least an hour to ejaculate, and when he did, there was some pain associated with it. When his doctors decreased the dose of the drug, his erection became firmer and he began to have satisfactory sexual intercourse once again.[29]

Case 3. Imipramine was given to treat the mild depression of a forty-three-year-old author. After a couple of weeks he reported, "There is no lessening of sexual drive, but it is almost impossible to attain ejaculation. The effects last two or three days after the last dose. There's no forewarning. I was quite unsuspecting when I attempted. As I said, there was no lessening of desire; however, as nearly as I can determine a subjective experience, there was no increase either. Try as I might, I was unable to attain ejaculation through intercourse and achieved ejaculation only through copious effort through masturbation. It was equally difficult to maintain tumescence. At first I was inclined to attribute these conditions to my psychic state, but whenever I stopped the medication, I was able to achieve the normal results of intercourse."[29]

Partly because of the adverse effects of imipramine on sexual function, physicians began to try other tricyclic antidepressants, especially amitriptyline (Elavil), to treat depression and symptoms of anxiety. In one group of fourteen patients given Elavil, only one patient reported he had experienced difficulty achieving an erection or ejaculation after taking the drug.[33]

There are other reports of Elavil causing a sexual problem though. After four weeks on the drug, one twenty-two-year-old man who was being treated for depression, had no ejaculate at all at climax. Fortunately, within a single day of being off the drug, the problem corrected itself.[30]

There are two reports of sexual problems associated with protriptyline (Vivactil). One of the cases, a fifty-four-year-old man, was given Vivactil to treat his depression. After two weeks, he found he was totally impotent, and even though the dose was decreased, the problem continued. Following removal of the drug altogether, his sexual potency returned to normal.[29]

Similarly, a fifty-two-year-old man was experiencing some decrease in sexual desire as a result of his depression. However, after a week of taking Vivactil, he said, "I have no sex emotions at all. I have difficulty in getting an erection and maintaining it. My mind wants it, but there is no erection to take part in it."[29]

Because antidepressants are prescribed very commonly—last year there were over 6.5 million new prescriptions filled for a tricyclic antidepressant, and about 2.5 million of the other kinds of antidepressants—it is important that people know that any problem they are experiencing with their sexual function may be related to their treatment and not to their depression.

In one study of sixty male patients on antidepressants, only three of the men volunteered that they were experiencing a sexual problem although about twenty of the men admitted it when they were asked directly.[29] Not all doctors will ask, so it is important for patients to know that, if they inform their doctor, the dose of the antidepressant may be decreased, or they may be switched to a different drug which can treat the medical problem without causing an adverse effect on libido or sexual performance. The antidepressants are not all alike, nor are the patients. A drug that causes a problem in one patient will not necessarily cause it in another, even at the same dose. One of the drugs in the antidepressant group may cause a problem and another may not, even though the two drugs are very similar in chemical structure.

Talking to their doctor about their sexual feelings and response may be particularly important for women. About 50 percent of women are considered to be depressed when they are menopausal, and many doctors give them antidepressants.[31,35] Because there is so little in the medical literature about the effect of the antidepressants on women's sexual function, physicians may be less likely to expect an adverse effect, or may associate a sexual change with the woman's depression or her age rather than the drug. However, there is no reason to believe that this group of drugs works any differently in women than it does in men, or that sexual dysfunction should happen any less often in women than men.

Patients should know that the antidepressants are powerful and important drugs which can help them function better at work and at home if they are suffering from depression. The experience of an adverse effect on their sexual function, which occurs in up to 30 percent of patients, depending on the particular antidepressant, should not cause them to discontinue taking a drug altogether, but to request that the dose be reduced or that a different antidepressant be tried.

ANTIPSYCHOTICS

Although antipsychotics, as a name for a group of drugs, suggest they are only prescribed for deeply disturbed persons, this is by no means the case. They are also prescribed for thousands of Americans with only minor psychological disturbances and for most persons in nursing homes, where they act as major tranquilizers. Loss of sexual function may not disturb most people in nursing homes very much, but loss of your sexual function may well disturb you. There is quite a difference among the antipsychotics with regard to their potential for affecting sexual behavior, so if you are taking one of these drugs now, or may be taking one in the future, you'll want to know which ones are the biggest troublemakers.

ANTIPSYCHOTIC DRUGS

Brand Name	*Generic Name*	*Component in*
Tindal	acetophenazine	
Repoise	butaperazine	
Chlor-PZ Thorazine Tranzine Promapar	chlorpromazine	
Taractan	chlorprothixene	
Haldol	haloperidol	
Permitil Prolixin	fluphenazine	
Lidanar Serentil	mesoridazine	
Trilafon	perphenazine	Etrafon
Compazine	prochlorperazine	Eskatrol
Navane	thiothixene	
Mellaril	thioridazine	
Stelazine	trifluoperazine	
Vesprin	triflupromazine	

The two most commonly prescribed antipsychotics are thioridazine (Mellaril) and chlorpromazine (Thorazine), but Mellaril has much more effect on sexual function than Thorazine. Mellaril interferes with ejaculation in men of all ages, including adolescents at almost any dose.[36] A man taking Mellaril may have a normal erection and a normal orgasm, but a decreased or perhaps no ejaculate at all.[5,36–41] About three-fifths of men taking Mellaril have problems with ejaculation,[5] and about half of them have problems with erections.[5,41,42] Some men become totally impotent, and others suffer from priapism.[43]

Here is what happened to two men who took Mellaril:

Case 1: A thirty-two-year-old man was given Mellaril to treat his anxiety, depression, panic, and irrational fears, but after taking it, he felt a decrease in his sexual desire. He had normal erections and reached climaxes, but he couldn't ejaculate. He tried several times but still remained dry. Nor did he succeed in producing an ejaculate with masturbation despite what was described as prodigious efforts.[41]

Case 2: A thirty-one-year-old single man taking Mellaril for schizophrenia remarked, "If you were with a woman you couldn't have a normal sexual intercourse. . . . If I take Mellaril, I do not like to masturbate; then I like to read, . . ."[41]

Women who take Mellaril may also find they don't have much sexual desire, and have trouble achieving orgasms.

No one knows why Mellaril is more likely than the other drugs in this group known as the phenothiazines to interfere with sexual function. About one-third of men have sexual problems after taking other phenothiazines, as compared to the three-fifths of men who have them with Mellaril. All of the phenothiazines have the same basic chemical structure, and all of them do their antipsychotic work by blocking chemical messengers in the sympathetic nervous system.

When Thorazine has an adverse effect on sexual function, it usually decreases libido, potency, and the amount of ejaculate.[38,40] Occasionally, it causes priapism.[5] Oddly enough, it has also caused hypersexuality as in the following case of a forty-four-year-old woman. After taking Thorazine she said to her doctor, "I am tormented by shameful thoughts. . . . I feel I will do something shameful to everyone I see. Whoever walks by I get these thoughts about. Do you think I'm going to do something about it? What'll you think of me?" The doctor prescribed a minor tranquilizer, Valium, instead of the phenothiazine antipsychotic drug Thorazine, and her bothersome sexual thoughts went away.[44]

Fluphenazine (Permitil, Prolixin) causes the majority of men to have problems with erections,[45] but there is no evidence that it blocks ejaculations. The other antipsychotics that do block or decrease the volume of ejaculate are mesoridazine (Serentil), perphenazine (Trilafon), trifluoperazine (Stelazine), butaperazine (Repoise), haloperidol (Haldol), chlorprothixene (Taractan), and thiothixene (Navane).

Stelazine and Haldol can also cause pain on ejaculation. A thirty-year-old father of two children was hospitalized when he evidenced deep psychotic episodes that were precipitated by smoking marijuana. He was given Haldol and then switched to Stelazine, but he had deep sharp pain with both of these drugs when he ejaculated. After he stopped the drugs, he had no more pain during intercourse.[46]

Sometimes a man will have a problem on one of these drugs but not another. For example, one patient did not have an ejaculatory emission at all with Mellaril, but when he was switched to Stelazine, he returned to normal.[36] In another case, a patient found that Stelazine blocked his emission, but when he was given an antidepressant instead, his normal function returned.[47]

All of the antipsychotics are very powerful; many of them have other serious side effects which can be permanent, as compared with their common disturbance of sexual functioning which is temporary. The antipsychotic drugs should be reserved for serious psychological disturbances, such as schizophrenia, and not for minor and transient depression, insomnia, or anxiety. The minor tranquilizers and antidepressants are better for these problems. Indeed, the side effects of the phenothiazine antipsychotics on sexual function are so frequent, they seem as likely to cause depression and anxiety as to alleviate them.

MISCELLANEOUS

Although most appetite depressants stimulate the central nervous system and alter sexual activity (see Chapter Six), there is one that has an adverse effect on sexual function. Fenfluramine (Pondimin) is not a central nervous stimulant, but depresses the appetite control center in the hypothalamus. Besides drowsiness, lethargy, bad dreams, and depression, this drug destroys libido and produces impotence. At least 85 percent of women have some loss of libido, and 6 percent of men become impotent, especially if the drug is taken over a long period of time and at high doses.[48]

Clofibrate (Atromid-S) is sometimes prescribed for people who have unusually high concentrations of lipids (fats) in their blood. There are several reports of this drug causing impotence in male patients.[49] Potency returns after the drug is stopped.

Naproxen (Naprosyn) is a nonsteroid anti-inflammatory agent that is taken by persons with rheumatoid arthritis. A forty-five-year-old woman who filled in the questionnaire (Appendix A) reported that this drug reduced her sexual arousal and reduced the number and quality of her orgasms. However, she recognized that she might have been psychologically influenced by her belief that sexual arousal is "inflammation of the genitals." This knowledge caused her to believe (mistakenly) that an anti-inflammatory agent could by its very nature decrease sexual arousal.

Disopyramide (Norpace) is a drug that treats the kind of irregular heartbeats that may predispose to heart attacks. The drug works by interfering with a chemical messenger in the parasympathetic nervous system. Most drugs aren't very selective and this is no exception. It also interferes with chemical messengers responsible for erection, so that a man on this drug may have sexual desire but have a dry mouth and be unable to perform.[50]

Cimetadine (Tagamet) has been touted as a miracle drug for persons plagued with gastric ulcers, but it's not so great for fertility. Doctors found that sperm production was decreased over 40 percent in men who took this drug for nine weeks, and it has also caused gynecomastia. The level of testosterone in the blood is not decreased by cimetadine. Thus, the effect on the sperm-producing tissues is probably direct.[51] Obviously, caution is advised when Tagamet is given to young men for prolonged time periods, and regular sperm counts should be taken.

CHEMOTHERAPY

Drugs used to treat leukemia and other kinds of cancer decrease fertility. Although all drugs are chemicals, many have fallen into the habit of referring to cancer-fighting drugs as chemotherapy to contrast drug therapy with other kinds of treatment, especially radiation. Sometimes patients take four or more different kinds of these chemotherapeutic drugs, also known as antineoplastics, at the same time. The antineoplastics have many other unpleasant side effects besides their effect on fertility. Because the illnesses they are treating are life-threatening, the effect of the drugs on fertility isn't very important, and most people willingly suffer the side effects for the chance to survive. Moreover, the decrease in fertility is probably temporary. Only one in seventeen of a group of young women with leukemia who had been treated with antineoplastics before puberty had any fertility problems. However, when the drugs were given after the first menstrual cycle, the young women had difficulties because of the adverse effect of the drugs on their hormones and ovaries.[52]

Antineoplastics do not affect libido or potency in men, but they do cause them to have a low sperm count or no sperm at all. About half of men return to normal in from two to seven years after taking the drugs, and half continue to have low sperm counts.[53]

Although fertility is decreased during the periods the drugs are taken, users of antineoplastic drugs should never count on them as a means of contraception.

In general, although there are many drugs that have side effects that interfere with sexual function, unhappily there are few that help it. This may be because there has been a lack of interest in the scientific community in investigating sexual function, but also perhaps because patients don't tell their doctors about the effects that drugs have on them. Also, researchers have simply thought that sex problems were not particularly important as compared with drugs for heart problems, diabetes, and other "real" illnesses. However, there are some drugs that specifically have been used to treat sexual dysfunction, hypersexuality, and infertility, and we'll have a look at those in subsequent chapters.

5

"THE PILL": HOW IT CAN AFFECT YOUR SEX LIFE

MINI PILL

Brand Name	*Generic Name*
Micronor 0.35 mg.	progestin
Nor-Q.D.	
Ovrette	

COMBINATION PILL

Brand Name	*Generic Name*
Brevicon	estrogen
Demulen	progestin
Enovid	
Loestrin	
Lo/Ovral	
Modicon	
Norinyl	
Norlestrin	
Ortho-Novum	
Ovcon	
Ovral	
Ovulen	
Zorane	

Whenever you see a very long list of brand names for the same drug, you can be sure of two things: there are a lot of people taking it, and there is no patent on it limiting its production to one manufacturer. The birth control pill is a good example. Since its introduction in 1960, the pill has been taken by millions of women throughout the world, and many drug manufacturers compete for the chance to sell it.

In the case of the pill, an initial sale is particularly important. A woman may need contraceptive protection for over forty years. Once satisfied with the pill, she may stick to a particular brand and generate profits for the manufacturer for a very very long time. It is no wonder that dozens of the companies have rushed in to compete in the oral contraceptive market. More than half of the people in the world are women, and most of them are concerned about unwanted pregnancies.

The early hopes for the pill as an answer to world overpopulation problems have diminished. Some of the difficulties have been economic, some have been cultural, and some have been political. In some Third World countries, distribution is next to impossible; women have trouble understanding that it is necessary to take one pill each day; and the prevailing religion may be opposed to any form of contraception at all. Although none of these problems has affected use of the pill to any extent in developed countries, the increasing concern about the safety and side effects of the pill has caused many women to have second thoughts about taking it.

Almost from the time the pill came onto the market, there have been reports stating that it decreases women's sexual desire. At first, there was just an occasional letter to a medical journal saying that the pill depressed some patients and decreased their libido. Other doctors countered by saying that, in their patients, the pill had quite the opposite effect. It was in effect an aphrodisiac. Others said that with so many millions of women taking the pill, of course there would be some women who would find it depressing, and who was to say the decrease in libido reported by some women was related to the pill? Maybe some women had deep feelings of guilt about using any contraceptive, and the guilt decreased their libido. Or, it was suggested, guilt and fear about the new freedom the pill gave them might have done it. Or suppressed anger about having lost the excuse not to have intercourse, which they really didn't like anyway.

As the number of reports in medical journals increased, underground knowledge about the pill began to spread among women. Some of the shared experience moved into the public arena as women formed "consciousness-raising" groups in the sixties and early seventies. Women began to demand more of an input into decisions that affected their bodies. Women wanted to know about all of the risks associated with the various methods of contraception so they could make up their own minds. More information began to appear in women's magazines and special books about women's health, some written not by doctors, but by the women themselves.

Although the medical journal reports of the pill's depressing libido were few relative to the number of women on the pill, they were likely to have represented the experience of thousands of women, simply because few doctors inquired into the sexual feelings or problems of their patients, and few women brought the subject up themselves.

One would imagine that a question over the side effect of a drug taken by millions of women would stimulate dozens of research projects. But no. Even by the late seventies, few, large, well-designed scientific inquiries had been made into the effect of the pill on women's sexual functioning. It is now known that women who take the pill increase their chances of a stroke, a pulmonary embolism, or a heart attack, any of which can be fatal, and printed warnings about these risks must be given out with oral contraceptives by pharmacists. An increase or decrease in sex drive is sometimes mentioned as an occasional reaction that has not been proved to be associated with the pill, yet depression of libido may be the most common reason women go off the pill.[1]

There are scientific reasons for believing that the pill may depress sexual function. One of the common components in the pill, ethinyl estradiol, is used to decrease hypersexuality in men. Another drug, cyproterone acetate, is a close chemical cousin of progestin which is in all of the oral contraceptives. Cyproterone acetate is used in Europe to treat male hypersexuality, sexual delinquency, and premature sexual development. It reduces the number of sexual thoughts and sexual activity in men and boys. If the progestin depresses sexual function in men, there is ample reason to believe that it can do it in women, too.

In all fairness, it is very hard to carry out good research to find out about the effect of the pill on sexual functioning. Because of the prominent place that psychological factors play in sexual activity, it isn't valid simply to have women take the pill, ask them about changes in their sexual feelings or activity, and then infer from their answers that the pill caused those feelings or activity. The scientific way is to give some women a placebo and others the pill, and then to ask about feelings and activity in each group, to see if the group that got the pill had more or less sexual activity on average than the group that got the placebos. This scientific method looks good on paper, but what woman would volunteer for an experiment in which she had even a one in ten chance of getting a sugar pill instead of a contraceptive pill?

In the early days of testing oral contraceptives, experiments took place in which placebos were given to women who were told they were getting contraceptives. These tests, to judge if the pill was more effective than a placebo in preventing conception, were carried out in Puerto Rico. The justification was that the women were using no contraceptive, so if any of them who got the placebo became pregnant, they were no worse off than they would have been without it. This kind of experiment could not take place today. Its questionable morality incensed many people and led to rules about the use of human subjects in experiments. These "informed consent" rules mean that all of the risks involved in an experiment must be explained, and that participation must be truly voluntary. Although one may salute and cheer these informed consent rules, they effectively prevent the carrying out of scientifically ideal oral contraceptive experiments. However, the feelings of women taking birth control pills can be compared with the feelings of women using other contraceptive methods, such as the intrauterine device (IUD), the diaphragm, or foams and jellies. This method of research involves having two groups of women continue to use one of these kinds of birth control methods, while one group takes the pill, and the other group takes placebos. Of course, they must all be told that they may be getting the pill and of the risks involved.

WILL THE PILL AFFECT MY SEX LIFE?

Most of the experts do not believe that birth control pills have a direct effect on sexual functioning. They argue that the progestin component sometimes causes depression and apathy, and that women who are depressed simply don't have much interest in sex.[2] They argue further that those who seem to have an increase in libido after taking the pill aren't really sexually stimulated, but are so relieved at not risking pregnancy they are much less sexually inhibited.[3]

Another theory is that the pill only appears to decrease sexual interest and response in some women. This is because some women really don't like sex very much. When they aren't on the pill, they can always use fear of pregnancy to avoid sexual relations. When they're on the pill, they've lost their excuse, so they blame the pill for their lack of interest.[4]

One study tried to sort out some of these factors by comparing three groups of women on different kinds of oral contraceptives with a group of women taking placebos. The researchers found that more of the women taking the pills had unpleasant mood changes than those taking the placebos, and that those women who were most depressed also said they experienced a decrease in their desire for sex.[2] Other studies have concluded that women taking the pill are more likely to be depressed if they are over twenty-five years old.[5]

You probably can't predict how the pill will affect you sexually. Depending on which article you read in the medical journals, depression occurs in from 5 to 46 percent of women who take the pill. Depression almost always affects people, both men and women, sexually. Doctors don't like to warn women that the pill can depress them and their sexual feelings, because they know that a suggestion by an authority figure like a doctor is very powerful, and if a doctor tells a woman that a medicine is going to harm her sexual desire or ability to achieve orgasms, she'll expect it and it becomes much more likely to happen. You can decide yourself whether you would rather have your doctor level with you and risk becoming depressed because your doctor told you about it, or leave it to chance and perhaps not understand what's happening.

Besides the possible loss of libido, both estrogen and progestin have side effects that are not considered serious by many doctors, but may be very unpleasant for the women who take them. The estrogen component causes nausea, vomiting, and breast tenderness. The progestin component causes headache, dizziness, depression, apathy, and fatigue. Weight gain and retention of fluids are also common. These side effects may subside after your body gets used to the pill. However, one-third of women switch to a different birth control pill, or stop taking them altogether because of their unpleasant side effects.[6,7]

WHAT IS THE PILL, ANYWAY?

At no time in history have more women taken chemicals that interfere with their normal body processes and known less about them. Only five years after the first pill, Enovid, appeared on the market, over 5 million American women were taking this or another pill. Although some women, frightened by reports of the pill's causing strokes and heart attacks, have given up the pill, over 30 million new prescriptions, not including refills, are dispensed each year. The pill works by tricking the pituitary gland into believing that the body is pregnant. When the gland accepts this, it refuses to send out two hormones, FSH and LH, that signal the ovary to release one of its eggs (ova). If there are no eggs released, there can be no pregnancy.

Most oral contraceptives contain an estrogen and a progestin. Estrogen occurs naturally in the body, but progestins are synthetic variations of the naturally occurring progesterone. Progesterone is not absorbed when it is taken orally, so synthetic forms that can be absorbed are put in the pill instead.

Briefly, this is how the normal menstrual cycle works:

1. The pituitary gland sends out FSH and LH.
2. FSH and LH tell the ovaries to release an ovum and to produce estrogen.
3. The ovum is released and the ovaries begin to produce progesterone as well as estrogen.
4. The progesterone and the estrogen tell the pituitary gland to stop releasing FSH and LH.
5. If the ovum is not fertilized, the ovaries decrease their production of estrogen and progesterone, and
6. menstruation occurs.

7. The low level of estrogen and progesterone tells the pituitary gland to start sending out FSH and LH, and back to Step One.

If estrogen is given at the start of the cycle, no ovum matures enough to be released because the estrogen tells the pituitary gland not to send out the FSH and LH that are responsible for the maturation and release of the ovum. With no ovum released there can be no pregnancy.

The progestin component of the pill, along with the estrogen, prepares the lining of the uterus for the baby just in case there might be one. After three weeks of the pill, the woman stops taking it. The decrease of estrogen and progestin signals the uterus that there's to be no baby after all, and the lining is sloughed off in the process known as menstruation.

Until a few years ago there were sequential oral contraceptives. In sequential therapy, a tablet containing only estrogen was taken for fifteen days, and then for the next five days a tablet was taken that contained both estrogen and a progestin component. There were more side effects, such as bleeding at the wrong time, with the sequential therapy, and more of a chance to take the wrong pill, so they were taken off the market.

Because of the increased risk of stroke and heart attack, especially for women over forty, that accompanies taking the pill, and because of the side effects, oral contraceptive manufacturers have produced pills with varying amounts of estrogen and progestin in the combination pills. You can get a high-estrogen, low-progestin pill and vice versa, or the pill can contain average amounts of each.

Recently, the "mini" pill has come on the scene. It has no estrogens whatever, and is somewhat less effective than the combination pill in preventing pregnancy. The "mini" pill not only prevents the egg from being released from the ovary, it makes the womb less receptive to any fertilized egg arriving there, but it has a tendency to cause irregular bleeding. There is as yet no evidence that it has fewer serious side effects than the combination pill.

WHAT SHOULD I DO?

The pill decision, to take or not to take, is certainly one of the most serious a woman has to make. Next to sterilization, which is rarely reversible, birth control pills are the most reliable form of contraception. If the pill is taken according to directions, the chance of a pregnancy is virtually zero.

If you are a young woman twenty-five or under, taking the pill is an easier choice than if you are older. In one study, only 9 percent of women under twenty-five found that their sexual desire was depressed by the pill, compared to 25 percent of women over twenty-five.[8]

Being unmarried makes a difference, too. Only 8 percent of single women reported a decrease in their libido after taking the pill, compared to 20 percent of married women.[8]

Remember, too, that many women actually find that the pill increases their sexual desire. This is almost certainly related to the effect of being freed of the fear of pregnancy. Without the fear, women can feel uninhibited, and their natural feelings can be expressed fully. In one study, one-fifth of single women actually had an increase in sexual desire, while one-fifth of married women found their sexual desire was depressed after taking the pill.[9]

For those young women who suffer from painful cramps during their menstrual periods, or whose periods are highly irregular, the pill is an additional bonus. The pill relieves the cramps, and by the way it's taken, regulates the cycle.

The pill can have an indirect effect on sexual fun. A woman will not get her period until she stops taking the pill. Sometimes it is inconvenient for a woman to have her period. She may have a big weekend coming up, or an important conference, or be running the Boston marathon, or whatever. Many women, it isn't known how many, use the pill to control the time of their periods for their own convenience. They shouldn't do this at all. Any deviation from the directions probably increases the risk of severe side effects in the long run.

Women over forty shouldn't take the pill. They most certainly should not do so if they smoke. Not only is general and sexual depression more likely, but the risk of stroke, heart attack, and side effects are markedly increased.

No woman should take the pill if she has any of the following: a history of thromboembolic disease (blood clots in the veins), liver disease, cancer, tumors in the uterus, migraine headaches, asthma, epilepsy, or any kind of blood disease.

If you decide to take the pill, there is still a decision to make about which pill. Even though a woman may be sexually depressed by oral contraceptives, there is no evidence that the pill decreases the number of times she has intercourse, if she is married, or increases the frequency of extramarital affairs by either her or her husband.[6] The failure of the pill to decrease the frequency of intercourse in married couples is probably because it is the husband who usually initiates sexual intercourse and the wife who goes along.[10]

Recently, however, a very interesting study was done among thirty-five college women. The study measured the number of times that the women initiated sexual intercourse with their partners, or on their own, masturbated, or had sexual fantasies. Some of these women were taking the pill, and the rest were using some other method of birth control. The researchers found that at the time of the women's ovulations, about the fourteenth day before the start of a menstrual period for most women, the amount of sexual activity initiated by the women who were not taking the pill was greater than the amount of sexual activity initiated by women who took the pill. These results suggest that the pill suppresses hormones that make women feel sexually aroused. The amount of male-initiated sexual activity was the same whether the woman was on the pill or not.[11]

Because it's the progestin component of the birth control pill that causes depression, women who want to use the pill, but get sad, weepy, and apathetic, should use a pill with a low dose of progestin.[12] Unfortunately, with estrogen alone, breakthrough bleeding often occurs, but even more importantly, high estrogen doses increase the risk of the formation of blood clots that can cause heart attacks.[5]

The kind of pill a woman should take is determined by the way her mood is affected by her normal menstrual cycle when she is not on the pill. If she usually is irritable just before her period, a pill with a low dose of progestin might cause her to be irritable throughout the whole cycle. Such a woman may be happier on a pill with a relatively high progestin dose.[2] If women are happier, it follows they'll be more likely to have a healthy appetite for sex.

In view of the potential side effects, most women are thinking at least twice about taking the pill. When and if they decide the benefits outweigh the risks, as compared with other means of contraception, women should know they don't have to take a pill that also makes them unhappy and depresses their sex drive. There are many different pills around—at least twenty combination and three "mini"—with different doses of different kinds of estrogen and progestin. If they can explain to the doctor how they feel during different phases of their menstrual cycle when they're not on the pill, they may be able to select one with minimal side effects at the outset. If not, it's nonsense for a woman to feel weepy all the time and to ruin her sex life to avoid having a baby. She should try a different pill, or switch to a different method of contraception. If her doctor is not sympathetic, she should switch him, too.

6

PRESCRIBED DRUGS: CAN THEY IMPROVE YOUR SEX LIFE?

Unfortunately, there are very few drugs prescribed by doctors that can help make your sex life better, and none that can make what is already pretty good into something great. If there were even 5 percent as many prescribed drugs that could help sexual desire or performance as there are drugs that can cause trouble, there would probably be a large number of doctors calling themselves sexologists, and they and the drug manufacturers would be rolling in money.

It does seem strange that there are so many drugs that can help in different ways, and that so few of them can help with sexual problems. In fact, none of the few drugs that seem to have some positive effects on sexual function was discovered as a result of looking deliberately for drugs capable of helping people with their sexual problems. Positive effects were found quite by accident as side effects of drugs developed to treat or prevent diseases.

Some people believe that the problem of sexual dysfunction has simply been too complicated a product of mind and body interaction for scientists to tackle. Others believe that our knowledge of body chemistry, especially the chemistry along the nerve pathways, is expanding so rapidly that we are on the threshold of major breakthroughs, and that it is only a matter of time before drugs that can improve sexual desire and performance are found and become used in everyday life. Other people are more cynical. They claim that the scientific knowledge to create such drugs has existed all along, but that social attitudes alone have prevented their development. Drugs such as tetrahydrocannabinol (the active ingredient in marijuana) and testosterone (a male hormone) have increased erectile capacity in laboratory animals, yet there has been no systematic search for human erectants.[1] The cynics argue that repressive ideas alone are responsible for the lack of drugs that can affect sexual desire and performance. Since virtually every aspect of human life can be influenced by drugs—drugs moderate sleep, aggression, hunger, and anxiety—why suppose that sex is different?

It is not politic, however, for governments to spend tax dollars for research on drugs to treat sex problems, nor can drug companies spend very much money on activities that instead could be spent to find and market drugs to help "sick" people.

If Calvinist antipleasure values have kept even persons with severe sexual dysfunctions from being defined as really sick so they could benefit from drug research, it is even more unlikely that drugs would be developed that simply helped people have more fun. Viewed in this way, the prescribed or over-the-counter aphrodisiac seems a long way off. Although more than one physician has argued that sexuality might be enhanced with drugs,[1,2] one suggesting that an enlightened medical community will overcome the past "medical and social morality and narrowness of outlook,"[2] there would surely be a public outcry against spending money to look for aphrodisiacs that could instead be spent for drugs to treat cancer.

Whatever the reasons, sex-enhancing prescription drugs are now largely confined to science fiction. In the real and present world, we have an extremely limited number of prescription drugs that have shown any positive effects on sexual function at all. Moreover, these few drugs don't do anything for persons whose sexual function is normal. Drugs may, and the word *may* should be emphasized, help some individuals who have problems such as lack of sexual desire, or failure to attain or maintain an erection, or to achieve an ejaculation, but they will do nothing for the normal person who wants more pleasure out of his sexual encounters, who wants to feel more desire, or who experiences occasional difficulties, such as erectile impotence or failure to achieve an orgasm.

It really is too bad there aren't any safe sex-enhancing drugs that are specifically for persons with occasional problems. There are surprisingly large numbers of them. Recently, a hundred well-educated, happily married couples were asked about the frequency of their sexual problems.[3] Although over four-fifths of them said their marital and sexual relations were happy and satisfying, two-fifths of the husbands said they occasionally had some erection or ejaculation problem, and over three-fifths of the women had problems with becoming aroused and achieving orgasm. In addition, half of the men and more than three-fourths of the women said they had other sexual difficulties sometimes. Either they weren't interested or they couldn't relax. It is probable that these normal couples would not consider themselves candidates for sexual therapy, and it is also probable that they would rather not have any sex problems.

At the present time, the medical community can offer normal people with sexual problems little but psychotherapy. Not only is psychotherapy very expensive and time-consuming, but if everyone in the population who had some sexual problem was treated, all of our health care resources would be used up for this problem alone. Although most sexual dysfunction may be caused by past experience, this does not mean that the treatment must necessarily be behavioral. Because experience sometimes causes adverse chemical changes in the body, the unwanted result of damaging experiences may be remedied most directly by chemical means. For example, a psychological study was made of 201 Swedish men being treated at an outpatient department of a hospital for impotence and premature ejaculation.[4] The conclusion was that the men were repressed and devoid of energy. They were likely to have been only children and to have been dominated by their mothers. Although the cause of the impotencies was psychological, and psychological counseling most often is used to treat people with sexual problems, there is no inherent reason why the damage could not be repaired by medicines. Consider how much better it would be if there were a safe pill or liquid that would remove sexual problems that might be minor and transient, but so often severely affect a marital relationship because they are misunderstood.

Sex-enhancing medicines appear to be a long way off. Few drugs are being tested in the sexual area, and it takes years before a drug gets from the laboratory to the marketplace.

The only prescription drug that is marketed in the United States and is used to treat impotence is the male hormone, testosterone. Female hormones, estrogens, are sometimes given to facilitate sexual intercourse after menopause.

A few drugs developed to treat specific health problems have aphrodisiac properties or increase sexual activity as a side effect. Among these are levodopa, a drug that is given for Parkinson's disease, and some of the anorexiants (appetite depressants). Bromocriptine (Parlodel) and clomiphene citrate (Clomid), drugs for female infertility, are being investigated to see if they can improve sexual activity. Afrodex, a combination drug containing methyltestosterone, has been given to treat impotence and premature ejaculation.

Not everyone with a sex problem wants a drug that would increase sexual activity. For men who suffer from premature ejaculation, taking a drug that depresses sexual activity actually enhances their sexual performance and pleasure.

Premature ejaculation is a common occurrence. Almost all men have experienced it at some time or other, and for some men it effectively rules out sexual intercourse altogether. For men with control problems, the side effects of drugs that can increase the time to ejaculation are welcome. The antidepressant group of drugs has been used to slow ejaculation time, and these also have the advantage of treating the depression and anxiety that make treatment of premature ejaculation so difficult. Sometimes, however, antidepressants don't just slow things down; sexual activity disappears altogether.

Another group of drugs can increase libido but their use is limited to narcotic addicts. Drugs known as narcotic antagonists do not play a direct part in sexual response. They work by reducing the anti-aphrodisiac effect of narcotics, which, in effect, releases the normal libido of narcotic addicts that has been depressed by the addiction.[5]

ANDROGENS

Brand Name	*Generic Name*
Anavar	mesterolone
Androdurin	methyltestosterone
Andrusol	oxandrolone
Atlatest	testosterone
Depoviron	
Lonavar	
Malogen	
Mertestate	
Metandren	
Neo-Hombreol-M	
Oraviron	
Oreton	
Synandrets	
Synandrol	
Synandrotabs	
Synerone	
Testate	
Testodet	
Testred	
Testora	
Testostroval	

ESTROGENS

Brand Name	*Generic Name*
Amen	conjugated estrogens
Amnestrogen	diethylstilbestrol
Amniotin	equilin
Co-Estro	estrone
Conestron	medroxyprogesterone
Congens	
Congesterone	
Conjutabs	
dep-Corlutin	
Depo-Provera	
Evex	
Femest	
Fem-H	
Femogen	
Formatrix	
Geneake	
Genisis	
Kestrin	
Menest	
Menogen	
Menotabs	

Brand Name	*Generic Name*	*Brand Name*	*Generic Name*
T-Ionate		Menrium	
Testrone P.A.		Milprem	
Vulvan		Oramestrin	
		Ovest	
		Palopause	
		PMB-200	
		PMB-400	
		P-Medrate-PA	
		Prelestrin	
		Premarin	
		Provera	
		SK-Estrogens	
		Sodestrin	
		Tag-39	
		Theogen	

It seems perfectly logical that sex problems should be treated with sex hormones, in view of what we know about the relationship of the sex hormones to sexual functioning.

A deficiency of the male hormone, testosterone, an androgen, invariably leads to sterility because testosterone is necessary for sperm production. Also, all of the obvious secondary male sex characteristics such as facial hair and deep voices, depend on an adequate supply of testosterone. This hormone, manufactured by the testes in males, is primarily responsible for physical development.

Not until 1849 was anything resembling a scientific experiment performed to study the effects of the secretions of testes on sexual development, although certainly the effects of castrating men and animals had been known for centuries. In 1849, a German physiology professor took the testes out of roosters and transplanted them into capons (castrated domestic male fowls). He didn't put the testes in the usual place; he put them in unusual positions in the capons, so there was no possibility that they could be controlled by the genital nerve system. Nevertheless, the capons developed roosterlike secondary sexual characteristics, suggesting that the testes produced substances that traveled through the body in the circulatory and not the nervous system. The results of the experiment also suggested that any substances that stimulate the testes into producing the masculinizing substances must travel to the testes in the blood.[6]

Later in the nineteenth century, a Frenchman caused quite a stir by injecting himself with the extracts made from the ground-up testes of dogs and guinea pigs. Articles in the press said that the "fountain of youth" had been found, but the French professor said that was absurd. He claimed the injections made him feel more vigorous, but that they would not stop the aging process.[7]

In the early 1900s, more transplants were done, and it was shown that if ovaries are implanted in a castrated male animal, or if testes are put in females after removal of their ovaries, the implanted sex glands will take over and determine the animal's physical and social characteristics. Not only will the female come to look like a male, but she will become more aggressive, whereas the male will lose his masculine appearance and become more docile.

Of course we know that males and females both produce male and female hormones. It is the balance that makes the difference. The predominant sex hormone promotes sexual characteristics, male characteristics by male hormones, and female characteristics by female hormones, and they also guard against the development of characteristics of the opposite sex. For example, there are special interstitial cells in between the sperm-producing cells in the testes that produce the male hormone, testosterone. But these cells also make tiny quantities of female hormones. If the interstitial cells stop making enough of the androgen, testosterone, the male becomes more feminine. In the female, the male hormone is produced by the adrenal gland.

Testosterone, or testosteronelike substances, promotes growth in women, and more important, relative to our interests, maintains their sex drives. In fact, testosterone has a greater influence on libido in both men and women than any other hormone.[8] Testosterone can restore libido in women if they have lost it after experiencing sexual gratification previously.[8]

The female sex hormones, estrogen and progesterone, are produced by the ovaries. These hormones regulate the menstrual cycle, and are responsible for secondary female characteristics. Their role in sexual desire and functioning is unclear, but they do maintain the lining of the vagina. During menopause, less estrogen is produced, and sometimes the vaginal lining becomes thin and dry so that sexual intercourse is painful and unpleasant. This condition has the unfortunate name, senile vaginitis. Often women are given estrogens to replace those that are no longer being produced by the body during menopause to treat the problem and other menopausal symptoms, such as hot flashes. Well over half of menopausal women take estrogens. About 60 million prescriptions for them were dispensed last year. One of them, Premarin, is one of the top twenty drugs sold in the United States.

During and after menopause, women may actually feel more sexual desire than before because their testosterone level is higher, relative to the decreased amounts of estrogens they are producing. It's kind of a dirty trick of nature that just when they may be feeling hotter sexually they're having hot flashes as well. Unfortunately, the drugs they take, while correcting the hot flashes, also may eliminate their newfound libido. A few women experience an increase rather than a decrease in libido after taking estrogens, but it is not as great as after taking androgens.

Another estrogen-related problem is more serious. In a series of articles over the past few years, researchers have concluded that women who take estrogens are much more likely to get uterine cancer than women who do not take them. In a recent article in the prestigious *New England Journal of Medicine,* the risk of getting uterine cancer was stated to be 1 to 3 percent of women taking estrogens, whereas nonusers had a risk less than one-tenth as great.[9] For women who smoke and take estrogens, the risk is much greater. Consequently, doctors are having second thoughts about prescribing estrogens to menopausal and postmenopausal women for long periods of time. The Food and Drug Administration now requires women to be given a pamphlet, the *Patient Package Insert* (PPI), warning them that there are risks involved with use of estrogens. These pamphlets are intended to encourage women to discuss with their doctors the risks and benefits involved with estrogen use. It is now believed that estrogens should be taken only for specific indications, such as hot flashes in specific individuals, and not as a routine matter over long periods of time. Treatment with antidepressant drugs for the depression and anxiety that often accompany menopause may be better than using estrogens.[10,11]

Because, incongruously, sexual desire in women is influenced more by androgens than estrogens, libido is usually not affected at all by removal of a woman's ovaries. If a woman had a good sex life before removal of her estrogen-producing ovaries, she should have one afterward. Sexual desire is decreased by removal of the adrenal gland, which is the major source of androgen production in women, and sometimes by removal of the hypothalamus, a gland that produces the chemicals, FSH and LH, that stimulate the adrenal gland into doing its job of producing testosterone.

Testosterone is rarely given to women because of its masculinizing effects. Sometimes it is given to women who have breast cancer to slow the growth of their tumors, and some of these women say they have had an increase in sexual desire as a result of taking it.[12]

Testosterone may also enlarge the clitoris. But the good side effects are far outweighed by the bad. Testosterone also causes acne, hoarseness, hairiness, baldness, oily skin, and it often stops menstruation.

Few women would think a slightly enlarged clitoris was worth these side effects.

For a long time it was believed that sexual desire and performance were directly controlled by the sex hormones. Now we know that appearance is much more related to these hormones, which are, in turn, governed by other hormones, than is sexual function. Sexual function has more to do with social and cultural factors and the way people think than with a lack of sex hormones. If you are a man, no matter how many sex hormones you have, you are unlikely to be turned on by a woman from a completely different culture, nor is she likely to be turned on by you. Think of some of the pictures you have seen in the *National Geographic* and you will understand at once.

Severe sex problems can rarely be corrected simply by giving hormones to men or women, but they are sometimes given to men in their middle and late years to help with declining sexual activity.

Testosterone production begins to decrease in men during their forties, and the decrease becomes significant in their fifties. About two-fifths of men over seventy have a testosterone level below that of the lower limit for normal twenty-year-olds.[13] If you are over forty and are having problems with impotence, *and* your problem is not psychological, which most are, but results from a diminished production of testosterone, you have a better than fifty-fifty chance of benefiting from testosterone.[14] As one doctor commented on the way he treats sexual dysfunction in men:

> . . . In general, if a man does not have any kind of erection including morning erection, masturbation or whatever, I would at least get a testosterone determination and look even more closely at his biological system. We have had some experience with using some form of testosterone . . . in treating sexual dysfunction. We get very equivocal results. It's very hard to tell whether what we're giving is a general sense of well-being or whatever. . . .[15]

In a study involving a hundred male patients, half of them got methyltestosterone and thyroid, and half of them got placebos. Only 40 percent of the men who took the placebos had a positive response from them, compared to 78 percent of the men who took the drug.[16] This result means that androgen therapy can provide real benefit beyond the psychological boost which may be needed to restore confidence. That 40 percent of the men benefited from placebos in the study shows the important relationship that psychology has for sexual function, and the difficulty of determining whether an improvement can be attributed to a drug.

The response to testosterone can be dramatic. One man, M.R., who was sixty years old, began having erections after having been totally impotent for ten years. He also had sexual dreams at night, erotic daydreams, and experienced a general feeling of euphoria. Testosterone was also given to a younger patient, D.P., who was thirty-five years old, and who had been impotent for two years. He developed a striking sexual appetite accompanied by three to four long-lasting erections every twenty-four hours. D.P. also had erotic dreams and nocturnal emissions. He found sexual abstinence intolerable, and begged for a weekend pass from the hospital so that he could be with his wife. The pass was granted, and the couple had normal sexual intercourse four times in two days.[17]

In both patients, M.R. and D.P., the testosterone was given with another drug (parachlorophenylalanine or PCPA). PCPA decreases tryptophan, a chemical that occurs naturally and moderates sexual activity in the body.[17] Tryptophan alone has been given experimentally to test its effect on sexual function, but the results are mixed.

In one case a forty-two-year-old university teacher took tryptophan for migraine headaches, but he found that the drug kept him from having orgasms and ejaculations. Sexual intercourse with his wife decreased to one or two times a month, whereas before he began taking tryptophan it was six to eight times a month. Sexual intercourse returned to normal after he stopped taking the drug.[17]

Tryptophan has been given to institutionalized schizophrenic male patients who became sexually uninhibited by the drug. Their conversations were dominated by sex topics; they began touching the female patients, and one patient assaulted a female patient.[18,19] However, when tryptophan was given to five hundred depressed patients, none of them showed any signs of hypersexuality.[20] These confusing contradictory results suggest that tryptophan may either increase or suppress sexual activity depending upon the preexisting chemical state in the individual, which may be natural or may be caused by other drugs or food the individual has taken.

Testosterone has little effect on young men with normal testosterone levels. Seven young men ages twenty to twenty-seven years were given testosterone for twenty-one weeks.[21] The drug did not affect their libido, sexual potency or their frequency of sexual intercourse, nor did it affect secondary sexual characteristics such as body hair. It did, however, decrease the sperm counts of the men, and most of them gained weight.

In young men who have had no disease or surgery that would limit testosterone production, decreased libido and impotence are almost always psychological, and hormone therapy won't help, although a placebo response is possible. No assumption can be made that increasing the amount of testosterone in the body will increase sexual activity.[22]

Over a hundred male university students, aged twenty to thirty years, had their sexual interest, thoughts, and frequency of coitus and masturbation compared to their testosterone levels. When testosterone was within the normal range, there was no association with the frequency of sexual activity or interest with its level. High sexual activity was just as likely to go with a low testosterone level and vice versa.[22]

Neither androgens nor estrogens will increase the sex drives in normal young adults. Moreover they can't make homosexuals into heterosexuals. There is no difference between homosexuals and heterosexuals in the levels of these hormones, or the chemicals that stimulate their production.[23] Hormones can help the sex organs to develop in those few individuals that fail to mature normally,[24] and they influence the frequency of sexual intercourse in couples. The testosterone level is highest in women at about the middle of their menstrual cycles, and women are more sexually responsive at this time. In couples, the male is more likely to initiate sexual activity when the female is most responsive, so couples tend to be more sexually active during the middle of the woman's menstrual cycle.[25]

LEVODOPA

Levodopa is one of the few drugs that has true aphrodisiac properties. Many patients who have taken levodopa have had an increase in their sexual desire and activity.

Levodopa is given to patients who have Parkinson's disease, an incurable illness that causes muscle rigidity, tremors, and mental depression. More men get Parkinson's disease than women. Some doctors have suggested that the increase in sexual desire by patients who have taken levodopa is only because the drug makes them feel so much better in general. However, there is a chemical basis for believing levodopa to be a true aphrodisiac.

LEVODOPA

Brand Name	*Generic Name*
Bendopa	levodopa
Biodopa	l-dopa
Dopar	
Laradopa	
Levopa	

Levodopa apparently either increases dopamine or decreases serotonin in the brain. Dopamine increases sexual activity while serotonin inhibits it. The reciprocal relationship between these two chemicals and their effect on sexual activity has been well demonstrated in laboratory animals.

Up to 100 percent of patients who have taken levodopa find they have increased sexual desire.[26,27] In one group with Parkinson's disease, all nineteen patients treated with levodopa reported they had an increase in their sexual functioning.[26] One of them was an eighty-year-old man who began having erotic dreams and nocturnal emissions.

Levodopa may cause too much interest in sex in some patients,[28] but brain disease probably has to be present for this to happen.[29] When levodopa was given to one group of mental patients, one woman tore off her pajamas and tried to seduce all the male patients and staff. Male patients who had been masturbating four to five times a week began doing it four to five times in a single day.[30]

Levodopa caused hypersexuality in a third of some patients at another psychiatric hospital. For example, after taking it, a thirty-seven-year-old alcoholic had unexpected erections when he was playing Ping-Pong with a nurse. It also caused a twenty-six-year-old homosexual patient to begin masturbating compulsively. However, one of the other patients who had had a problem achieving erections for a long time gratefully welcomed a return of his normal abilities after he began taking the drug.[31]

Hypersexuality also occurred in a seventy-six-year-old man hospitalized with Parkinson's disease. As his dose of levodopa increased, so did his interest in sex, to the extent that his advances to the nurses resulted in his removal to a different floor, presumably where the nurses were more tolerant. He was given a major tranquilizer in the hope that his sexual activity would be controlled, but the tranquilizer had no effect, and he was discharged after his relationships with the staff had deteriorated markedly because of the amorous advances he was making, not only to the nurses, but to young female patients as well. At home he continued to be "restless," and eventually declared that he would rather put up with the symptoms of Parkinson's disease than the constant sexual stimulation caused by the drug.[32]

Caution. There is no reason to believe that levodopa will cause stronger sexual feelings in those who are already functioning normally. Nor is there much evidence that it can correct impotency problems. When doctors have given levodopa specifically to treat impotence, the drug increased the number of spontaneous nocturnal erections, but the patients were still not able to sustain erections long enough for intercourse to occur. Nor is levodopa guaranteed to increase libido.

This only happens in about one-third of patients who have taken levodopa for sexual response problems.[29]

Levodopa is a potent drug that has serious side effects other than its effect on sexual function, and, like all prescribed drugs, it should only be taken under the guidance of a physician.

DIET DRUGS

The appetite depressants, called anorexiants by doctors when they're talking to each other, and uppers or speed by drug abusers, may stimulate sexual desire indirectly. As appetite controllers, they work by increasing the production of a chemical messenger in the sympathetic nervous system. The chemical messenger in turn cuts off the appetite-regulating center in the brain. After taking an amphetamine or amphetaminelike drug, your body stops screaming at you, "Feed me. I'm hungry." At least it stops for a few days and may for as much as two weeks. Gradually, your body adapts to the interference, and finds a way to let you know that it wants food. For that reason, appetite depressants are not recommended to be taken over longer periods than two weeks.

APPETITE DEPRESSANTS

Brand name	*Generic name*	*Component in*
Amphedrine Benzedrine	amphetamine	Biphetamine
Dexedrine Apetain	dextroamphetamine	Bamadex Biphetamine Dexamyl Eskatrol
Tenuate Tepanil	diethylpropion	
Sanorex	mazindol	
Desoxyn Obedrin Desoxedrine Desyphed Methedrine	methamphetamine	Fetamin
Ritalin	methylphenidate	
Cylert	pemoline	
Preludin	phenmetrazine	

Of course, appetite depressants don't make you lose weight at all. It's cutting out the food that does that. Their only purpose is to help you stay on your diet, at least at the beginning while you get through the first few days.

The appetite depressants include Benzedrine, Dexedrine, methamphetamine (Obedrin, Desoxyn, Methedrine), phenmetrazine (Preludin), methylphenidate (Ritalin), diethylpropion (Tenuate), pemoline (Cylert), and mazindol (Sanorex).

Because appetite depressants don't make a beeline for the appetite regulating center in the brain, but circulate through the body, they have other effects as well. Only the "appestat" gets depressed; the drugs wake up everything else. The whole nervous system is stimulated so that people become hyperactive, and have trouble sleeping. For this reason, amphetamines and their chemical cousins have been the drug of choice for truck drivers and students studying for exams. They are also taken by athletes for the illusion of power and energy they bestow.

If people take these drugs for several weeks, they may become dependent on them. They tend to like the "jumped-up" feelings they get from the drugs, and to feel down and depressed without them. For these people, the choice becomes hard. Either take the drugs and feel nervous and perhaps weepy, or not take them and feel dragged out, depressed, and sleepy. Because of our national hysteria about slimness, women are particularly susceptible to becoming dependent on amphetamines or other weight-control drugs.

The general central nervous stimulation accounts for the increase in libido and sexual aggression that appetite depressants cause in about 5 percent of women. In one instance, a forty-five-year-old woman was given an amphetaminelike drug, Sanorex, for weight control. The drug suppressed her appetite for food, but her appetite for sex increased to an extent that she was almost insatiable. Until then, her husband had held a job over a hundred miles distant, returning home on weekends only. After his wife began taking Sanorex, he gave up his job for a lower paying one closer to home, so that he could satisfy his wife's craving.[33]

Amphetamines can stimulate the sexuality of men, too. In one example, three men were being treated for failure to ejaculate.[34] Neither tranquilizers nor placebos helped, but they achieved their goal with amphetamines. Others have found that amphetamines can increase libido and prolong erections.[35]

The effect of amphetamines on stimulating sexual function is entirely dose related. At the normal dose taken to suppress the appetite, the drug may seem to be an aphrodisiac, but the chronic use of high doses by drug abusers may lead to a decrease in sexual abilities and interest in both men and women.[35] A single massive dose when injected may produce marked sexual arousal.[36]

Paradoxically, although amphetamines stimulate adults, they seem to do quite the opposite in children, and are given to them for hyperactivity. They are a means of social control of children who disrupt the classroom and drive their parents crazy. Some doctors think too many children get these drugs and that the fault lies with the classroom and the homes rather than with the children. They argue that the minimal brain damage that is supposed to cause the hyperactivity is poorly defined, and that giving drugs for social convenience is arbitrary and perhaps immoral.

Some people don't think these drugs should be on the market at all, or they think that their use should be limited to hyperactive children, because the potential for abuse is so great. They claim that the appetite depressants only work for a couple of weeks anyway, and that use over a long period does not affect weight loss, but does encourage dependence. In any event, it would be foolish to take them for their effect on sexual feelings. The odds are that you'll only feel wide awake.

BROMOCRIPTINE

Bromocriptine (Parlodel) is a drug related to the alkaloids of ergot, a drug used to treat migraine headaches that can induce abortions. Bromocriptine is not a hormone, nor is it similar to levodopa. So far, there are only a few studies suggesting that bromocriptine can improve male sexual functioning and cure infertility. One study done in Europe concluded that bromocriptine increased the sexual activity of male patients who had tumors of their pituitary glands.[37] Pituitary gland tumors may decrease the production of FSH and LH which stimulate the production of testosterone by the testes, as well as sperm production. Bromocriptine is believed to work through its relationship with dopamine, one of the chemical messengers, in the central nervous system. In another study, no increase in testosterone was found in the patients who took bromocriptine nor was there any increase in their sexual activity.[38] These studies suggest that the drug may be useful to treat male infertility but not lack of sexual interest or ability to perform.

The Food and Drug Administration has not approved bromocriptine for use in this country because so few studies have been done that its safety and efficacy are both in doubt. Currently, it is being investigated for a large number of disorders, such as menstrual difficulties and Parkinson's disease, in addition to the research on its potential for treating sexual dysfunction and infertility.[37]

CLOMIPHENE

Clomiphene (Clomid) is a fertility drug. It is given to women to stimulate their ovaries into producing ova so they have an increased chance of becoming pregnant. Sometimes this is overdone, which accounts for the increased number of twins, triplets, quadruplets, and more that are born these days.

Clomiphene works by causing the hypothalamus to produce more FSH and LH which stimulate the ovaries into releasing their eggs. However, FSH and LH are also the hormones that induce the testes to put out more testosterone. Recently, when clomiphene was given to men, their testosterone levels rose almost 300 percent on average. Their testosterone increases in turn caused increased libidos, increased sexual potencies, and increased feelings of well-being.[39]

Again, it should be stressed, there is no reason to believe clomiphene will do anything for the man who already has a normal level of testosterone. The hormone system in the body is a delicate and interacting one that is not fully understood. Interfering with it should be left to physicians with special training. Specialists in this field are called endocrinologists.

Afrodex, a combination product consisting of nux vomica, yohimbine, and methyltestosterone, was marketed for the treatment of male impotence. The Food and Drug Adminstration removed its approval because there is no scientific reason to believe that two of the ingredients are useful in the treatment of erectile difficulties.

Several studies in the sixties concluded that Afrodex was better than a placebo in treating impotence.[40,41] These studies followed a report on 4,000 men which concluded that Afrodex helped them, but which had no placebo group to compare them with. Therefore, one couldn't know for certain whether it was the Afrodex that helped or just the expectation that something was being done to help them.

In a better designed study for twenty-two impotent men aged twenty-nine to sixty-two years, Afrodex was two to five times better than placebos as measured by the number of erections and orgasms.[40] A similar study in fifty impotent men aged twenty-six to seventy-three years concluded that Afrodex was four times better than a placebo in increasing the number of orgasms. In both studies, the improvement tended to be maintained once the increase was achieved.

With what seemed to be irrefutable evidence that Afrodex helped men overcome their impotency problems, one might well want to know why big brother Food and Drug Administration pulled it off the market. It was done because Afrodex is an irrational combination of drugs. The effective ingredient is the methyltestosterone, and there is not one shred of evidence that adding nux vomica and yohimbine contributes to the correction of impotency problems.

Nux vomica consists of extracts of the dried ripe seeds of a tree, *Strychnos nux-vomica*. The extract contains the alkaloids, strychnine and brucine, which in large doses causes death.

The theory behind the use of these apparently very dangerous drugs is that in small doses, they will stimulate the central nervous sytem, which, in turn, will stimulate the muscles that are needed to maintain an erection. However, at doses low enough not to be dangerous, strychnine and brucine cannot increase muscle tone.[42]

Yohimbine is also an alkaloid obtained from a plant, the bark of a tree, *Corynanthe yohimbi*. Because yohimbine can cause blood vessels to dilate, theoretically it is supposed to work by increasing the flow of blood to the penis to assist in achieving and maintaining an erection. Although there has long been a myth that yohimbine is an aphrodisiac, probably because of the sensation of warmth it gives, there is no evidence that it can help overcome impotence.

ANTIDEPRESSANTS

One effect, which would be considered an adverse and unwelcome side effect by men taking drugs to treat depression, is welcomed by men who are not generally depressed but have premature ejaculations. These men who are too fast off the mark want a drug that can slow them down and give them a chance to enjoy the experience of intercourse and satisfy their partners.

As recently as the 1940s, doctors did not consider premature ejaculation to be a real sex problem. Their view was that men who had it were actually superior because they were so responsive. Instead, the blame was laid on women for being so slow to reach climax.

Probably every man has ejaculated sooner than he would have liked at some time or other, but this sometimes occurrence is hardly the reason to take drugs. For a minority of men the problem and the threat of the problem effectively render normal intercourse impossible. These men benefit from the tricyclic antidepressants. At the same time, the drugs may lift the depression caused by the anxiety and embarrassment that frequently accompany an inability to perform sexually.

TRICYCLIC ANTIDEPRESSANTS

Brand Name	*Generic Name*	*Component in*
Elavil Endep	amitriptyline	Etrafon Triavil
Norpramin Pertofrane	desipramine	
Imavate Janamine Presamine SK-Pramine Tofranil	imipramine	
Aventyl Pemlor	nortriptyline	
Triptil Vivactil	protriptyline	

Although the antidepressants may sometimes help slow down the time to ejaculation, they may cause problems of their own. This is what happened in one case:

A fifty-nine-year-old man was prescribed an antidepressant to treat his premature ejaculation, and he was very pleased with the results. After a few weeks, however, his orgasms were accompanied by considerable pain, so his doctor switched him to a different antidepressant, mebanezine. Things went from bad to worse. Within ten days, the patient had no orgasm at all, and he didn't have one again for four weeks. In fact, he said he had "no feeling" and "no sensation." He stopped taking the drugs because of the erection problem "it does on me."[43]

NARCOTIC ANTAGONISTS

Narcotic addiction destroys sexual desire. It follows that if drugs were given that could interfere with the narcotic and keep it from working, normal or near normal sexual desire and activity might return.

Narcotic antagonists are sometimes given to persons dependent on the opium derivatives, heroin and morphine. An addict who shoots heroin or morphine after he has taken naloxone (Narcan) or cyclazocine feels no effect from the narcotic. The antagonists are blocking agents.

The theory is that, if there is no effect, no euphoria, the addict will not bother to take a narcotic. A powerful inducement might seem to be a return of the sexual desire and abilities that were destroyed by the addicting drugs.

Libido does seem to return after addicts take narcotic antagonists. Addicts don't like them very much though. For one thing, they don't stop the craving for narcotics. For another, they have very unpleasant side effects, if the addict takes a narcotic after taking one of them. And for another, not all addicts want their sexual desire back. Some persons become addicts in the first place because they have sexual problems, and narcotics are a way of escaping that unpleasant reality.

In any event, the narcotic antagonists aren't for your average person with libido problems. They are not aphrodisiacs. They only work by blocking narcotics and releasing the addict's normal sexual capacities.

However, it must disappoint those who have sexual difficulties that there are no legally prescribed drugs except for the male hormones that specifically can correct loss of libido in either men or women, or increase the likelihood that either men or women will reach sexual climax, or improve erectile or ejaculatory capacity in men. Unless there is a disease or surgery related need, the male hormones are limited to use in men suffering from impotence, when their impotence has resulted from the lack of testosterone production in their later years.

To date, the focus of research on sex-enhancing drugs has been on finding drugs to correct infertility, not on finding drugs to correct problems with desire or performance in otherwise normal persons. There are no prescribed drugs available that are specifically for sexual pleasure or to increase sexual desire in normal men and women.

7

HOW PRESCRIBED DRUGS ARE USED TO DECREASE SEXUAL ACTIVITY

The occurrence of sexual problems in the form of lack of interest, failure to achieve orgasms, or to achieve and maintain erections is so common and has such a devastating impact on marital relationships and self-images, that most people give little thought to the problem of hypersexuality. Hyper- or oversexuality may only catch our attention when we read in the newspaper about crimes of aggression such as rape, pederasty, and sodomy. We may think these kinds of crimes are caused by some "oversexed" biological condition such as a man's having too high a level of male hormones, but actually, sexual crimes may be committed by persons with normal hormone levels and psychopathic personalities. Somehow, sexual desire in these persons is translated into sexual aggression.

There are other sorts of crimes that may be related to hypersexuality, but for the most part these crimes fall into the category of embarrassing violations of social rules, rather than causing physical harm to anyone. The classical image of this kind of person is the "flasher," the man in the trench coat who exposes himself to unsuspecting women and children as they pass him on the street or in a hallway. Other common examples are voyeuristic peeping Toms, and men who make obscene phone calls. These vicarious adventurers rarely cause real harm to anyone—they seldom "act out" their feelings—but they do cause considerable fear and anxiety.

Women are also guilty of these kinds of violations. The woman who commonly undresses with her bedroom light on and the shades up, the woman you see on the bus sitting with legs spread wide without visible evidence of underwear, the braless woman in the see-through blouse, all of these may be exhibiting hypersexuality as well as themselves.

If we examine social-rule violation crimes closely, we see that the demarcation between rule violations and rule-bending is confused and constantly shifting. For example, is a person who leaves an obscene graffito in a public toilet hypersexed or merely vulgar? Are the women who go topless on the beach at Cannes exhibitionists, or are they observing the rules of local custom? How about the same state of undress on the beach at Atlantic City? The key, of course, is the extent to which people break social customs regarding sexual behavior whatever these customs, and how silly they may seem in retrospect. This being said, it is not certain whether either criminal or social rule-breaking behavior relates to the amount of sex hormones produced in the body, whether experiential and personality factors are more important, or whether there is some kind of interaction effect.

An interaction effect might exist, for example, when a man with more than the average amount of male hormone, testosterone, had had a particularly unhappy childhood that made him deeply angry at his mother and resentful toward women in general. Such an individual might be much more likely to commit a rape than either the average man with a high testosterone level, but a normal childhood, or the average man with an average testosterone level, but a similarly unhappy childhood.

Testosterone, the hormone most often associated with aggression, occurs in men in the population according to a normal curve, so that some men are in the upper 5 percent range of possible levels of testosterone, and some are at the lower 5 percent range, and so on.

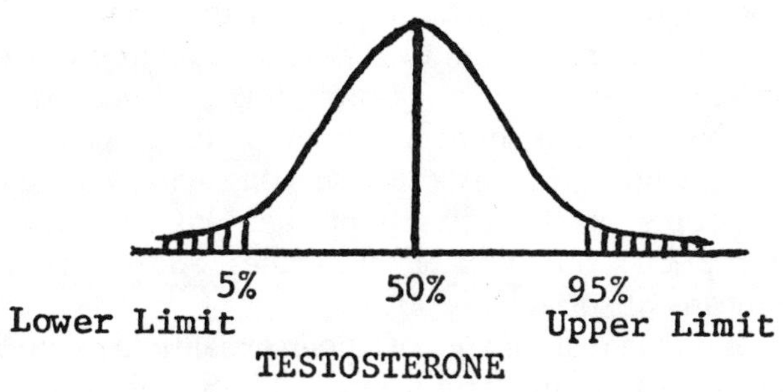

The curve for testosterone is developed by measuring the level of testosterone in each man. Obviously, that can't actually be done, so a random sample of men is taken that is assumed to represent the population. The number of men at each level is counted. The 50 percent point on the curve represents the average. It is the highest point on the curve because more men have an average level than any other. Curves such as this one help doctors tell how likely it is that an individual has an unusually high or low hormone level. For instance, if your level puts you in the upper 5 percent range, you could be considered to be hypersexed. If it puts you in the lower 5 percent, you may be hyposexed. The probability of your lying at either one of these extremes is ten in one hundred, or one in ten. It is five in one hundred, or one in twenty that you will be hypersexed, and similarly, one in twenty that you will be hyposexed.

For hormones, a series of curves for each age group is necessary because the average level is higher in younger men than older men. If only a single curve were used, most of the young men would be on the right side of the curve, and most of the older men would be on the left. Although the level of testosterone, or place on the curve, may be important, it is not all-important. Most of the experts believe that it is the willingness to observe social rules that matters far more than anything else.

The relationship of sexual misbehavior and rule-breaking is apparent in mental institutions and in institutions for mentally retarded persons. People are defined as mentally ill and are institutionalized because they have failed to observe social rules. Their behavior is at the extreme of the normal curve for acceptable behavior, and it has become intolerable for others in society. Few things are guaranteed to admit you to one of these institutions faster than breaking a sex rule.

In addition to sex rule-breakers, people are institutionalized because they are too mentally deficient to cope with society or to care for themselves. There is no reason to believe that retarded or mentally ill persons have imbalances of sex hormones, yet these persons often engage in public sexual activities such as fondling, masturbation, and exhibitionism. Although many of these same activities are carried out by normal people in the privacy of their homes, when they are performed in public, they violate social rules, and drugs may then be given as a means of social control.

For most of us the relationship of hypersexuality to crime and mental illness is not very relevant, and we probably have little concern about the use of drugs to modify antisocial behavior. However, if we really look at the meaning of hypersexuality, we may come to believe that it is a common social problem that causes much misfitting of sexual desire and response in couples. Some of the disparity is related to age. For males, the peak of sexual activity is in the late teens, and for females it is in the early thirties. This mismatch is exacerbated by the custom of men marrying women younger than themselves. The rest of the differences are simply related to variations in sex drive, whether hormonally or socially determined. For whatever reasons, whenever there is a pair in which one person has a stronger sex drive than the other, that person is hypersexed *relative to the other*, as the other is hyposexed relative to the person who has the most drive. This does not mean that one person is unusual or abnormal or sick, or that drugs should be taken by either, but it does indicate that within couples, hypersexuality is common, and that it is frequently a cause of infidelity, aggression, discord, and divorce. A rather dramatic example was brought to the public's attention when a woman in Oregon charged her husband with rape and took him to court.

Even normal sexuality can be too much, or hypersexuality, when it is unwanted, when there are rules against it, or when the normal sexual outlets are unavailable. The persistent belief of army recruits that their food has been laced with saltpeter, a food preservative mistakenly believed to be an antiaphrodisiac, is testimony to man's recognition of his sex drive as an almost constant presence in his life. As such, it is sometimes an interference with other valued activities, and one over which he often wishes he had more control. Who can blame him for imagining that his sex drive is so important that when normal sexual outlets aren't available, it must be dealt with by an official agent of the government?

The relationship between sex and aggression is close, and men have often thought that if they did not expend their energies on sex, they could somehow channel all of their energies into becoming stronger, and they would become better athletes or warriors. Remember General Ripper in *Dr. Strangelove* eschewing women so he could preserve his "vital juices"? Or the manager in *Rocky* saying that women make the legs weak? Or the team in winter training where no women are allowed? How many women over the years have been blamed for men's failures on the athletic field? Even a scientific study showing that sexual intercourse the night before an athletic event had no adverse effect on the event's outcome, and, indeed, might have improved it, has not laid this myth to rest. Some drugs, on the other hand, especially the steroid hormones taken by athletes, may have a positive effect on the strength of athletes, but a negative effect on their sexual abilities.

Some persons are morally indignant at the idea of some people controlling others' behavior by chemical means. Others argue that in any case all of behavior is governed by chemical reactions in the body. Through no fault of their own, some people's chemical systems have gone awry, resulting in behavior damaging to the social order. Logically, whether they have been defined as criminals or mentally ill, their chemical imbalances if located, and understood, could be repaired. But science has not advanced that far. However, we do give people drugs that have enabled many to live normal lives outside of prisons and mental institutions, and this is a far better arrangement for society and for the individuals involved than keeping them locked up.

The argument for giving drugs to persons in institutions is weaker. The contention is that drugs control the behavior of mentally ill persons so that they are accessible to psychotherapy. However, psychotherapy is expensive and thus infrequent for most persons institutionalized with mental illness. For those in prison, the argument is untenable. If prisoners are mentally ill, they do not belong in prison. To these and thousands of mentally ill and retarded persons, drugs are given as a commonplace to control behavior. They are administered purely for the convenience of the staffs so that the inmates are docile and easier to manage. Some of these drugs such as chlorpromazine (Thorazine) and thioridazine (Mellaril) are major antipsychotics which are approved by the Food and Drug Administration for persons with severe mental problems. They have side effects that may be permanent if they are taken for a long period of time.

Antipsychotics are used to control the embarrassing sexual activity of elderly persons in nursing homes as well. Not only do many persons who become senile "revert to their childhood," they also revert to their adolescence, albeit without the modesty that accompanied that earlier life phase. Overt sexual behavior in the elderly is poorly tolerated by relatives and staff who find it easier to control with drugs than with other means.

Another example of the use of major antipsychotics for mind control was reported in the press in 1978 in connection with the mass suicide and murders at the Reverend Jimmy Jones's Peoples Temple in Guyana. The reporters who investigated the death camp found an enormous cache of mind-bending drugs, among them large quantities of major and minor tranquilizers. Reports from the few survivors said that these drugs were used to control individuals who began to complain about their treatment and wanted to leave. They may also have been given to the Temple members before they were asked to drink to their deaths. The deadly Kool-Aid concoction most certainly contained tranquilizers as well as strychnine. Apparently, persons who complained about the way things were being done at the camp were sent to a kind of reeducation infirmary where they were dosed with major tranquilizers until they found the place more to their liking. As noted previously, a side effect of these antipsychotic agents is their adverse effect on sexual function.

Because a side effect of the major tranquilizers is the depression of sexual function, they serve a dual purpose in prisons and institutions. They keep the inmates quiet and they help control and prevent exhibitionism, masturbation, and sexual crimes such as sodomy and rape.

The sex offender has long been a problem for society. The child molester is particularly abhorrent. Sometimes child molesters are highly productive members of society except for their unfortunate aberration. For these persons, a drug that controls their urge to yield to their antisocial impulses is welcome. They and society benefit. The drug answer may be distasteful, but it is better than prison. Although many persons deplore society's tendency toward medicalization, defining people as sick instead of bad can be the humane approach.

A number of drugs are used to control sexual behavior and even sexy thoughts. The latter as a measure of a drug's success doesn't seem very scientific. The frequency of sexy thoughts in average persons or how they vary with age is certainly not known. Moreover, in order to measure a drug's success, we must rely on the voluntary self-report of cooperative and even eager drug taking subjects. Still, sexy thoughts are used by doctors to measure how an antisex drug is working, and is undoubtedly better than no measure at all.

The following drugs or their combinations are used as antiaphrodisiacs to control sexual behavior: cyproterone acetate, estrogens, antipsychotics, and antidepressants.

CYPROTERONE ACETATE

Cyproterone acetate is given to men who have committed sex crimes such as rape, exhibitionism, and pederasty. Cyproterone acetate is a true antiandrogen; it blocks the action of male hormones in the body. After men take cyproterone, their average level of testoserone falls to one-fiftieth of its former level.[1] In addition to its effect on sexual behavior, it may cause gynecomastia and infertility. In time, however, the amount of ejaculate tends to increase, and men have been known to father children while taking cyproterone.

In some European countries, sex offenders are given the choice: take cyproterone or go to jail. Known as the sexual tranquilizer, it also helps relieve the anxiety and guilt that go with hypersexuality in both men and women.

Although cyproterone acetate is most often given to men who have committed sex crimes, it is sometimes requested by individuals for rather surprising reasons. One case involved a woman who asked her family doctor to prescribe it for her husband so he would keep his hands off other women.[2]

Valid—meaning doctors' interpretations of valid—requests are similar to the following: a pedophilic homosexual was picking up young children several times a week and forcing them to fellate him. He was given cyproterone acetate, and although he still "fancies young boys," the drug keeps his behavior under control.[2]

A thirty-five-year-old homosexual schoolteacher took the drug to control his appetite for his students. He had married to "cure his sinful tendencies." Although the responsibility of marriage did keep him from committing overt sexual acts against his students, he was unbearably miserable and was considering suicide. Although cyproterone acetate "decreased the color in his life," he had no more troublesome erections at school.[2]

Cyproterone was given to thirty-six institutionalized boys who had committed sex crimes. Although the drug produced mild cases of breast development and decreased the sperm counts of the delinquents, they became much easier to handle. Their former aggressiveness and antisocial behavior became more stable and cooperative.[3] Many persons would disagree with the involuntary use of a drug to control hypersexuality, but the voluntary use is certainly welcomed by some individuals whose sex problems effectively keep them from having happy, fulfilling lives. One European doctor suggested that cyproterone acetate is suitable for cases of the following:

compulsive masturbation
indecent exposure
exhibitionism
aggressive alcohol-related sex behavior
sado-masochism
hetero- or homosexual pedophilia

The doctor went on to say that cyproterone acetate may be suitable for cases where a husband is much more highly sexed than his wife. The doctor's point is that if the couple wishes to preserve their marriage, the drug may be a better answer than extramarital affairs, or unhappiness, which in time may lead to hostility and divorce.[2]

FEMALE HORMONES

ESTROGENS

Brand Name	*Generic Name*
Atladiol	ethinyl estradiol
Aquadiol	estradiol
Delestrogen	estradiol benzoate
Dimenformon	estradiol cyprionate
Diogyn	estradiol valerate
Diogynets	
Estate	
Estinyl	
Estrace	
Estraval	
Feminone	
Femogen	
Inestra	
Ionate	
Lynoral	
Organon	
Progynon	

Because a male hormone, the androgen testosterone, is mainly responsible for libido and associated aggressive tendencies, an obvious answer to hypersexuality is to counterbalance the testosterone in hypersexed men by giving them a female hormone, an estrogen. Estrogens along with tranquilizers and counseling are often recommended for sex offenders. Estrogens decrease the sex drive without altering its direction.[4] Men who take estrogens will still prefer women as sexual partners, if they preferred women before they took estrogens, and they will still prefer men, if men were their sexual inclination before taking estrogens.

The estrogen, estradiol, or some form of it, tends to produce the unwelcome side effect of gynecomastia in men. There is little more certain to discourage men from taking it than developing breasts, so some doctors recommend giving the hormone in the same combination that is in oral contraceptives to help control gynecomastia.

ANTIPSYCHOTICS

Benperidol is the antipsychotic (major tranquilizer) that has been given most often in Europe to decrease sexual activity, and sex-related antisocial behavior. Benperidol is a powerful sedative that is used for its side effect. Like the other antipsychotics, it may decrease sexual pressures, especially sexual thoughts and masturbation, but it is probably not strong enough to control antisocial behavior. When an erotic film and slides were shown to twelve child molesters who had taken benperidol, they had as many erections as men who had not taken the drug. In the absence of sexual stimuli, sexual activity is apparently reduced by the antipsychotics, but in the presence of sexual stimuli, the potential for antisocial behavior remains.

ANTIPSYCHOTIC DRUGS

Brand Name	*Generic Name*
	benperidol
Thorazine	chlorpromazine
Prolixin Permitil	fluphenazine
Mellaril	thioridazine

None of the antipsychotics in the above list is an antiandrogenic drug as is cyproterone acetate. Although antipsychotics are given to control hypersexuality, their antiaphrodisiac properties were discovered as side effects of drugs used to treat psychosis and depression. During the process of treating people with these drugs, many of the patients reported sexual function difficulties, and when the drugs were given to hospitalized patients, the staff observed changes in their sexual behavior. It was not long before these drugs began to be used primarily for hypersexuality.

The practice of giving drugs for their side effects is not unusual in medicine. Once a drug has been approved by the Food and Drug Administration to treat a particular problem, there is nothing to prevent doctors from prescribing it for unapproved (known as unlabeled) problems. Drugs must go through a rigorous testing process to gain approval for any unapproved use, a process similar to that required to earn the original marketing approval. Some drugs never go through this second approval process, but they are used for unlabeled indications anyway. Such is the situation with respect to using antipsychotics to treat hypersexuality. They are not labeled by the Food and Drug

Administration as approved for the treatment or control of sexual problems, but they are still prescribed to treat and control sexual problems.

Sometimes the antipsychotic agents, such as thioridazine (Mellaril) and fluphenazine (Prolixin, Permitil), are given in combination with estrogens such as ethinyl estradiol to decrease the drive of sex offenders. On their own, patients tend to be poor compliers with either kind of therapy. Having an uncontrollable sex drive may get men into trouble, but for the heterosexual male, it is tied up with a macho image, one which men are proud of, and one they are reluctant to relinquish. To overcome the poor compliance problems, the antipsychotic is sometimes injected instead of being given in tablets or capsules.

Twenty-six men in one group of sex offenders were given fluphenazine (Prolixin, Permitil) by injection.[4] The majority of them lost their sex drives. Their loss of libido was confirmed by their wives and girlfriends. None of the men in this particular group developed gynecomastia which is the most psychologically distasteful side effect produced by both the antipsychotics and the estrogens.

ANTIDEPRESSANTS

If you think you've seen the tables listing antidepressants before, you're right. Because they have side effects that depress sexual function, they're used to treat premature ejaculation and to control hypersexuality. For most people, the sex activity depressing component is highly unwelcome. But for people who are constantly bothered by their domineering sexual states, the side effects of antidepressants may be relatively welcome.

ANTIDEPRESSANTS

Brand Name	*Generic Name*	*Component in*
Elavil Endep	amitriptyline	Etrafon Triavil
Norpramin Pertofrane	desipramine	
Imavate Janamine Presamine SK-Pramine Tofranil	imipramine	

Brand Name	*Generic Name*	*Component in*
Aventyl Pamelor	nortriptyline	
Entonyl	pargyline	
Triptil Vivactil	protriptyline	

Unlike an antipsychotic, an antidepressant may also lift the spirits of those who are down in the dumps over the effect that being hypersexed is having on their lives. For hypersexed persons, the primary effect of an antidepressant is a side effect.

Case 1: A nineteen-year-old male came to his doctor for help. He was deeply anxious and depressed and was suffering extremely from the guilt he felt over his compulsive masturbation. He felt like masturbating all the time, even all day at work. After two weeks of taking pargyline, he wasn't masturbating nearly as often, and after one month on the drug, he was considered to be normal.[5]

Case 2: A thirty-seven-year-old male was given Elavil because he was anxious and depressed over what he regarded as a lack of control over his compulsive desire to have sexual relations six or seven times a week. After taking the antidepressant drug, Elavil, for a week or two, he felt much less compulsion, and he was having sexual relations three to four times a week.[5]

Because the effect of the antidepressants on sexual function is really only a side effect, it doesn't work on everyone. It is one of those kinds of drugs that doctors try on you and hope they'll work. They certainly are not suitable for people who have committed sex crimes. They may be suitable for people who are depressed, and who have compulsive sexual feelings that dominate their lives and threaten their normal home and work relationships.

Besides cyproterone acetate, which is not approved for use in the United States, there is no drug that is specifically an antiaphrodisiac. The estrogens are used, but they have unpleasant feminizing side effects. The antipsychotics are most often given for their combined effects of sedation and of producing a decrease in sexual activity.

Those who complain about the lack of research to find an aphrodisiac might voice a similar complaint with respect to antiaphrodisiacs. Failure to fund research to find a drug to control hypersexed criminals obviously cannot be blamed on antipleasure Calvinist values. However, the attitudes toward supporting any research directed at finding drugs to enhance or suppress sexual behavior might relate to deep-seated feelings about interfering in bodily systems used for procreation.

8

OVER THE COUNTER, IN THE DRUGSTORE AND THE BEDROOM

Not all of the drugs that are capable of affecting your sex life or reproductive system are prescribed by your doctor or are obtained on the illegal drug market. You can buy some of them over the counter (OTC) at the drugstore or supermarket, and you've probably got some of them in your kitchen. Of course alcohol is the most important sex-affecting over-the-counter drug of all, so important, in fact, that Chapter Nine is entirely devoted to it. In this chapter we will discuss vitamins, cold remedies, caffeine, nicotine, household spices, ginseng, and a chemical called tryptophan that's a big seller in health food stores.

VITAMIN E, VITAMIN E, VITAMIN E, AND OTHER VITAMINS

Have you taken a close look at vitamin commercials on television lately? The not-so-subtle sell is that if you're not getting your quota or perhaps megaquota of vitamins, you're in trouble sexually. The words potency, drive, and energy are all mixed in with other clue words like caring, pleasure, love, and enjoyment. No longer are these messages directed at doddering old folks whom we suspect (probably wrongly) wouldn't be interested anyway, and have long ago decided on separate bedrooms, nor are they directed at the nutritional anxieties of the mothers of young children, but to young, attractive, vital, and clearly sexual young couples. Nor are these couples always married. No, indeed. There is now Geritol for "living togethers." We who are "such good friends" need these "potent" vitamins so we can go on "being together." Touching touchingly, our Madison Avenue couple gaze into each other's eyes as they tell how much they mean to each other, and how much these vitamins, which we once thought were for the near senile, mean to their meaningful relationship. We begin to worry. If this couple—so glowing, so in love—so obviously near the peak of their sexual capacities—take Geritol, what about those of us who are relatively "over-the-hill"? Thoughts of playing it safe begin to cross our minds, if we're not playing it safe already. After all, vitamins aren't really very expensive, and we've never actually met anyone who's been harmed by them and what if, just what if, those vitamins are actually making those people feel and behave as they appear on the living-room screen?

There's no doubt that if you did not get any vitamins at all, your sexual system would be seriously impaired, but so would your entire body. Vitamins are absolutely essential for human life. Since most people get an adequate amount from even moderately well-balanced meals, and any number of common foods, such as breads and cereals, are vitamin-boosted, the questions remain whether extra vitamins can do anything special for sexual function, and if so, for whom, which vitamins in particular, and exactly what can they do.

Vitamin E, often called the sex vitamin, is the subject of a great deal of controversy both inside and outside the medical community. Vitamin E has its loyal supporters, but others will tell you sooner than you can say vitamin, that it's a load of rubbish and a gigantic rip-off.

Recently, thirty-five people volunteered for an experiment to test the effects of vitamin E. Some of the volunteers were given vitamin E and some were given placebos. After twenty-eight days, there was no difference in the reported sex behavior or arousal between the people who took the vitamin and the people who took the placebo.[1]

Since the early 1920s, vitamin E, or alphatocopherol as it's called in medical circles, has been touted as the answer to sterility and lack of virility in males. The entire scientific support for the view that vitamin E is important in human sexual function rests on rats. Yes, rats; not people, but rats. The person who said "A drug is a substance that when injected into a rat produces a scientific paper" rather understated reality with this one. It's produced thousands of men who are convinced that vitamin E is the secret to continued success in the sack, a source of energy, a key to health and well-being, and helpful for baldness, potbelly, liver spots, varicose veins, and other symptoms of age-related deterioration.

With regard to those rat experiments, if rats are totally deprived of vitamin E, they are incapable of producing progeny. They are sterile. It has not been possible to demonstrate any relationship between vitamin E and sexual function, including impotence, pregnancy, and fertility in humans. For one thing, you simply can't find any human beings who have been totally deprived of vitamin E. It's found in common foods: grains, fish, meat, eggs, milk, butter, cheese, green leafy vegetables, margarine and vegetable oils. Just try and get through life without eating at least one of these. Not only is it pretty much impossible to avoid, but it's a really stable vitamin that keeps its activity during normal cooking.

Because of its curious relationship to rat reproduction, vitamin E has proved to be an exceedingly embarrassing vitamin to the scientific community which feels there must be a use for it in humans but hasn't been able to determine exactly what. Most physicians would agree that it should be given to premature babies and persons who have difficulty digesting fats. A few physicians think that vitamin E helps with nighttime leg cramps or "restless legs," and perhaps poor circulation, and the cramps that sometimes occur during and after exercise. No responsible physician will tell you that vitamin E can help your sex life. Even a book called *Vitamin E Questions and Answers,* published by a company that makes vitamin E, states: "Enjoyment of sex is, in good part, mental. If you believe vitamin E will help, maybe it will. There is no evidence, however, that it will cure impotence or infertility in humans."[1] Nevertheless, there are many men, especially men in their second half-century, who will tell you, sometimes with a wink, that vitamin E is terrific, and that they've never felt—or performed—better since taking it.

The argument of those who sell vitamin E is that people vary, and even though an average person may be getting enough vitamin E, not everyone is average. Some people may not absorb all the vitamins that they get in their normal diets, or their bodies may not use them very well after they're absorbed. Those touting supplementary vitamins also claim that supplementary vitamins may be needed to achieve a complete sense of physical, mental and social well-being, which they argue is some state beyond and more desirable than a state in which there is merely an absence of detectable illness.

Vitamins A and D probably do play a part in sex hormone chemistry, especially vitamin D, which may stimulate the production of estrogens.[2] These vitamins certainly stimulate the general metabolism and thus affect the ovaries, the adrenal cortex, and the pituitary gland, which produces the hormones responsible for secondary sexual characteristics, reproduction, and libido. In general, well-being, including sexual well-being, is dependent on vitamins, and minerals too, but there simply isn't any reason to believe that taking extra or megadoses increases well-being beyond a level provided by an average diet. The body simply uses what it needs and excretes or stores the rest.

Given the strength of the placebo effect, if you believe very strongly that vitamin E or any other vitamin can help your sexual prowess, it probably will, and conversely, if you disbelieve, it probably won't, and you probably won't take it faithfully either.

If you take a multiple vitamin tablet every day you won't hurt anything but your wallet. However, high doses of the fat-soluble vitamins, which include vitamin E—the others are A, D, and K—can be harmful, because they accumulate in the tissues and may damage the eyes, cause dangerously high calcium levels, and cause birth defects, if they are taken during pregnancy.

Iron is the one mineral that clearly has a sex factor. Women do need more than men during their fertile years because of menstruation. However, they don't need anywhere near the amount that television commercials would lead you to believe, and they certainly don't need some special kind for women only. Iron is iron, whether it be in the sulfate, fumarate, or gluconate form. During menstruation, women need about 0.5 to 1.6 mg. of iron a day while men and postmenopausal women need from 0.5 to 1.0 mg. Even during pregnancy women need no more than 2.0 mg., and only in very rare conditions would as much as 4.0 mg. be needed by anyone.[3] The supplemental vitamin and mineral combinations seem to provide overkill. For example, the One-A-Day Plus Iron brand provides 18 mg. of iron, but only 10 percent of the oral forms is absorbed by the body.

Vitamin C also has a sex relationship, but that is only for women who are taking contraceptive pills. Oral contraceptives cause vitamin C to be used by the body more quickly, so that women on the pill have up to 30 percent less vitamin C in their blood than other women. Some doctors believe that the bad side effects of the pill, for example, blood clots in the legs, may be a consequence of the depletion of vitamin C, caused by the pill, and not a direct effect. This means that women on the pill should probably take extra vitamin C as a precaution.

Oral contraceptives also decrease the amount of vitamin B_6 (pyridoxine) that is in the body, and sometimes folic acid and B_{12}.[4] Vitamin B_6 is needed for tryptophan metabolism and tryptophan is a precursor of serotonin. Although some researchers believe that vitamin B_6 depletion may be the reason some women on the pill become depressed, the chemistry of these systems is highly interrelated, and interdependent, and science hasn't progressed far enough to fully understand it.

A mixture that sounds like a vitamin but isn't is Gerovital #3. This drug, which contains procaine, an anesthetic, is purported to slow the aging process. There's no scientific evidence that it does, but it's stirred up considerable controversy, with the FDA refusing to allow it on the market, and one state, Nevada, allowing it to be sold. The procaine may decrease pain, and thus make persons who take it feel better, but that's hardly the same thing as finding a fountain of youth.

DRUGS FOR COLDS

When you've got a cold about the only thing you want to go to bed with is a hot water bottle, so you probably won't care very much if the cold remedy you've taken puts your sexual response to sleep. Actually the amount of anticholinergic drug these combinations often contain is probably too small in the recommended dosages to affect your sexual response. The most common anticholinergic is belladonna, which is supposed to relieve nasal stuffiness. If you get a high enough dose of it to work (the manufacturer's recommended dose is not high enough) you could experience the same kind of problems that are caused by the prescribed anticholinergics (see Chapter 4). Since these anticholinergic combination cough and cold products aren't recommended for colds, and people with hypertension should never take them anyway, why take a chance? Read labels. Ask your pharmacist if the product you're about to buy contains any anticholinergics. If you must take one, buy a product containing a simple decongestant instead of a combination for colds. Try phenylpropanolamine, phenylephrine, or pseudoephedrine (Sudafed, D-Feda) as recommended by the American Pharmaceutical Association.* Check with your doctor or your pharmacist if you have hypertension and want some relief from a cold.

DRUGS FOR SLEEP

One of the main ingredients, also an anticholinergic, in most OTC sleeping drugs is our old friend scopolamine, one of the hallucinogenic alkaloids in plants of the Solanaceae group, belladonna, henbane, datura, and mandrake. Scopolamine is the most active of the "belladonna" alkaloids and was the one used not only in witchcraft in the Dark Ages but in modern times as a truth serum, and for "twilight sleep." In the 1920s, cigarettes made from datura leaves, Asthmadors, were on the market for asthma sufferers. Now we have "Take Sominex tonight and sleep. . . ." What some people have while they're sleeping,

---

*The best, up-to-date, all around book on cough and cold and other OTC remedies is *The Handbook of Nonprescription Drugs*, 6th Edition, published by the American Pharmaceutical Association, 2215 Constitution Avenue, Washington, D.C., 1979.

especially if they greatly exceed the recommended dosage, is hallucinations, nightmares, confusion, and disorientation, sometimes accompanied by sexual excitement. In the recommended dosage, Sominex and other scopolamine containing drugs simply don't work any better than a placebo,[5] and may actually worsen insomnia by interfering with REM (rapid eye movement) sleep that is so important to achieve a feeling of having rested. Therefore, the temptation is great to exceed the recommended dose and risk the side effects which have only a small chance of being a pleasant experience. The other drugs containing scopolamine are Nite Rest and Seedate.

In view of their failure to help people sleep and the side effects of OTC sleep medications, forget them. For a serious sleep problem, see your doctor. Otherwise, try exercise, reading, warm milk, or counting sheep. When you feel better, wake up your partner and tell him or her that you need a little therapeutic loving. Or perhaps try tryptophan. Tryptophan, an amino acid that occurs naturally in the body, may be the ideal sleep producer. In fact, it is the tryptophan in milk that may be the reason milk is the favorite folk remedy to produce sleep. It's also been found useful to treat severe migraine headaches.

Tryptophan is one of the chemical messengers in the serotonin/dopamine complex, and that makes it one of the actors in sex chemistry. Strangely enough, it's been found both to dampen down sexual expression and to stimulate it in combination with another drug. In one case, it took care of headaches and hypersexuality in the same patient:

A forty-eight-year-old physician, A.B., with an unusually vigorous sexual appetite since his childhood, found his sexual compulsion with accompanying headaches an interference in his work. Moreover, partners weren't always available when he wanted them, and he found masturbation unsatisfactory. After he took tryptophan, his headaches disappeared and his unpleasant erotic tendencies became normal so that he was engaging in sexual activity only three to four times a week. When he stopped taking tryptophan, both his headaches and his sex problem came back.[7]

In the instance in which tryptophan stimulated sexual response, it was given along with a monoamine oxidase M.O.A.I. antidepressant drug to seven schizophrenic women. Five of the seven exhibited sexual excitatory behavior which was believed to result from the combination of the antidepressant, which decreased the serotonin level, and the tryptophan. The effect would not be possible with tryptophan alone.

Tryptophan is under investigation to treat depression, which is believed to result from an imbalance in brain neurotransmitters, especially dopamine, serotonin, and tryptamine. Tryptophan has been shown to be as effective in treating depression as tricyclic antidepressant drugs such as amitriptyline in some studies.[7] If it is a successful treatment for depression, however, it should restore normal sexual interest in those persons whose depression is characterized by a decrease in libido. This would make tryptophan an unusual drug; one that could correct an abnormality and dampen hypersexuality or increase libido in some patients while decreasing libido in others.

Tryptophan may be an ideal drug. Readily available, cheap, safe. If it can put people to sleep, take away migraine headaches, and diminish hypersexuality for those who have such problems, in time it may have a proper place in household medicine cabinets, and replace saltpeter as the suspected substance in army and boarding school food.

TOBACCO

Kissing someone who smokes may be akin to kissing a dirty ashtray, but aside from its negative esthetic qualities, at least to nonsmokers, is there any good or harm that smoking can do to sexual function? Certainly, tobacco addicts—unless they chew—suffer from decreased lung capacity in the long run, and to the extent that stamina is required, huffing and puffing may not be conducive to optimal sexual performance. Smokers also are more prone to heart attack, and this may combine with the extra stress put on the heart during intercourse, particularly extramarital intercourse, to increase the likelihood that a heart attack will occur.

There is considerable evidence that heavy smokers have less sexual activity than nonsmokers. Some believe that this is because smokers are less fit. Others believe, at least for men, that the situation is more complex with smokers exhibiting low testosterone levels and decreased sperm production and motility, especially in association with alcohol.

It's the nicotine in the tobacco that may have a direct effect on sexual function. Nicotine is a drug that constricts the blood vessels. The constriction may decrease the amount of blood that flows to the penis to keep it erect and to the pelvic area of the female during the preorgasmic phase. Nevertheless, the effect is probably minor and most of the negative effects of tobacco on libido can be blamed on the feelings of nonsmokers about the smell and taste of smokers. Nonsmokers rarely find smoking sexy, and so if you are a smoker, your partner is likely to be one too.

Former smokers usually find they have an increased interest in sex after they stop smoking. Of course, they have more time for it too.

CAFFEINE

Caffeine, that little pepper-upper that comes in coffee, tea, and chocolate, has a stimulating effect on sexual function and may increase fertility.

Depending upon the way it's made, a cup of coffee has about 75 to 120 mg. of caffeine, a cup of tea about half that, and a six ounce bar of chocolate about 25 mg. Cola drinks also contain caffeine, about 40 mg. in 10 ounces. Caffeine is the main ingredient in OTC stay awake pills such as No-Doz, and is found in most OTC diet pills in amounts up to 100 mg.

Because caffeine stimulates the central nervous sytsten, in high doses it may produce sexual arousal. Its ability to keep people awake may facilitate sexual activity in persons who otherwise would be disinterested because of mental or physical fatigue. On the other hand, the stimulation in mental activity may make it difficult for some people to concentrate on the job at hand. As they say in Australia, the mind tends to "go walkabout."

At least one individual has suggested that one of the reasons people take so many other drugs to help them cope with life in general and sexual function in particular is that they're so jumped-up all the time by their caffeine addictions.

The stimulation effect of caffeine may increase fertility, not by increasing the number of sperm, but by making those that are produced swim faster and survive longer, an effect that lasts from four to five hours after a man has drunk some tea or coffee.[8] A normal man produces several hundred million sperm in a single day, and the average ejaculate is less than a teaspoonful, yet it contains about 300 million sperm. Given those mind-boggling figures, it is hard to understand why sheer numbers wouldn't ensure that at least one sperm made it to its ovum goal. But some men produce less than the average amount, and some sperm swim more sluggishly than others. Also, some women put up more barriers to sperm because of physical abnormalities or the pH and viscosity of mucus at the mouth of the cervix. For these persons, anything that gives the sperm a better chance increases the chances of parenthood. Making a cup of coffee may be the first step toward making a baby!

Chocolate was considered to be a terrific aphrodisiac by the Aztecs, whose history records not only the first known written mention of chocolate but its first use in association with sexual activity. Montezuma, the Aztec king, is reported to have drunk fifty cups of chocolate a day in an effort to attain the energy needed to satisfy his seven hundred wives.

SPICES ARE NOT ALWAYS JUST FOR COOKING

Nutmeg and mace, two of the most common household spices, contain alkaloids that have hallucinogenic properties. Mace is the ground up seed covering, and nutmeg is the seed of the same plant, an evergreen tree *Myristica fragrans,* that grows in the East Indies. However, you are not going to get high on your holiday eggnog or your Thanksgiving pumpkin pie. The amount of nutmeg or mace required to produce even a minor buzz is so large that would-be spice ingestors usually gag and turn nauseous long before they attain it. For this reason, nutmeg and mace are known as the hallucinogens of last resort. And for this reason, even though many drug subculture experimenters have tried them, they are used most frequently by prisoners who simply resort to spices because they can't get anything else.

To get even a minor euphoria takes about one-third of an ounce of nutmeg or mace. Considering that the average kitchen container holds one and a half ounces, you can readily imagine the challenge in gagging down that much of the dry powdery stuff. Those able to stomach two-thirds of an ounce may approach heavy intoxication with euphoria, time and space distortion, and disorientation, but the heavier dose also increases the chance of nausea, headache, constipation, cold, clamminess, dry mouth, fear, and a heavy depressive hangover that may last one to two days. For only a few people is the experience so pleasant as to include erotic dreams and visions. In prison, the practice is to mix the spice in a glass of very hot water to make the stuff more palatable.

Considering the potential unpleasantness at the outset, during, and after an attempted nutmeg or mace trip, only those who will try anything to escape the realities of their existence can probably say that "spice is nice."

Although you may have heard that banana skins have hallucinogenic or aphrodisiac properties, it's a lot of humbug. Anyone claiming to have tripped on banana skins certainly was referring to a fall or experienced a placebo effect. The only sexual property of a banana is its phallic symbolism.

Green peppers too enjoyed a brief fling in the sixties. People were inhaling regular cigarettes through rotten green peppers and claiming to get slightly high. Although the FDA looked into the claims, it concluded that, although there is a serotoninlike chemical in banana skins and some other fruits and a tryptaminelike chemical in green pepper, these foods have no psychoactive, let alone sex-related, activity.

GINSENG

The aphrodisiac non pareil in ancient Chinese pharmacology is the ginseng root, now available to smoke, chew, or make into a tea, and sold in modern health food stores as well as traditional Chinese herb stores. Ginseng comes in a powder, a liquid, or the dried root. Like the almost mythical mandrake root, the more the ginseng root resembles the human form, the more powerful an aphrodisiac it is believed to be, and the more expensive it is—up to $1,500 an ounce for anthropomorphic tubers with testis-like protrusions. Ginseng is reported to restore and maintain potency as well as guard well-being and extend the life span. These claims have not been confirmed, but on the other hand, they haven't been disproved either. In this respect, ginseng is the Oriental counterpart to vitamin E.

Experiments have shown that the active ingredients in ginseng help the body adapt to stress and correct adrenal and thyroid dysfunction.

The most common psychological effect of ginseng is euphoria. In one study, only 9 of 133 persons who had used ginseng over a two-year period reported that it enhanced their sexual performance.[9]

Today ginseng is one of the main ingredients in so-called "legal grass" which also contains yohimbine and hops plus some other "natural" herbs, damiana and lobelia. When smoked, the mixture smells almost like marijuana, but doesn't have anywhere near the latter's psychoactivity.

PART IV

RECREATIONAL DRUGS: HOW THEY CAN HELP (OR HARM) YOUR SEX LIFE

9

ALCOHOL: WHAT IT DOES TO YOUR SEX LIFE

Without question, no drug in present or past use has done more to harm marriage and sexual relationships than alcohol, despite its place as the number-one drug used as an aphrodisiac. Alcohol wins hands down on both counts. Paradoxical, yes, confusing, no. It's simply dose-related. A little alcohol can be (but is not always) a help, while a large amount is damaging to sexual function; chronic alcoholism, drinking large amounts over a long period of time, is totally destructive (see table on page 142.)

The only way that alcohol can help is to release some of the inhibitions that are bottled up in individuals, and this is at some expense to physical response. If you don't have any inhibitions, liquor won't do a thing for you on the positive side. If you do have some inhibitions, alcohol can indeed be an aphrodisiac, both increasing or, more accurately, releasing desire and increasing the chance the performance will take place.

> Sherry, my dear? Why yes
> But two at the very most
> Because three puts me under the table
> And four puts me under my host.

These lines in an old song suggest that wine, in fact a lot of wine, is a super seductive agent that can lead a woman into debauchery. "Candy is dandy, but liquor is quicker" is less subtle but puts across a similar point. Let a woman get a little drunk and you've half got her into bed. Although there is some truth to this, men often fail to watch the

EFFECTS OF ALCOHOL ON SEXUAL FUNCTION BY SEX AND AMOUNT OF ALCOHOL*

	Small Dose	*Moderate Dose*	*Large Dose*	*Chronic Alcoholism*
WOMEN:	Release of inhibitions Feelings of warmth Increased aggression Increased desire Increased enjoyment of foreplay Increased quality of orgasm	Fewer or no orgasms Decreased quality of orgasm Longer foreplay Decreased lubrication	No orgasm Lassitude No lubrication	Loss of libido Loss of menstruation Frigidity Infertility
MEN:	Release of inhibitions Increased aggression Increased desire Increased arousal Control of premature ejaculation Decreased penile tumescence	Longer foreplay Increased time to erection Difficulty in maintaining erection Uncertain orgasm Decreased penile tumescence	Impotence, both erectile and ejaculatory Thoughtlessness Unpleasant ejaculation Aggressiveness	Loss of libido Loss of sexual satisfaction Erectile impotence Decreased testosterone Infertility Breast development Decreased body hair Shriveled testicles

*The amount of alcohol ingestion depends on how strong the drinks are made, how fast they are drunk, the amount of food and drink in the stomach, other drugs taken, weight and age.

amount they are drinking themselves while at their seductive pursuits, so that when the sought after moment finally arrives, they are literally not up to the task at hand.

How does it work? The answer is related to both the depressant action of alcohol in the body, and to alcohol's ability to dilate the blood vessels. Most persons, and particularly women, in our society have suppressed sexual feelings. Alcohol tends to release those feelings and loosen control by depressing the centers in the brain that are responsible for control. As blood vessels dilate, more blood comes to the surface of the body, causing the moderate drinker to experience a feeling of warmth and well-being. These two effects account for the disinhibiting qualities associated with alcohol, and the increase in libidinous feelings experienced by moderate imbibers.

Because there is a forty-five-minute to two-hour delay before all the alcohol that is drunk is absorbed into the bloodstream, individuals, particularly inexperienced young people, tend to drink too much before they feel the effects, and then it is too late. The nervous system becomes severely depressed and sexual functioning is considerably diminished.

Zombies, Black Russians, wine, white or red, mulled cider, mai-tais, vodka martinis, draft beer—does it make any difference? Which works best?

Outside of the questionable romantic appeal in a drink called a "bullshot" or in a large, dripping mug of beer, which almost inevitably will produce a negative placebo effect in a woman who is an object of desire, the form in which alcohol is served makes very little difference. It's the total amount of alcohol that's drunk that counts the most, not the kind of drink that it comes in. Even though wine has been the leading aphrodisiac of alcoholic beverages throughout recorded history, there is nothing in wine other than the alcohol that makes it more likely than hard liquor to increase sexual desire. The apparent association of wine to increased libido is related to the relatively modest alcohol content. When a person takes in small to moderate amounts of alcohol, sexual inhibitions are decreased and suppressed desires and sexual feelings are released. Because wine contains a lower percentage of alcohol than hard liquor, such as Scotch, gin, bourbon and vodka, people are likely to get less alcohol in the same period of time when they drink wine. They will probably start to feel the effects before they have had too much alcohol. Their feelings are more likely to remain pleasant because they stop drinking or cut back sooner, and they are more likely to feel sexually aggressive and aroused and to associate these feelings with the wine they drank. Hard liquor in moderation and drunk slowly would accomplish the same thing, but people tend to have a drinking pace, and unless the drink is unpleasantly strong, they tend to keep that pace whether they are drinking soda pop or mixed drinks. Hard liquor has not attained the cachet of wine as an aphrodisiac simply because drinkers have too frequently zipped right through the modest amount of alcohol that is most conducive to sexual arousal, and into a phase that is unpleasant or in which sexual performance is adversely affected. Hard liquor is fine, of course, if you stick to one or two weak ones and learn how to sip. But if you want romance, why not stick to wine? Its reputation is established and you'll get favorable expectations along with it, especially if you enhance the milieu with candles and soft music.

In terms of its alcohol content, beer is on a par with wine, but it has never made it as the beverage of romantics. It isn't as esthetically appealing as wine, tends to cause embarrassing burps, and results in numerous trips to the bathroom. There is little more guaranteed to break a mood as progress toward the peak experience is made than discovering that one has a full bladder. Such a discovery, requiring an announcement, a breaking off of activity and departing the room for relief, returning and then trying to resume the activity at the same level is considerably problematical. Any disruption as demanding as that generally puts a woman back to "start" on the arousal road, while the man remains about where he was. Moreover, the woman in a couple which hasn't been together long tends to be somewhat embarrassed and to put off as long as possible the announcement of the discomfiting bladder. It is strangely true that many couples who enjoy the most intimate access to each other's bodies have difficulty acknowledging bodily functions such as urination, defecation, menstruation, or even flatulence. In the case of urination, early childhood parental admonitions, "Now be sure to go to the toilet before we start," are likely to evoke at least a modicum of guilt and a feeling of failure at a time when such feelings are least wanted and can do the most damage. Probably for these reasons, beer tends to be associated with men, macho, and sports, and has left totally untapped its possible potential as an aphrodisiac.

The other reason that wine is better as a disinhibitor is that it is usually drunk with food. The presence of food in the stomach, especially carbohydrates, slows down the absorption of alcohol, and what is most desirable is slow absorption over a considerable period of time, so that inhibitions will be released, but performance will not be seriously impaired. Moreover, beer and wine themselves contain nutrients that slow down absorption as compared to, say a Scotch on the rocks or bourbon and water. Soda water actually increases the rate of absorption.

Other factors that contribute to how much is too much, and make it impossible to say how much is enough in terms of the number of drinks and period of time, are how much a person weighs, individual body chemistry, and the psychological setting. A heavy person simply has more blood and other fluids in the body to dilute the liquor, so that the same amount drunk at the same speed over the same period of time will not affect him or her as much as it will a person weighing less. Persons have their own special body chemistry, too, that affects the sobriety per drink level. Some individuals seem to tolerate a fairly high level of alcohol and remain quite sober, whereas in others even small amounts seem to act as a poison, causing nausea, vomiting, and headaches.

There is no drug like alcohol when it comes to changes in a person's behavior that arise from an interaction between his psychological state and his drinking surroundings. Depending if he's with a pretty girl in a romantic atmosphere or at a boring business meeting, at a bar with "the boys" or by himself, the same amount of alcohol could turn a man into a garrulous lover, a hostile argumentative aggressor, or he might become pensive and withdrawn.

The professional literature is loaded with information about how many people are alcoholics, how alcohol is metabolized and affects the body, alcohol associated crime statistics, the debilitating effects of chronic alcoholism, and the costs of alcohol consumption to the moral fiber and pocketbook of the nation. Not very much can be found about how people feel when they've been drinking, or how alcohol makes them feel through the various stages leading up to and through an act of sexual intercourse. Although some studies carried out under laboratory conditions have concluded that some of the ways people respond sexually after drinking is because of their expectations and not because of the pharmacological effects of alcohol, it does not mean their responses are less real or less satisfying.

Moreover, laboratory conditions are not the bedroom or the beach or the back seat of a car or wherever. No one has ever measured in a scientific way what the interaction is between the body chemistry and alcohol metabolism in a sexually aroused man or woman under natural conditions. In the absence of a scientifically designed study, the next best thing is to design a questionnaire and go out and ask people.

WHAT DRINKERS SAID

Alcohol was the most commonly mentioned drug of all those that people said had an effect on their sexual function. Frequently, however, alcohol was not used alone but accompanied the use of other drugs, such as marijuana or amphetamines. We are sticking to alcohol alone in this chapter. You can find the responses of people who used alcohol in conjunction with other drugs in the following chapters.

No one said they drank alcohol primarily because of the way it affected their sexual function. Both men and women of all ages said their primary reason for drinking was social, to have a good time, to relax, or because they liked the taste. One forty-three-year-old woman, however, said her primary reason for drinking was to "inspire bravado" which she said was dependent upon the number of drinks she had. One drink was usually enough to inspire some of the bravery. With several drinks she might either submit to a sexual advance or be willing to initiate one herself. Another woman, twenty-three years old, said she sometimes needed alcohol to decrease her inhibitions and make sex more adventurous.

Only one person, a thirty-six-year-old man, said that alcohol decreased his sexual desire and arousal, and only one man said that alcohol actually increased the number of erections he had. Most men said they were difficult to achieve. All of the rest of the men and women said that alcohol increased their desire, and most of the women, unlike the men, added that drinking made them more forward or into more aggressive partners.

Alcohol-related desire seems to be situational. There is an interaction among the alcohol, the individual, and the environment, all modified by the amount of alcohol drunk. Examples of comments are: "The effects of alcohol vary with the circumstances. When there is a nice woman around, I will be more likely to flirt, but if not, I may get philosophical or grumpy or just relaxed."

"If there is no appropriate woman around, it [sexual desire] is not aroused and instead I get sleepy."

Most of the men reported that alcohol delayed the time it took them to reach orgasms with a partner, and the younger men also commented that fewer orgasms were possible over a night. A typical comment, in this case from a forty-one-year-old man, was that without alcohol he usually reached orgasm in about twenty minutes, whereas four to six drinks either extended the time about 50 percent, or he didn't reach orgasm at all. A thirty-year-old man also mentioned the diminished quality of alcohol influenced orgasms: "The quality is such that it is sometimes unclear whether or when I have had one."

Only occasionally can a man distinguish between having an orgasm and an ejaculation. If they are normal, they occur simultaneously and are perceived to be part of the same process. It is when a man has an organic problem or has taken certain medicines that the distinction becomes clear. In these situations, a man sometimes achieves an orgasm without having any ejaculate. Alcohol does not seem to affect the ejaculation as distinct from orgasm. Both may be delayed or prevented, they may occur with diminished quality, or they may even be unpleasant.

Women, too, experience delayed orgasms after drinking, but the experience of quality is mixed: "I often do not achieve orgasm after drinking a lot, if achieved, only so-so." "Occasionally the quality and depth will increase—I will as a rule come harder after drinking." "Took patience and imagination on his part, orgasm was disappointing—finally." "Orgasm took longer to achieve—then only one—too tired—less in quality." Some women commented that they observed a decrease in the amount of lubrication prior to and during intercourse.

It seems likely that those women who are relatively uninhibited without alcohol, and find it easy to achieve orgasm, notice that alcohol diminishes their sexual functioning similar to what men experience. More inhibited women may use alcohol in moderate amounts because it seems to help them achieve orgasms which they are not as likely to achieve without some aid that facilitates their getting past their inhibitions.

The following comments were not elicited from the more formal questionnaires (see Appendix A), but from an informal survey of employees at a university medical center. The question was "What effect do you think alcohol has on sexual desire and performance?" The answers are quoted below to illustrate the wide range in responses that are evoked by such a question and some of the variations in attitudes toward and feelings about alcohol and sex.

On average, for those who drink moderately and socially, with only an occasional one-too-many, alcohol is experienced as a stimulant to sexual desire. However, no one put it better than Shakespeare in *Macbeth,* Act 2, Scene 3:

Macduff: What three things does drink especially provoke?
Porter: . . . Lechery, sir, it provokes and unprovokes; it provokes the desire, but it takes away from the performance . . .

Women

Age 23: "Well, I think a few glasses of wine really sets the mood. When I want a really super night, I do the whole bit—chilled wine, candles, and soft music—a good, but light dinner. That half bottle of wine is just right to make me feel like making love all night."

Age 25: "Hey, booze makes me feel more loving, you know, and more like having sex, but I think it makes men selfish. A few drinks and they just want to get it on, get it off, and go to sleep."

Age 30: "Of course if I really have too many, I'm sick—I have whirly beds, and I'm not interested. But with a couple, yeah, I think I'm more interested. I don't think it makes me have orgasms more often though."

Age 35: "Yeah, well liquor loosens me up, all right. But my husband, sometimes he has too many and then he wants to make love. Well, he used to take hours. It's some kind of macho thing—just like Candice Bergen in *A Night Full of Rain*, Well, I finally learned it was O.K. to just shove him off."

Age 51: "Well, when I got married, I just didn't know anything. I was so shy. Well, I found that the only time I really enjoyed sex was after a party when I'd had a few drinks. The rest of the time I couldn't have cared less. It doesn't make any difference one way or the other now."

Age 63: "Oh, I don't drink, but it turns my old man into a lover. He loves up every woman in sight. I have to grab him by the ear and lead him home."

Men

Age 20: "It all depends on how much you have, what else you have, who you're with, and where you are."

Age 22: "Hey, no effect at all. I like sex anytime, anyplace, booze or no booze."

Age 30: "Frankly, I have this tendency to, you know, come too fast before my wife is ready. So a couple of drinks really seems to help. We even have these clue words between us. 'How about a couple?' means 'How about some sex, honey?'"

Age 34: "A few drinks and the right music can increase the whole sexual atmosphere at a party—but if you drink too much, forget it."

Age 49: "Liquor? It makes me feel like I want to more, but behind it, I know I can't. As for women, who knows? I've been married twenty-three years and I still don't understand women's sexuality."

Age 56: "I used to drink a lot—I guess I was an alcoholic. When I was drunk which was a lot of the time—I was useless to my wife. Now I don't drink at all. But my wife—she has a couple and I'm pretty sure it makes sex more pleasurable for her. I don't know why. Guess she's more relaxed."

ALCOHOL AND SEX IN THE LAB

All of the surveys that have been written up in medical journals have concluded that the average person finds a moderate amount of alcohol to be an aphrodisiac.[1–5] However, not all of the information on the effects of alcohol on sexual performance has relied only on people's perceptions of their feelings and physical states. Some effort has been made to measure the effects of alcohol on sexual response in both male and female volunteers under controlled laboratory conditions.[2,3]

To measure libido in studies of male response to alcohol, a combination technique is usually used. Volunteers are asked to give their subjective opinion of the level of sexual arousal they experience, and a sensitive mechanical device indicates both the amount of time it takes them to achieve an erection, and the degree of their penile tumescence.[2] Measuring penile tumescence is simply a way to measure the size of the penis during an erection. The size of the penis as it becomes engorged with blood is believed to indicate the degree of sexual arousal.

One study involved sixteen young adult males who, after they had drunk varying amounts of alcohol, were shown erotic films depicting a variety of sexual acts between men and women. The results indicated that, on the average, the time to attain an erection did not increase until the subjects had had three drinks. However, even the first drink decreased penile tumescence about 50 percent of the degree possible without any alcohol. One of the young men could only attain 23 percent of his normal tumescence after his third drink.[2]

In contrast to those objective results obtained by using the mechanical device, which showed that alcohol depressed sexual abilities, six of the young men reported they believed alcohol increased their ability to respond sexually, and they still held that belief at the end of the experiment. The scientists conducting the experiment suggested that the delaying effect of alcohol may work to the advantage of those young men who tend to come to erection and ejaculation too quickly. The alcohol induced delay may give these men more time to stimulate their partners and bring them to orgasm. Their improved abilities as partners may lead them to believe alcohol helps their functioning. Of course it is possible that some of the young men do better in the bedroom with live partners than they do hooked up to machinery in the laboratory, watching movies.

In another laboratory study, forty-eight undergraduate men, who judged themselves to be social drinkers, were divided into two groups.[6] One group was told they were drinking malt beer and the other was told they had a nonalcoholic malt beverage. Actually half of each of the groups got the real thing and half got the fake, so that there were four groups, those with real beer who were told they had it, those with real beer who were told it was nonalcoholic, those with fake beer who were told it was real, and those with fake beer who were told it was fake. After the malt drinks were consumed, the groups listened to three erotic recordings. On one of them was a representation of mutually enjoyable sex, on the second, a forcible rape scene, and on the third, a scene representing sadistic aggression.

After hearing the recordings the men were asked to what degree they were aroused, and their responses were compared with the physical responses measured by penile tumescence. The men who believed they had drunk the alcoholic beverage regardless of whether it had actually contained any alcohol, reported a greater degree of sexual arousal during the rape and sadism tapes than did the men who believed they had had a nonalcoholic drink. Not only did they report stronger sexual arousal, but the measurement of penile tumescence confirmed it. These results suggest that beliefs about what alcohol does has a greater effect on the sexual response, at least at low levels of alcohol, than the alcohol itself. Apparently, the men who believed they had been given alcohol expected to lose some self-control, and this permitted them to respond to the tapes describing forcible rape and sadism. They were able to say to themselves, "See, it isn't my fault if I respond to these bad scenes; it's the alcohol doing it." The men who thought they had the nonalcoholic beverage felt more responsible for exerting self-control, and were able to do so, even when they had actually consumed the alcoholic drink.[6]

To measure libido in laboratory studies of the effects of alcohol on female sexual arousal and function, a similar combination of questioning and a mechanical device is used. The instrument measures the pressure of the pulse in the vagina. In one study, sixteen university women volunteers drank alcohol before they were shown an erotic film. One-half of the women were told that the alcohol would increase their sexual arousal, and the other half were told that alcohol would decrease it. The results of the experiment indicated that women believed alcohol increased their sexual responses regardless of what they were told to expect. However, as the amount of alcohol intake increased, the sexual responses of the women, as measured by their vaginal pulses, decreased.[4] Apparently, the feeling of relaxation, warmth, and loss of inhibition that accompanies moderate alcohol use is interpreted as increased sexual desire by some women, and this feeling overcomes the decrease in actual physical response.

In another laboratory experiment, the vaginal pulses of forty university women, age eighteen to thirty-five, were evaluated.[7] Twenty of the women were given alcohol and twenty were not, but as in the study of the effect of men's expectations and drinking on their sexual arousal, half of the women in each group were told they had alcohol, and half were told they had a nonalcoholic drink. Then they were shown an erotic film. On average, those women who said they felt intoxicated also said they felt sexually aroused. Surprisingly, regardless of whether the women actually drank alcohol, if they believed they did, their sexual arousal was less as measured by their vaginal pulse than if they believed they had a nonalcoholic drink. This suggests that women expect alcohol to arouse them sexually, so they exert some control to guard against it. They may have heard other women warn that they are in danger of behaving in ways that they will be sorry for later, so they are wary, which translates into decreased response, even though they are not aware of it and say they are experiencing sexual arousal. As the researchers pointed out, women are not as able as men to identify their own physical signs that indicate they are sexually aroused.

Most women say that the effect of alcohol is to disinhibit and to reduce anxiety and its associated tension. A laboratory study tried to find out whether alcohol really reduces women's anxiety, or whether it is a myth. Women may have learned from others that reduction of anxiety is supposed to happen, and so find it happening when they drink. In the experiment, some college women were given vodka and tonic, and some were only given tonic water. The drinks were mixed in the presence of the women, but one vodka bottle only contained more of the mix for half of the volunteers. After the drinks, both of the groups, the one with the real drinks and the one with the fakes, were asked some questions. When the answers of the two groups were compared, there were no significant differences between the two groups. Both groups reported that the drinks had decreased their anxiety and tension; moreover, both groups also reported they experienced an increase in sexual arousal. The researchers observed that the women were noticeably uncomfortable in the research situation, which may have accounted for some of the results. If the anxiety of the women was created by the laboratory situation, they may have been unconsciously looking for a way to reduce it. Because they believed that alcohol would reduce anxiety, they were likely to find it happening in the anxiety-provoking situation.[8]

Overall, we must conclude that a little alcohol is favorable to libido, at least mentally. It loosens people up so they permit themselves to be less inhibited. However, it tends to decrease actual physical responses in both sexes, and it delays ejaculation, which can be a benefit to some men. A lot of alcohol at once, or over a long period of time, leads to sexual problems. In one of their studies, Johnson and Masters found that a specific incidence of drunkenness or a pattern of excessive drinking was the second most frequent cause of men failing to achieve and maintain erections.[9]

HEAVY DRINKING

Alcohol is the most abused drug in the United States. It has been estimated that at least 7 percent of Americans drink enough to be classified as alcoholics. Although only a small fraction of alcoholics are skid row types, the rest drink enough to impair their work and social and family relationships.[10] For alcoholics in this group, sexual desire and performance are almost certainly decreased, and for many they are destroyed forever.

Alcohol may cause temporary or permanent frigidity, and sterility in women,[11] and impotence, sterility, and even feminization in men.[12]

Of 17,000 alcoholics treated at one hospital, at least 8 percent of the males complained of impotence. In one-half of these, the problem of impotence persisted even after years of sobriety. The damage that alcohol does can be permanent, unlike most drugs. Many of the men felt considerable guilt that they were unable to satisfy their wives and girlfriends. As an exalcoholic put it, "I drank Early Times, but the result was Old Granddad."[13]

In a study at a state-operated hospital out-patient clinic, seventy-nine alcoholic male and female patients were asked about their sex lives.[14] Although no patient was more than fifty-one years old, most said they were interested in sex only rarely, and twelve patients said they were never interested. The following are typical of comments made by the patients:

Case 1, a twenty-four-year-old male: "I don't care much for girls. I would rather be with fellows. I have intercourse once in a while. I have had it about thirty-five times in my life. But I'm not interested nor get satisfaction from it."

Case 2, a thirty-nine-year-old male: "I never go for that sort of stuff. Whenever I feel like that, I had much rather go someplace and get drunk."

Case 3, a thirty-seven-year-old male: "Sex is disgusting. You get a woman, you get infected, and the girl may get pregnant."

Case 4, a thirty-eight-year-old woman: "I have never had an orgasm."

Case 5, a thirty-nine-year-old woman: "I have no sexual feelings toward men; in fact, I don't like to have anything to do with sex."

Alcohol use may mask already existing sexual problems or it may decrease the interest in sex altogether. These reports are a clue that many alcoholics had sexual problems before turning to drink. Others have less sexual satisfaction, but do not have different attitudes toward sex than nonalcoholics. Alcoholic men may in fact have more interest in sex than other men, but find sex disappointing because they are impotent some or all of the time, and have trouble finding sexual partners.[15]

Alcoholics may refuse to recognize that booze is affecting their sexual abilities. In one laboratory study eight male alcoholics were given four drinks as they watched an erotic movie.[16] None of the men said that they would be affected by that much alcohol, but they were wrong. Each experienced a decrease in his penile tumescence which was correlated with the amount he drank. Thus, alcoholics may not recognize the effect alcohol has on them until they are almost nonfunctional.

Some individuals, both men and women, have homosexual tendencies, and they may use alcohol to mask or cope with their feelings of inadequacy and guilt.

However, it is difficult to know whether alcoholism causes sexual problems, whether sexual problems cause alcoholism, or whether other problems cause both. For example: Although homosexual women are more likely to be alcoholics than heterosexual women, there is no reason to believe alcohol causes homosexuality. The extra stress put on homosexuals in society may cause them to become alcoholics.[17]

Chronic alcoholism may change secondary sex characteristics and cause aggressiveness in men by interfering with the production and metabolism of the male hormone, testosterone. As early as 1926, there were reports of finding feminization, shriveled testicles, and breast development in male alcoholics.[18] Alcohol can also alter the distribution of body hair, so that a man becomes more feminine in appearance. The development of secondary female characteristics is directly associated with decreased levels of the male hormone, testosterone.[19,20]

Even in cases where the testosterone circulating in the blood is not decreased, alcohol can lead to infertility. Apparently alcohol has a direct effect on the testes which causes atrophy and decreased or no sperm production.[21]

In a study under controlled laboratory conditions, alcohol was given to eleven normal male volunteers, aged twenty-one to forty years, over a four-week period. All of the men had significant reductions in testosterone in their bodies at the end of the study.[19] Eight males, aged twenty-eight to forty-seven years, who had been heavy drinkers for at least five years were also studied. After six days without alcohol, they were given up to a quart of liquor a day for ten days. Following this drinking period, they again spent about a week without any alcohol. It was found that all of these men had significantly decreased testosterone levels during their drinking periods.[20]

Because of finding feminization so frequently in older male alcoholics, some people used to believe that alcohol was used by already effeminate men to help them cope with their problems of sexual identity. However, a study of 144 adolescent boys and girls did not support this theory. Nondrinking boys represented themselves as more feminine than drinking boys. Indeed, heavy drinking among boys was associated with "machismo." Among girls, there was no relationship between drinking and their perception of themselves as relatively feminine or masculine.[22]

Chronic alcoholism has a devastating effect on the sexual function of women too. Alcoholic women seem to lose their interest in sex, although it is likely that the relationship is circular. Sexual problems may be part of a set of social problems that lead to drinking which then creates more sexual problems, and so on. There is no reason to believe that the preexisting sex problem was lack of libido. In women it may be guilt for having sexual desires that they've been taught are bad or evil and should be suppressed. Alcoholic women are likely to have little appeal as sex partners, which further lowers their self-image and increases the chance that they will continue to drink.

If drinking becomes heavy and chronic, eventually the hormonal cycle of women is so disturbed that their menstrual periods stop and, of course, they become infertile.

ALCOHOL AND SEXUAL CRIMES

Because alcohol decreases the amount of testosterone, which has been thought to be responsible for sexual aggression as well as secondary sex characteristics in men, it seems logical that alcohol should decrease the chance that a person would commit a sex crime, but this is certainly not the case. Up to 50 percent of convicted rapists had been drinking heavily before committing their crimes, and about a third of these could actually be classified as alcoholics.[23]

The relationship among alcohol, testosterone, and sex-related crimes is very confusing. Alcohol apparently releases deep-seated angers and hostilities, and removes whatever block existed to prevent those angers from becoming aggressive crimes of violence; moreover, high levels of testosterone have frequently been found in persons who have committed rapes or crimes against children.

To explain the puzzle, scientists have come up with a new theory about testosterone and its relationship to aggression. Scientists noted that both alcohol and marijuana had been reported to decrease the levels of testosterone in the body. However, people who drink tend to get aggressive while people who smoke grass become passive. Therefore, it appeared likely that alcohol increases or releases another factor that accounts for aggression.

By performing experiments in the laboratory in which subjects were given various amounts of alcohol, some researchers came up with the theory that another hormone, known as luteinizing hormone (LH), causes the alcohol-related aggression. The theory suggested that when people drink, LH levels increase in the body while testosterone levels decrease, but when people smoke marijuana, both the level of testosterone and the level of LH decrease.[20] More recent experiments with marijuana, however, have not found that it decreases levels of either testosterone or LH.

SHOULD YOU DRINK?

If you choose to drink, make sure it really is a choice, and that you remain responsibly in control. Alcohol is the only legal and socially approved disinhibitor around, but it's no secret that many people do things they're sorry for after drinking. For too many couples, that one-for-the-road has resulted in one for the nursery. Don't get "swept away." Plan the amount and kind of alcohol you're going to have (if any) ahead of time, and stick to it. Then sip up, and enjoy your own and your partner's sexuality.

Drinking too much too often? Stop fooling yourself. Get professional help before you've permanently altered your sexual abilities and thus permanently damaged one of life's greatest—and cheapest—pleasures.

10

MARIJUANA: WHAT IT DOES TO YOUR SEX LIFE

And then followed a dream of passion like that promised by the Prophet to the East. Lips of stone turned to flame, breasts of ice became like heated lava, so that to Franz, yielding for the first time to the sway of the drug [hashish], love was a sorrow and voluptuousness a torture, as burning mouths were pressed to thirsty lips, and he was held in cool serpent-like embraces.

Alexandre Dumas: *The Count of Monte Cristo.*

The United States *Dispensatory,* published in 1851, stated, "Extract of hemp is a powerful narcotic causing exhilaration, intoxication, delirious hallucinations, and in its subsequent action, drowsiness and stupor, with little effect upon the circulation. It is asserted also to act as a decided aphrodisiac." The *United States Pharmacopeia,* which contains the most selective listing of the nation's drugs—no drug is admitted without the approval of a panel of independent expert physicians and pharmacologists—contains a monograph on "Extract of Hemp from 1850 to 1942." In the first half of this century, marijuana was prescribed for a wide range of medical conditions ranging from gout to insanity, and especially for migraine headaches, and was contained in six widely prescribed products.

Six major government commissions, the last one being the National Commission on Marijuana and Drug Abuse in 1970, have carried out independent investigations of marijuana use. Their conclusions are remarkably similar. Why do people smoke marijuana?

"Simple pleasure, similar to that claimed for the moderate use of

MARIJUANA

Scientific Name	*Active Ingredient*	*Street Name*	
Cannabis indica	Cannabidiol	bang	marihuana
Cannabis ruderalis	Cannabinol	bhang	marijuana
Cannabis sativa	Tetrahydro-cannabinol (THC)	charas	Mary Jane
		crystal-T	Mary Weaver
		dagga	m.j.
		dawamsec	moocah
		dope	mota
		ganja	mu
		goof balls	muggles
		gouge	muta
		grass	pot
		grefa	punta roja
		hash	red oil
		hasheesh	reefer
		hashish	sinsemilla
		hemp	smash
		herb	stick
		Indian hemp	tea
		kif	thai stick
		maconha	weed

alcohol, or food, or sex, is frequently offered as the general explanation for most current drug [marijuana] use."

"A major factor appears to be the simple pleasure of the experience. . . . We do it for fun. Do not try to find a complicated explanation for it. We do it for pleasure."

"In the case of cannabis, the positive points which are claimed for it include the following: it is a relaxant; it is disinhibiting; . . . increases sensual awareness and appreciation; it is a shared pleasure . . ."

The moral outrage against marijuana in the early part of this century, which led to the ban of the drug, was not based on its use in medical practice, but because of a social revulsion against people using drugs recreationally. Alcohol was well entrenched in American society and survived prohibition as a legal psychotropic drug. Marijuana did not.

Next to alcohol, and often with it, marijuana is the most commonly used recreational drug in the United States and probably the world. By 1970, the government's estimate of the number of citizens who had tried it was twelve to twenty million, which at its upper limit is almost

10 percent of the population. A more recent survey performed by NIDA (National Institute of Drug Abuse) of HEW found that nearly 10 percent of high school seniors smoked grass on a daily basis, with nearly a third of students this age having smoked it at least once during the month before the survey. About half of students in professional schools, medicine and law, are believed to use marijuana on a regular basis.

Nor is grass the special turf of students. A study carried out of San Francisco residents in the late sixties concluded that marijuana smoking was related to age, but that within each age group just as many nonstudents were smoking grass as students.[1] It's apparent that those who began smoking marijuana in the sixties as students are now adults in businesses and professions so that as *The New York Times Magazine* said, "The most important reason for the sudden outbreak of marijuana use in the adult working world is that young people have grown older."[2] The author of the article went on to say that he had interviewed four psychoanalysts who belonged to the New York Psychoanalytic Society, and they agreed that 95 percent of their colleagues in their own age group used marijuana and that all whom they knew under thirty-five years of age smoked pot on a regular basis, many of them every day. The incidence of marijuana use was reported to be similar among psychiatrists in Boston. Because sexual activity is also a widespread activity, it is certain that hundreds of thousands and probably millions of Americans have had sexual experiences while high on marijuana.

But is marijuana an aphrodisiac? The mere fact that many people have sex after smoking grass does not make it one. Most grass smoking is not followed by sexual activity. The predominant pleasant effects of marijuana for most people is not sexual arousal but garrulousness, giddiness, warmth, mild euphoria, bouts of hilarity, heightened sense perceptions, enhanced visual and musical perceptions, time distortions, a feeling of good will, and what may be best described as a serene "spaciness."

Nevertheless, marijuana is probably as close to being an aphrodisiac as any legal or illegal drug available. And that is if aphrodisiac is defined as a drug that modifies the experience of sexual activity in pleasurable ways. Marijuana affects perceptions and feeling states during sexual activity; at the most it may be predispositional to sexual activity under certain conditions; it does not cause people to commit sexual acts or crimes. As one scientist has commented, the problem is semantic. Does aphrodisiac mean to enhance manifest impulses, or does it mean to trigger preexisting impulses?[3] Marijuana, it seems, fits the former but not the latter definition.

WHAT'S THE EVIDENCE?

Not only because of its widespread use, but because of the frequent mention of marijuana in association with sex in Middle and Far Eastern erotic literature, and because of its popularity with the love generation of the sixties, some scientists have tried to investigate the relationship of pot to sexual function. Because marijuana is an illegal drug, it is very difficult to perform the kind of experiments in the lab that have been done with alcohol, where sexual arousal is measured in terms of penile tumescence and vaginal pulse rate. It has only been since 1970 that a standardized marijuana, grown at the University of Mississippi under a government contract, has been available to researchers who need to know the exact amount of the active ingredients in any natural substance that is used in an experiment. As you can imagine, most of the federal pot is smoked by monkeys and rats, who are then "sacrificed," so their brains and other organs can be studied. Providing standardized grass to researchers who wish to study its effects on the sexual function of humans has a low priority, certainly far behind studies of the effects of marijuana on glaucoma and anticancer drug-induced nausea. Consequently, the sex and marijuana research that has been done has consisted of interviewing persons who are willing to admit they have used marijuana and are willing to reveal their perceptions of how it affected them sexually.

In the late sixties, Dr. Erich Goode of the State University of New York asked two hundred marijuana users to fill in a twelve-page questionnaire about how the drug affected them.[4] Almost 70 percent of the respondents said that marijuana enhanced their sexual response. Fewer, but more women than men, said that pot could excite their sexual interest. Half of the women and 39 percent of the men said that smoking marijuana could make them more interested in having sex, but this was only if the person they were smoking with was sexually desirable. If the person they were with was distasteful, the effect of marijuana was to make the person more repugnant. It seems that grass can not only heighten senses of smell, taste, and hearing, but can exacerbate sexual desires of some persons for others.

Both women and men said that grass had a pronounced effect on the quality of their physiological response during sexual intercourse. Women used terms like "intense," "ecstatic," "rhapsodic," some saying they experienced orgasm for the first time with grass. They said that grass made sex more beautiful, more spiritual, that there was greater sharing than without it. One woman stated that the quality of her orgasm was related to the quality of the marijuana. At its best, she felt "little tongues of flame licking at the clitoris, rippling back and forth in waves, radiating through my genitalia and on to my entire body. It was system total. Usually like a brief sunburst and sunset . . . this was a continuum of sensation. I could actually feel it taking me over—as if I were surrendering to it."

Men said smoking grass extended the time of foreplay, that sex was more adventurous, that they could go on and on, lingering, enjoying every detail of the experience, that they had more control over ejaculation, and that when it happened it was a total, intense, orgasmic experience. One man said that sex lasted longer "by the clock."

Regular marijuana users said they were more sexually affected than those who had only used it a few times. This difference suggests two possibilities. Perhaps those who use marijuana only occasionally are more closely monitoring their feelings and are thus more aware of and distracted by the wide range and variety of their sensations. Or it may be that marijuana has more positive sexual effects on some persons than others, and that an initial positive experience has encouraged them to continue to use grass to enhance and explore its relationship to their sexual function. Undoubtedly the kind or quality of grass, the way it was smoked, whom it was smoked with, and when it was smoked contributed to the likelihood that an individual would find pronounced aphrodisiac properties in grass. A third possibility is that marijuana cannot further disinhibit those who are already disinhibited. For those who find it possible to attain full expression of their sexuality easily, openly, and joyfully, the marijuana may be perceived as an unnecessary and even unwelcome intrusion.

Goode offered another reason, suggesting that the aphrodisiac "myth" itself is influential. He said that when a man and woman smoke marijuana together, they already share a covert understanding and expectation. There is a tacit agreement that if they smoke together, they will bed together. Women, who are more reluctant to reveal frank sexuality, having been inhibited by societal prohibitions, may be able to use grass as an excuse for their behavior, thus absolving themselves from guilt and blame because the marijuana was responsible. Also the general circumstances in which two people are sharing an illegal activity may contribute to an excitement that is translated into a general feeling of euphoria and sensuality. Moreover, as Wells has commented, "If the individuals are relative strangers, then sexual abandon is probably a less likely sequel than if they are already sexually familiar with one another and experiment in the use of the drug."[3]

In another survey investigating the sexual effects of marijuana, 750 questionnaires were given to students who were asked to pass them along until they fell into the hands of "experienced" marijuana users, i.e., those who had smoked grass on twelve or more occasions. Just over a fifth of the questionnaires were mailed back in, and of those, 72 percent of the marijuana users said they had also taken LSD. Most of the persons wrote that marijuana very favorably enhanced their sexual pleasure, reporting in particular that their orgasm had developed new and more exciting qualities. They felt that the quality of their interpersonal relationships was improved, as well as physical sensations such as touch and taste. Commonly they reported that their sexual desire was increased in those situations where they would have been at least somewhat responsive, and that marijuana did not affect their sexual desire in those circumstances where it was inappropriate or if they did not like the persons who were potentially available. The survey concluded that "for practically all experienced users, marijuana intoxication greatly intensifies the sensations experienced in sexual intercourse."[5]

In a 1973 survey of students at the University of California at Berkeley, 71 percent of students had tried marijuana and a third of students smoked it at least weekly. Three percent used it several times a day. Forty percent of marijuana smokers found it "very satisfying," which compared to only 29 percent of alcohol users who found drinking "very satisfying."[6]

Someone once remarked that the whole of American psychology is built on the responses of college students. That is nearly the case with sex and marijuana investigations. There are two more surveys of college students. In one of them, of sixty-two men aged twenty-one to twenty-seven years, the scientist carrying out the survey tried to find out if there were any psychological or other differences among three groups: those who were chronic users of marijuana, those who had never used it, and those who were occasional users.[7] He was unable to detect any significant differences between the group of twenty-five men who had never used marijuana, and the group of twenty-eight "sometimes" users. However, the nine chronic users in the group were different in two respects. They tended to regard marijuana as the single, strongest factor determining the pattern of their lives, and they were more likely to have formed a stable relationship with a woman, either a wife or girlfriend.

Eighty-four graduate students, over three-fourths of whom were male, were queried about the effects of marijuana on their sexual enjoyment in the late 1970s.[8] Most of the subjects had used marijuana more than fifteen times, and about two-fifths of the group had had sexual intercourse while they were "stoned." Almost 90 percent of the experienced smokers said they believed that grass increased their sexual pleasure, and more than half of the nonsmokers believed that it did. The majority felt that smoking grass did not affect the frequency of sexual intercourse in either direction. As shown in the table below, almost half of the experienced smokers believed that when they were stoned, they were able to increase the pleasure of their partners. Although 42 percent of the experienced smokers said that being stoned increased their satisfaction and enjoyment of oral-genital sex, three-fourths of them did not believe being stoned contributed to their engaging in more varied sexual behavior. Very few of the graduate students asked believed that smoking grass could either decrease their sexual pleasure or have any deleterious effect.

THE EFFECTS OF BEING STONED ON THE SEXUAL ACTIVITY OF FIFTY-NINE EXPERIENCED MARIJUANA USERS.

*Questions**	
When you are stoned:	*Yes*
Is your partner's pleasure increased?	48%
Is oral sex more enjoyable?	42%
Do you engage in more varied sex?	24%
Do you have oral sex more often?	36%
Is the intensity of orgasm increased?	58%
Is there more pleasure if you and your partner are both stoned?	76%
Marijuana increases sexual pleasure and is therefore an aphrodisiac	61%

*Table adapted from information in Dowley (see note 8).

The only survey reported in medical journals that was not primarily made up of college students consisted of hippies who attended the free medical clinic in the Haight-Ashbury section of San Francisco.[9] The director of the clinic asked known heavy drug users about the aphrodisiac properties of the various drugs they were using. Twenty-five men and twenty-five women were interviewed. Forty of the fifty men and women said that grass was the drug that most enhanced sexual pleasure. They said that sexual pleasure is only decreased in those few persons in whom marijuana causes anxiety or mild paranoia. On balance the consensus for the relationship of sex to grass is "It's the one drug that's better than natural."[10] As one person put it, "Alcohol may make you think you want to more, but when you do it, you don't do as well. With grass it's just the opposite. It doesn't make you want to do it more, but when you do, it's better."

HOW DOES IT WORK?

Although most people think of marijuana or grass as the dried leaves that are smoked in cigarettes or pipes or bongs (water pipes that cool the smoke), the powdered leaves and seeds are sometimes eaten, and the resinous hashish and hash oil are also smoked. Hashish or hash is the resinous exudate that is scraped from the leaves of the cultivated plants. Hashish is from five to ten times more potent than marijuana. Hashish and hash oil are the cannabis products that have the potential of producing hallucinogenic and psychoticlike symptoms on a regular basis.

Hash oil contains a much higher percentage of active ingredients, chiefly THC (tetrahydrocannabinol) than hash. Most of the marijuana available on the street contains from 3 to 5 percent THC and it may be less than 2 percent. "Good" hash, from plants grown in Afghanistan, starts out with 8 to 15 percent of THC but by the time it reaches the States oxidation has markedly reduced the amount of active ingredient. The THC ratio of hash oil to hash is about five to one and to grass about twenty-five to one. According to *High Times*, the oil is made by boiling powdered marijuana leaves or hashish in alcohol, either methyl or ethyl. The oil dissolves in the alcohol which is then strained from the fiber parts and when the alcohol evaporates, the oil is left. Besides THC the oil principally contains cannabinol and cannabidiol. Pure THC, which is considered to be pot's principal psychoactive ingredient, was not isolated until the midsixties. Since then about forty cannabinoids have been isolated, and it is generally accepted that the effect of marijuana depends on their balance. Although pure THC (crystal-T) is offered on the street, a buyer is more likely to get PCP, a cheap, inferior, and probably more dangerous synthetic street substitute.

The activity of marijuana is mainly that of a minor psychedelic, but the effects are complex, and the drug also possesses the characteristics of sedatives and stimulants. Space and time are distorted and other sensations—feel, sound, and smell—are increased, but only rarely at high doses does marijuana induce hallucinations, in which the sense of reality is temporarily lost. Although THC has strong hallucinogenic properties, and although the subjective experience is similar, its chemical structure does not resemble that of any of the other known hallucinogens, such as LSD, DMT, PCP, STP, mescaline, or psilocybin.

The percentage of THC in the plant is related to the plant's sexuality. There are male, female and even hermaphroditic cannabis plants. The most potent grass comes from mature female plants that have not been pollinated. If all of the male plants are destroyed, sinsemilla (Spanish for without seeds), whose well-developed flowering tops are coated with glittery starchy THC containing resin, is produced. If the female plant is pollinated it stops making the potent resin. That George Washington wrote in his diary about the removal of the male plant from his hemp crop is sometimes cited as evidence that more than Indian tobacco may have been smoked by the Founding Fathers. Others disagree, citing evidence that removing the male plants following pollination was believed to increase the seed yield needed for the following year's crop.

In addition to the anxiety state and feelings of fear and paranoia that marijuana produces in some people (bad trips!), other unpleasant side effects that have been associated with smoking grass are giddiness, rapid heartbeat, elevated blood pressure, loss of memory, delusions, nausea, throat and chest pains, dry mouth, and cold hands and feet.

It is hard to classify as good or bad that side effect known as "the munchies." Since most Americans are dieting, it's probably viewed with mild but amused displeasure.

There is a raging debate over whether the time of foreplay and intercourse is really extended by marijuana intoxication, or whether the couples involved have had their sense of time and space modified so that they only perceive they are taking more time.[8,11–13] Some persons feel their consciousness is altered like a slowed-down movie so that they feel disembodied and floaty and all movement has a dreamlike quality. Some may begin to feel depersonalized and unreal or lost in time. This sense of time distortion is so common that individuals sometimes add "by the clock" when responding to a question about the effect of being stoned on the duration of intercourse.

The argument over whether more time is really spent on a sexual activity seems silly. It is the perception of reality that matters. A "separate reality" as argued by Carlos Castaneda is no less in its implications and consequences for those who experience it.

In addition to time distortion, the principle effect of marijuana that contributes to increased sexual pleasure is probably that of touch. As Gawin has argued, the subjective sensory enhancement that is felt is an increase in sensuality which has implications for persons who are so inhibited they feel little or nothing in response to their partner's nongenital caresses.[14] Sex therapists rely on exercises in which the whole body is stroked and aroused, but some persons are so inhibited they cannot respond. Some individuals have been able to learn total body erotic pleasure after using marijuana before sexual intercourse. Dr. Gawin urges that a systematic study of sex and marijuana be undertaken to see what valuable results may be obtained. Apparently, as with women who experience orgasm for the first time while high, feelings that are experienced under the influence of marijuana are learned and may be repeated more easily at a later time without marijuana.

The most important sex organ is the mind. If a drug like marijuana affects the mind, it is a certainty that it will affect sexual function too. Whether the effects are perceived as good or bad depends on preexisting states, circumstances, and moral judgments.

"Sexual orgasm has new qualities, pleasurable qualities. When making love I feel I'm in much closer mental contact with my partners; it's much more a union of souls as well as of bodies. I have no increase in sexual feeling unless it's a situation that I would normally be sexually aroused in, and then the sexual feelings are much stronger and more enjoyable. I feel as if I'm a better person to make love with when I'm stoned."[12]

The above remarks are attributed to a college student by Dr. Solomon Snyder, Professor of Psychiatry and Pharmacology, of The Johns Hopkins University School of Medicine. They are typical of the kind of responses made by people when they are asked the general question "How does marijuana affect making love?"

WHAT WOMEN SAY

All of the women who filled in one of the questionnaires (Appendix A) said they had used marijuana more than ten times. The youngest was twenty-one, and the oldest was forty-six. Few women said that they smoked marijuana primarily for the way it affected them sexually. Typical responses were:

"Social enjoyment—I like the reaction."

"I enjoy smoking grass and do so most of the time."

"Just to have a good time."

"To relax."

"Enjoyment, relaxation—it's really part of our life-style."

"Relaxation, or as part of a social function."

"Because it made things flow easier; for several years now I've had difficulty unwinding and relaxing to get into sex."

"Just to get high."

"Enjoy sensation. Never used for the purpose of improving sexual function."

"To relax, be social; because I enjoy the way it makes me feel."

Two of the women said they sometimes used marijuana for its effects on their sexual function. One, aged forty-three, said, "At my age, sex is sometimes boring. I like to smoke grass to change the experience. I get more excited just thinking about it." Another said, "When alone with my lover—it made me feel closer to him and more in love with him."

Women use grass at parties or under the same kind of circumstances and apparently for the same kinds of reasons that people have a drink. The reasons are hedonistic, but do not represent any unusual association of drugs with sex for most women.

However, there are some women who get high so commonly, and have been doing it for such a long time, that they can't say what effect the drug has on their sexual response, because they don't know what it is like to have sex without being high:

"Because I've been smoking marijuana regularly for about eight years (since age sixteen) I don't remember the last time I had sex without it. It relaxes me. Due to the fact that I've been getting high and having sex for about the same amount of time, I couldn't image one without the other."

Grass is more likely to be reserved for use in a group than alcohol. Women will have a drink alone, but grass is usually to be shared or at least used in the company of others:

"I almost always reserve marijuana for social gatherings. . . . I'd be more inclined to use alcohol by myself rather than at a party."

"I sometimes have one joint at home—my partner does not smoke."

"We usually smoke three joints a day varying with how many people are with us—if we're with a large group more pot is smoked."

"A moderate dose of fairly high quality cannabis at parties as well as alone with a lover."

There was quite general agreement among the women that marijuana increases sexual desire and arousal in those circumstances in which they had already decided they were going to make love.

"Nothing happens on grass that isn't going to to begin with."

But, "Sometimes it makes sex more adventurous."

Once the decision is made, marijuana "makes me horny and generally makes me desire long-drawn-out foreplay and intercourse."

"Desire was increased greatly; felt more relaxed and, therefore, better able to be aroused; arousal time *seems* to be longer than usual but actually is not; touching and kissing seem more sensual and more arousing."

"Increases desire and feelings of closeness."

"Increases physical sensations, so sex is more intense; it becomes totally absorbing."

"Lessened my inhibitions and subsequently increased my arousal and passion."

"Increased gratification."

"Increased the number of times I can get aroused."

"It helps take away sexual tension, so I am able to achieve a new sexuality; I used to make love in the dark but not now, but I don't look at it as a necessary crutch."

"It breaks down my feelings of isolation and releases my libido."

"Enhanced my sexual desire and I had more energy to put into it, but my arousal level seems to be about the same."

"Foreplay is better than usual, and unless I'm extremely tired, I can usually last much longer."

Only one woman, aged twenty-four, said that marijuana sometimes lessened her desire and arousal.

The effect of marijuana on orgasm is extraordinarily mixed. Some women say that there is no effect at all, others say that orgasms are reached sooner but that quality is not affected; others report a marked effect—increase in orgasmic intensity and number of orgasms and so on. The wide range of responses suggests that the women who filled in the questionnaire have reported the actual perceptions of their experiences and not what they have learned from others is supposed to happen.

"The drugs [alcohol and marijuana] increase my desire for sex but they don't actually cause me to climax faster or have more orgasms, nor do they improve quality."

"More intense orgasms—it's easier to let loose and enjoy orgasm—but with very excessive use, am unable to achieve any orgasm."

"It takes me less time to reach my single orgasm when under the influence of pot. The quality is not significantly different."

"Orgasm achieved at normal time expectancy two to ten times."

"Regular orgasms and similar timing as when drug not used."

"Orgasms vary—sometimes within a minute, but can be extended to fifteen minutes to achieve. Usually have one per sexual contact—often intense and long lasting."

"I don't always have one. If I do, the intercourse usually goes on for a long time beforehand."

"Orgasms were more intense—sensitivity is definitely heightened."

"Makes the orgasm more intense."

"Increases the number of orgasms which are also stronger."

"Length was increased, or rather desire for act to last a long time."

"Longer to achieve than under normal circumstances. Often more than one and the quality is much better. Alcohol lessens quality."

"It is not as difficult to achieve orgasm when I'm high. . . . I find sex more enjoyable when high, even if an orgasm is not achieved."

"It took longer than normal for both of us to achieve orgasm—there was no change in the number or quality of my orgasm."

Only one of the women mentioned having unwelcome side effects. She observed that marijuana seemed to dry out the lining of her vagina as well as her mouth, and for her, this detracted from the experience of intercourse.

A twenty-three-year-old said she believed that for her, as a moderate marijuana user, marijuana functioned chiefly to "decrease the inhibitions associated with various aspects of sex. . . . Verbal communication during sex is much easier when 'under the influence.' I'm much more relaxed, and feel more comfortable about verbally expressing myself. I think part of the reason for this (aside from the direct effects of the drug itself) is that when I've been smoking I have an 'excuse' for any behavior I don't normally indulge in. My normal sexual functioning is relatively unaffected (i.e., the quality or number of orgasms) by pot use. My enjoyment of the whole is increased by use of drugs because I am more able to explore those areas of sex in which I am inhibited."

Two of the female respondents commented on how they perceived pot affected the sexual function of their partners, one saying that marijuana alone didn't seem to impair their functioning, but that the combination of pot and alcohol could prevent her partner from reaching a climax, the other saying she believed pot enhanced the quality of her partner's orgasms. Few women reported masturbating when high, but those that did said they had reponses similar to those with a partner.

"Can achieve orgasm much quicker when masturbating and can come continually for five to ten times. Orgasms are intense but short lasting—usually want to do it again."

"Not as much fun without partner."

"Masturbated using vibrator. [Marijuana] Relaxed me in order to achieve maximum pleasure."

One of the women commented on the difference between smoking and eating marijuana, saying in effect that smoking is better for sex, because it's easier to control the amount you get and it works faster.

"A small amount of grass is good for sex, but if I have too much, I'd rather just sit around and tune in to the sights and sounds."

Only one of the women commented on the distinction between the grass "we usually get" and "high quality hash."

"High quality hash changes everything in the most wonderful way so that I love everything and especially sex when I'm really high. Everything is languid and your body feels like it's floating in space. All of your body is alive—every lingering caress is a delight. If you look in the mirror you can see yourself moving like in a slow motion movie. You hear your voice more inside your head, and others sound more tinny. It's not frightening at all because you know what you're seeing is created by the drug and you're not out of touch with reality. You feel you would like it to go on forever, and that you'd like everyone to feel it with you and to be happy with you. Orgasms rise up and go on and on—you feel every part of them all over your body—your skin is so sensitive it's an exquisite pleasure to be touched. Finally you float off to sleep, and when you wake up it is a wonderful memory and you wish your body were light and floating again. I think a lot of women try grass and don't feel very much, if anything, so they think it's all humbug. They don't know what they're missing."

WHAT MEN SAY

"Moreover the sentiment of love itself could not have intensified the bliss, and a hashish Romeo would have forgotten his Juliet. I must acknowledge that for a *hachichin,* the loveliest lady of Verona is not worth the bother."[15] Thus wrote Théophile Gautier of his experience at a gathering of the all male Club des Hachichins in Paris in 1844. The specialty of the club, whose members included Victor Hugo, Honoré de Balzac and Charles Baudelaire, was a kind of green jam called *dawamesc* whose principal ingredient was hashish. So much for hashish as an aphrodisiac. However, the lack of romantic inclination may have lain with Gautier and the lack of a proper stimulus. Baudelaire wrote that "Hashish will be for a man's familiar thoughts and impressions a mirror that exaggerates but is always a mirror,"[15] and went on to say:

> What about love-making? I have heard people actuated by a schoolboy inquisitiveness ask some such questions of experienced hashish-takers. What can become of the intoxification of love, powerful though it be in a man's natural state, when shut within this other intoxication, like a sun within a sun? . . . It is well known of course that the most common result of a man's abuse of his nerves, and of nervous stimulants, is impotence. Since then, we are not here considering physical potency, but emotion or susceptibility, I shall merely ask the reader to remember that the imagination of sensitive man, intoxicated moreover with hashish, is tremendously enhanced and as unpredictable as the utmost possible wind-force of a hurricane; and that his senses have been refined to a point almost equally difficult to determine. It is therefore permissible to suppose that a light caress of the most innocent description—a handshake for example—may have its effect multiplied a hundred times by the state of the recipient's soul and senses, and may perhaps conduce, even quite rapidly to that syncope which is regarded by vulgar mortals as the *summum bonum.*[15]

Baudelaire believed that hashish only lets out those feelings that already exist, a belief that is entirely in keeping with contemporary beliefs about the effects of the products of cannabis. "Marijuana doesn't make you do anything you wouldn't do without it," wrote one of the men who returned a questionnaire.

The ages of the men who filled in the questionnaire about their use of marijuana in association with sexual activity ranged from twenty-two to fifty-six. All but one were experienced marijuana users, and most of them said that they had used the drug with alcohol. One of the men, aged forty-eight, said he had tried smoking pot three times and the experience was so unpleasant he would never try it again. He said his heart pounded, and he became very frightened:

"The room I was in was on the sixth floor. I felt that if I got out of my chair something terrible would happen—I might fall or jump out of the window. Then my wife came home and I wanted to make love because I had heard it was great with grass and I thought it might help. But she wouldn't because she was angry with me, and didn't understand why I was frightened, and I didn't want to tell her, so I got in bed and stayed there until the feelings went away. I don't think anyone should smoke grass by themselves for the first few times."

Like the women, the men said they did not use marijuana primarily for sex, but just because they enjoyed getting high. Still they recognized the contribution that marijuana could make to sexual pleasure.

"I am extremely sensitive to THC and it's not unusual for me to hallucinate after smoking one joint. The drug enables me to enter realms of my mind which are usually repressed (or suppressed) by the demands of society. Not only are certain cerebral functions increased, but all sensations, thus sex is intensified. However, my primary reason for smoking is a fascination with my mind's ability to create, to analyze, and even to enter new dimensions."

"Being high enhances any pleasurable sensations, making the sexual act just that much more enjoyable. Sex is immensely enjoyable anyway, but being high intensifies it."

"I smoke marijuana regularly and often combine it with sex. It acts as an aphrodisiac for both of us."

"To grasp for sensitivity and awareness not normally present."

"Marijuana has an aphrodisiac effect, so sometimes I use it for this reason."

"It is just different—a separate way."

"The sexual aspects are just an added benefit to a pleasurable experience."

"Sometimes I do [use it primarily for sex] because it's good for sex—but it's also good for other things."

Men report that pot is usually smoked at parties, before parties, or with another person, one man describing the parties where he smoked pot as orgies: "With a large dose, there are large orgies, and with a small dose, there are small orgies."

"Smoking is just a way of life. There is always grass around. Most of the time I get high, I don't have sex, but most of the time I have sex, I am high."

"Well everywhere: party, alone in my room, walking or sitting outside; all circumstances; doses ranged from two hits to five joints."

Men believe marijuana contributes to their sexual desire and arousal, and particularly their ability to become stimulated. Responses ranged from a simple "increased both," to the more descriptive:

"Of all the psychotropic drugs I've used, marijuana has the greatest ability to stimulate my sexual desires, and especially after two or three successful attempts at coitus, it has the ability to renew my sexual interest. My touch becomes more sensitive, as though I had never touched the person before. My sexual desire increases and I have the opportunity to perform more coitus."

"The effect was a strong feeling of closeness with the girl even though I hardly knew her. I felt like I loved her tremendously even though we were just having sex on a one night stand."

"Usually any thought of sex while high would lead me on a pretty sustained track of desire and arousal."

"My desire is vastly increased—especially when the person was in the room and had very few clothes on."

"Although other drugs and alcohol increase my sexual drive too, marijuana seems to have the greatest effect on the height and renewal of desire and arousal."

Orgasms are reported to increase in quality as well as number, several of the men attributing the difference between sex with marijuana and without it to changes in time perception.

"Due to changes in temporal perspective, and the sensitizing nature of marijuana, orgasms are lengthy and very enjoyable."

"The time it takes to have one depends more on the person I'm with. The quality is damn good."

"The amount of time spent in foreplay and the quality of orgasm seemed to be increased. Perhaps this is due to altered time perception."

"I tend to spend more time in foreplay—massaging, performing cunnilingus—when I am high. Such foreplay tends to enhance the quality of the total sexual experience. Climax is more intense after such foreplay."

"There is more control and the orgasm lasts longer—it seems more dramatic and explosive and it feels better."

"If I am very stoned, it will prolong my orgasm but not alter its intensity."

"First orgasm achieved faster than when not high (2–3 minutes); second and third orgasms prolonged (10 minutes)."

When asked about the effect of marijuana on erections and ejaculations, the answers were somewhat more equivocal. Several men said it didn't have any effect at all, but one of these was the least enthusiastic about its effect on orgasm, saying only that "I guess it enhances its quality by opening your mind to the rush of emotions that you feel."

Others said erections were "stronger," "longer," "as many as orgasms," "increases size and hardness."

Ejaculations were "better," "maybe better—feels good," "very strong." "I tend to perceive more sensations during ejaculation when high." "Sometimes would last a long time."

Few men admitted to masturbating while high. Of those that did, a typical response was:

"Adds substantially to masturbating. Seems to stretch the rush of the orgasm out so that rather than a quickie up and down, you can lie back and enjoy the rush."

Another said, "Marijuana improves my ability to fantasize, and therefore masturbation is much more enjoyable." And another, "Time to achieve took longer than usually as a string of fantasies would go on longer than usual. Number—greater as my sheer horniness was greater. Quality—no real difference."

One man said, "Are you kidding—do you think I'd smoke dope and get horny if no one was around to give me some release?"

The perceived effect of marijuana on women was described by a few men. For example:

"Pot tends to lower inhibitions in women. Longer periods of time are spent engaging in oral sex. I have found that women spend much less time performing fellatio when they are not under the influence of drugs [marijuana and alcohol]."

Somewhat surprisingly, no man distinguished between moderate and hallucinogenic doses of marijuana or hash. Nor were any sexual partners described as "glowing like jewels," or experiences believed to be "glimpses of paradise." Either the earlier users of marijuana and hash were more poetic or pot is now used more conservatively—to get a little high, to relax, and to enjoy sex a little more. It is also possible that very little hash available "on the street" is strong enough to produce hallucinations or psychosislike states.

IS IT HARMFUL?

"Is it harmful?" is one of those questions that cries out for a question in return, "Compared to what?" It is generally recognized that anything can be harmful sometimes, at some quantities, to some people. At least three cases of deaths due to compulsive water drinking were reported in medical journals in 1979. Aspirin has caused gastric bleeding that has led to death. Almost all medicines, alcohol, and tobacco are teratogenic—they have the potential for damaging babies before they are born. Certain foods such as milk, shellfish, strawberries, produce extraordinarily violent allergic reactions in some people, causing them to swell up, to break out into hives, to have asthmatic attacks. The effects of the excessive use of alcohol and tobacco are well known.

To simply acknowledge that marijuana can cause harm justifiably earns a yawn and a "What doesn't?" The issue must be pushed farther, "To whom?" "When?" "How much?" "What kind?"

The good news is that marijuana produces no physical dependence. That means that when habitual users stop, they have no physical symptoms or cravings such as those that develop with narcotic addiction. Nor does tolerance develop. That means that people do not need larger and larger doses to feel an effect. If anything, the reverse seems to be true; habitual users need less to feel an effect. Marijuana produces no hangover or, indeed, any morning-after feelings at all.

What about the bad news? Marijuana has been accused of decreasing testosterone levels in males, of causing birth defects when used by pregnant women, of precipitating automobile accidents by impairing temporal and spatial judgments, of undermining the moral fiber of American youth by turning them into promiscuous lawbreakers and hedonists, of precipitating heroin use, and of overturning the work ethic.

Quite a stir was raised when Kolodny reported that marijuana decreases testosterone levels and causes breast development in males.[16] He claimed, in addition, that six of seventeen chronic marijuana users he studied also had lower than average (although within normal) sperm counts, and that two were impotent. However, no sooner did this study hit the press than it was attacked for its methodology and dismissed.[17] Two studies since then have not been able to reproduce Kolodny's results[18,19] relative to testosterone depression, but one did find sperm production somewhat depressed.[19] Said one wag after reading about Kolodny's study, "I always knew I was headed for a bust, but this is ridiculous."[20]

In the study that observed a marijuana-related decrease in sperm count, sixteen university students smoked five to twenty NIDA joints (2 percent THC) for a month, while hospitalized to make sure they didn't cheat.[18] At the end of the month, not only did the students show a decrease in their sperm counts, with no change in testosterone levels, but the sperm were less lively and more deformed sperm were present. At the end of the next month, which was smokeless, all had returned to normal.

The amount of THC in one to three reefers a day when given to rhesus monkeys produces a high rate of hyperactive offspring, birth defects, stillbirths, and low birth weights. Monkey studies have also shown that hormones involved in reproduction, LH and FSH, are decreased by THC at one to two joints a day. Of course, a rhesus monkey does not weigh anywhere near as much as a human, so it's likely that a higher dose would be required to produce the same effect.

Similar results have been produced in mice, rats, and rabbits. In one mouse experiment, THC totally stopped lactation. In others, lactation was decreased, but not stopped altogether.

The effects of grass on the lung and brain have also been investigated. After rats "smoked" one to two joints a day for a year, lung tissue breakdown was found, and the ability of the lung to deal with bacteria was impaired.

The brain work was also done on monkeys. After one joint a day, five days a week, for three months, a monkey brain shows evidence of structural damage and a slowing down of nerve impulses.

In one of the more interesting monkey experiments, it was found that after a placid "stoned" period of several months, chronic marijuana smoking monkeys became irritable and aggressive, and monkey mothers showed less concern for their babies than undrugged monkey mothers.

Because THC and other cannabis by-products are fat soluble like vitamins A and D, they are stored in the body and it takes a month for them to be entirely eliminated. Some people believe this is why it takes chronic marijuana users less to get high—their bodies already have some stored up.

It is true that a few persons have highly unpleasant cannabis-related experiences, usually marked by rapid heartbeat, cold hands and feet, and paranoia. These atypical responses may reflect underlying psychological states, anxieties in the individual that are somehow released by the ingredients in marijuana.

On balance, the evidence is that, except for pregnant or trying-to-get-pregnant couples, cannabis is no worse and is probably better than most recreational drugs, if used moderately and occasionally. Those physicians who write about it say doctors should convey to their patients the risks and benefits associated with the use of any medicines or recreational drugs, and that patients should then decide if they wish to accept the social and legal risks. In this respect, of course, cannabis impairs judgment and reflexes. Individuals who are high should not drive or operate any kind of machinery.

Physicians are ambivalent about the relationship of marijuana and sexual function. In a survey, 52 percent of doctors said they believed that marijuana "increased sexual pleasure or performance," and 63 thought the same for alcohol. However, 72 percent of the doctors said that a woman who used alcohol or a mood-altering drug like marijuana was "a poor choice" for a sex partner; 14 percent thought she would be hypersexed. These latter responses reflect the general feelings in society about drugs, sex, pleasure, and women.

The question of marijuana undermining society by promoting promiscuity and sensuality at the cost of other values is of course a value judgment. Many people believe that a moderate alteration of perceptions and increased pleasure in sexuality are not threats to the general well-being of the state or even the work ethic. No one has shown that students who smoke marijuana, any more than those who drink beer, have different values regarding fairness, work, honesty, achievement, and so on than those who don't.

Moreover, several studies have concluded that marijuana does not add to alcohol use like one and one make two. Marijuana users do use alcohol sometimes, but marijuana tends to substitute for alcohol use. Persons, including students, who use only alcohol, drink far more of it on average than do those who get high on grass. Some have suggested that the recent increase in alcohol drinking among high school and college students is in response to parents who sighed with relief, "Thank God, it's not marijuana." The highly regarded *Consumers Union Report, Licit and Illicit Drugs*, published in 1972, said that "A knowledgeable society, noting a few years ago that some of its members were switching from alcohol to a less harmful intoxicant, marijuana, might have encouraged the trend. At the very least, society could have stressed the advantages of cutting down on alcohol consumption if you smoke marijuana. But no such effort was made here. It may yet not be too late to present that simple public-health message."[21]

In 1894, the *Indian Hemp Drugs Commission Report* concluded that "the moderate use of these drugs is the rule, and that the excessive use is comparatively exceptional. The moderate use practically produces no ill effects. In all but the most exceptional cases, the injury from habitual moderate use is not appreciable." No evidence has appeared since 1894 to challenge this statement.

CANNABIS AND CRIME

Although young people who smoke pot and drink have more sexual activity than those who don't, studies of youth, sex activity, and cannabis have concluded that stoned students cannot be induced into sex orgies, and that even a large overdose cannot induce an individual to commit a rape, violent sex, or sexual perversions.[22] The association of teen drug-and-sex orgies is a myth.

The same conclusion was reached by the *LaGuardia Committee Report* (1939–44). The LaGuardia commission, a committee of eight physicians, a psychologist, and four New York City health officials, studied marijuana use in the city's "tea pads" and brothels, and concluded that, in opposition to much public expectation and speculation, cannabis was not a direct causal factor in stimulating debauchery, prostitution, or hypersexuality despite the fact that people were getting stoned in houses of "ill repute."

Marijuana, by diminishing inhibitions, may be like the medal given to the cowardly lion in *The Wizard of Oz:* it arouses enough bravery so that people may enter into sexual relationships. For those who have aberrant sexual problems, the relationship may be with a prostitute.

In this regard, as a psychological crutch, marijuana may be a step on the road to the use of other drugs such as heroin, given preexisting psychological problems such as a poor home relationship. Almost all marijuana users have used beer or wine and tobacco before they used marijuana. Only a small percentage of marijuana users subsequently use other drugs such as LSD or heroin. Here is one of these atypical cases:

A young teenage boy was friendly and relaxed with boys, but very shy with girls. After trying beer and wine with the boys, he tried marijuana at age fourteen and found he was much less timid. At age sixteen he tried heroin and believed it made him very successful at decreasing his anxiety when he was with a girl. As his heroin addiction increased, he began to experience delayed ejaculation. Finally he became impotent and sexually indifferent.

Marijuana did not drive this young man to heroin, his social and sexual problems did.

The strongest and saddest relationship of marijuana to sexual crimes is the result of laws prohibiting possession and sale of marijuana, and the inability of our penal system to enforce laws within prison walls. Countless young men have been busted for breaking marijuana laws and have been subjected to homosexual rape and degrading sexual acts while in prison. Thus the relationship of marijuana to sex crimes is not a product of any pharmacological property of the drug, but a product of the laws of the land. In the absence of prison reform, it is a compelling reason for decriminalization of the weed.

11

UPPERS: COCAINE, AMPHETAMINES, VOLATILE INHALANTS, OTHERS

COCAINE

Generic Name	*Street Name*	
cocaine	bernice gold dust	happy dust
	"C"	lines
	cecil	snow
	coke	snowbirds
	flake	speedball (with heroin)
	girl	stardust

"The Kogi ideal would be to never eat anything besides coca, to abstain totally from sex, to never sleep."[1]

"The C-charged brain is a berserk pinball machine flashing blue and pink lights in electric orgasm."[2]

Who can you believe, the Kogi Indians of South America, who for centuries have chewed the leaves of *Erythroxylon coca*, the tall plant once the property of Inca royalty, or William Burroughs' *Naked Lunch?* The apparent contradiction parallels that of marijuana, which at one time was declared to be an antiaphrodisiac because ascetics in India smoked it to control their sexual urges,[3] and the contemporary belief that marijuana enhances sexual pleasure.[4] Cocaine, like marijuana, does not cause anyone to engage in a sexual act or to have a spontaneous sexual response. It only modifies sexual activity and perceptions of it. If there is a value for abstention in the society in which it is used, cocaine will exert its pharmacological effects of central nervous system stimulation and appetite suppression, but it will not act as a sexual stimulant. If the societal values permit or encourage full sexual satisfaction and exploration, cocaine's stimulant effects will make people feel and respond differently during sexual activity, just as it does during other activities.

Despite their different routes of ingestion (cocaine is commonly "snorted" while amphetamines are swallowed or injected), the physiological effects of cocaine and amphetamines are very similar. Moreover, they resemble in an exaggerated way their more pedestrian cousin, caffeine. The most widely used pharmacology textbook, Goodman and Gilman's *The Pharmacologic Basis of Therapeutics* (1965 edition), said of cocaine:

> The subjective effects of cocaine include an elevation of mood that often reaches proportions of euphoric excitement. It produces a marked decrease in hunger, an indifference to pain, and is reported to be the most potent anti-fatigue agent known. The user enjoys a feeling of great muscular strength and increased mental capacity.

Goodman and Gilman (1970 edition) said of amphetamine:

> The main results . . . are as follows: wakefulness, alertness, and a decreased sense of fatigue; elevation of mood, with increased initiative, confidence, and ability to concentrate; often elation and euphoria; increase in motor and speech activity. Performance of only simple mental tasks is improved. . . . Physical performance, for example, in athletics, is improved.

It appears that if one paragraph were exchanged for the other, few would notice the difference.

The departure of cocaine from amphetamine in terms of its effects is that cocaine is a very strong local or topical anesthetic that has a pronounced numbing effect on the eyes, the gums, the inside of the nose, and other mucous membranes. For this reason, cocaine is sometimes applied to the glans of the penis. If men have a problem with premature ejaculation or merely want to have intercourse for a longer time than is usually possible, a little cocaine applied topically desensitizes and delays the time to reach ejaculation. Similarly, women may apply cocaine to the clitoris and genital mucosa or take a cocaine douche so they can have intercourse for a longer time. Those of you who are aware of the price of cocaine, from $1,600 to $2,500 an ounce or about $100 per gram, and much of this cut with inactive ingredients, would probably just as soon use cold showers. Others have solved their "problems" with topical sprays that contain benzocaine which are the sort sold to dull the pain of sunburn.

Two countries, Peru and Bolivia, grow about five million pounds of coca each year. Nine-tenths of it, usually containing less than 1 percent of the active alkaloid cocaine, is chewed by the local Indians, 90 percent of whom are estimated to use it daily. Chewing leaves of coca lifts their spirits, keeps them from being hungry, and provides them with vitamins B and C.

The alkaloidal extract is much more efficient to smuggle than the leaves, so the extraction process takes place near the coca fields in enormous vats, holding tons of leaves. The final product, one that is soluble and quickly absorbable by the mucous membranes, is cocaine hydrochloride, a refined extract of the paste dissolved from the leaves. The more it is cleaned, the more refined it becomes. Pharmaceutical crystalline cocaine must be at least 99 percent pure, but illicit "flake" cocaine is from 80 to 86 percent pure. Most of this is further cut by sugar, salt, and local anesthetic drugs for the retail or illegal market.

The recreational topical use of cocaine is probably relatively rare. Most coke is sniffed because it is absorbed quite rapidly through the mucous membranes of the nose. Swallowing is the slowest route; smoking is faster than sniffing, but wasteful; and injecting is the quickest way to get "hit."

AMPHETAMINES

Brand Name	*Generic Name*	*Street Name*	
Amphedrine Apetain Bamadex Biphetamine Desyphed Eskatrol Desoxedrine Deaxmyl Dexedrine Obedrin-LA	amphetamine dextroamphetamine	bennies black beauties black B's cartwheels Christmas trees coast-to-coast copilots dexies footballs forwards hearts L.A. turn-abouts	leapers oranges peace pills peaches pep pills pinks RJS's roses speed uppers ups white crosses
Desoxyn Methedrine	methamphetamine	bombida crank crystal	meth speed water

The first amphetamine, Benzedrine, came on the market in 1932, and by the seventies about thirty amphetamine and amphetamine combination products were available. Amphetamines were prescribed for fatigue, heroin addiction, and appetite suppression. They had several advantages over cocaine: they could be taken orally in tablet or capsule form; they had a longer and more sustained effect; they did not carry the moral opprobrium and legal status of cocaine; and patents could be obtained so they could be sold and promoted under various brand names by the drug companies. As amphetamines began to be used recreationally they had another advantage. Black market branded or kitchen and garage amphetamines could be sold for a fraction of the cost of imported cocaine and at far less risk.

Amphetamines, as drugs of abuse, and "speed freaks" came on the scene in the sixties. Chronic amphetamine, unlike chronic cocaine, users build up tolerance for the drugs so that eventually whole handfuls may be swallowed. Although excessive doses may cause psychoses, millions of Americans have taken amphetamines for nonmedical reasons with few or no ill effects. The intravenous use of amphetamines, however, is one of the most damaging sorts of drug use, leading to profound intellectual disorientation. The injectable amphetamines, methamphetamine (Desoxyn, Methedrine), are no longer available on the legal retail drug market.

The rush or high attained by snorting cocaine or mainlining speed has been compared to sexual stimulation or orgasm. When either is injected a man may have a spontaneous erection. When used before sexual intercourse, cocaine and amphetamines may facilitate a more intense experience and prolong the period until orgasm in both men and women. Women report that they experience an increase in the contractions of their vaginal muscles during orgasm.[5] These effects are dose related. Although the effects are generally correlated with the dose, larger doses being associated with more pronounced effects of sexual stimulation, increased energy, euphoria, and mental lucidity, large chronic doses often result in impotence, insomnia, confusion, and anxiety, and eventually with amphetamines, little or no interest in sex.[6]

OTHER STIMULANTS

Brand Name	*Generic Name*	*Street Name*
Ritalin	methylphenidate	Ciba
Preludin	phenmetrazine	bam

A number of nonamphetamine stimulant drugs are also on the market, some used medically for weight control, and others for hyperactivity in children. These drugs, such as phenmetrazine (Preludin), and methylphenidate (Ritalin) are also sold in the illegal market and are used alone or in combination with other drugs, such as heroin. About half of users claim that nonamphetamine stimulants are aphrodisiacs, that they greatly heighten perceptions and delay the time to and increase the quality of orgasm.[7]

WHAT'S THE EVIDENCE?

There are surprisingly few investigations into the effects of amphetamines on sexual function, and none of cocaine, except as incidental to multiple drug use reported in medical journals. There is no mention of lab research with human beings, but people who have come to drug clinics and programs have been surveyed several times. The reports of users are purely subjective and in many cases, the effects are "impure" because other drugs, especially alcohol and marijuana, were used concomitantly.

In one instance, two women, aged nineteen and twenty-two years, and one man, aged twenty-nine, all multiple drug users, were asked to tell about the effects that all the drugs they had used had had on their sexual function. Because their reports were inconsistent, i.e., the man said cocaine stimulated and amphetamines decreased his sexual drive, and one of the women said amphetamines increased her sexual desire, the interviewer concluded that there was no readily discernible relationship between drug ingestion and sex behavior, and that any change in sexual behavior that occurred after drug use was related entirely to the ability of drugs to weaken controls and inhibitions. He went on to suggest that with young persons, drugs and not sex were the focus, but that older users may be trying to capture an earlier level of sexuality through drugs or attain a level of sexuality that they never had, but they think the young of today have.[8]

In a larger study of sixty patients being treated for amphetamine abuse, a minority said that amphetamines affected their sexual functioning.[9] Nine of the forty-five patients who had been using an average of 165 mg. a day (thirty-three tablets—the average dose is three tablets per day) said that amphetamines increased their sexual desire and seven said that they associated amphetamine use with delayed ejaculation. Most of the fifteen women patients said that the drug increased their libido and let down some of their inhibitory defenses, one claiming that she became a compulsive masturbator whenever she got amphetamines. Others in the group reported engaging in marathon sex, and sadistic and perverted sexual practices such as cunnilingus with dogs. Men reported various sexual deviations, such as public masturbation, paedophilia, and penis mutilation. However, the doctor treating the patients made it very clear that these people had preexisting sexual tensions and problems that were exacerbated by amphetamines, which acted as an aphrodisiac in the very persons who needed it least.

In all of the studies of amphetamine addiction, the conclusions are similar. Both the drug use *and* the sexual pathology derive from common personality variables. Depending on the person's state before drug abuse, amphetamines will be associated with a decrease in sexual feelings, whereas in others, a marked increase occurs, sometimes accompanied by perverse sexual expression.

For example, in one group of amphetamine users, one-fifth said they had no change in libido whatever; 30 percent had a decrease, and 50 percent an increase.[5] One woman who had been frigid and had little sex experience prior to her drug use, said:

"I had more sex in six months than in my whole life. I would have a compulsion at times, and would have sex even if there were a crowd of others in the room."

And another female patient said:

"I was in a constant state of lust. My whole body felt like my sex right before orgasm. I thought they were playing with my mind. I became a nymphomaniac from a completely frigid state. I wanted men to beat me. I had multiple orgasms but no satisfaction in terms of release from tension."[5]

Of those who associated amphetamine use with an increase in libido, some said that the drug releases sexual fantasies. One man became an ardent fan of women's wrestling.

In another investigation of fourteen male and eleven female amphetamine abusers, both tended to be promiscuous, but to be generally negative and unhappy about sex, and to have low images of themselves. Men complained of their inability to "keep a girl," and women that they felt "used."[10]

Depending on the way they are taken and the amount, both cocaine and amphetamines can be used simply to increase the experience of sexual feelings and pleasure, or as substitutes for sex. Navy recruits said they used amphetamines to relieve pressure and boredom, and cocaine to enhance their sexual fantasies and pleasure.[11] When clients of the Haight-Ashbury Free Medical Clinic in San Francisco were asked, half of them said they enjoyed sexual relations more while straight than high, but three-fourths of the rest said they enjoyed sex more since they began drugs. On their list of aphrodisiacs were cocaine and amphetamines at low doses. These were said to increase libido, to decrease inhibitions, and to enhance enjoyment. At large doses, amphetamines were said to decrease sexual activity.[12]

The clinic patients who described themselves as heavy drug users said that the needle used to inject amphetamines and cocaine was a phallic symbol, and that the act of injection had marked sexual overtones. Injected cocaine was "electricity to the brain," a marked "exhilaration." If shot right before intercourse (a time that is required because of the rapid excretion rate), men could have multiple orgasms. Therefore, some men saved it for sex, and that was the reason it was called "girl" and "the pimp's drug." If rubbed on the penis for anesthesia, it prolonged sex, but sometimes resulted in priapism and could also inflame the vaginal mucosa of their partners.[13]

Thirty of thirty-six Haight-Ashbury clinic patients said that speed generally increased their sex drives, especially if used intravenously. Injected amphetamines (usually methamphetamine) gave a "flash," a "rush," the whole body was "orgasmic." Over half of the men got erections with the injection, and a few women experienced orgasms. Speed was said to be "the sexless sex drug"; users became "supermen." Both cocaine and amphetamines were associated with a "pleasure-pain" syndrome. Genitalia would be rubbed raw probably due to the inhibition of secretions; muscle spasms hurt. After amphetamine highs there were "brutal comedowns" with teeth-grinding, insomnia, weight loss, depression, and paranoia.[14]

Heavy amphetamine use can stop orgasm in men without stopping erectile capacity, but eventually it leads to complete impotence.[15]

Although athletes usually are turned on to amphetamines to give them energy and improved performance, the drug can also substitute for sex. Some male athletes believe that "old husbands' tale" that sex debilitates them physically, and that they will perform better on the field if they abstain from performing in bed. For them, the drug they take to help them play better turns into a substitute for coitus.[13]

WHAT USERS SAY

When cocaine and amphetamines are used in moderation, the primary reason is usually for the stimulation effect, the feeling as put by Aleister Crowley in *Diary of a Drug Fiend,* that "one is master of everything, but everything matters intensely."[16]

In response to the questionnaire (see Appendix A) women said:

My primary reason [to use cocaine] was:

"To feel euphoric. But this drug is a fantastic stimulant, and of course the more energy a person has, the better the sex is."

"Just to get high," but sometimes, "I've used cocaine directly on the genitals which greatly prolongs the time to achieve orgasm."

"To feel full of energy."

"To have the exhilaration."

"Just to feel great and that I can do anything and enjoy everything including sex."

"It's like getting a shot of power and confidence, so I feel more confident about sex too."

Cocaine, like marijuana, is a social drug, but probably less so than marijuana. People who would not smoke at work because of the distinctive marijuana odor can easily dip into a small box of white powder and sniff a line or two. When associated with sex, however, it's most likely to be used by a couple or a small group, where about a half to a gram, depending on the strength, will be divided between two persons.

There were mixed reports of the effect of cocaine on women's desire and arousal, a minority stating that cocaine made it more difficult to become aroused or had no effect at all. Typical remarks were:

"The drug made it harder to be aroused, but my sexual desire was higher, and after arousal, sex was much better and I felt more aggressive."

"Sexual desire was enhanced, and I had more energy to put into it. My arousal level seemed to be the same."

"It doesn't make me think about having sex more, but once I decide to, I have lots more energy to put into it, so I feel more aroused."

"I am very sensitive and extremely horny."

"It depends on who I'm with and where we are. The stimulation I get with cocaine can make me talk more, or dance more, work more, or feel like having sex more."

"Drugs such as cocaine, marijuana, and hallucinogens, seem to heighten sexual arousal."

Generally women said that cocaine had a positive effect on their orgasms:

"Orgasms were definitely better, longer and more of them; the length to achieve them was approximately the same."

"Cocaine makes everything go on forever—you really get into one thing and don't want it to stop. Everything is pleasurable. Orgasms, if achieved, are momentous and often several. Cocaine is a rare drug because of the expense."

"The best thing is to snort one to two lines (depending on the quality) and after one great orgasm, to put a little on the genitals to keep going and eventually have more orgasms."

"Increased the number of orgasms which were also stronger."

Effects that are noted with a partner are consistent with those felt with masturbation:

"Can achieve orgasms much quicker when masturbating and can come more than one time which is not the case when I haven't any drugs."

"Orgasms are intense but short-lasting—I feel like my whole body is involved instead of just my pelvic area."

"It's the only drug that gives me enough energy to want to do it by myself."

Most probably agree that:

"Cocaine is too expensive to waste by myself."

Those women who commented on it were uncertain about the effects of cocaine on their partners, one saying she thought "men have difficulty performing under the influence," and another "cocaine is like alcohol in its effect on the male, but great fun for the female, but the high is short-lived."

Two women who filled in the questionnaire mentioned taking amphetamines in the oral tablet form:

"I get too crazy to appreciate sex."

"Can have either positive or negative effects. If you're too speedy, sex is impossible and mainly not desirable. You can't concentrate on anything long enough. Sex is impossible and frustrating. If you're not too high, the effects are fast and fun. Orgasm is usually not achieved."

There is a considerable difference between taking cocaine injections and snorting it in the effect on sexual response, and the same is true of amphetamines. Most users of either are casual recreational users who exhibit not a whit of psychological dependency, meaning they are not trapped into the cycles of hyperactivity followed by depression that are associated with chronic and high dose use of stimulant drugs.

Persons who inject amphetamines, usually methamphetamine (Methedrine) report much more exaggerated sexual effects, often with masochistic overtones. For example, from Cohen's *The Amphetamine Manifesto*:[17]

"Meth orgasms are like winding a spring for hours building tension."

"Gives you convulsive total orgasms, it's like a grand mal seizure—violent spastic, involuntary contractions down to the toes."

"Like an aphrodisiac. Tightened muscles, fired sensations . . . unblocked passageway to libido . . . No filter . . . no blocking . . . no censor . . . are capable of any erotic behavior."

"I abstracted myself from my flesh, from pain. I went out with this girl; she'd gotten into a sex thing. Every time I'd get off, she wanted to get off. After I hit her, we'd wind up in bed."

"Women become ferocious in pursuit of orgasm but frustrated."

"[Methamphetamine is a] beautiful love potion; you could fuck all night with an eternal hard-on, but you can't come. You make yourself sore; it's a meat/flesh thing."

A strong shot of amphetamine can lead to "blue balls" or impotence; erections are prolonged but there is often no climax. Used over a long period of time, amphetamine transmutes the sex drive altogether.[17]

Some women start on the amphetamine road through the legitimate drug system. One woman wrote:

"You can get any kind of downs and ups from any doctor. . . . If you can bullshit, you can get anything you want anywhere in the world which I did. . . . Since I was sixteen, I used ups (black beauties, Dexedrine) to lose weight. The first time with my parents' permission. I couldn't think straight on the medication so I figured since drugs helped you I self-prescribed tranqs. But it became more advanced . . . I was doing grass, acid, ups and downs and red ones to direct the traffic. . . . Now for the reason I am writing. Drugs fuck up your sex life. They fuck up your feelings, your emotions, and in conclusion your response. You make love through a misty haze of highness. . . . Ironically I never realized how drugs were seeping into the very essence of my being. I guess I was so drugged up most of the time I didn't notice the job it was doing on my sex drive. . . . My sex drive has been coming back . . . but you must understand the very essence of sex had left me due to drugs."

More men than women, and ranging from twenty to thirty-six, told about the effects of cocaine use in response to the questionnaire, and some men also wrote about the effects of amphetamines.

Cocaine was usually taken along with marijuana or alcohol and always snorted. The drug was usually taken at a small party or in private with one other person. One man, however, said:

"After snorting coke, experienced fellatio in a nightclub beer closet."

About half of the men said they took cocaine primarily because of the way it affected them sexually, and the rest just because they enjoy the way it makes them feel. In general, cocaine heightens sensory perceptions and delays climax.

"It was offered and nobody turns down a free toot."

"I like to experiment with drugs."

"To avoid premature ejaculation."

"Endurance—to come until it hurts."

"To create a new euphoria."

"So the mind can amplify sexual fantasies."

Almost all of the men reported that cocaine increased their sexual desire and arousal, but the effect on orgasms was mixed.

"Cocaine is a strong aphrodisiac. It increased desire and aroused sexual organ."

"Prolonged them [orgasms]" and "sustained" erections. Ejaculation was "held off."

"One perfectly controlled winner."

"Loosened up inhibitions and increased my desire and performance."

"Had three orgasms. Normal size."

"Coke seems to have a more physical effect on sex in delaying orgasm and my erection doesn't shrivel as soon as normally."

"Four to five orgasms over two hours of excellent quality." Erections were "constant." "Lost track" of ejaculations.

The latter remark was made by a man who said he used a minimum of a gram and sometimes as much as two grams "at a small gathering ending in an orgy situation."

However, one man said that the dose of cocaine doesn't matter because "it's basically a head trip—and a nice one which carries over." Thus "cocaine seems to be the most pleasant." Too much amphetamine, on the other hand, "makes it impossible. Speed seems to leave you unsatisfied, ready to jump up and move on to something else. I felt rushed—also like I hadn't done anything." He went on to say that he couldn't tell if his partner's desire was more easily satisfied or not satisfied at all.

One man, an alcoholic truck driver who took amphetamines "to stay awake to make miles," wrote from prison that with alcohol alone he could get very aroused, but that "When I mixed, for some reason or another, I couldn't become aroused."

Another man, aged twenty, said he took amphetamines (and coffee) "to study" but sometimes "I do more than study," and "I become wildly aggressive." However, orgasms were said to be of "a substandard quality." He noted that "the effects are not necessarily due to the drug."

Said another, who also said he'd used LSD as well as marijuana and alcohol, "I believe that stimulant drugs have an aphrodisiac effect on either partner and can be used to release inhibitions that might otherwise be repressed. Total sexual freedom can be very rewarding."

Phenmetrazine (Preludin)—and sometimes methylphenidate (Ritalin)—is commonly used to boost the effect of heroin or methadone. Preludin, like amphetamines, may also be used alone and is perceived as a sexual stimulant by multiple drug users. A thirty-six-year-old man said:

"Preludin will stimulate you with the fact that you can't get enough of your partner. It arouses my sex drive and I have a constant erection."

CAN THEY HURT YOU?

Speed, though it rarely kills, is far more dangerous than cocaine. Cocaine, especially when taken by chewing coca leaves, causes no physiological dependence and, many have argued, less psychological addiction than caffeine. Many highly productive people have used it to increase their capacity for work and to help them feel cheerful and energetic. The director of the Harvard Botanical Museum, Richard Evans Schultes, is reported to have chewed coca daily for eight years with no ill effects.[18] In the nineteenth century, the country was awash with drinks containing the energizing cocaine, among them the famous Coca-Cola.

Persons who occasionally take cocaine in moderation do not become dependent on it. However, some individuals get into a cycle where they increase the amount they use to avoid the letdown or depressions they experience after their highs. The repeated use of large doses of cocaine produces a characteristic paranoid psychosis in all or almost all users who trap themselves in this cycle. In this sense, for these people, cocaine is an addicting drug. When persons who are customarily taking high doses of cocaine stop taking it, they may suffer from a depression from which they wish to escape by using more cocaine. A further characteristic of high chronic dose use of cocaine is the hallucination that tiny bugs are crawling around just under the skin. This characteristic is shared by amphetamines. Persons dependent on amphetamines are often seen picking at the "bugs" until their skins are raw and bleeding.

Another unpleasant side effect of cocaine is a tender, running nose. Cocaine dries up the mucous membranes initially, but eventually the irritation leads to sores and bleeding, blocked nasal passages, and finally to perforated septums which require surgery.

Cocaine is a short high, the effects of a moderate dose—euphoria, increased energy, and sexual stimulation—lasting about a half an hour. With large chronic doses opposite effects, confusion, insomnia, and impotence, may be produced.

The short-lasting effects of cocaine are a major reason it is a popular social drug. People can take it and be confident they will be "back to normal" and "ready to drive home" by the time the party or the night or whatever is over.

Although cocaine is a legal drug, its production is highly controlled, and it is almost impossible to obtain on the legal retail market. Amphetamines, in contrast, although more restricted than they once were, are widely available in tablet form under several brand names, and are often prescribed for dieting. At one time, pharmaceutical amphetamines were widely available on the black market, but tighter controls have decreased their availability, and adverse publicity has made physicians more wary of prescribing them.

That cocaine was designated a narcotic under the Controlled Substances Act at a time when amphetamines were not is attributable to history, irrationality, and the ingenuity of the American pharmaceutical industry.

Tolerance to amphetamines usually develops rapidly so that higher and higher doses are required to attain the highs that are produced by the drug's ability to release and sustain adrenaline and adrenaline-related chemicals in the body. Amphetamines are among the most dangerous and damaging of all the abusable drugs. Even moderate chronic use can cause high blood pressure, abnormal heart rhythm, irritability, insomnia, anxiety, and aggression. There is a saying that barbiturates make you feel like hitting someone, and amphetamines give you the energy to go out and do it. As use continues and dosage increases, the user develops a marked personality change, severe weight loss, and paranoid psychoses with delusions and hallucinations, and may have a compulsion to engage in repetitive, bizarre, purposeless tasks such as folding and unfolding clothing. Although the most terrible consequences are seen most often in those who inject methamphetamine, the "speed" of abusers, the same effects can be achieved with oral use. However, the gratification of shooting speed makes it a substitute for sex that is not a characteristic of the oral use, but is one of the reasons that people with depressive personalities and existing sexual problems find it attractive.

If you want to damage all of your responses, including your sexual ones, chronic high use of any drug or alcohol is a way to do it. Amphetamines, for any purpose, except possibly hyperkinesis in children, for whom they work as a sedative, have little to recommend them. Of the two principal stimulants in use, cocaine carries the least physiological risk but clearly the greater legal risk, the laws for possession and sale being more punitive, even though at least one judge, Judge Elwood McKinney, of Roxbury, Massachusetts, said in 1976 that cocaine was "an acceptable recreational drug," and that "cocaine regulation as it now stands is clearly unconstitutional," calling cocaine a "benign drug" and saying that it is "an irrational addition to federal and state narcotic laws. Cocaine is not a narcotic drug," the misclassification resulting from "generations of ignorance, from myths connected with the drug and from blatantly racist attacks on cocaine users, all of which are now destroyed by reliable scientific data."

VOLATILE INHALANTS

If your kid's got a can of Toilet Water in his room, but the room still smells like dirty socks, it isn't because the Toilet Water isn't doing its job, it's because it is doing its job. The kid, along with at least half a million other folks, is into one of the volatile inhalants, probably butyl nitrite. Judging by the list below of cute little brand names, the competition for the inhalant dollar is fierce. Notice that the list of names, probably incomplete considering the rate at which the volatile nitrite inhalants have been hitting the market, is much longer than the list of street names. This is because there was no widespread use until recently, and because one of them, butyl nitrite, is a legal nonprescription "room odorizer." Apparently, the market does not lack for manufacturers to exploit the potential demand for a cheap recreational chemical, especially among the young who like to live moderately dangerously and, in this case, sniff at authority. With butyl nitrite, they think they've really put one over.

VOLATILE INHALANTS

Brand Name	*Chemical Name*	*Street Name*
Aroma of Man	amyl nitrite	poppers
Ban Apple	butyl nitrite	snappers
Black Jac	isobutyl nitrite	
Bolt		
Bullet		
Cat's Meow		
Cum		
Dr. Bananas		
Gas		
Hardware		
Heart On		
Hi Baller		
Jac Aroma		
Krypt Tonight		
Loc-a-Roma		
Locker Room		
Oz		
Rush		
Satan's Scent		
Shotgun		
Toilet Water		

Amyl nitrite, a vasodilator, is a drug that relaxes smooth muscle so that the small blood vessels are expanded and the blood pressure is lowered. It is sometimes taken to relieve the heart pains of angina pectoris victims. Amyl nitrite also relaxes the sphincter muscles of the anus and this is one of the reasons that it is a popular drug among male homosexuals who inhale it. However, this is not the only reason that amyl nitrite is used in association with sexual function. It has a direct effect as well, producing a short but intense magnification of orgasm that is very pleasurable. Although some believe this is only because of the effect on the blood vessels of the sexual organs, others say that the subjective experience of pleasure is too great for vasodilation to be the only reason, and that there must be a direct effect in the central nervous system as well.[19–21] Thus, amyl nitrite is not an aphrodisiac in the sense of increasing libido, but in the sense of modifying the sexual experience in pleasurable ways.

Amyl nitrite, a volatile flammable liquid, was a prescription drug until 1960, when it became an over-the-counter drug. It was sold in small (0.3 ml.) glass ampules, which when crushed so that the vapor could be inhaled, made a popping noise, hence the street names "popper" or "snapper." Because of concern that amyl nitrite was being used nonmedically, poppers were again made a prescription drug after only nine years. So up popped the chemical cousin of amyl nitrite, butyl nitrite (or isobutyl nitrite).

Butyl nitrite is not licensed or regulated by the FDA as a drug, but as a "room odorizer." However, unlike the floral or spice bouquets that one has a right to expect of a room odorizer, this one stinks of stale locker rooms and unwashed tennis shoes. As a room odorizer it is total humbug. As a recreational drug it has the same action as amyl nitrite, which smells a great deal better.

Butyl nitrite is not sold in neat little ampules, but in squat, wide-mouthed, screw-capped bottles that hold less than half an ounce. The label of at least one brand entices with its warning, "Danger. Excessive use may cause euphoria." The fumes may be sniffed directly from the bottle or through an inhaler that even has a lanyard attached, so it can be carried around the neck. This lanyard probably only gets in the way during lovemaking, but it is a useful appendage for those who sniff while they're on the dance floor in the throes of disco and butyl nitrite fever.

Both amyl and butyl nitrite seem to be remarkably nontoxic. Although the death of a teenage boy who had sniffed butyl nitrite was reported in the *Washington Post* in 1979, the boy probably died because he sniffed the stuff in a plastic bag. Experienced volatile substance sniffers know that this is the surest way to O.D. (overdose) oneself to a status of D.O.A. (dead on arrival). Pharmacologists do say, however, that butyl nitrite decreases the oxygen-carrying capacity of the blood, which increases the danger in inhaling the stuff from a closed container.

Dr. T. P. Lowry, a clinical professor of psychiatry at the University of California, has reported the conclusions of a symposium on the recreational nitrites.[20] A questionnaire was sent to over 3,000 emergency room specialists and over 200 pathologists. The pathologists who responded said they had never seen a patient who had died as a result of inhaling nitrites. Only thirteen of the emergency room doctors had seen any toxic reactions and these, headache, fainting, and low blood pressure, were short-lived.

The Department of Justice has a Drug Abuse Warning Network (DAWN) which gets reports from hospital emergency rooms. Of well over a million drug-related visits that have been reported, only sixty-seven could be attributed to the sniffable nitrites. These visits were brief, no one was hospitalized, and there was not a single death. In contrast, there were 350 deaths and 17,600 visits attributable to aspirin in a recent year. In fairness, many more people take aspirin than sniff nitrites, and we are not certain what the nitrite-related visit rate would be if as many people sniffed nitrites as swallow aspirin.

When people sniff these nitrites, they feel flushed, somewhat dizzy, and their hearts pound. In other words, they have the same kind of feelings they might have from frenzied dancing without nitrites. However, with the inhalant and dancing or sex at the same time, they are really stimulated so that they feel strongly excited and passionate or wildly thrilled and ecstatic.

The most common side effect is a headache, which about a third of nitrite inhalers have experienced at least once. Other unwanted effects—nausea, nasal irritation, cough, pounding pulse, dizziness, erectile impotence, and loss of emotional control—are relatively rare; they occur in 10 percent or fewer of users. None of these effects lasts; only the headache may hang over to the next morning.[19] Although the blood pressure falls and the heartbeat rate increases almost immediately upon inhalation, they both return to normal within two minutes.

According to Dr. Lowry, who surveyed 255 nitrite sniffers living in the San Francisco Bay area, "The majority of volatile nitrite users have had at least one orgasm while under nitrite influence and report the experience to be intense, pleasurable and free of serious side-effects."[19]

Occasionally, men have a temporary loss of erection after inhaling the stuff, but that's not surprising considering that the volatile nitrites expand the blood vessels. After all, the penis is only held erect or tumescent because it is engorged with blood. If the passageways for blood expand and no more blood flows in to maintain the pressure, or if the expansion allows some of the blood to flow out, the pressure will drop and the penis will collapse just like a balloon with some of the air let out. This kind of effect, a temporary detumescence, is always pleasing to men who suffer from premature ejaculation.

Although not as visibly obvious, there's a parallel situation in women. Pooling of the blood in the genital area may be lessened so that the attainment of orgasm is inhibited. This suggests that women would not like the nitrites very much, but apparently some of them enjoy the overall body rush and heightened perceptions associated with the drug.

Actually, it's hard to imagine women sniffing something that smells like decaying gym socks, as does butyl nitrite, and finding it romantic. That may be why there are more male than female nitrite sniffers, and why male users sniff more often than their female counterparts. During his survey, however, Dr. Lowry found one woman who said she'd been sniffing amyl nitrite for twenty-six years.[20] Of course, amyl nitrite smells much better than butyl nitrite.

"Poppers" and "room odorizers" are often sniffed just before the sexual climax. This method of operation seems O.K. for men who are relatively undistractible as they approach orgasm. Forget it for women though. If women are interrupted as they proceed toward orgasm, they tend to lose their edge and must almost start over to build toward climax. An interruption to take a whiff may be more of an interference than a welcomed adjunct.

WHAT USERS SAY

Although not generally touted as an erotic arouser, the nitrites are sometimes said to lower inhibitions and to break down social barriers.[19–22]

A thirty-five-year-old male, replying to the questionnaire, said of butyl nitrite:

"All your senses are heightened. The visual is not to be believed. Looking at your partner's body, your own, or pornography is terribly exciting. Inhibitions leave as quickly as your clothes and one can become extremely inventive with oneself or one's partner. Watching and being watched is very trippy. The sex drive is so strong that all paranoia leaves and you simply get down to things. One of its greatest values is that both partners don't have to do it—but both will enjoy it. The drug does not add desire that is not already there, it simply intensifies it to the point where it must manifest itself and that can be one hell of a turn-on to the partner who is not doing the drug. She will find herself so turned on by her partner's lust that it won't matter who took the drug."

Another questionnaire respondent, also male, but older, fifty-eight years, said he used amyl nitrite to maintain rather than arouse his libido. He believes that the drug helps him in his pursuit of younger partners.

"I have unlimited sexual prowess and use poppers to stimulate young lady foxes."

His primary reason for using the drug is to "release tensions and hostilities," but also for "conquest of younger partners who can only get into sex by using artificial stimuli. I have found that the amplification of my sexual prowess by the use of poppers has increased my popularity. It is a common denominator for those younger than I am to achieve sexual release, and more importantly for them, sexual and social acceptance."

Amyl nitrite is sometimes described as a head and body trip. When sniffed just before climax, the increase in blood flow causes a warm rush to the genitalia so that orgasms seem more intense, and the mind can seem to "zoom off" for up to three to four minutes. The rush is said to be similar to cocaine but of shorter duration and greater intensity.[22] Almost three-fourths of the respondents to Dr. Lowry's survey of nitrite users (97 percent male) said that there was increased intensity of feeling during orgasm; 15 percent perceived that time slowed down, and almost one in fifty mentioned that the nitrites facilitated variations in sexual experience, such as fellatio and anal intercourse.[19]

The effects of the inhalable nitrites on women's sexual function is mixed. Although orgasm may be delayed, when it does happen it may feel more intense. Without orgasm, amyl nitrite still seems to be enjoyed. As one young woman told Dr. Lowry:

"I enjoy the sensations; my whole skin becomes sensitive; being kissed all over while sniffing amyl is like a wonderful dream, but I can't get off. I get right at the edge and then my orgasm slips away. It sounds funny, but sensuousness is all over my body, but for me orgasm has to be focused."[19]

Another, more successful and more poetic in achieving orgasms on amyl nitrite, said:

"It's like being shot through the stars in a rocket. The orgasm is truly awesome. I can feel my whole body accelerate; my climax keeps building up and building up, all the rest of the world just disappears and it seems to go on forever. Words are no good to tell you how I get lost in the sensations. My inhibitions evaporate and almost every kind of sex seems possible and desirable. My whole body throbs. In the center of my vision is The Flower, a bright yellow center with deep purple petals radiating out. With the right person, it's like a religious experience, ecstatic, transcendent."

Although the nitrites have only been getting a big play in the press in recent years, amyl nitrite has been used recreationally for over a quarter of a century. Since it is unlikely that all those people during the last twenty-five years inhaled amyl nitrite to relieve the pain of angina also had sexual experiences at the same time, it is likely that the circumstances and expectations that are associated with its use are more important than the physiological effects on the body, which are also said to include fits of giggling.

12

DOWNERS: BARBS, LUDES, HEROIN, OTHERS

As the amphetamines are to cocaine, so the barbiturates are to alcohol. Barbs, like amphetamines, are legal drugs prescribed for a variety of problems. As amphetamines mimic the stimulant effect of cocaine, so barbs mimic the intoxication effects of alcohol. Indeed, the *Consumers Union Report* titled a chapter, "Alcohol and Barbiturates: Two Ways of Getting Drunk."[1] There is cross-tolerance between alcohol and barbiturates; if you can handle a lot of one, you can handle a lot of the other. Withdrawal symptoms are the same. Hangovers are the same. Behavior is the same. Thus we should not be surprised to find that barbs affect sexual function very much the way alcohol does. Like alcohol, barbs increase desire but diminish performance.

Methaqualone, known widely under one of its brand names, Quaaludes or simply "ludes," was touted on the market as a synthetic "safer" substitute for barbiturates. In 1965 it was the sixth most frequently prescribed drug in the United States, but soon it became apparent that methaqualone carried its own risks and could also cause serious poisoning, convulsions, coma, and even death, and that continued heavy use could lead to development of tolerance and dependence.[2] Now it's rarely prescribed by doctors, but is the "love drug" of the sex and drug subculture where it enjoys considerable popularity on the illegal drug market.

There are other nonbarbiturate downers, chloral hydrate (Noctec, Somnos), glutethimide (Doriden), and ethchlorvynol (Placidyl), which produce similar sedative and sleep-inducing effects, and which some users find produce a state of languid lethargy or a depressant high which is conducive to sexual activity.

BARBITURATES

There are literally hundreds of barbiturate drugs and their combinations. The major differences among them are the variations in the length of time before they take effect and in the length of time their effects last. They are all central nervous system depressants, and until the benzodiazepine tranquilizers and hypnotics such as Valium, Librium and Dalmane, came on the market, they were the principal drugs prescribed for nerves, anxiety, and insomnia. Phenobarbital is also used to prevent epileptic seizures.

BARBITURATES

Brand Name	*Generic Name*	*Street Name*
		barbs goof balls goofers
Amytal	amobarbital	bluebirds blue devils blue heaven blues
Butisol	butabarbital	
Nembutal	pentobarbital	nimbys yellow jackets yellows
Luminal	phenobarbital	
Seconal	secobarbital	pinks red birds red devils reds seccy
Tuinal	amobarbital with secobarbital	double trouble rainbow tuies

Phenobarbital is a long-acting (up to sixteen hours) barbiturate with a relatively slow (up to one hour) onset of action; thus, it is not popular for recreational use. Any situation for which a barb might be wanted would usually be over before a phenobarb user had felt the drug's effect. Nor are the ultrashort injectable barbs popular. Their rapid onset of action, within a minute, and very short life severely limit their use for nonmedical purposes.

The most popular barbs, and those that sometimes are used in association with sexual activity, are the short and intermediate ones, in particular amo-, pento-, and secobarbital. The onset of action of these is fifteen to forty minutes, and their downer effects last up to six hours.

Barbiturates, once used in moderation to calm nerves and help people sleep, became known as "thrill pills" in the 1940s. As more warnings about their potentially damaging effects appeared in the press, the more popular they became. It has been estimated that at least half of the legitimate production of barbiturates in the United States ends up in the illicit drug market.[3]

Today, one is unlikely to find young drug abusers who use only barbiturates. Barbiturates are used with, or alternated with other drugs, or used to counteract the effects of other drugs.

Because of their similarity to alcohol, barbiturates, in small doses, enhance libido through the release of inhibitions. At doses large enough to induce heavy sedation and sleep, it would seem that barbiturate users wouldn't be interested in much of anything including sex. But large doses of barbiturates produce a feeling of euphoria, called a downer high in many persons, and it is this feeling that is sometimes associated with sexual stimulation. In others, the same size dose produces only depression and apathy. Chronic use, like chronic alcohol use, often leads to impotence, loss of libido, and a prolongation of the time to climax.[4]

Like most potentially abusable drugs, and unlike the "love drug" downer, methaqualone, barbs are rarely used specifically for their effects on sexual desire or performance.[5–7] Barbs are most likely to be used to relieve stress and pressures related to getting along in the world and sometimes to counter the effects of uppers.

Of course, one of the problems that causes stress and pressures is inadequate sexual adjustment, and barbs might be taken to help people cope with them. A couple of studies have looked into the possibility of such an association, and have concluded that there is a correlation between barbiturate dependence and sexual inadequacy, but these studies weren't able to determine for certain if the dependency led to the poor sexual adjustment or the other way around, with poor sexual adjustment predisposing to barbiturate dependence.[8,9]

In one study, one hundred Australian barbiturate-dependent women were asked about their sex lives and were found to have many more sexual problems than a group of women who were not dependent on drugs. Seventy-four of eighty-eight married barbiturate-dependent women said they were either frigid or had stopped having sexual relations altogether.[8] In another study of seventy men and women in a drug treatment program, those who preferred barbiturates had many more guilt feelings about their sexual feelings and behavior than those men and women in the program who preferred stimulants or those who didn't care whether they used barbs or stimulants such as amphetamines.[9] Both of these studies suggest that some people hide behind barbiturate drugs to avoid facing their sexual needs and problems.

When young people in the drug subculture are asked about barbiturates, they say that barbs act like alcohol.[7,10] In small doses they decrease inhibitions and can produce euphoria, but they tend to make for sloppy sex, they delay ejaculations, and if the dosage is large enough, they cause impotence. The consensus is that, on average, barbs decrease sexual pleasure.

Respondents to the questionnaire also reported alcohol-like effects:

"I find I get less inhibited, but I get too hooched out."

"Depressants make sex rather undesirable and sloppy— Sometimes it's just too much to do if you're downed out. On the occasions when sex has been completed, the act was very unsatisfactory (no real pleasure, sensations, or orgasm). The effect of alcohol is similar."

"Downers tend to decrease sexual functioning for me. The desire is there, but not the energy."

There is little to recommend barbiturates in recreational drug or legitimate medical circles. As sedatives or sleep-inducers, they have been preempted by the safer benzodiazepine tranquilizers and hypnotics. Reactions to barbs are highly unpredictable. As with alcohol some people become sad, some are loud, funny, belligerent, talkative, mean, silly, sentimental, and a few are even horny.

Alcohol and barbs together are additive and deadly. Doses of barbiturates larger than those recommended for mild sedation produce an intoxication resembling alcoholic intoxication in almost all respects. Barbiturate intoxication produces impaired judgment, slurred speech, and lack of coordination, and as dosage increases, progresses through successive stages of sleep and coma to death, primarily from failure of the respiratory system. Moreover, chronic barb users become physically and psychologically addicted, an abrupt withdrawal producing effects similar to those seen after alcohol withdrawal.

Chronic barbiturate users build up a tolerance and eventually may be taking ten to twenty times the recommended dose, a risky process because there is a very narrow range between the dose required to produce the desired effect and the lethal dose. Moreover, the cross-tolerance between alcohol and barbiturates means that as the dosage of one of them is increased, one achieves the ability to take larger doses of the other. Alcohol and barbs taken in combination have resulted in many unintentional deaths because of the difficulty in judging how much is enough and the narrow range between a response-inducing and a lethal dose.

THE LOVE DRUG

While barbs have fallen out of favor, and barb freaks are looked upon with disdain as sloppy, crude, and rude, the downer cousin of the barbs is enjoying a popularity as the aphrodisiac par excellence. Many, however, and among them, experienced recreational drug users, who usually have their heads about them, claim that methaqualone or "ludes" do the same number on their sexual performance that the other downers, alcohol and barbiturates, do. This raises the suspicion that the expectations associated with methaqualone do a number on the mind which makes its effects that of a most successful placebo.

LUDES

Brand Name	*Generic Name*	*Street Name*
Parest	methaqualone	love drug
Quaalude		ludes
Somnafac		vitamin Q
Sopor		

An editor of *High Times* said, "Methaqualone did for seduction what McDonald's did for hamburgers," and some have assigned it almost mystical sexual properties, but pharmacologists have noted that it is a sedative, and that sexual performance after sedation is almost certain to be diminished rather than enhanced.[11] Underground sentiment has it that ludes are such strong disinhibitors that at parties "formerly repressed women have been known to make their erotic needs the subject of public announcement."[12] This is the stuff that inflames erotic natures and causes the hormones of panting adolescent studs to surge in hopeful expectation. No longer need one long for the romantic days of Spanish flies; one lude in her diet cola and she will be yours, if not forever, at least for the night. And what of the young lady? If she, after taking a "love drug," were to behave in a way encouraged by her flooding hormones, but against her personal expectations, why, could she be blamed? Ah no, for who could be strong enough to resist the lure of an attractive young man and the power of such a drug at the same time? All is forgiven.

Methaqualone's aphrodisiac powers derive solely from its disinhibiting factors. One to two ludes are said to impart a feeling of warmth, a glow of well-being; everything and everyone is lovable. The tongue is loosened, the hands wander, the body yearns. Critical faculties and guilts are dismissed as the mind bends toward hedonistic self-indulgence. Never mind that speech is slurred, vision is blurred, and movements uncoordinated, or that the object of one's luded heart may seem less than attractive tomorrow.

If the sexual properties of methaqualone are entirely attributable to its disinhibiting effects, which seems to be the case, it will not act as an aphrodisiac for those persons who are totally free in their sexual expression. However, if disinhibition is equated with increased libido, methaqualone will appear to produce or enhance orgasm for those persons who have sexual blocking. In this sense, ludes can be seen as akin to opening the sluice gates in a dam. The water is always there, but unless the gates are opened, the water doesn't turn the generators to make any electricity.

Methaqualone is especially popular with women, who seem to require disinhibiting more than men. Some women have reported that it not only makes it easier to achieve orgasm, but increases their ability to have multiple orgasms.[13] Among a group of fourteen men and eleven women heroin addicts, who were asked about drugs they associated with favorable effects on their sex lives, the men picked amphetamines, but the women said they preferred methaqualone.[14]

Two other surveys that looked into the effect of methaqualone on sexual arousal and activity came to different conclusions. A group of ninety-five men and women, aged twenty-one to twenty-nine years, all clients of the Haight-Ashbury Free Medical Clinic of San Francisco, were asked about drugs that had an effect on their sexual enjoyment. The consensus of this group was that methaqualone use decreased sexual activity.[7] In contrast, twenty-five undergraduates reported methaqualone gave them feelings of increased sexual arousal, along with feelings of light-headedness, dizziness, detachment, weakness, and loss of control.[15]

There was no reason to believe that methaqualone was taken by the students to cope with psychological or sexual problems. The group of undergraduates who used it scored no differently on personality tests than did undergraduates who were not drug users.[15]

All but two of the female Quaalude users who responded to the survey viewed it positively. One of the two women who viewed it negatively said that it was just like the other downers, a downer for sex as well as everything else. The other said she didn't have any sexual desire while on Quaaludes, Valium, Librium, or alcohol which she took to cope with stress, and which she recognized as also decreasing her interest in sex.

Some of the rest of the women said their reasons for taking Quaaludes were:

"To relax."

"To relax and let go completely. Not to think. It's fun to be stupid and extremely sexual."

"Because I really loved a man and wanted to please him. I got hooked on sex."

As for sexual desire and response:

"It was almost immediate."

"Loosened me up. I felt like I was melting inside."

"I had multiple orgasms behind Quaaludes."

"Taken with marijuana (an extremely potent aphrodisiac), the sexual experience was the best ever."

"Methaqualone was a popular sedative/hypnotic being used by college peers who usually took three or four at a time to totally uninhibit the user."

"Actually single orgasm after a long aphrodisiac experience."

"This man taught the use of aphrodisiacs [Quaaludes and wine] and the ability of anonymous sex to fulfill my fantasies. One time I thought Jesus fucked me. I was going to die and he kept yelling, 'Here comes Jesus.'"

"Each time I have taken it I have experienced an intense desire for sexual activity. Perhaps it just relaxes my inhibitions, but it seems much more than that."

"Very euphoric in effect."

"At a high dose, it decreases vaginal secretions."

"It enabled my sexual partner to maintain an erection for literally hours, no matter how many times ejaculation occurred."

The following was written by a man about the effect of methaqualone on his partners:

"Quaaludes seem to make [them] willing to accept anything—desire is at a very much less buried level. The greater the dose (up to five) the more spaced, the more willing to accept anything and get satisfaction from it."

Men tended to agree that ludes are pleasant and disinhibiting, but they are uncertain about its effects on their actual performance:

"The lude high can bring amazing pleasures."

"Sexual response is fluid and exciting."

"Ludes give you the randies like marijuana gives the munchies, but not with a very high dose."

"Vibes from the mild euphoria are delightful."

"Increased desire and seemingly faster arousal, but I'm sure it was only my altered perceptibility."

"Less arousal but more desire."

"Long and slow in coming."

"I think the number and quality of orgasms is unchanged."

"I never get off and it's hard to get it up."

"Erections are longer-lasting, and I think female orgasms are bigger and better. It numbs the extremities, so that the skin feels rubbery."

Methaqualone is very popular, but drugs vary in fashion, and methaqualone may be merely fashionable for the present. The argument will not be settled here. What is evident is that it is a drug that is used specifically to increase libido and to enhance sexual pleasure, unlike many other recreational drugs for which sex is incidental.[16]

Glutethimide (Doriden) is, like Quaalude, a nonbarbiturate drug taken for insomnia. However, it has not attained any notoriety as a love stimulant. Nevertheless, a woman who filled in the questionnaire said that Doriden caused her to have a significant increase in her sexual arousal every time she took it. She said she had first been prescribed the drug over ten years ago, and since then has taken it specifically to increase her sexual feelings. "Each time I have taken Doriden, 500 mg. or half—I have experienced an intense desire for sexual activity. Perhaps it just relaxes my inhibitions, but it seems much more than that."

NARCOTICS

Opium, the analgesic addictive derivatives of opium, such as heroin and morphine, and the synthetic substitutes, such as methadone and meperidine (Demerol) or hydromorphone (Dilaudid), are all central nervous system depressants. They are downers. They are downers for sex. Few drugs have the potential for making men impotent and women uninterested as do the narcotics. Potential, however, is a critical word. Sexual functions may be damaged for those who are addicted—who are junkies—who use narcotics as a way of life—whose lives are run by their habit. For some of these persons, narcotics are a substitute for sex. For others, they are an escape from their sexual inadequacies.

OPIATES AND SYNTHETIC NARCOTICS

Brand Name	*Generic Name*	*Street Name*
	heroin	"H" junk Harry horse joy powder Mexican mud smack snow speedball (with cocaine) sugar white stuff
Dilaudid	hydromorphone	
Demerol	meperidine	
Adanon Dolophine	methadone	
	morphine	hard stuff "M" Miss Emma morph unkie
	opium	black stuff hop op pen yan tar

For some men, the dampening effect that narcotics have on their sexual performance is enjoyed and welcomed; ejaculation can be blocked altogether or considerably delayed so that sexual intercourse can be prolonged almost indefinitely. This is one of the reasons that opium was very popular in India in the 1800s.

Opium was also popular in the Orient to stimulate erotic dreams, visions, and voluptuous thoughts. The older Chinese gentleman did not need to be concerned that he had no partners or that his sexual powers had diminished. Opium vapors became his ethereal mistress—"The drug does not put the heart to sleep but his sexuality."[17]

Opium is a natural product, a dried juice that runs out of the capsule (seed-pod) of the opium poppy *(Papaver somniferum)*. Opium is usually taken by mouth or smoked. Opium is not actually smoked. The bowl of the pipe is warmed, the vapors are driven off, and these are inhaled. Opium may also be taken in a suppository route, favored by those who like opium with sex.

As one of the most widely used medicines in the United States in the nineteenth century, with a wide range of therapeutic qualities, opium was sometimes called "God's own medicine." At that time, there were no synthetic tranquilizers or hypnotics, so opium was the drug of choice for nerves, sedation, and insomnia. There were no synthetic antidepressants, so opium was used by some people to produce euphoria. It was also important for pain relief. Few drugs have superseded morphine, the potent pain-killer ingredient in opium, for its analgesic properties. For diarrhea and for cough suppression, opium, or its active ingredients, remains important, and is still in use. Opium was widely grown in the United States and innumerable patent medicines contained it. They were advertised as soothing syrups, cough syrups, women's friends, pain-killers, consumption cures, and nerve tonics. Most pharmacies in the country had their quota of habitual or dependent users of one or more of these tonics, and opium was prescribed freely by physicians. At one time there was no moral reprobation attached to its use. The junkie of yesterday was not a poor black urban male in his early twenties, but a middle-class, white, rural, middle-aged female. She may have been using opium to cope with symptoms of menopause, but she was unlikely to have been using her habit-forming patent medicine to affect her libido or sexual performance.

The opium den, blue with smoke, and filled with reclining people nodding dreamily over their pipes in languid tranquility has passed from the American scene. Some, who saw the opium pipe as one of the few pleasures left to the elderly, bemoaned its passing. They pointed out that opium smoking is much less likely to result in addiction than other routes of ingestion, and that the laws outlawing it were based on anti-Chinese propaganda, drug-associated "white slavery" fears. The anti-Chinese feelings that swept the country in the 1800s actually resulted from the competition the Chinese represented in the depressed labor market of 1875. Stories that white women were enticed into opium dens and sold into slavery by yellow men who had seduced them helped turn public opinion against the "yellow peril." In this kind of climate, a simple association, a few prostitutes confessing they had smoked opium, were enough to convince many frightened people that opium caused debauchery.

In general, the occasional and modest use of opium in association with coitus has pleasant erotic results. By delaying climax, orgasm in both men and women may be deeper and more profound. However, immoderate and excessive use can weaken and destroy sexual capacity. The danger, of course, as with any truly addictive drugs, those that produce physical withdrawal symptoms when habitual use is stopped, is that occasional use will insidiously lead to chronic use and addiction, as it does with tobacco.

At the time that opium was becoming a public issue, morphine, especially injected morphine, was becoming the opiate of choice. Morphine is the chief active ingredient, and is about 10 percent of opium, so that it is about ten times stronger by weight than opium. Because it is a pure chemical that forms a soluble salt, it is injectable, unlike opium. Heroin, which is also injectable, is made in turn from morphine, and is about ten times stronger than morphine in terms of its pain-relieving ability. Heroin, the junk of the addict, is illegal in the United States.

There is a strange history of opiates being used, or more appropriately misused, to treat addiction. Morphine was once prescribed to cure opium addiction, and heroin was subsequently prescribed to cure morphine addiction. Eventually the quality of cross-tolerance and cross-addiction among narcotics became appreciated by the medical community, as it was early done by drug addicts. Nevertheless, along came methadone, another addicting drug, designed to substitute for heroin. Despite a prodigious search, for the financial rewards would be considerable, the pharmaceutical industry has yet to produce a drug that has the analgesic, but not the addictive, properties of the opiates.

When morphine, heroin (in other countries), or other narcotics are given medically, they are usually injected under the skin. By this subcutaneous route, the maximum pain-killing effect is reached in about half an hour, and the effect lasts from four to six hours. Actually narcotics don't so much kill pain, in the sense of a local anesthetic, as they alter the perception of it. With narcotics, people know they are experiencing pain, but they feel detached from it. Anxiety drops away. Pain doesn't matter. Recreational narcotic users or addicts prefer to mainline the drugs into a vein, because they get an immediate jolt, flash, or "rush" to the central nervous system. It is this rush that is often described in sexual terms and has caused the needle and the process of injection to take on sexual symbolism. The effects of narcotics shot into a vein have been described as "a total orgasm," or "an orgasm in the stomach." Heroin gives the strongest rush, morphine the second best, and methadone little, if any.

As tolerance to heroin builds up, it takes more and more to achieve a rush, and eventually a chronic high-dose user must usually settle for the mellow euphoria, the cool detachment, and the pleasant dreamlike imagery that opiates induce. The occasional heroin user, and there may be more of these than there are occasional cigarette smokers, does not build up tolerance, so he always experiences the rush at a low and cheap dose.

Addiction means that the body cannot function normally without drugs. As a diabetic needs insulin, and experiences physical symptoms when he does not get his injection, so a narcotic addict experiences symptoms, such as restlessness, irritability, yawning, running nose and eyes, fever, chills and sweats, nausea, vomiting, diarrhea, insomnia, anorexia, and involuntary ejaculations, if he is suddenly detached from his drug. Despite the unpleasantness, addicts commonly detoxify themselves so they can regain the flash they enjoy at a price they can pay.

Drug addicts are not great lovers. They may even have difficulty becoming parents. Which is just as well. The economic struggle required to maintain a habit is hardly conducive to parenthood. Moreover, addicts are selfish. Feeding the habit can come before feeding the baby. Of at least equal concern is the fact that an addicted pregnant woman produces an addicted infant.

Study after study has shown that long-term heroin and methadone addicts have substantial sex-related problems. Addicted men commonly experience erectile impotence, delayed ejaculation, failure to ejaculate, decreased nocturnal emission, and loss of sensitivity and sexual desire. Sperm motility is also suppressed.[6,13,18–20]

Women may experience difficulty attaining orgasm and have loss of libido.[21] Failure to menstruate is a common experience of female addicts.[22] However, they may actually become pregnant more often than nonaddicted women because they become inattentive to the need for contraception.[13]

The needle pain is often associated with masochistic symbolic orgasms. The injection substitutes for sex.[23] Thus, for those who have personality problems that mean they have difficulty forming relationships with others, junk can become a substitute for a sex partner. The junkie risks neither failure nor rejection. Junk is demanding but it always comes across.

Multiple drug users say that, like alcohol, the barbiturates, and large doses of amphetamines, heroin use leads to decreased sexual activity.[7]

"Junk short circuits sex."[23]

In one study, 68 percent of the male heroin addicts asked said that heroin delayed climax to the extent some couldn't ejaculate at all about half of the time. The rest said it took more than twenty-five minutes, whereas when they were off drugs they were completely normal and ejaculation took from four to less than twenty-five minutes. As shown in the following table, heroin addiction causes more libido problems but fewer potency problems than methadone:[24]

Addict Category	*Normal Libido*	*Normal Potency*
heroin	39%	61%
methadone	74%	24%
formerly addicted	100%	100%

Notably, all physical sex problems rapidly disappear when an addict goes drug-free. The problem is that sex is an inadequate substitute for drugs. The addict would rather have drugs than sex.

A minority of heroin and methadone addicts say that sex is improved on the drug.[25] They are likely to be those for whom premature ejaculation is a problem. Premature ejaculation is a common complaint of addicts when they are drug-free.

WHAT USERS SAY

Two kinds of narcotic users answered the questionnaire, the occasional user and the former addict.

The occasional users indicated they didn't use heroin for sex, but to get high, one saying that opium was better for sex. Heroin taken intravenously tended to decrease desire, and for males, to delay ejaculation. The quality of the sexual experience:

"Entirely depended on my partner."

Orgasms were said to be "normal" and even "irrelevant; I was interested in the drug experience not the sex experience."

Only one former addict indicated that heroin had been used alone. Preludin was the additional drug most often referred to, but some addicts had also used cocaine. Some of the former addicts continued the "sex as irrelevant" theme, and some men indicated that heroin could substitute for sex.

"Heroin is sex."

"That drug became my lady, but she ran my life."

"I didn't really care if I had sex or not; when I did it didn't seem different."

"Listen, when you're really hooked and need a fix, you want IT, not a fuck."

"Methadone makes me feel horny sometimes, but with heroin it doesn't seem to matter."

"If you can understand that 'a blow' is an addict's term for a shot of dope, you'll understand that all these questions aren't worth a shit."

"Addicts don't need women."

"The yen I got for drugs was always greater than the yen I got for a woman."

"You do not have a sexual desire; [heroin] takes away all of your sexual desire."

One man simply indicated that he had no desire, erections, or ejaculation with heroin.

No former addict indicated that he or she took heroin for sexual reasons. Reasons given were simply that it made them feel good, or to enjoy the high or to escape:

"I just liked the feeling; makes you feel like you own the world."

A few men mentioned the delaying effect of heroin which they liked:

"Sometimes junk helped me. My erections could last much longer than usual, but I never took heroin for that reason."

"Was able to perform sex longer. One orgasm, but under drugs, it took longer."

"Time to achieve was lengthened; the number of times was usually two to three and the quality was intensified."

"I don't think it affected my usual arousal—with the exception of cocaine [used with heroin]. Cocaine stimulated my sexual arousal. No problems [with erections and ejaculations]."

"Before becoming addicted, drugs acted as a stimulant; when addicted, it was the only way I could become aroused." This former addict said he had taken amphetamines, barbs, and morphine with heroin, and that on drugs, his orgasms were "long and good," and his erections were "quick."

Former female addicts, aged twenty-three to forty-six, responded to the questionnaire. Most mentioned heroin addiction, but some also had used Dilaudid. Both of these drugs were usually used with Preludin. Some women said that their sexual desire wasn't affected, others that it was increased and others that it was decreased:

"It [heroin and bam] made me want to have sex more."

"I had a very strong drive."

"[Heroin and bam] took away my sexual desire."

"To the highest peak. Depends on who I am with, but [orgasm] usually doesn't take too long."

"Suppressed sex desires. [Orgasms] were seldom and took a long time to achieve."

"It was good, but it took me a long time to reach a climax."

"It [heroin and bam] made me want to have sex more."

"When I was really down from drugs I was really fucked up. I didn't want sex, and I didn't enjoy it when I had it."

"I used to be a prostitute, and I did all the drugs. They helped me stand what I was doing, but drugs really destroyed my mind."

Perhaps no one who filled in a questionnaire said it better than Cocteau in 1930 in *Diary of a Cure:*

". . . there is no mistress more exacting than this drug which takes jealousy to the point of emasculating the addict . . . not only does it cause impotence, but what is more, it replaces these somewhat base obsessions by others which are somewhat lofty, very strange and unknown to a sexually normal organism."[26]

13

PSYCHEDELICS: LSD, PCP, STP, DMT, OTHERS

LSD is a synthetic, chemical, major hallucinogen that resembles its natural cousins mescaline, the active ingredient in the peyote cactus, and psilocybin, the "magic mushroom." They are all alkaloids that are similar in structure. Three are said to be aphrodisiacs or sex experience enhancers, but they are also said to diminish sexual activity or interest in sex during the hallucinatory phases of their effects. LSD has been used to treat frigidity and homosexuality, but the strongest and most consistent claim for a hallucinogen and sex relationship is that the drug-induced perceptions of cosmic or religious experiences open up the mind so that inhibitions, prohibitions, and socially induced restrictions drop away, and a full expression of sexuality is experienced as natural, beautiful, and as a spiritual as well as physical bond that is suffused with love.

There is no evidence whatsoever that the natural plant hallucinogens are somehow better or safer than the synthetic ones. They are simply different or stronger. The only reason that natural drugs may be better is if the synthetic drugs are not what they are purported to be. A person who buys drugs in an illegal market has little way of knowing whether the LSD he has purchased is pure or has been adulterated with amphetamines, PCP, or strychnine (a natural drug!), for example, whereas a peyote button is unmistakable. However, even marijuana may be, and often is, adulterated with synthetic PCP, and most people can't tell a "magic mushroom" from a garden store variety impregnated with PCP. To the body, a chemical is a chemical whether its origin was a plant or a test tube. Each must be judged on its own merits for its effects and its safety and not by some misguided claim that it is organic or natural.

LSD AND NATURAL PSYCHEDELICS

Common Name	*Street "Brand"*	*Street Name*
ALD-52 LSD LSD-25 LSD-59	blotter blue cheer chocolate chip clear light double domes flying A four-ways microdots orange wedges pink swirls purple haze sunshine windowpane white lightning	acid cubes Sugar big D Lucy in the sky with diamonds "25"
mescaline		buttons divine cactus peyote plants
psilocybin		flesh of the gods magic mushroom sacred mushroom

If you didn't know what you got, you probably wouldn't be able to tell the difference between LSD and mescaline or pscilocybin, although they do vary in the amount needed to produce an effect and in the length of time their effects last. Cross-tolerance exists among them, and tolerance develops rapidly, so it is impossible to stay on a trip for long periods of time, say four days, even though higher and higher doses are taken and one switches around from one of these psychedelics to another.

There is a great deal of misunderstanding about the meaning of hallucinogen by people who have not taken LSD or any similar drug. The hallucinogens have even been called psychotomimetic which suggests that they cause psychotic states. However, for the most part, LSD and its cousins distort reality, but the trippers are aware that what they are experiencing is a distortion caused by the drug. They have pseudohallucinations. They do not ordinarily believe that their drug-induced visions are real. In contrast, a schizophrenic person believes that the voices he hears really exist, and he may act on the advice they give him. That an LSD tripper is aware of what he is experiencing does not necessarily protect him from "bad trips," which are usually represented by a state of paranoia or extreme fear. After all, people who are afraid of heights realize that tall buildings are not likely to collapse, and that they are not really going to fall out of the windows, but they are still terrified, many of them enough to keep them from going into tall buildings. The possibility of a terrifying experience which happens to some trippers every time and, eventually, to almost every user, is why experienced users say that the drug should never be taken alone, but always with a friendly "guide" who can help the individual interpret his experiences and lead him into a different "set." Moreover, the prospective user should be told (programmed?) ahead of time so that he'll know what to expect and will not be frightened or think he's truly gone over the edge.

The LSD underground grew out of psychiatrists turning themselves and their friends on, not all of which was therapy. The word and the rumors spread. Exaggerated claims ranging from creation of a "union with God" to "unlimited orgasms in a single night" were made for LSD, first by the grapevine and then by the underground press. However, most of LSD's popularity must be attributed to strong cult figures, Drs. Leary and Alpert from Harvard, the poet Allen Ginsberg, and the writer Ken Kesey *(One Flew Over the Cuckoo's Nest)*, who led the drug and antiestablishment revolution in the sixties. At that time, there was a coming together of various social forces, the Vietnam War, an increase in college attendance to avoid it, and a decrease in economic growth, so that young people perceived they didn't have much of a chance to do better than their parents, and gained a media-enhanced diffusion of the understanding that man-made rules govern social activity, and that the rules that man makes vary, change over time, and can be unmade and broken. Some persons believe that if conditions are right, leaders will be propelled to the head of new movements. During the sixties, the followers were ready, the leaders became the heads all right, and the drugs and sex revolution tripped away to acid rock.

By 1973, many were still tripping. A survey of students at the University of California found that 27 percent of students had tried it, and 2 percent used it every week.[1]

LSD AND SEX

Many persons, because of the hippies and their so-called love-ins of the sixties, associate hallucinogens with notions of hypersexuality, group sex, promiscuity, and the breakdown of conventional morality. However, as one student of the drug scene has pointed out, the evidence is entirely of the associational type, and not of the causal type.[2] This simply means that because two kinds of behavior appear in the same person there is not enough evidence to say that one kind of behavior caused another. It is no more logical to say that hallucinogens caused a specific sexual behavior than it would be to assume that the skills of a successful businessman derive from drinking expensive Scotch. Both behaviors are part of a life-style that for businessmen includes secretaries, tax deductions, and working long hours. In the sixties, the use of so-called "mind-expanding" drugs was one of a number of activities engaged in by the counterculture—"tune in, turn on, drop out"—which, bolstered by the strong social support groups it created, began to examine the conventional social rules embodied in the work ethic and sexual inhibitions and found them wanting, created by human beings, and thus possible to challenge. The exploration into drugs formed part of the general exploration into new experiences whose pioneers were reexamining, overturning, and redrawing the boundaries of permitted behavior. One of these up-for-reexamination areas was sex, now reordered as an activity that, "as long as it doesn't hurt anyone, and feels good, do it," and drugs, "as a way to fully understand who you are," and both sex and drugs for their novelty and sheer enjoyment.

Evaluating the effects of LSD on libido and sexual function is not easy. Once again, as with all illegal drugs, there have been no controlled experiments, and with LSD there is considerable disagreement. Timothy Leary, a recognized LSD expert and guru, claimed in an interview given to *Playboy* magazine in 1966 that LSD was the aphrodisiac nonpareil,[3] but most writers say that LSD has few specific effects on sexual function, is rarely used specifically for sex, and that its ability to modify the perception of what is happening often, but not always, is in pleasurable ways. For example there is one report of a man becoming impotent on LSD when he hallucinated that his partner had become a shark.[4] Not that he really believed she had become a shark, but the impression was so unpleasant it was enough to cause detumescence. Some writers have even suggested that some people take LSD to avoid having to engage in sexual relations.

Although Leary, when describing the effects of LSD, specifically spoke of the effects of LSD on orgasm, a careful reading suggests that

Leary has reinterpreted the meaning of the word orgasm from what is generally regarded as a focused localized genital response with specific observable physiological effects. The intense involvement of his nervous system and heightened sensitivity under LSD seems to have been interpreted by Leary as a continuing all-encompassing orgasm:

> Leary: Touch becomes electric as well as erotic. . . . Rosemary [his wife] leaned over and lightly touched the palm of my hand with her finger. Immediately a hundred thousand end cells in my hand exploded in soft orgasm. Ecstatic energies pulsated up my arms and rocketed into my brain, where another hundred thousand cells softly exploded in pure, delicate pleasure. . . . Wave upon wave of ethereal tissue rapture—delicate, shuddering—coursed back and forth from her finger to my palm.
>
> Playboy: And this was erotic?
>
> Leary: Transcendentally. An enormous amount of energy from every fiber of your body is released under LSD—most especially sexual energy. There is no question that LSD is the most powerful aphrodisiac ever discovered by man.
>
> Playboy: Would you elaborate?
>
> Leary: I'm simply saying that sex under LSD becomes miraculously enhanced and intensified. I don't mean that it simply generates genital energy. It doesn't automatically produce a longer erection. Rather it increases your sensitivity a thousand percent. Let me put it this way: Compared with sex under LSD, the way you've been making love—no matter how ecstatic the pleasure you think you get from it—is like making love to a department-store-window dummy. In sensory and cellular communion on LSD, you may spend a half hour making love with eyeballs, another half hour making love with breath. As you spin through a thousand sensory and cellular organic changes, she does, too. Ordinarily, sexual communication involves one's own chemicals, pressure and interactions of a very localized nature—in what the psychologists call the erogenous zones. A vulgar, dirty concept, I think. When you're making love under LSD, it's as though every cell in your body—and you have trillions—is making love with every cell in her body. Your hand doesn't caress her skin but sinks down into and merges with ancient dynamos of ecstasy within her. . . . Merging, yielding, flowing, union, communion. It's all lovemaking. You make love with candlelight, with sound waves from a record player, with a bowl of fruit on the table, with the trees. You're in pulsating harmony with all the energy around you.
>
> The three inevitable goals of the LSD session are to discover and make love with God, to discover and make love with yourself, and to discover and make love with a woman. You can't make it with yourself unless you've made it with the timeless energy process around you, and you can't make it with a woman until you've made it with yourself. The natural and obvious way to take LSD is with a member of the opposite sex, and an LSD session that does not involve an ultimate merging with a

person of the opposite sex isn't really complete. One of the great purposes of an LSD session is sexual union. The more expanded your consciousness—the farther out you can move beyond your mind—the deeper, the richer, the longer and more meaningful your sexual communion. . . .

Only the most reckless poet would attempt [to describe the sensation of an orgasm under LSD]. I have to say to you, "What does one say to a little child?" The child asks, "Daddy, what is sex like?" and you try to describe it, and then the little child says, "Well, is it fun like the circus?" and you say, "Well, not exactly like that." And the child says, "Is it fun like chocolate ice cream?" and you say, "Well, it's like that but much, much more than that." And the child says, "Is it fun like the roller coaster, then?" and you say, "Well, that's part of it, but it's even more than that." In short, I can't tell you what it's like, because it's not like anything that's ever happened to you—and there aren't words adequate to describe it, anyway. You won't know what it's like until you try it yourself and then I won't need to tell you. . . .

In a carefully prepared, loving LSD session, a woman can have several hundred orgasms. . . . This preoccupation with the number of orgasms is a hang-up for many men and women. It's as crude and vulgar a concept as wondering how much she paid for the negligee.

Playboy: Still, there must be some sort of physiologic comparison. If woman can have several hundred orgasms, how many can a man have under optimum conditions?

Leary: It would depend entirely on the amount of sexual and psychedelic experience the man has had. I can speak only for myself and about my own experience. I can only compare what I was with what I am now. In the last six years, my openness to, my responsiveness to, my participation in every form of sensory expression, has multiplied a thousandfold. . . . I feel I'm free at this moment to say what we've never said before: that sexual ecstasy is the basic reason for the current LSD boom. When Dr. Goddard, the head of the Food and Drug Administration announced in a Senate hearing that 10 percent of our college students are taking LSD, did you ever wonder why? Sure, they're discovering God and meaning; sure, they're discovering themselves; but did you really think sex wasn't the fundamental reason for this surging, youthful social boom? You can no more do research on LSD and leave out sexual ecstasy than you can do microscopic research on tissue and leave out cells.

To Leary, then, the entire experience of LSD is erotic, and the aphrodisiac properties lie mainly in the flood of sensory perceptions that magnify sensitivity. However, he does go on to warn "of this tremendous personal power in LSD. You must be very careful to take it only with someone you know really well, because it's almost inevitable that a woman will fall in love with the man who shares her LSD experience. Deep and lasting neurological imprints, profound emotional bonds, can develop as a result of an LSD session—bonds that can last a lifetime." However, psychologists have long known that strong bonds are forged between people who share unusual and particularly emotional experiences, and that the gratitude and dependence that people have for those who have helped them and to whom they have revealed areas of their private worlds have often been translated as love. This is the classic case in psychiatry, and one that psychiatrists are trained to manage. It is not surprising that as Leary initiated young people into LSD in his "research," he found they were falling in love with him and each other to the extent he viewed it as a problem.

> For this reason I have always been extremely cautious about running sessions with men and women. We always try to have a subject's husband or wife present during his or her first session so that as these powerful urges develop, they are directed in ways that can be lived out responsibly after the session.

Although this remark suggests that Leary believed LSD to be the kind of aphrodisiac that awakens and stimulates sexual desire, he also says:

> LSD is not an automatic trigger to sexual awakening. The first 10 times you take it, you might not be able to have a sexual experience at all, because you're so overwhelmed and delighted—or frightened and confused—by the novelty; the idea of having sex might be irrelevant or incomprehensible at the moment.

Thus, although Leary says that sex under LSD must be tried to be understood, it seems that it may have to be taken many times before its aphrodisiac properties are manifested. It seems unlikely that those who have had bad trips, "become frightened," would care to continue beyond "the first 10 times," or the first one or two times, on the chance of having a "words aren't adequate to describe" sexual awakening, and one must conclude that, regardless of Leary's claims for LSD's ability to cause "several hundred orgasms" in a single night, it has no specific sexual properties. It may be uninhibiting, and it surely modifies sensations during sexual experiences.

Although many have associated LSD with the sex and drug culture and especially promiscuity and group sex, Leary is very specific on this point: ". . . I've been extremely monogamous in my use of LSD over the last six years."

He goes on to say that the sexual power of LSD is so great that it must be used responsibly and with respect between mutually agreeable persons. Moreover, he makes a claim for LSD that rules out its use to exploit a potential sex partner:

> . . . if you use LSD to make out sexually in the seductive sense, then you'll be a very humiliated and embarrassed person, because it's just not going to work. On LSD, her eyes would be microscopic, and she'd see very plainly what you were up to, coming on with some heavy-handed, moustache-twisting routine. You'd look like a consummate ass, and she'd laugh at you, or you'd look like a monster and she'd scream and go into a paranoid state. Nothing good can happen with LSD if it's used for power or manipulative purposes.

This claim is unequaled by any pharmacological product known. There are certainly drugs that uninhibit people so they are more likely to say things than they would otherwise, and drugs that may help people with memory, but a drug that enables a person to see into the mind of another is highly unlikely and has no basis in scientific theory. Most psychoactive drugs, including those that act like LSD to block serotonin in the brain, tend to make people somewhat more self-centered rather than sensitive to others. They tend to be preoccupied with the novelty of their drug-induced sensations. They may want to share their experience with others; they may feel warm and more loving, but this is not the same thing as having an ability to read another's thoughts or intentions.

The other claim for LSD made by Leary that, if true, would make it totally unique pharmacologically is that LSD can "cure" homosexuality. Not only did Leary deny that LSD could release latent homosexual impulses in heretofore heterosexual persons, he said that "LSD is a specific cure for homosexuality." Of course this would imply, in contradiction to the position taken by the American Psychiatric Association, that homosexuality is a disease. Leary referring to homosexuality as a "sexual perversion" that was the result "not of biological binds but of freaky, dislocating childhood experiences of one kind or another," and citing the poet Allen Ginsberg as an example, said that LSD can turn people on to members of the opposite sex, even though their past sexual preference has been entirely for those of their own sex.

Leary's claim that LSD is a panacea for frigidity and impotence is not so dissimilar from claims made for other uninhibiting drugs. If the problems are mental and result from psychological blocks caused by fears, embarrassment, shame inculcated by rigid social mores and childhood prohibitions, it is not theoretically unreasonable that a drug could help overcome them. Whether LSD is the best drug for this problem or can help with it in even a minority of cases is questionable. If it is true that persons who are rigid and fearful are the most likely to experience fear and paranoia with LSD, it seems unlikely that LSD could help them, unless it was given carefully under the supervision of trained psychotherapists who are completely familiar with the effects of LSD.

Constance Newland has written a book about her use of LSD to overcome frigidity in psychotherapy. She claimed that during twenty-three LSD sessions she was able to relive childhood experiences and gain insight into the relationships between her mind and her body, and this insight enabled her to dissolve her "ego images" and achieve full sexual satisfaction.

The remarkable sexual claims that Leary made for LSD are not supported by others. However, as Brian Wells wrote, Leary's views should not be ignored since his experience with LSD is vast, and he "personally introduced hundreds, and possibly thousands, to the use of LSD."[2] Nevertheless, when Gay and Sheppard interviewed experienced drug users attending the Haight-Ashbury Free Clinic about the effect of various recreational drugs on sexual function, forty-four of forty-eight hippies asked said that LSD is not an aphrodisiac, and only four claimed that it increased desire;[5] however, when asked to list aphrodisiacs and antiaphrodisiacs, LSD and PCP were among the former while barbiturates, methaqualone, heroin, alcohol, and high doses of amphetamines were among the latter.[6] In another survey of four multiple drug users, two persons, a twenty-two-year-old female and a twenty-nine-year-old male, said that LSD increased sexual drive, a nineteen-year-old male said that LSD decreased it, and a twenty-two-year-old female said it had no effect.[7]

In an extraordinary inquiry, a medical investigator, went to a psychedelic training center established by Leary in Mexico to investigate his claims for LSD.[2] At the end of his study, he concluded that not only was LSD not an aphrodisiac, it was an antiaphrodisiac. At the most, it increased mental eroticism, and exaggerated or augmented sexual experiences when they did occur, but it had a negative effect on the frequency of sexual intercourse. The investigator asked both men and women at the center about the sexual effects of LSD, and then checked their reports by asking hotel employees about the sexual behavior of the trippers. The men who took LSD said that repeated use of LSD led to a decrease in their sex drives, and two men said that LSD was a sexual downer, it made them impotent. Except for one woman, who said her inhibitions were lessened, LSD was said to have had no effect at all on the erotic drives of the women. The hotel employees made corroborating statements saying that there was less sexual activity among the group than they had expected, and certainly no more than any other group of people on vacation.

The inconsistencies between Leary and the medical investigator may only be one of semantics. There simply are no drugs that cause people to engage in sexual activity more often or fall in love with another person or commit sexual crimes, and LSD is no exception. LSD, like other hallucinogens, distorts the perceptions of sexual activities, perhaps enlarging the appearance of the genitals, extending time, increasing sensitivity, making sex more novel and more pleasurable for some people. If the LSD and sex pleasure are great and shared, it is not surprising that individuals may "fall in love," if they haven't already. In this redefined sense, LSD may be an aphrodisiac for some people. The argument that drug-induced eroticism is not real, and thus a fake, is not compelling since all sensations are perceived and regulated by the chemistry of our bodies. The modified perception, albeit transient, by an outside rather than an endogenous chemical, is only less real when it occurs in the sense that the distortions are not perceived by others who have not modified their body chemistries similarly. This is the lesson that Castaneda seemed to have so much trouble grasping in his three-volume account of hallucinogen drug use under the surprisingly patient tutelage of the Yaqui Indian, Don Juan.

Others, including the Canadian Commission of Inquiry (1970) have come to similar conclusions about the sex-linked properties of LSD.[8] LSD is neither a sexual stimulant nor an inhibitor; it modifies all perceptions, not simply those related to sexual activity. Some may find sex more satisfying, while others lose interest in it. LSD may be helpful in removing psychological blocks that have produced frigidity, reticence, inhibitions, and poor sexual relations. For example, although a woman who had taken LSD would have no increase in orgasms in the usual sense, she might say that she was in a state of satisfying bliss extending for hours, that LSD was a source of sensuous, rapturous delights, and that she was wholly satisfied. Specifically, for some people, LSD seems to be able to decrease defensiveness and sex-related anxieties, extend sensations so that stroking may produce orgasmiclike feelings over a large area of the body, and prolong time so that the user "luxuriates" in the experience.[10]

Two researchers, Bernard Aronson and Humphrey Osmond, studied the use of LSD in one homo- and two heterosexual groups in the psychedelic underground in the sixties.[11] The homosexual group grew from four women friends, one of whom had been initiated into LSD with Leary, and who introduced her friends to it. Friends and acquaintances, ranging in age from nineteen to forty-five, were added until there were seven core and twenty-five peripheral members of whom seventeen were female, and fifteen were male. Most were single and twelve were professionals. Before a new member was given LSD, he was required to read Leary's *The Psychedelic Experience,* was told what he would feel, and asked to observe a group session.

The group met about once a week and had LSD sessions of two kinds, work and play, once a month. The work sessions, "housecleaning," were supposed to help free participants of their psychological "hang-ups." For this type of sessions, one person concentrated on his problems during the week prior to the session. During the sessions "guides," who took lighter doses than he, helped him with what he was experiencing. Marijuana was usually smoked while waiting for the LSD to take effect, and sometimes to break up LSD effects. After the work session, which could last all night, the group got together to interpret what had happened.

Play sessions were spontaneous as well as planned. They were parties at which dancing, eating, drinking wine, and smoking marijuana took place. Sometimes the play session was an outing to a movie, museum, park, or concert.

Although the group was affectionate and talked about loving each other, the love was said to be like that of a family and LSD was not used for sex. While three women had once had a sex orgy with one man, which was said to have been "beautiful" and "interesting," the members were generally disapproving of sex-oriented groups. Members took LSD for such reasons as to attain personal growth, explore ESP, develop creativity, attain freedom to make choices, and understand their homosexuality.[11]

The heterosexual groups were smaller. The purpose of one group with a core of two men was not sex, but to explore mysticism and God. Eight to nine other men in their twenties took LSD with them, but most of the others participated only once over the year of the LSD sessions.

The second heterosexual group, with a core of two men and the girlfriend of one of them, met over six months. Again the sessions which took place on Sundays were not primarily for sex, but to share the experience, and included going to parks and museums while high. Sometimes the couple would absent themselves for "sexual intensification" and "total involvement," although the male said that he was sometimes impotent with LSD. Impotence was said to have been more frequent during his first trips.[11]

There is nothing in the reports of members of the three groups to suggest that LSD is a fantastic aphrodisiac, and it is certainly not a cure for homosexuality. In fact, the central pair of men in the first heterosexual group developed a homosexual thread to their relationship during the year they were experimenting with LSD.[11] The warmth and support of the groups may have helped the members to grow and to change through the mechanism of shared experiences, but it is not certain that this can be directly attributed to LSD. The nature of LSD trips is markedly affected by the participant's expectations.

HOW LSD WORKS

The LSD trip is a long one compared to some of the other hallucinogens. The time it takes, as much as the possibility of "bad" trips and the need of prudent trippers for "guides," is probably a major reason that LSD was in less favor in the seventies than it was in the sixties. Moreover, the desire for the LSD experience became less as the underground passed the word that the Leary claims were overblown. If you're not creative and religious or sexy somewhere inside yourself already, LSD is not going to make you that way.

It is very difficult to describe the effects of LSD. No other hallucinogen is as powerful, dose for dose, and no other drug produces the variety of contradictory responses as LSD. Thus, one LSD tripper reports euphoria and another depression; one is anxious, another calm; one says his sensitivity is increased, another says his is lost; one is tranquil, the next is irritable. For some the sex drive is increased, for others depressed. The most common attribute is that the experience is highly personal and indescribable. While the inner world of the brain is opened up by LSD, the brain is flooded by stimuli from outside so that the user almost drowns in perceptions, visions, colors, sounds, smells, all streaming and changing so rapidly that time is virtually stopped and minutes pass like hours.

The LSD experience proceeds in three stages. It takes about a half to three-quarters of an hour for LSD to "turn on." "Turning on" for those who never have is suddenly becoming aware that something is different. One feels slightly "shifted" in space and time. Somewhat "set aside." Sounds become somewhat "off" and "echoey." The nearest nondrug-induced feeling, only without the dizziness, is that caused by a fever. The marijuana "turn-on" seldom proceeds past this stage. During the next hour with LSD, however, the sensory circuit begins to become flooded with exploding imagery. Smells, sight, sound, tactile sensations, moods are exaggerated and change rapidly so that all are distorted in a pastiche of kaleidoscopic patterns that constantly move and shift and blur. Colors ripple about. The eyes fill up with what has been called a "retinal circus." Sound seems to merge with other senses, so that music seems to control or produce visual imagery. One may become acutely conscious of the working of one's body—breathing and heartbeat, for example. In this first sensory stage, trippers may also have identity loss, so that they feel they have merged with the cosmos. Mind, body, and universe may seem to have become one, or the tripper may feel he is floating or flying out of his body. Time slows so that it is hard to believe so much has happened in so short a time. Time travel may seem to occur. The past, the present, and the future may be perceived to blend. The experience of reliving one's childhood or even one's birth may happen.

The peak LSD experience, sometimes called the rebirth or transcendence, the "clear light" or the "brilliance," occurs after about three hours. One feels insightful, all-knowing, compassionate, tolerant, wise, wonderful, infinite, and loving at this time. The LSD effects in the first phase and the "peak experience," if any, are dose related. As can be imagined, it is impossible to have or even think about sexual relations while space and time are jumping around, and one is imagining that one is being reborn. At least in the first and second phases, and at high doses, LSD is more of a head than a body trip.

The last three to four hours of the twelve- to fourteen-hour trip is the come-down or reentry phase. The tripper goes back and forth between feeling like himself and somebody else, somewhere else. He may feel sad at coming back to reality, and it is at this time that making love is most likely to happen. Many people say they feel more loving and want closer interpersonal relationships after using LSD. These feelings may extend for months beyond the LSD experience.

WHAT USERS SAY

The men who replied to the sex and drugs questionnaire range in age from twenty-one to thirty-five. Although LSD was usually taken alone, a few said that they had smoked marijuana or had some wine as well. Every one of the men said that LSD increased their desire and arousal, several mentioning the head trip or "whole" experience that was more than genital:

"Increased arousal in the presence of a stimulus in the form of a young, willing female with a well-proportioned body."

"Increased sensitivity to touch; felt as if I was feeling through my partner, reaching down into her very being. Between visions and hallucinations, I felt very close to my partner, as if I could play with the sexual act for a long period of time."

"It seemed to make it [desire and performance] more intense. Also an emotional sense of omnipotence."

"Created a great need for physical contact."

LSD was never used primarily because of the way it affected their sexual functioning either by men or women. The primary reason given was simply "to get high," although sex was sometimes a part of it.

The responses to questions about erections indicated some vagueness and uncertainty apparently related to the time distortion, several men mentioning the possibility of multiple orgasms over the time of the trip, and the enhanced quality which extended to the whole body:

"I don't believe I stayed extremely erect for long if at all, but it didn't seem to impede the sexual urge or act."

"Seemed to continue almost immediately after ejaculation."

"Multiple."

"Made them last much longer but *most* importantly . . . made it more of a religious and caring experience."

"Would become erect again approximately five minutes after ejaculation."

"One erection seemed to last a very long time."

Of orgasms and ejaculations it was said:

"I only remember when I ejaculated I felt as if I was coming with my whole body and soul. Somehow it seemed more than just a bodily act."

"I had over six orgasms, one in particular which I felt was truly sublime."

"Had two, but no idea how long it took as the perception of time was somewhat distorted."

"Seemed very strong. Very hard to judge the time. They seemed more prolonged, but I'm sure they were faster."

"Exquisite."

"Lost in delirium of ecstasy."

"The mere thought of engaging in a sexual act would almost cause an immediate orgasm; once the first one was completed the second would and could take another thirty or forty minutes."

"Several in a night's course with each seeming to be greater and more forceful than the preceding one."

Both men and women mentioned the overall experience, and the importance of the preexisting state, and the context in which LSD is taken:

"LSD can tend to be a more transcendent, holistic experience, thus making sex seem less important."

"Raw physical sex is trivial compared to the psychological impact of LSD and sexual contact."

"The effect depends entirely on the environment and one's emotional state going into the drug experience which can carry over if it was strong. Hallucinations accompany all acts including sex, and can be terrifying depending on your condition (emotional primarily), and your partner's as well as the way you see your partner. Feelings of mistrust or fear will certainly be intensified (with accompanying hallucinations—a witch, for instance). Basically it tends to speed up and intensify the whole act while making it appear more prolonged. If you were strongly enough convinced that you could go forever, you'd be well on your way. In an ambiguous situation, I can easily see one being unable to perform and more unwilling."

Although women mentioned the same merging and enhancement of psychological as well as physical experiences, they tended to be more cautious about sex and LSD than men, several saying that they couldn't concentrate enough on what was happening to achieve orgasms. One said that LSD seemed to bring out all her underlying fears and hang-ups about sex:

"I saw my partner as enormous and it became very threatening."

"Things just happen too fast to get into sex except at the end of the trip, and then I'm usually too tired."

"I like the sharing and the closeness, but not necessarily physical sex."

On the other hand:

"LSD enhances sex—it can go on for hours and I will never get bored as long as hallucinations don't overrun everything."

"Sex is often very desirable and the longer and more stimulating the better."

"Orgasms are usually nonexistent, but if they do come, they are well worth waiting for because of their intensity and long-lasting after-effects."

The responses to the questionnaires do not vary from the explanations of how LSD affects sex given by Dr. Joel Fort in his book *The Pleasure Seekers*:[12]

> Strong emotional bonds or positive feelings for each other, changes in time . . . perception, unusual genital sensations, diminished inhibitions and symbolic overtones can be part of an LSD experience and will in some circumstances produce a mystical or ecstatic sexual union which may seem endless. . . . Such an experience would derive mainly from the underlying characters of the lovers, discriminate and experienced use of the LSD, the setting and chance factors. Many instances have been reported of lessened sexual interest and involvement while under the influence of an LSD-type drug, and no instances have been authenticated of repetitive male orgasms resulting from taking the drug.

CAN LSD HURT YOU?

LSD, d-lysergic acid diethylamide, was first put together at Sandoz laboratories in Switzerland in 1943. Early experience, largely by psychiatrists, established that the drug is not addicting, and it was soon the object of wide experimentation within psychiatry and by the army which thought the drug might join its chemical warfare arsenal.[13] Although LSD has been largely discredited through its association with hippie groups and bad trips in the fifties and sixties, it was used to treat alcoholism, cancer-related pain, and neuroticism, as well as various mental illnesses. Many still consider it to be valuable in psychiatry. In 1969 over half of British psychotherapists were still using it, but it is a very time-consuming and thus expensive form of therapy.

In 1966, Dr. Sidney Cohen inquired into the harmful effects of LSD by sending a questionnaire to sixty-six researchers who had given over 25,000 doses of LSD to over 5,000 men and women.[14] Not one instance of physical damage or prolonged side effects was reported, but there were psychological problems which Cohen divided into two groups, immediate and subsequent effects. The problems included loss of insight into the situation so that the individual acts on paranoid ideas, panic episodes, and fears of not being able to get back to one's original state.

Many LSD users experience extreme fear during their trips, and psychiatrists say the most common problem is unmanageability. In the first phase, the perception that the identity is gone may make users afraid they will never get back to their normal feelings or selves. Being given LSD without knowing it almost inevitably leads to extreme terror that the mind has been irretrievably lost. Providing guides and setting the psychological and physical stage does not always guard against a paranoid state. LSD can also have an unpleasant physical effect before it begins to take effect. Many persons have nausea, anxiety, nervousness and feelings of hyperactivity, pounding hearts, and sweaty palms. During the experience, LSD users become very aware of their bodily processes and may feel they may stop working—that they will stop breathing or their hearts will stop beating. Somehow the autonomic processes come to be seen as under conscious control, and there is a fear that control will be lost and death will occur.

As LSD came to be used under unsupervised conditions, the knowledge that a bad trip could happen led people to be apprehensive about it, and their expectations were borne out. People may jump out of windows under LSD if they think it can happen. Overdosage can also lead to acute psychotic reactions.

After even a "good" trip, the user may have an LSD hangover, accompanied by a headache, extreme tiredness, and a general state of malaise.

The effects of LSD can be stopped by one of the major antipsychotic drugs, chlorpromazine (Thorazine), or more gently by niacin.

MDA, DMT, PCP, STP

SYNTHETIC HALLUCINOGENS

Brand Name	*Generic Name*	*Street Name*
	DMT	businessman special lunch-hour trip
Ketaject Ketalar Ketavet	ketamine	green jet "K" mauve 1980 supergrass purple special LA coke super acid super C
Sernylan	PCP	angel dust angel mist crystal crystal points cyclone dust elephant tranq flakes hog horse track KJ KW peace weed super weed surfer "T" Tic Tac wacky weed
	STP (DOM)	serenity tranquility and peace

DMT (dimethyltriptamine), STP (methyldimethoxyamphetamine), and MDA (methylenedioxamphetamine) are LSD-like drugs in their action but amphetamine-like in their chemical structures. Like LSD, they depress serotonin in the brain. In low doses all of these drugs stimulate sexual activity in laboratory animals, and in high doses sexual activity is depressed.[15]

STP, also a synthetic drug, is even more powerful than LSD. It is metabolized much more slowly so that the peak can last up to twelve hours, and its effects up to three days. The uncontrolled psychic energy, accompanied by perceptual distortions, trembling, and shaking, makes for some terrifying trips. Because the LSD antidote only makes a bad STP trip worse, STP fell from popularity within a year of its introduction.[16]

DMT is the quickie psychedelic that's almost identical with naturally occurring tryptamines found in the resin of several South American trees and used by the Indians in the snuff, *cohoba,* and in the drink, *yage.* Instead of being eaten, DMT is dried onto parsley and smoked—quite frequently along with marijuana. The "turn-on" takes place within seconds, peaks in three to ten minutes, and the whole experience lasts about thirty minutes. The same, only perhaps milder, effects that occur with LSD take place with DMT. If a bad trip occurs, at least it is over soon. The whole thing happens so fast, there is hardly time to have a sexual encounter along with it, and it's not considered to be among the better sex enhancers.

MDA, an illegal drug which was promoted as "speed for lovers" in the sixties, is a psychedelic amphetamine (methylenedioxyamphetamine) that is a derivative of an oil found in sassafras and nutmeg. According to the *High Times Encyclopedia of Recreational Drugs,* MDA is "very much a body psychedelic, coupling feelings of euphoria and emotional closeness with increased tactile sensitivity. It does not produce the depersonalized and hallucinatory states of other psychedelics, but enhances feelings and makes users very communicative with each other."[17] An MDA trip lasts about eight hours. MDA has serious overdose potential, and users are warned to use very small doses until establishing their toxicity level.

Dr. Frank Gawin has argued that MDA has "a significant potential for sexual benefit" because it combines the "sexual enhancement and increased pleasure derived from stimulants such as cocaine or amphetamine with the ability to enhance affect, facilitate self-insight, and enhance interpersonal empathy in a manner common to hallucinogens, but without the perceptual alterations, depersonalizations, or disturbances in thought which often prevent the hallucinogens from being useful therapeutically or as consistent aphrodisiacs."[18] He goes on to say that several researchers have found that MDA brings feelings expressed as "love" to the surface. This quality with its stimulant activity might make MDA a useful drug to treat sexually dysfunctional persons, and that idea should not be dismissed out of hand, because of some notion that "aphrodisiacs do not exist."

Only one person, a twenty-two-year-old homosexual man, reported the effects of MDA, the hallucinogenic amphetamine, on sexual function. He said he sometimes used marijuana or alcohol with it and noted, correctly, that MDA was promoted as "the love drug" in the sixties. This MDA user claimed that MDA greatly increased his sexual desire, and that with MDA he was capable of multiple orgasms.

"MDA is a mood lifter and can make any situation enjoyable. It increases your sensual awareness and your sexual desire. I do MDA mainly because it makes me feel good all over, and I enjoy myself immensely on it—but I also do it because intimate contact can be very special and sensuous on it. MDA will make me go sexually for several hours after I've lain down with my partner. It is the only time I think I've achieved multiple orgasms and will do so several times (two to four) before going to sleep only to wake up and make love again. Another thing I love to do on MDA is dance—music seems to sound better, and it's much easier to get into when on MDA."

PCP is often pawned off on would-be LSD users, who hardly have anyone to complain to, as the real thing. PCP (phencyclidine) is not a psychedelic like LSD or mescaline, even though it's pushed as such. Underground chemists can get away with this because teenage experimenters don't have any experience of psychedelics to compare it with, and because at that age, they'll try almost anything for kicks or because it's illegal. Too bad, because PCP is a long way from aspirin and coke.

Taking PCP is like giving yourself schizophrenia. Very mild doses produce a little "spaciness" with strong feelings of mind and body separation. More produces a full-blown psychosis. The symptoms are there: amnesia, paranoia, delusions, and violently aggressive behavior. Except for the spontaneous "cure," which may take up to two weeks, doctors can't tell the PCP-induced psychosis from the real thing. Chronic users say it may take years to recover from it.

PCP is called "hog" because it's a veterinary tranquilizer. It's called "KW" for killer weed because of the way it affects people. Sernylan (PCP) came on the market in the fifties. It was tried on human beings, but the psychotic reactions and unmanageable experimental subjects soon led the manufacturer to restrict it to animal use where its advantage is that it can dull the central nervous system without stopping the reflex action that keeps saliva from flowing into the lungs.

PCP is very attractive to basement and garage chemists. About $150 of raw materials can be turned into $58,000 or more (not counting the parsley onto which it's dried), and it's easy to make. In addition to parsley, it's also dried on marijuana and tobacco, and may be ingested in gelatin capsules. The effects come on slowly and last four to six hours. Because of the slow onset, inexperienced users often overdose.

PCP is not primarily or secondarily taken for lovemaking, although at the "mild spaciness" stage some people might be more uninhibited. PCP, though, simply does not make people feel friendly and loving like marijuana often does. It just makes them feel crazy.

In its July 13, 1968, issue, *Rolling Stone* reported that it had interviewed a woman from the barrio who said that PCP was given to young women until they reached psychotic states and then the women were used as prostitutes. This seems unlikely for several reasons. Undrugged prostitutes are available, and who would want to have intercourse with a partner who was confused, disoriented, dizzy, and possibly nauseated, gagging, and foaming at the mouth, or aggressive and screaming?

The backyard chemists continue to be ingenious. Just as the word on PCP began to get around with the kids learning about its crazy-making effects, up pops a new mind-bender. This one is ketamine. Like PCP it's an animal anesthetic, and like PCP it causes psychotic states. However, its effects seem to be milder than PCP and to last a shorter time. Besides delusions and confusion, over 10 percent of users get hallucinations. As with PCP, sex with ketamine is probably irrelevant. Far from being a sex enhancer, it's more likely to be used as a substitute for sex or a way of avoiding human contact, communication, warmth, and closeness.

PART V

SEX THROUGH CHEMISTRY IN THE PRESENT AND THE FUTURE

14

DRUGS AND SEX APPEAL

Many individuals use drugs on a regular, often daily, basis for the singular purpose of making themselves more attractive, more appealing, more sexy. They might even be said to be psychologically dependent on these drugs. But don't dismiss these people out of hand as narcissistic, self-indulgent and wasteful. These people are probably you. At least they are you if you use perfume or cologne, or deodorant, or the so-called feminine hygiene sprays, or vitamin- or hormone-enriched creams. They're also you if you take any drug to change or control your growth or appearance in any other way—for example, if you're an athlete and take steroids or a menopausal woman and take estrogens or rub in creams that are supposed to fade those ugly brown—BUT WHAT'S A WOMAN TO DO?—spots.

Some of the drugs that change the way you look or smell are terrific. Ever work in a hot room with someone who didn't believe in underarm deodorants? Some are merely a waste of money, for instance, feminine "hygiene" sprays, and some of them are dangerous, for instance anabolic steroids.

DRUGS FOR SMELLS

There are two classes of drugs for odors, one to add to your natural odors, and one to make them go away. That is, there are two classes of drugs used deliberately for these purposes. Unbeknownst to you, other drugs you take may be changing the way you smell and subtly influencing the persons you attract and even the time when you have sexual relations.

Odors rule sexual activity in the animal world. A Labrador retriever doesn't walk up to a poodle and say, "How about it?" or study her for coy clues indicating her willingness. The odors she gives off are so powerful that they absolutely control his behavior. When she's not in heat, he's not interested. When she is, he has no more control over his behavior than he does over the beating of his heart. He's driven to try to impregnate her. This animal enslavement by odors is one of the principle differences between people and their pets.

Although olfactory choice seems to have given over to visual choice in human beings, scientists believe that odors have more of an effect on our sexual behavior and choices than we think. In the animal world, the chemical sexual excitant has been dubbed a pheromone. Scientists are convinced that people produce pheromones as well, but there is only indirect evidence.

Not only are the volatile pheromones turn-ons and turn-offs on the farm and in the game park, but they seem to be capable of regulating the fertility cycle of females. For example, take pigs. When female pigs are kept together, eventually the estrus cycle of all of the females will be the same. They will all come in heat at about the same time. It has been suggested that this cyclical clumping is a functional adaptation for pigs which increases the chance that pigs will always be around. Thus, if all the pigs are ready at the same time and a wandering boar trots by, he can impregnate all of them during the same visit. It may also be that a boar is more likely to wander by if all of the lady pigs are wafting their come-hither pheromones across the countryside together.

There is quite solid evidence that women put out pheromones too. When women live together in groups, the same clustering effect occurs. After a period of time, all or most of the women will be getting their menstrual periods at about the same time, and the longer the women are together, the closer their periods become.

Some physiologists think that the variation in the rates of sexual intercourse among couples during the menstrual cycle is due in part to subtle pheromone messages secreted by women. Normally, there is a decrease in the frequency of intercourse among couples during the woman's luteal phase which is about the eighteenth to the twenty-fifth day. However, if women are on the pill, this decrease is not observed, and the frequency is the same throughout the cycle, except for the actual days of menstruation. Scientists have interpreted this pill-related change to pheromones, suggesting that during the luteal phase, when progesterone is being produced, either a sexual turn-off pheromone is also produced, or more likely, women's turn-on pheromones stop being made. The pill suppresses the production of progesterone, so that the male gets the same pheromone messages throughout the cycle and maintains the frequency of intercourse.[1]

The identification of pheromones in humans may go a long way toward explaining the vagaries of sexual attraction. So far no one has been able to explain why there is a kind of electric magnetism between two people and not others, or why some people have more capacity for attraction than others. Beauty has something to do with it, but not everything.

A *New York Times* headline recently announced that "Women Respond to Sex Attractant Isolated from Male Sweat." The article went on to say that a pheromone called alpha androstenol has been isolated from the perspiration of human males by an English research team. When purified the substance was said to smell like sandalwood and to be an extraordinary turn-on for women.

Some believe that the popularity of perfumes made from animal excretions is not because they smell nice, but because they also contain pheromonelike chemicals that are out of the smelling range we can identify, but that affect us despite our inability to detect them. We know that many animals, dogs for instance, have a much more sensitive sniffing system than we do. Since much of sexual appeal seems to be beyond our ability to control, it seems perfectly logical that we are being led around, not by our noses, but by undetectable scents that get past our noses and stir our genitals.

Everyone has a unique scent that is as obvious and identifiable to even the most ill-bred of canines as a fingerprint is to an FBI agent. Body scents are also influenced by the diet—meat-eaters smelling different from vegetarians—race, and of course, sex. Age may also have a distinctive odor. If so, the older woman of the future may compete more successfully with younger women for the attention of men—if she cares to—by using pheromones obtained from younger women.

One of the attractions of animal-secretion-based perfumes is the way they change depending on how they interact with the natural skin chemistry. The right perfume on the right skin has been recognized as an aphrodisiac almost forever. The ancient Egyptians were especially known for their fondness for perfumes. Fragrances have been found in tombs over 3,000 years old. Tutankhamen's tomb, dated 1350 B.C., contained a perfumed ointment apparently thought necessary for the final trip of royalty. Cleopatra and her court considered perfume to be absolutely essential for the well-turned-out courtesan or mummy, whether alive or dead.[2]

There are four kinds of animal ingredients that are perfume bases. Flower parts, though they may have it for bees, just don't make it for humans. Ambergris, a ball of waxy grayish substance that is vomited up by sperm whales, has been the most highly prized ingredient in fine perfumes for eons for its aroma and aphrodisiac properties. Anyone who finds one of these balls adrift on the sea or washed up on a beach will be as happy as if he had found a bottle with a genie in it. Ounce for ounce it's more expensive than gold, and is certainly one of the most expensive items that occurs naturally.

The anal glands of the male musk deer are the source of one of the world's most popular aphrodisiac scents. In fact, the sex scents of animals, such as the civet cat and the beaver, are, along with ambergris, the most popular of perfume bases. The Empress Josephine was said to entice with musk to the extent she sometimes got complaints from Napoleon, who apparently was extremely sensitive to odors as well as power. The Arabs liked the musk odor all around them, so they put it in the mortar when they constructed their buildings. When the sun shone and the bricks warmed up, the air became heavily perfumed.[2] It seems like an excellent idea, and one that any old building could benefit from. Certainly better musky than musty.

Considering their source, it is obvious why the animal-based perfumes are so costly, and why they are not the choice of cosmetic manufacturers who have preyed on our fears of offending to the point that we smell like variations of Right Guard from our hair to our toenails. The average woman of today is a walking olfactory confusion. Her shampoo, her hair spray, her cosmetics, her soap, her toothpaste, her mouthwash, her underarm deodorant, her depilatory, her body lotion, her cuticle softener, and her perfume all smell different, and that's not all. Lately she's fallen for a perfumed douche, for spraying her crotch with a perfumed "feminine hygiene spray," and for using deodorant tampons. With all that "protection" it seems a self-respecting pheromone trying to get out and wing its way to a receptive male would hardly have a chance. Of course, it might not get by his hair spray and shaving lotion and cologne and deodorant and jock itch powder et cetera anyway.

The so-called feminine hygiene spray has nothing hygienic about it. Most of these products are nothing but perfume, an emollient (skin softener), and a propellant. Some have flavors. Few contain an antibacterial agent since the ban on hexachlorophene, which was found to be absorbable and dangerous, and the manufacturers admitted the antibacterials didn't do a thing anyway.[3-5] Besides being a rip-off these sprays can produce swelling, itching, and eruptions of the vulva and the area around the vulva. These unpleasant side effects are not confined to the recipient of the directed spray. The user's consort may also end up with a contact dermatitis.[3] Despite the popularity of these items, especially with the self-conscious high school set, everything points to plain soap and water as the "feminine hygiene" product of choice.

Some of the douches contain vinegar and some contain perfume. Normal women need neither. The vagina, even more than the nose and the ear, is self-cleansing. Use of the perfumed douche risks an allergic reaction. It, like the spray and various types of contraceptives, has no effect on the bacteria of the vagina.[5] Moreover, douches are risky forms of contraceptives. Sperm may not swim faster than you can run, but they're much closer to their target than you are to the bathroom.

A research project concluded that vaginal odors do vary in intensity and pleasantness through the menstrual cycle, as judged by both men and women who were asked to sniff vaginal secretions at various cycle stages.[6] On average, odors were judged to be weaker and more pleasant early in the cycle. There was no indication that either sex found the odors erotic. Nor, however, is there any evidence that the secretions of vaginas could be erotic if they'd been sprayed with cheap perfume or stuffed with deodorant tampons.

DRUGS FOR ATHLETES

Want to have a superb body so that heads turn when you walk by on the beach? Want to have muscles that ripple in the sun and to look like you've spent all your life eating health foods and doing pushups? Want to be strong so nobody will push you around? Want to look like a sex object? You, too, can do what so many athletes who need brawn have done. Forget your brains. Take anabolic steroids and look gorgeous but ruin your sex life.

ANABOLIC STEROIDS

Brand Name	*Generic Name*
Maxibolin	ethylestrenol
Dianabol	methandieone
Decadurabolin Durabolin	nandrolone
Anavar	oxandrolone
Neodrol	stanolone
Winstrol	stanozolol

Talk to young football players or weight lifters or throwers and they'll tell you that everybody takes body-building drugs, and that they have to do it to compete.

Anabolic steroids, Dianabol for example, are synthetic derivatives of the male hormone, testosterone, which were put on the market to combat senility and loss of appetite in the elderly and to help build up people who were debilitated from long illnesses, or long stays in prisoner-of-war or concentration camps. Because of their muscle-building properties, more than ten times greater than methyl-testosterone, steroids were soon the darlings of athletes, especially for those events that require super strength and stamina. By 1968, it was probably impossible to do well in national or international competition in some sports without the edge given by these drugs. The attraction to athletes in addition to muscle development is that on steroids they are less susceptible to fatigue so they can train harder and longer and are less likely to get tendon injuries. When they do get hurt, they seem to heal faster.[7] The steroids affect protein metabolism so that athletes in training build muscles faster and increase their strength.[8]

But the cost for this chemical boost, which for some is probably the difference between fame and anonymity, can be very high. Testicles shrivel, breasts may develop, and libido drop along with the sperm count and the volume of ejaculate. And these sex-related side effects aren't all. Anabolic steroids also cause acne, nausea, hypertension, headache, urethritis, vomiting, loss of appetite, and liver damage that can be serious and permanent. The sex-related side effects are reversible upon discontinuance of the drugs. Some men find that, rather than decreasing their libido, it may be somewhat increased if the drug has been taken in small doses.[7] However, body builders usually take large doses.

There is increasing evidence that an effect of anabolic steroids is indirect and deadly. It seems they may be capable of causing cervical cancer in the partners of the men who have been taking them. Women beware! Inquire into the drug habits of your athletic partner.

Not just men, but women athletes, too, are using steroids, and they're getting some androgenic side effects as well as muscles. Most of them develop some facial hair and voice deepening. Some of them experience clitoral enlargement and menstrual irregularities. Presumably they should have some increased libido as well, but it seems this side effect can go either way. Many doctors believe that women who take steroids are running the risk of destroying their child-bearing potential and developing cancer, especially if the drugs have been taken before the woman has reached her full growth development.

HORMONES FOR GROWTH AND AGING

Hormones are needed for sexual development. In women the clitoris, labia majora and body hair are under the control of male hormones, so when they take androgenic anabolic steroids they are increasing their maleness. Other areas of their bodies, the labia minora, vagina, cervix, uterus, fallopian tubes, and breasts are responsive to estrogens. Sometimes the body makes too many hormones, which results in sexual precocity, children developing sexually far younger than normal. Sometimes the body doesn't make enough hormones so that growth is delayed and there is sexual immaturity. Sometimes hormones are taken inadvertently affecting normal development, and sometimes hormones are taken by menopausal and postmenopausal women to combat senile vaginitis and aging skin, as well as hot flashes and brittle bones.

In girls, sexual maturity takes place approximately between nine and twelve years, beginning with breast development and proceeding to pubic hair, underarm hair, and menstruation. Boys begin to mature a bit later than girls. Their average age of puberty is from eleven to fifteen years. That's when their testicles and penis increase in length, they develop pubic, facial, and other body hair, their voices deepen, and sperm production begins.

There is rarely an organic problem in girls who are sexually precocious. If they develop sexually before nine years, it is rare that something needs to be done to correct the situation. Boys are different. Over half of them who mature before age eleven have some problem with their adrenal glands, their central nervous system, or their testes. The problem is often a tumor. All cases, whether girls or boys, of sexual precocity should be taken to a doctor.

Sexual precocity has occurred in girls as young as two years, and there are cases of girls producing babies at age five. Sometimes, if no tumor can be found, sexually precocious girls are given medroxyprogesterone (Depo-Provera). This drug will stop menstruation and breast development, but not body growth. Moreover, it may increase rather than decrease body hair and inhibit future ovulation. Therefore, it is not recommended unless a sexually precocious child is younger than eight years old.[9]

Some cases have been reported of inadvertent sexual precocity caused by cosmetic lotions and creams. Some of these contain estrogens and progesterone. If they are used frequently on a child, the hormones will be absorbed into her system. She will develop brownish black pigmentation of her nipples and begin sexual development. These hormones may also appear in vitamin combinations in foreign countries.

If no organic problem can be found, sex hormones are usually given to boys and girls when they fail to develop on schedule. If girls have not begun to menstruate by the time they are fifteen, they are put on the pill, a combination of estrogens and progesterone. Boys who don't have tumors that have caused their sexual immaturity are given an androgen, oxandrolone (Anavar), for example, as well as lots of emotional support and assurances that soon they will be as sexually appealing as their fellow adolescents.[10] The androgen will work if the boy has a normal amount of growth hormone in his body.[11]

In addition to being prescribed to sexually immature and precocious children, hormones are given to transsexuals to change the way they look. Sometimes a man feels like a woman in a man's body and is determined to become a woman. If he is given estrogens and progestins, with or without castration, he will develop breasts, a smooth, soft skin, more scalp hair, less of a beard and other body hair, a smaller prostate, less acne, and less libido. His testes will shrivel, if he still has them, and his potency will drop.

The rush of hormones during adolescence, which makes girls women and boys men, also produces the dreaded "greasies" and the loathed acne, both considered by teenagers to be sexual turn-offs. Some doctors prescribe an antibiotic, tetracycline, for acne, but others are reluctant to prescribe antibiotics for long periods of time. Women who take them often develop a vaginal yeast infection as a side effect, and long-term use of antibiotics leads to the development of antibiotic-resistant bacteria so that antibiotics don't work when you most need them. There has been some success with vitamin B_6 for acne that flares up in women just before menstruation. The best product for severe acne is tretinoin (Aberal, Retin-A), a prescription drug that peels and dries the skin, but that takes a considerable amount of patience, including a "worse" period, before it works. Some people try it but give up too soon when they find their acne is not only not improving, but apparently thriving. Perseverance, faith, and following directions should produce a skin with as much sex appeal as the next in about three months.[12]

The most common use of female hormones besides oral contraceptives is for postmenopausal symptoms. Although the most common and disconcerting symptom is the hot flash, the hormones are also taken for two reasons related to sexual function and appearance. The first of these is senile vaginitis. During menopause women stop producing hormones that ruled their menstrual cycles, and this affects the surface lining of cells in their vaginas, which get thin and dry and may cause sexual intercourse to be painful. Replacement estrogens may fix this problem so that a normal sex life can be enjoyed. One way of getting them is by using a vaginal estrogen-containing cream instead of taking them orally. The estrogens are readily absorbed from the cream through the vaginal wall and can also provide some lubrication.[13]

The second reason is to soften the skin and retain a youthful appearance. Too bad—it probably doesn't work. There's no evidence that estrogens will keep your skin young.

Because long-term use of estrogens increases the danger of uterine cancer, women are advised that they should only take them for severe menopausal symptoms and probably not for long periods of time.[14]

DRUGS TO CHANGE THE WAY YOU LOOK

Unfortunately there probably are more drugs that can decrease sex appeal by affecting appearance adversely than there are drugs that can help it. Many drugs and alcohol change body hair distribution and cause breast development in males—hardly a sexual turn-on. Some drugs cause female adolescents to grow beards and moustaches.

Alcohol is one of the worst offenders in terms of a change in body hair patterns and producing gynecomastia in men. Heavy drinking damages the liver and reduces testosterone levels. Thus, the feminization. Gynecomastia also happens naturally in aging, and may occur as a result of taking reserpine, digitalis, digoxin, spironolactone, and hormones.[15]

Digitalis interferes with hormone production in men. It has estrogenlike effects which decrease the production of testosterone and LH, by causing the Leydig cells that make testosterone to shrivel. A postmenopausal woman who takes digitalis may develop hard and horny patches on her skin and vaginal lining.

A drug taken to prevent epileptic seizures, diphenylhydantoin (Dilantin) may cause facial hair to grow on young women by interfering with their normal hormone metabolism.

One of the most useful over-the-counter drugs that you can buy is a good sunscreen. Used faithfully throughout a lifetime of outdoor activity, sunscreens will do more to keep you looking young and lovely into your old age than any cosmetic regardless of its claims, regardless of its contents, and regardless of the price. You don't have to fade age spots if you don't get them in the first place. You probably won't get them if you read labels, and only buy sunscreening lotions that contain para-aminobenzoic acid (PABA). This stuff is better than all the baby oil, coconut oil, vitamin-enriched and hormone creams you can buy. Not only will your skin look better if you use it, but you'll markedly decrease the risk of skin cancers.

If it's too late for you, and your skin is beginning to resemble an alligator's, is there anything you can do? You could get a chemical peel or dermabrasion on your face. That's expensive, it hurts, and it still leaves your legs, hands, and arms unchanged. Creams such as Porcelana and Esoterica require diligent application twice a day for months and then only fade spots a little. Most people don't stick to the routine so they don't find out that they wouldn't have had much luck anyway. The most effective thing to do is to pretend they're freckles and that everybody would look better if they had them.

Probably the best way to look good is to feel good inside. Feeling good about yourself means you probably will take care of yourself, care for your appearance, and wear a smile on your face and your disposition. Everyone's beautiful who does that. Make sure you understand what your drugs can and can't do, and what they're supposed to do. Try to understand their risks and benefits. Keep feeling well and you'll keep looking well. And that's the real key to sex appeal.

15

DRUGS AND SEX IN YOUR FUTURE

"What is needed is a new drug which will relieve and console our suffering species without doing more harm in the long run than it does in the short. Such a drug must be potent in minute doses and synthesizable. If it does not possess these qualities, its production, like that of wine, beer, spirits and tobacco will interfere with the raising of indispensable food and fibers. It must be less toxic than opium or cocaine, less likely to produce undesirable social consequences than alcohol or barbiturates, less inimical to heart and lungs than the tars and nicotine of cigarettes. And on the positive side, it should produce changes in consciousness more interesting, more intrinsically valuable than mere sedation or dreaminess, delusions of omnipotence or release from inhibition." A recent remark on the state of pharmacology and a guide to the drugs of the future? Hardly. This statement is from *The Doors of Perception,* written by Aldous Huxley, and published in 1954. A quarter of a century later we seem to be no closer to happiness through chemistry than we were then.

The only legal, freely obtainable drugs capable of modifying states of consciousness are alcohol and tobacco, despite their well-documented, economic and personally devastating effects in terms of liver, lung, heart, and sexual function, as well as the deaths and disabilities incurred by drunken drivers.

All of the mind-altering drugs whipped up by basement and garage chemists are illegal. All of the psychedelics, euphorics, narcotics, and tranquilizers that occur naturally in berries, roots, bark, leaves, and flowers are either illegal or are available only by a doctor's prescription.

Although some of these may alter sexual function in pleasurable ways for some people, doctors do not prescribe them for such reasons.

Doctors treat or prevent illness—organic lesions, breakdowns in normal biological processes. Although sometimes permitted to treat unhappiness, e.g., psychiatric neuroses, and unwanted physical states, e.g., big noses, doctors must usually be seen as alleviating or preventing a problem. They must play by the social rules constructed by society and their profession or they will be in danger of losing their quite special positions in the social hierarchy. Doctors are rarely allowed to change physical states that are viewed as normal or average. Treating menopause is O.K. because all aging has been defined as sickness and as something to be avoided as long as possible. Breast augmentation or subtraction is marginal and only entirely approved of if the breasts are very small or very large, and preferably to treat cases of the latter. Otherwise such surgery is suspect and its practitioners are viewed as being at the fringe of acceptable practice.

Breast surgery and face-lifts may both be justified by the claim that they are necessary for persons who have them to maintain their professional or business positions, or to prevent depression and psychological breakdowns. Penile implants and surgically exposing hooded clitorises are only marginally O.K. because the erect penis and the ability to have orgasms are normal states. But just go into your physician's office and say, "Doctor, I am a responsible person not given to excesses. I have never been drunk and my driving record is exemplary. I have confined my use of mind-altering drugs to the modest and social use of alcohol, and without going out of my way to purchase it, have had a few puffs of marijuana, which I found to be mildly euphoric. I also took Valium when you prescribed it for my somewhat elevated blood pressure, but I'm afraid I didn't take it as often as you asked me to, and I didn't get the prescription refilled. My sex life is pleasurable, and as far as I know, completely normal for a person my age. But, Doctor, I would like to add a little more spice and adventure to it, and do not want to buy drugs in the illegal market. My wife and I would like to try cocaine. We understand that it is a fast- and short-acting drug, relatively free from physical damage or side effects unless it is used frequently over long periods of time. We only want to have a few hits, maybe once a month, in the privacy of our bedroom. We have shown ourselves to be responsible citizens and would behave responsibly with cocaine." You know already that there's no way that your doctor's going to prescribe cocaine or any other legally prescribed drug to make a normal sex life into one that is more fun or more aggressive or more whatever. We simply don't have the social rules that permit it.

It is the social climate, not the pharmacological capabilities, that governs the future development and availability of aphrodisiacs. Irrationally, it is easier to bring a new mind-altering drug to market than to change laws that rule out old ones. Research and technological development dollars are getting harder, not easier, to come by. When there is competition for them, they end up on projects that are trying to develop drugs for illness and disability. Any deviation from this—at least with federal money—puts them in the running for Senator William Proxmire's "Golden Fleece Award."

Despite the political reality of the unlikelihood of a breakthrough in pharmacological aphrodisia in the immediate future, there are considerable discoveries in the world of molecular biology that have the potential for decreasing the harmful side effects of drugs on sexual function, and for dealing with organic abnormalities that produce impotence, ejaculatory problems, and infertility. In the past, most drugs that altered states of consciousness were discovered by accident; there has been no understanding until recently of how they work, or why drugs that treat different kinds of illness have similar effects on sexual function. In the past, scientists changed the structure of a drug known to possess some desired quality—appetite suppression, for example—and then they gave it to animals to try it out. Sometimes they discovered other uses for the new drug in this way. Now, with the recognition that the brain has specific receptors for chemical neurotransmitters, new drugs are tested on brain cells in the test tube, to see how they bind to the receptor sites.

Much of the sexual-response chemistry in the body relates to the dopamine-serotonin complex, two neurotransmitters that work in tandem to govern much of the brain's activity. You will recall that drugs that block serotonin, LSD and other psychedelics, for example, are aphrodisiacs, at least in the sense of modifying perceptions and often increasing pleasure during sexual activity.

This is how it works. There are specific nerve cells that take up dopamine, for example. Now, if a drug is given that binds to the places that are supposed to be for dopamine, then there will be excess dopamine loose in the brain. Moreover, the cells that make dopamine can tell that the cells which were supposed to take up dopamine aren't doing it, so they make more and more dopamine until the brain is flooded with it, and the body becomes stiff and trembling. This is a greatly oversimplified picture. There are actually two kinds of dopamine receptors, and the way that serotonin and other neurotransmitters, such as histamine, are interrelated, is not fully understood. There is an understanding, however, that drugs that increase serotonin, such as antidepressants, seem to depress sexual function and vice versa. Research is now proceeding rapidly in brain chemistry and holds out the hope of finding drugs that can correct specific problems without producing disagreeable side effects. Probably less than 5 percent of the brain's neurotransmitters have been found so far. One of these is an analgesic substance, an enkephalin, that is produced naturally by the brain, binds to specific "opiate" receptors, and may account for the way acupuncture works.

To date, most brain drug research has been directed at finding antischizophrenic drugs, i.e., major antipsychotic drugs like chlorpromazine, that do not produce Parkinsonlike effects or menstrual abnormalities. As this research proceeds, it is likely that drugs will be found that do not interfere with sexual function, and more will be found that can correct sexual problems. Some of these are likely to be found by chance as a result of the effort toward specificity in drugs, and the effort to understand the entire chemistry of the body. For example, there is a parallel effort in basic science to understand the body's hormonal system, that is, to understand how the secretions of the pituitary gland affect the uterus, ovaries, and testes, and how their secretions in turn affect sexual function, secondary sex characteristics, and fertility. The brain chemistry research is beginning to interface with the hormone chemistry research. A contraceptive for males is being tested now, and is expected to be on the market soon. This drug does not work directly on sperm-producing tissues, but indirectly by blocking the neurotransmitters in the brain that are responsible for sending messages to the sperm-producing tissues.

The most fruitful research with the potential for correcting male impotence and female infertility involves brain neurotransmitters. A substance known to increase the production of LH and FSH has also been found to stimulate sexual desire. The substance is LRH (luteinizing release hormone).

A pioneer in LRH research, Dr. Robert Moss of the University of Texas, and others have traced the path of LRH, which is produced naturally by the hypothalamus and has long been known to control the production of LH and FSH which in turn control the production of ova and sperm, and have linked it to a sexual desire, arousal, and mating center in the brain. When LRH has been given to men whose sexual appetites have been depressed because of psychological reasons, in most cases, sexual desire and activity have returned.

In Europe, LRH has also corrected delayed puberty in young men, has induced potency in previously impotent men, and has elevated sperm counts to increase male fertility.

In women, LRH has been given to treat infertility. Because LRH is natural, it stimulates the production of only one ovum in each cycle.

The fertility drugs currently on the market such as Clomid, stimulate the release of many ova. When this happens, the chance of multiple births is high with few, if any, of the babies surviving.

LRH is very expensive, perhaps $100 a dose, but synthetics are being made that may reduce the cost to a few cents. Although they are being considered by American drug companies, they will probably be on European pharmacy shelves first.

Although neurobiology, neurotransmitters, and cerebral wonder drugs are the current darlings of research, the sex system is so complex, it can be challenged in almost any system. Thoughts affect blood volume affect nerve affect brain affect respiration and so on. Someday we'll have an understanding of how a pretty face and a pheromone wafting through the air can produce a pooling of blood in the genitals of a surprised teenager, and why it happens to some individuals and not others.

Armchair pharmacologists enjoy musing over the drug future and making lists of the best bets for the future. In 1968, the members of the American College of Neuropsychopharmacology amused themselves by making lists of the drugs they thought would be available to normal human beings by the end of the century. Many of the envisioned drugs were seen as coping with the stresses and strains of a restless, highly mobile and bored leisure society, and some were seen as treating an increasingly aging population. One participant thought aphrodisiacs would be generally available in response to an increasingly "sensually oriented culture," and another thought drugs would "regulate sexual responses."[1] The predictions are not unlikely in themselves, but the length of time in which they will happen seems optimistic. It takes ten years to bring a new drug to market and we are a long way from making this type of drug generally available. Indeed, the social climate toward use of any drug except alçohol for its aphrodisiac or recreational properties is punitive, and drug laws remain unchanged despite any number of government and private reports concluding they are irrational and counterproductive.[2]

If and when we have aphrodisiac drugs, they may come in through the back door of gerontology. By the end of the century, about 20 percent, or about twice as high a proportion as there is now, of American citizens will be over sixty-five. Most of these people will be highly active. They are playing tennis and jogging and swimming now, and they are not ready to become sexually inactive. This trend should increase. There is a precedent in our culture for defining aging as an illness that should be corrected if possible. Thus we have hormones for menopause and an increasing acceptance of wrinkle-removing surgery. Methyltestosterone is given now (not very effectively) to treat impotence associated with aging. Thus, aphrodisiacs such as LRH that help sexual performance should be highly acceptable and salable, with aphrodisiacs of the attractant sort perhaps not so far behind.

For sex-attractant drugs, pheromones have been suggested, some scientists hypothesizing that a sex-attractant pheromone for post-menopausal women might be made from the vaginal secretions of young women.[3]

A pheromone in a shaving lotion or cologne is apparently almost on drugstore shelves. Commercial perfume manufacturers are competing to be the first to put alpha androstenol, the pheromone isolated from male sweat that is sexually arousing to women, into male cosmetics.

Older women may soon have more sex appeal, for not only are they gaining economic security, they may become brighter and more interesting as they remain in the work force. We seem to be on the threshold of marketing drugs that will increase memory. It seems probable then that there might soon be drugs that prevent the deterioration in recent memory capacity that is associated with aging. If persons remain bright, clever, and vital in their later years, we will have gone a long way toward keeping them attractive and sexually active. The only problem with this is that there are about twice as many women as men over sixty-five. If all women want to be sexually active, in their later years, some are going to have to share, or there is going to have to be some rethinking of lesbianism and masturbation. A generation jogging its way into old age may not take kindly to being told it should forgo sex, sit in a rocker and enjoy drug-induced erotic dreams, however pleasant they may be.

Some visionaries believe that the sexual imbalance in the elderly will take care of itself as a result of the recent disclosure that some women are having amniocentesis to learn the sex of their babies when they find they are pregnant, and then having abortions if the sex of the fetus is not what they wanted. In two to one of these instances, the aborted fetus is female. If this process should continue, and there is little to stop it—abortions, whether legal or illegal have always been available—the sex ratio in society may be altered in favor of men, so that the ratio would become more equal during the later years.

Abortions after fetal sex determination might not be the only way to alter nature's ratio of men to women. It is conceivable that a drug could be found that would make it more likely that a male- (or female-) determining sperm would find its way to the ovum, depending upon the preference of the parents-to-be.

Not only will the kind of drugs change in the future, with the development of problem-specific drugs most likely, but there will be changes in the way they are taken. Tiny little drug-soaked pellets will be implanted under the skin so that a steady drug dose can be obtained throughout the day. Contraceptive drugs for both men and women, and drugs to correct mental problems, epilepsy, diabetes, and hormonal imbalances are particularly likely to be given in steady doses.

Drugs will also be tailored according to the sex of the patient. Over two dozen drugs in current use are known to vary in effects that depend on the recipient's sex.[4] More attention will be given to the patient's weight and circadian rhythms when dosing with highly potent and specific drugs. These will be problems for the clinical pharmacologist or pharmacist whose expertise in pharmacokinetics is rapidly making him indispensable in modern hospitals. In the future, it is almost a certainty that one of these persons will tailor drugs to you, based specifically on your diagnosis, drug history, sex, age, weight, and life-style, and that this will happen in ambulatory as well as institutional care. Moreover, he or she will monitor your progress and adjust your dosage, or react to drug-related problems. In addition to asking for drugs to treat your ills, eventually you may be asking for drugs for psychic stimulation or for dreamy weekends.

There is likely to be an increased blurring between cosmetics and drugs, with no decrease in the emphasis on physical appearance. The biggest breakthrough here will be in weight control. Fat will be conquered by a drug that controls the appetite-controlling center—the appestat—in the brain. An additional help to dieters will be in the form of drug foods that fill you and fool you, but aren't turned into energy and pounds.

Meanwhile, the trend will continue toward drugs that are supposed to give you more sex appeal by peeling you, tanning you, softening you, coloring you, curling and removing your hair, firming you, freshening you, stimulating you, smoothing out wrinkles on your face, eyes, lips, legs, knees, elbows, etc. Drugs will certainly be developed that may be taken informally to curl hair, prevent cavities, change skin color, and prevent the loss of skin elasticity during aging. There will be a better understanding of the role of vitamins and minerals and your requirements throughout life, and whether large doses are beneficial for particular illnesses or during specific age or physical states, such as infancy or pregnancy. For example, a way will be found to stop the calcium depletion in elderly women without incurring the risk of cancer that is now associated with estrogen replacement.

Not that all of these pharmacological changes are just around the corner. Many of them will not come to market unless there are profound changes in society. If you want to have legal drugs that have aphrodisiac properties whether for sexual attraction or for the modification of sexual function or the perception of it, or even drugs that correct sexual dysfunction, you have to create a social climate that makes them possible. As it is now, some of the most harmful drugs are legal, and some of the most benign drugs are illegal. Sex should be good and fun—a source of joy and a binding force between people throughout life. Not all recreational drugs are addictive. Some recreational drugs may only create, as Carlos Castaneda put it in his book, *A Separate Reality*.

At the least, society should support consumers having greater knowledge about the drugs that adversely affect sexual function, and should encourage physicians to have more concern about the sexual side effects of the drugs they prescribe. This one is easy; swallow your embarrassment—think of the potential benefits—screw up your courage—and bring the subject up whenever you get a new drug. Make your drugs and their effects on your sex life a subject that matters to your physician as well as yourself and your partner.

APPENDIXES

APPENDIX A
Questionnaire

I AM WRITING A BOOK ABOUT THE EFFECTS OF DRUGS, ALCOHOL AND MEDICINES ON SEXUAL FUNCTION. IF YOU HAVE EXPERIENCED ANY CHANGE IN YOUR SEXUAL DESIRE OR PERFORMANCE THAT YOU ASSOCIATE WITH A DRUG OR MEDICINE, COULD YOU PLEASE TAKE A FEW MINUTES TO FILL OUT THIS QUESTIONNAIRE AND RETURN IT TO ME? PLEASE GIVE AS DETAILED ANSWERS AS POSSIBLE. ATTACH ADDITIONAL SHEETS OF PAPER AS NEEDED. IF YOU CAN'T COMPLETE THE QUESTIONNAIRE, PLEASE PASS IT ON TO SOMEONE YOU BELIEVE HAS HAD SOME EXPERIENCE. THANKS VERY MUCH FOR YOUR HELP.

Patricia J. Bush, Ph.D.

SEX: M ____ F ____ AGE: ____ YEARS

NAME OF DRUG ____

WAS THE DRUG USED WITH OTHER DRUGS? YES __ NO __

IF YES, PLEASE NAME OTHER DRUGS ____________________

HOW DID THE DRUG(S) AFFECT YOUR:

SEXUAL DESIRE AND AROUSAL? __________________________

____

____

ORGASMS? (Time to achieve, number, quality, etc.)

WITH PARTNER ____

____

____

PARTNER WAS OPPOSITE SEX? YES __ NO __

WITHOUT PARTNER ____

____

____

ERECTIONS ____

____

____

EJACULATIONS ____

____

____

COULD YOU PLEASE DESCRIBE THE CIRCUMSTANCES, i.e. whether the drug was used at a party, at a large or small dose, etc.

____

____

____

____

I USED THIS DRUG *PRIMARILY* BECAUSE OF THE WAY IT AFFECTS MY SEXUAL FUNCTION YES ___ NO ___, MY PRIMARY REASON WAS ______________________________________

____

SOMETIMES (Explain) ____

____

OTHER COMMENTS:

I HAVE USED THIS DRUG: ONE TIME __________

2-10 TIMES __________ OVER 10 TIMES __________

PLEASE USE THE REST OF THIS SPACE TO ELABORATE ON YOUR COMMENTS OR TO ANSWER THE SAME QUESTIONS ABOUT THE WAY OTHER DRUGS HAVE AFFECTED YOUR SEXUAL DESIRE AND FUNCTION.

APPENDIX B
A Summary Table of Sex and Drugs

Drugs That *May* Increase Libido*

alcohol—in small amounts
amphetamines (Amphedrine, Apetain, Benzedrine, Dexedrine)
androgens, e.g., methyltestosterone
anticholinergics—rare
  e.g., atropine, scopolamine, belladonna
barbiturates—in small amounts
bromocriptine (Parlodel)
cocaine
DMT
glutethimide (Doriden)
hashish/hash oil
levodopa (l-dopa)
LSD
marijuana
MDA
mescaline
methaqualone (Quaalude, Sopor)
peyote
psilocybin
STP
thioridazine (Mellaril)—rare
tranylcypromine (Parnate)
tricyclic antidepressants—rare
  e.g., Elavil, Norpramin, Tofranil
tryptophan

Drugs That *May* Decrease Libido

alcohol
amitriptyline (Elavil)
amphetamines—high chronic use
  (Amphedrine, Apetain, Benzedrine, Dexedrine)
anabolic steroids
barbiturates
chlordiazepoxide (Librium)
cyproterone acetate
desipramine (Norpramin, Pertofrane)
diazepam (Valium)
diethylpropion (Tenuate)
estrogens

*Most of these drugs can also decrease libido in some persons, especially at high doses.

fenfluramine (Pondimin)
heroin
hydromorphone (Dilaudid)
imipramine (Tofranil)
mazindol (Sanorex)
meperidine (Demerol)
methadone
morphine
nicotine
nortriptyline (Aventyl)
oral contraceptives
phenmetrazine (Preludin)
phenoxybenzamine (Dibenzyline)
protriptyline (Vivactil)
tryptophan

Drugs That *May* Increase Potency and the Number and/or Quality of Orgasms

androgens, e.g., methyltestosterone
clomiphene (Clomid)
cocaine
DMT
ginseng—rare
hashish/hash oil
levodopa (l-dopa)
LSD
marijuana
MDA
mescaline
methamphetamine (Desoxyn, Opedrine, Methedrine)
methylphenidate (Ritalin)
peyote
psilocybin
STP

Drugs That *May* Decrease Potency and the Number and/or Quality of Orgasms

alcohol
amitriptyline (Elavil)
atropine
barbiturates
belladonna
bethanidine
chlorpromazine (Thorazine)
chlorthalidone (Hygroton)
clofibrate (Atromid-S)
clonidine (Catapres)
desipramine (Norpramin, Pertofrane)
disopyramide (Norpace)
estrogens
fenfluramine (Pondimin)
fluphenazine (Permitil, Prolixin)
furosemide (Lasix)
guanethidine (Ismelin)
heroin
hydralazine (Apresoline, Lopress)
hydromorphone (Dilaudid)
imipramine (Tofranil)
isocarboxazid (Marplan)

mebanazine (Actomol)
meperidine (Demerol)
methadone
methantheline (Banthine)
methaqualone (Quaalude, Sopor)
methyldopa (Aldomet)
morphine
nicotine—heavy smoking
nortriptyline (Aventyl)
opium
oral contraceptives
pargyline (Eutonyl)
phenelzine (Nardil)
propantheline (Probanthine)
protriptyline (Vivactil)
thiazide diuretics, e.g., Hydrodiuril
thioridazine (Mellaril)
tranylcypromine (Marplan)
triamterene (Dyrenium)

Drugs That *May* Cause Ejaculatory Problems

alseroxylon (Rau-Tab, Rautensin, Rauwiloid)
atropine
belladonna
bethanidine
butaperazine (Repoise)
chlordiazepoxide (Librium)—rare
chlorprothixene (Taractan)
cyproterone acetate
deserpidine (Harmonyl)
guanethidine (Ismelin)
haloperidol (Haldol)
heroin
hydromorphone (Dilaudid)
isocarboxazid (Marplan)
mebanazine (Actomol)
meperidine (Demerol)
mesoridazine (Serentil)
methadone
methantheline (Banthine)
pargyline (Eutonyl)
perphenazine (Trilafon)
phenelzine (Nardil)
phenoxybenzamine (Dibenzyline)
prochlorperazine (Compazine)
propantheline (Probanthine)
rauwolfia, e.g. Raudixin, Raupena, Rauserpa
rescinnamide (Moderil)
reserpine, e.g. Raused, Reserpoid, Serpasil
scopolamine
thiazide diuretics (e.g., Hydrodiuril)
thiothixene (Navane)
trifluoperazine (Stelazine)

Drugs That *May* Change Perceptions During Sexual Activity

amyl nitrite
butyl nitrite

DMT
hashish/hash oil
ketamine
LSD
marijuana
MDA
mescaline
nitrous oxide
PCP
peyote
psilocybin

Drugs That *May* Cause Male Breast Development (Gynecomastia)

alcohol
cyproterone acetate
digitalis
digoxin
spironolactone (Aldactone)

Drugs That *May* Cause Menstrual Irregularities

alcohol—chronic high use
anabolic steroids
androgens
heroin—chronic use
hydromorphone (Dilaudid)—chronic use
meperidine (Demerol)—chronic use
methadone—chronic use
morphine—chronic use

Drugs That *May* Increase Fertility

bromocriptine (Parlodel)
caffeine
clomiphene (Clomid)

Drugs That *May* Decrease Fertility

alcohol—chronic high use
antineoplastics (cancer drugs)
cimetadine (Tagamet)
cyproterone acetate
heroin—chronic use
hydromorphone (Dilaudid)—chronic use
meperidine (Demerol)—chronic use
morphine—chronic use

REFERENCES

Chapter 1

1. Wedeck, H. E. *Dictionary of Aphrodisiacs*. New York: Philosophical Library, 1961.
2. Davenport, J. *Aphrodisiacs and Love Stimulants*. Ed. by A. H. Walton. New York: Lyle Stuart, 1966.
3. Wells, H., Fink, P. J., Rugar, K., Fisher, R. M., Woodruff, D. S., Herschmann, K. Sexual problems in general practice. *Med. Aspects Hum. Sex.* 6(9): 102–27, 1972.
4. Weiss, H. D. The physiology of human penile erection. *Ann. Intern. Med.* 76:793–99, 1972.
5. *Drugs of Abuse*. United States Department of Justice Drug Enforcement Administration. Washington, D.C. (n.d.).

Chapter 2

1. Wolf, S. The pharmacology of placebos. *Pharmacol. Rev.* 11:4, 1959.
2. Bush, P. J. The placebo effect. *J. Amer. Pharm. Assoc.* NS14:671–74, 1974.
3. Cousins, N. Mysterious placebo; how mind helps medicine work. *Saturday Review*, 1 Oct. 1977, pp. 9–16.
4. Skipper, J. et al. Children, stress and hospitalization. *J. Health Soc. Behav.* 9:275, 1968

Chapter 3

1. Gawin, F. H. Pharmacologic enhancement of the erotic: implications of an expanded definition of aphrodisiacs. *J. Sex Res.* 14:107–17, 1978.
2. Masters, R. E. L. *Forbidden Sexual Behavior and Morality*. New York: Lancer Books, 1969.
3. Davenport, J. *Aphrodisiacs and Love Stimulants*. Ed. by A. H. Walton. New York: Lyle Stuart, 1966.
4. Walton, A. H. *Stimulants for Love: A Quest for Virility*. London: Tandem Books, 1966.

5. Attributed to Paracelsus by Walton, ibid., p. 16.
6. Walton, op. cit., pp. 67, 68.
7. Ibid., p. 70.
8. Ibid., pp. 41, 42.
9. Attributed to Draper, *The Intellectual Development of Europe,* vol. II, pp. 235–56, by Walton, ibid., p. 52.
10. Walton, op. cit., pp. 73, 74.
11. Wells, B. *Psychedelic Drugs.* Baltimore: Penguin Books, 1974.
12. Wilson, R. A. *Sex and Drugs.* Chicago: Playboy Press, 1973.
13. Walton, op. cit., pp. 95, 96.
14. Guerra, F. Sex and drugs in the 16th century. *Brit. J. Addict.* 69:269–90, 1974.
15. Brecher, E. M. et al. *Licit and Illicit Drugs: The Consumers Union Report on Narcotics, Stimulants, Depressants, Inhalants, Hallucinogens, and Marijuana—Including Caffeine, Nicotine and Alcohol.* Boston: Little, Brown and Co., 1972.
16. Aldrich, M. R. Tantric cannabis use in India. *J. Psychedelic Drugs* 9:227–33, 1977.
17. Cohen, S. Cocaine. *J. Amer. Med. Assoc.* 231:74–75, 1975.
18. De Ropp, R. S. *Drugs and the Mind.* New York: St. Martin's Press, 1957.
19. Allegro, J. *The Sacred Mushroom and the Cross.* New York: Doubleday, 1970.
20. *High Times Encyclopedia of Recreational Drugs.* New York: Stonehill, 1978.
21. Guerra, F. *The Pre-Columbian Mind.* New York: Seminar Press, 1971.

Chapter 4

1. Schwartz, N. H., Robinson, B. D. Impotence due to methantheline bromid. *NY State J. Med.* 52:1530, 1952.
2. Bulpitt, C. J., Dollery, C.T. Side effects of hypotensive agents evaluated by a self-administered questionnaire. *Br. Med. J.* 3:485–90, 1973.
3. Zarren, H. S., Black, P.M. Unilateral gynecomastia and impotence during low-dose spironolactone administration in men. *Military Med.* 140:417–19, 1975.
4. Greenblatt, D. J., Koch-Weser, J. Gynecomastia and impotence complications of spironolactone therapy. *J. Amer. Med. Assoc.* 223:82, 1973.
5. Mills, L. C. Drug-induced impotence. *Amer. Fam. Pract.* 12:104–6 (Aug) 1975.
6. Laver, M. C. Sexual behaviour patterns in male hypertension. *Aust. N.Z. J. Med.* 4:29–31, 1974.
7. Oaks, W. W., Mayer, J. H. Sex and hypertension. *Med. Aspects Hum. Sex.* 6:128–37 (Nov) 1972.
8. Bauer, G. E., Hull, R. D., Stokes, G. S., Raftos, J. The reversibility of side effects of guanethidine therapy. *Med. J. Aust.* 1:930–33, 1973.
9. Seedat, V. K., Pillay, V. K. G. Further experiences with guanethidine—a clinical assessment of 103 patients. *S. Afr. Med. J.* 40:140–43, 1966.
10. *Diagnosis and Management of Hypertension.* National Heart, Lung and Blood Institute. DHEW Pub. No. (NIH) 79–1056, Washington, D.C.: U.S. Government Printing Office, 1979.

11. Wilson, G. M. Toxicity of hypotensive drugs. *Practitioner* 194:51–55, 1965.
12. Newman, R. J., Salerno, H. R. (Letter) Sexual dysfunction due to methyldopa. *Br. Med. J.* 4:106 (Oct) 1974.
13. Alexander, W. D., Evans, J. I. (Letter) Side effects of methyldopa. *Br. Med. J.* 2:501 (May) 1975.
14. Johnson, P., Kitchin, A. H., Lowther, C. P., Turner, R. W. D. Treatment of hypertension with methyldopa. *Br. Med. J.* 1:133–37, 1966.
15. Horwitz, D., Pettinger, W. A., Orvis, H. Effects of methyldopa in fifty hypertensive patients. *Clin. Pharmacol. Therap.* 8:224–34, 1967.
16. Kohn, R. M. Nocturnal orthostatic syncope in pargyline therapy. *J. Amer. Med. Assoc.* 187:229–30, 1964.
17. Raftos, J., Bauer, G. E., Lewis et al. Clonidine in the treatment of severe hypertension. *Med. J. Aust.* 1:786–93, 1973.
18. Kahn, A., Camel, G., Perry, H. M. Clonidine (Catapres) a new antihypertensive agent. *Curr. Ther. Res.* 12:10–18, 1970.
19. Clonidine (Catapres) and other drugs causing sexual dysfunction. *Med. Letter* 19:81 (7 Oct) 1977.
20. Greenberg, H. R. Inhibition of ejaculation by chlorpromazine. *J. Nerv. Ment. Dis.* 152:364–66, 1971.
21. Hughes, J. M. Failure to ejaculate with chlordiazepoxide. *Amer. J. Psychiatr.* 121:610–11, 1964.
22. Vinarova, E., Uhliro, Stika L., Vinar, O. Side effects of lithium administration. *Activ. Nerv. Suppl.* (Praha) 14:105–7, 1972.
23. Segraves, R. T. Pharmacological agents causing sexual dysfunction. *J. Sex. Marital Therap.* 3:157–76 (Fall) 1977.
24. Wieland, W. F., Yunger, M. Sexual effects and side effects of heroin and methadone. In Proceedings National Conference on Methadone Treatment, New York, Nov. 14–16, 1970. Washington, D.C.: U.S. Government Printing Office, 1970.
25. Shochet, B. R. Medical aspects of sexual dysfunction. *Drug Therapy.* (Jun) 1976, p. 37.
26. Gwin, R. D., O'Hara, G. L. Drug-induced changes in sexuality. *Apothecary* (Jan/Feb) 1978, pp. 11–60.
27. Ruskin, D. B., Goldner, R. D. Treatment of depressions in private practice with imipramine. *Dis. Nerv. Syst.* 20:391–99, 1959.
28. Wyatt, R. J., Fram, D. H., Buchbinder, R. et al. Treatment of intractable narcolepsy with a monoamine-oxidase inhibitor. *New Engl. J. Med.* 285:987–91, 1971.
29. Simpson, G. M., Blair, J. H., Amuso, D. Effect of anti-depressants on genito-urinary function. *Dis. Nerv. Syst.* 26:787–89, 1965.
30. Nininger, J. E. Inhibition of ejaculation by amitriptyline. *Amer. J. Psychiatr.* 135:750–51, 1978.
31. Bodnar, S., Catterill, T. B. Amitriptyline in emotional states associated with the climacteric. *Psychosomatics* 13:117–19, 1972.
32. Clarke, F. C. The treatment of depression in general practice. *S. Afr. Med. J.* 43:724–25, 1969.

33. Couper-Smartt, J. C., Rodman, R. A technique for surveying side-effects of tricyclic drugs with reference to reported sexual effects. *J. Int. Med. Res.* 473–76, 1973.
34. Greenberg, H. R. Erectile impotence during the course of Tofranil therapy. *Amer. J. Psychiatr.* 121:1021, 1965.
35. Kerr, M. M. Amitriptyline in emotional states at the menopause. *N.Z. Med. J.* 72:243–45, 1970.
36. Greenberg, H. M., Carrillo, C. Thioridazine-induced inhibition of masturbatory ejaculation in an adolescent. *Amer. J. Psychiatr.* 124:991–93, 1968.
37. Kotin, J., Wilbert, D. E., Verburg, D. et al. Thioridazine and sexual dysfunction. *Amer. J. Psychiatr.* 133:82–85, 1976.
38. Ditman, K. S. Inhibition of ejaculation by chlorprothixene. *Amer. J. Psychiatr.* 120:1004–5, 1964.
39. Greenblatt, D. J., Shader, R. I. Rational use of psychotropic drugs. III. Major tranquilizers. *Amer. J. Hosp. Pharm.* 31:1226–31, 1974.
40. Blair, J. H., Simpson, G. M. Effect of antipsychotic drugs on reproductive functions. *Dis. Nerv. Syst.* 27: 645–47, 1966.
41. Haider, I. Thioridazine and sexual dysfunctions. *Int. J. Neuropsychiatr.* 2:255–57, 1966.
42. Carlson, B. E., Sadoff, R. L. Thioridazine in schizophrenia. *J. Amer. Med. Assoc.* 217:1705, 1971.
43. Dorman, B. W., Schmidt, J. D. Association of priapism in phenothiazine therapy. *J. Urol.* 116:51–53, 1976.
44. Seeman, M. V., Denber, H. C. B., Goldner, F. Paradoxical effects of phenothiazines. *Psychiatr. Q.* 42:90–103, 1968.
45. Bartholomew, A. A. A long-acting phenothiazine as a possible agent to control deviant sexual behavior. *Amer. J. Psychiatr.* 124:917–23, 1968.
46. Berger, S. H. (Letter) Trifluoperazine and haloperidol: sources of ejaculatory pain? *Amer. J. Psychiatr.* 136:350, 1979.
47. Shader, R. I. Sexual dysfunction associated with mesoridazine besylate (Serentil). *Psychopharmacologia* 27:293–94, 1972.
48. Pinder, P. M., Brogden, R. N., Sawyer, P. R. et al. Fenfluramine: a review of its pharmacologic properties and therapeutic efficacy in obesity. *Drugs* 10:241–323, 1975.
49. Schneider, J., Kaffarnik, H. Impotence in patients treated with clofibrate. *Atheroscler.* 21:455, 1975.
50. McHaffie, D. J., Guz, A., Johnston, A. Impotence in patient on disopyramide. *Lancet*, 16 Apr. 1977, p. 859.
51. Van Thiel, D. H., Gavaler, J. S., Smith, W. I. et al. Hypothalamic-pituitary-gonadal dysfunction in men using cimetadine. *New Engl. J. Med.* 300:1012–15, 1979.
52. Siris, E. S., Leventhal, B. G., Vaitukaitis, J. L. Effects of childhood leukemia and chemotherapy on puberty and reproductive function in girls. *New Engl. J. Med.* 294:1143–46, 1976.
53. Sherins, R. J., DeVita, V. T., Jr. Effect of drug treatment for lymphoma on male reproductive capacity. Studies of men in remission after therapy. *Ann. Intern. Med.* 79:216–20, 1973.

Chapter 5

1. Herzberg, B. N., Draper, K. C., Johnson, A. L. et al. Oral contraceptives, depression, and libido. *Br. Med. J.* 3(773):495–500, 1971.
2. Cullberg, J. Mood changes and menstrual symptoms with different gestagen/estrogen combinations. A double blind comparison with a placebo. *Acta Psychiatr. Scand. Suppl.* 236:1–86, 1972.
3. O'Dwyer, W. F. (Letter) Oral contraceptives, depression, and libido. *Br. Med. J.* 3(776):702, 1971.
4. Dennerstein, L., Burrows, G. Oral contraception and sexuality. *Med. J. Aust.* 1:796–98, 1976.
5. Grant, E. C. Metabolic effects of oral contraceptives. *Br. Med. J.* 3(719):402–3, 1970.
6. Rodgers, D. A., Ziegler, F. J. Changes in sexual behavior consequent to use of noncoital procedures of contraception. *Psychosom. Med.* 30:495–505, 1968.
7. McCauley, E., Ehrhardt, A. A. Female sexual response. Hormonal and behavioral interactions. *Primary Care* 3:455–76, 1976.
8. Hall, D. M., Hall, S. M. Side effects of the pill. *Br. Med. J.* 3(871):105, 1973.
9. Gambrell, R. D., Jr., Bernard, D. M., Sanders, B. T. et al. Changes in sexual drives of patients on oral contraceptives. *J. Reprod. Med.* 17(3):165–71, 1976.
10. Udry, J. R., Morris, N. M., Waller, L. Effect of contraceptive pills on sexual activity in the luteal phase of the human menstrual cycle. *Arch. Sex. Behav.* 2:205–14, 1973.
11. Adams, D. B., Gold, A. R., Burt, A. D. Rise in female-initiated sexual activity at ovulation and its suppression by oral contraceptives. *New Engl. J. Med.* 299:1145–50, 1978.
12. Carey, H. M. Principles of oral contraception. 2. Side effects of oral contraceptives. *Med. J. Aust.* 2:1242, 1971.

Chapter 6

1. Dille, J. M. Aphrodisiacs: a project in search of a sponsor. *Psychopharmacol. Bull.* 11(3):43–44, 1975.
2. Gawin, F. H. Pharmacologic enhancement of the erotic: implications of an expanded definition of aphrodisiacs. *J. Sex. Res.* 14(2):107–17, 1978.
3. Frank, E., Anderson, C., Rubinstein, D. Frequency of sexual dysfunction in "normal" couples. *New Engl. J. Med.* 299:111–15, 1978.
4. Lidberg, L. Social and psychiatric aspects of impotence and premature ejaculation. *Arch. Sex. Behav.* 2:135–46, 1972.
5. Goldstein, A., Hansteen, R. W. Evidence against involvement of endorphins in sexual arousal and orgasm in man. *Arch. Gen. Psychiatr.* 34:1179–80, 1977.
6. de Kruif, P. *The Male Hormone.* New York: Harcourt Brace, 1945.
7. Walton, A. H. *Stimulants for Love: A Quest for Virility.* London: Tandem Books, 1966.
8. Greenblatt, R. B. The psychogenic and endocrine aspects of sexual behavior. *J. Am. Geriatr. Soc.* 22:393–96, 1974.

9. Jick, H., Watkins, R. N., Hunter, F. R. et al. Replacement estrogens and endometrial cancer. *New Engl. J. Med.* 300:218–22, 1979.
10. Kerr, M. M. Amitriptyline in emotional states at the menopause. *N.Z. Med. J.* 72:243–45, 1970.
11. Bodnar, S., Catterill, T. B. Amitriptyline in emotional states associated with the climacteric. *Psychosomatics* 13:117–19, 1972.
12. Kennedy, B. J. Effect of massive doses of sex hormones on libido. *Med. Aspects Hum. Sex.* 7(3):67, 70–71, 74, 1973.
13. Stearns, E. L., MacDonnell, J. A., Kaufman, B. J. et al. Declining testicular function with age. Hormonal and clinical correlates. *Am. J. Med.* 57:761–66, 1974.
14. Reiter, T. Testosterone implantation: A clinical study of 240 implantations in aging males. *J. Am. Geriatr. Soc.* 11:540–50, 1963.
15. Panel Discussion II. In Oaks, W. W., Melchiode, G. A., and Fisher, I. (eds) *Sex and the Life Cycle.* New York: Grune and Stratton, 1976.
16. Hoffer, A., Osmond, H. *The Hallucinogens.* New York: Academic Press, 1967.
17. Sicuteri, F. Serotonin and sex in man. *Pharmacol. Res. Commun.* 6:403–11, 1974.
18. Egan, G. P., Hammad, G. E. (Letter) Sexual disinhibition with l-tryptophan. *Br. Med. J.* 2(6037):701, 1976.
19. Hullin, R. P., Jerram, T. (Letter) Sexual disinhibition with l-tryptophan. *Br. Med. J.* 2(6042):1010, 1976.
20. Broadhurst, A. D., Rao, B. (Letter) L-tryptophan and sexual behavior. *Br. Med. J.* 1(6052)51–52, 1977.
21. Mauss, J., Borsch, G., Bormacher, K. et al. Effect of long-term testosterone oenanthate administration on male reproductive function: clinical evaluation, serum FSH, LH, Testosterone, and seminal fluid analyses in normal men. *Acta Endocrinol.* (KBH) 78:373–78, 1975.
22. Brown, W. A., Monti, P. M., Corriveau, D. P. Serum testosterone and sexual activity and interest in man. *Arch. Sex. Behav.* 7:157–73, 1978.
23. Friedman, R. C., Dyrenfurth, I., Linkie, D. et al. Hormones and sexual orientation in men. *Amer. J. Psychiatr.* 134:571–72, 1977.
24. Werff Ten Bosch, J. J. Van. Manipulation of sexual behaviour by anti-androgens. *Psychiatr. Neurol. Neurochir.* 76:147–49, 1973.
25. Persky, H., Lief, H. I., Strauss, D. et al. Plasma testosterone level and sexual behavior of couples. *Arch. Sex. Behav.* 7:157–73, 1978.
26. Bowers, M. B., Jr., Van Woert, M., Davis, L. Sexual behavior during L-dopa treatment for Parkinsonism. *Amer. J. Psychiatr.* 127:1691–93, 1971.
27. Greenburg, J. Side effects of L-dopa treatment. *Pa. Med.* 74(4):55–56, 1971.
28. Benkert, O. Pharmacological experiments to stimulate human sexual behavior. In Ban, T. A. et al., *Psychopharmacology, Sexual Disorders and Drug Abuse.* Amsterdam: North Holland, 1973.
29. Markham, C. H., Treciokas, L. J., Diamond, S. G. Parkinson's disease and levodopa. A five-year follow-up and review. *West. J. Med.* 121(3):188–206, 1974.

30. Angrist, B., Gershon, S. Clinical effects of amphetamine and L-dopa on sexuality and aggression. *Compr. Psychiatr.* 17:715–22, 1976.
31. Zarren, H. S., Black, P. M. Unilateral gynecomastia and impotence during low-dose spironolactone administration in men. *Military Med.* 140:417–19, 1975.
32. Shapiro, S. K. Hypersexual behavior complicating levodopa (L-dopa) therapy. *Minn. Med.* 56(1):58–59, 1973.
33. Friesen, L. V. (Letter) Aphrodisia with mazindol. *Lancet* 2(7992):974, 1976.
34. Rowan, R. L., Howley, T. F. Ejaculatory sterility. *Fertil. Steril.* 16:768–70, 1965.
35. Hollister, L. E. Drugs and sexual behavior in man. *Psychopharmacol. Bull.* 11(3):44, 1975.
36. Louria, D. B. Some aspects of the current drug scene with emphasis on drugs in use by adolescents. *Pediatr.* 42:904–11, 1968.
37. Stohs, S. J. Drugs and sexual function. *U.S. Pharmacist*, Nov./Dec. 1978, pp. 51–66.
38. Saidi, K., Wen, R. V., Sharif, F. Bromocriptine for male infertility. *Lancet* 29:250–51, 1977.
39. Sy, L. V., Fang, V. S. Restoration of plasma testosterone levels in uremic men with clomiphene citrate. *J. Clin. Endocrin.* 43:1370–77, 1976.
40. Miller, W. W., Jr. Afrodex in the treatment of male impotence: a double-blind cross-over study. *Curr. Ther. Res.* 10:354–59, 1968.
41. Sobotka, J. J. An evaluation of Afrodex in the management of male impotency: a double-blind cross-over study. *Curr. Ther. Res.* 11(2):87–94, 1969.
42. Salomon, C., Maitr, A., Pelat, J. et al. Clinical study of Sargenor in secondary sexual impotence. *Psychol. Med.* 4:541–59, 1972.
43. Goodman, L. S., Gilman, A. *The Pharmacologic Principles of Therapeutics.* New York: Macmillan, 1970.
44. Simpson, G. M., Blair, J. H., Amuso, D. Effect of anti-depressants on genito-urinary function. *Dis. Nerv. Syst.* 26:787–89, 1965.

Chapter 7

1. Harcus, A. W. Effect of oral cyproterone acetate on urinary FSH and LH levels in males being treated for hypersexuality. *J. Reprod. Fertil.* 33:356–57, 1973.
2. Boas, C., Van, E. Cyproterone acetate in sexualogical outpatient practice. *Psychiatr. Neurol. Neurochir.* 76:151–54, 1973.
3. Werff Ten Bosch, J. J. Van. Manipulation of sexual behaviour by anti-androgens. *Psychiatr. Neurol. Neurochir.* 76:147–49, 1973.
4. Bartholomew, A. A. A long-acting phenothiazine as a possible agent to control deviant sexual behavior. *Amer. J. Psychiatr.* 124:917–23, 1968.
5. Simpson, G. M., Blair, J. H., Amuso, D. Effect of anti-depressants on genito-urinary function. *Dis. Nerv. Syst.* 26:787–89, 1965.

Chapter 8

1. *Vitamin E Questions and Answers*. Minneapolis, Minn.: Henkel Corp., 1975.
2. Vara, P. The climacterium from the gynaecologist's point of view. *Acta Obstet. Gynecol. Scand.* Suppl. 1 P. Suppl. 1:43–55, 1970.
3. Callender, S. T. Iron absorption. *Biomembranes* 48:761–91, 1974.
4. Larsson-Cohn, U. Oral contraceptives and vitamins: a review. *Amer. J. Obstet. Gynecol.* 121:84–90, 1975.
5. Kales, J., Kales, A. Are over-the-counter sleep medications effective? *Curr. Ther. Res.* 13:143–51, 1971.
6. Sicuteri, F. Serotonin and sex in man. *Pharmacol. Res. Commun.* 6:403–11, 1974.
7. Colvin, C. L-tryptophan for treatment of depression? *Amer. Pharm.* NS19 9:24–25, 1979.
8. Schoenfeld, C., Amelar, R. D., Dubin, L. Stimulation of ejaculated human spermatozoa by caffeine. A preliminary report. *Fertil. Steril.* 24:772–75, 1973.
9. Siegel, R. K. Ginseng abuse syndrome. *J. Amer. Med. Assoc.* 241:1614–15, 1979.

Chapter 9

1. Freedman, A. M. Drugs and sexual behavior. *Med. Aspects Hum. Sex.* 1(3):25–31, 1967.
2. Rubin, H. B., Henson, D. E. Effects of alcohol on male sexual responding. *Psychopharmacologia* 47:123–34, 1976.
3. Wilson, G. T., Lawson, D. M. Effects of alcohol on sexual arousal in women. *J. Abnormal Psychol.* 85:489–97, 1976.
4. Athanasiou, R., Shaver, P., Tavris, C. Sex. *Psychol. Today* 4:37–52, July 1970.
5. Gay, G. R., Newmeyer, J. A., Elion, R. A. et al. Drug/sex practice in the Haight-Ashbury or "the sensuous hippie." Proc. 37th Annual Scientific Meeting, Committee on Problems of Drug Dependence. Washington, D.C., May 19–21, 1975.
6. Briddell, D. W., Rimm, D. C., Caddy, G. R. et al. Effects of alcohol and cognitive set on sexual arousal to deviant stimuli. *J. Abnormal Psychol.* 87:418–30, 1978.
7. Wilson, G. T., Lawson, D. M. Expectancies, alcohol, and sexual arousal in women. *J. Abnormal Psychol.* 87:358–67, 1978.
8. Abrams, D. B., Wilson, G. T. Effects of alcohol on social anxiety in women: cognitive versus physiologic processes. *J. Abnormal Psychol.* 88:161–73, 1979.
9. Masters, W. H., Johnson, V. E. *Human Sexual Inadequacy*. Boston: Little, Brown, 1970.
10. *Alcohol and Health: Report from the Secretary of Health, Education and Welfare.* New York: Charles Scribner, 1973.
11. Corrigan, E. M. Women and problem drinking: notes on beliefs and facts. *Addict. Dis.* 1:215–22, 1974.

12. Van Thiel, D. H., Lester, R. (Editorial) Sex and alcohol, a second peek. *New Engl. J. Med.* 296:835–36, 1976.
13. Lemere, F., Smith, J. W. Alcohol-induced sexual impotence. *Amer. J. Psychiatr.* 130:212–13, 1973.
14. Levine, J. The sexual adjustment of alcoholics. *Q. J. Stud. Alcohol* 16:675–80, 1955.
15. Whalley, L. J. Sexual adjustment of male alcoholics. *Acta Psychiatr. Scand.* 58:281–98, 1978.
16. Wilson, G. T., Sawson, D. M., Abrams, D. B. Effects of alcohol on sexual arousal in male alcoholics. *J. Abnormal Psychol.* 87:609–16, 1978.
17. Saghir, M. T. et al. Homosexuality. IV. Psychiatric disorders and disability in the female homosexual. *Amer. J. Psychiatr.* 127:147–54, 1970.
18. Mello, N. K. Alcoholism and the behavioral pharmacology of alcohol: 1967–1977. In Lipton, M. A., DiMascio, A., and Killan, K. F. (eds) *Psychopharmacology: A Generation of Progress.* New York: Raven Press, 1978.
19. Gordon, G. G., Altman, K., Sauthren, A. L. et al. Effect of alcohol (ethanol) administration on sex-hormone metabolism in normal men. *New Engl. J. Med.* 295:793–800, 1976.
20. Mendelson, J. H., et al. Effects of alcohol on pituitary-gonadal hormones, sexual function and aggression in human males. In Lipton, M. A., DiMascio, A., and Killan, K. F. (eds), op. cit.
21. Manheimer, D. I., Mellinger, G. D., Balter, M. B. Marijuana use among urban adults. *Science* 166:1544–45, 1969.
22. Zuckker, R. A. Sex-role identity patterns and drinking behavior of adolescents. *Q. J. Stud. Alcohol* 29:868–84, 1968.
23. Rada, R. T. Alcoholism and forcible rape. *Amer. J. Psychiatr.* 132:444–46, 1975.

Chapter 10

1. Manheimer, D. I., Mellinger, G. D., Balter, M. B. Marijuana use among urban adults. *Science* 166:1544–45, 1969.
2. Blum, S. Marijuana clouds the generation gap. *The New York Times Magazine,* 23 Aug. 1970, p. 28.
3. Wells, B. *Psychedelic Drugs.* Baltimore: Penguin Books, 1974.
4. Goode, E. *The Marijuana Smokers.* New York: Basic Books, 1970.
5. Tart, C. T. *On Being Stoned. A Psychological Study of Marijuana Intoxication.* Palo Alto, Calif.: Science and Behavior Books, 1971.
6. Fort, J. Youth: drugs, sex and life. *Curr. Prob. Pediatr.* 6(11):1–42, 1976.
7. Zinberg, N. E., Weil, A. T. A comparison of marijuana users and non-users. *Nature* 226(241):119–23, 1970.
8. Dowley, H. H., Winstead, D. K., Baxter, A. S. et al. An attitude survey of the effects of marijuana on sexual enjoyment. *J. Clin. Psychol.* 35: 212–17, 1979.
9. Gay, G. R., Newmeyer, J. A., Elion, R. A. et al. Drug/sex practice in the Haight-Ashbury or "the sensuous hippie." Proc. 37th Annual Scientific

Meeting Committee on Problems of Drug Dependence. Washington, D.C., May 19–21, 1975.
10. Gay, G. R., Sheppard, C. W. Sex in the "drug culture." *Med. Aspects Hum. Sex.* 6:28–50 (Oct) 1972.
11. Lewis, B. *The Sexual Power of Marijuana.* New York: Peter H. Wyden, 1970.
12. Snyder, S. H. *Uses of Marijuana.* New York: Oxford University Press, 1971.
13. Piemme, T. E. Sex and illicit drugs. *Med. Aspects Hum. Sex.* 10:85–86 (Jan) 1976.
14. Gawin, F. H. Pharmacologic enhancement of the erotic: implications of an expanded definition of aphrodisiacs. *J. Sex. Res.* 14(2):107–17, 1978.
15. Ebin, D. (ed). *The Drug Experience. First Person Accounts of Addicts, Writers, Scientists and Others.* New York: Orion Press, 1961.
16. Kolodny, R. C. et al. Depression of plasma testosterone levels after chronic intensive marijuana use. *New Engl. J. Med.* 290:872–74, 1974.
17. Chauson, A. M., Saper, C. B. (Letter) Marijuana and sex. *New Engl. J. Med.* 291:308–10, 1974.
18. Mendelson, J. H. et al. Plasma testosterone levels before, during and after chronic marijuana smoking. *New Engl. J. Med.* 291:1051–55, 1974.
19. Huang, H. F. S., Nahas, C. G., Hembree, W. C. Morphological changes of spermatozoa during marijuana induced depression of human spermatogenesis. *Fed. Proc.* 37:739, 1978.
20. *High Times Encyclopedia of Recreational Drugs.* New York: Stonehill, 1978.
21. Brecher, E. M. et al. *Licit and Illicit Drugs: The Consumers Union Report on Narcotics, Stimulants, Depressants, Inhalants, Hallucinogens, and Marijuana—Including Caffeine, Nicotine and Alcohol.* Boston: Little, Brown and Co., 1972.
22. Schofield, M. *The Strange Case of Pot.* Baltimore: Penguin Books, 1971.

Chapter 11

1. Martin, R. T. The role of coca in the history, religion, and medicine of South American Indians. *Economic Botany* 24:422–38, 1970.
2. Burroughs, W. *Naked Lunch.* New York: Grove Press, 1959.
3. Taylor, N. The pleasant assassin: the story of marijuana. In D. Solomon (ed) *The Marijuana Papers.* New York: Panther, 1969.
4. Wells, B. *Psychedelic Drugs.* Baltimore: Penguin Books, 1974.
5. Ellinwood, E. H., Jr., Rockwell, W. J. K. Effect of drug use on sexual behavior. *Med. Aspects Hum. Sex.* 9:10–32 (Mar) 1975.
6. Hollister, L. E. Drugs and sex and behavior in man. *Psychopharmacol. Bull.* 11(3):44, 1975.
7. Louria, D. B. Some aspects of the current drug scene with emphasis on drugs in use by adolescents. *Pediatr.* 42:904–11, 1968.
8. Freedman, A. M. Drugs and sexual behavior. *Med. Aspects Hum. Sex.* 1:25–31 (Nov) 1967.
9. Angrist, B., Gershon, S. Clinical effects of amphetamine and L-dopa on sexuality and aggression. *Compr. Psychiatr.* 17:715–22, 1976.
10. Greaves, G. Sexual disturbances among chronic amphetamine users. *J. Nerv. Ment. Dis.* 155:363–65, 1972.

11. Nail, R. L., Gunderson, E. F., Kolb, D. Motives for drug use among light and heavy users. *J. Nerv. Ment. Dis.* 159:131–36, 1974.
12. Gay, G. R., Newmeyer, J. A., Elion, R. A. et al. Drug/sex practice in the Haight/Ashbury or "the sensuous hippie." Proc. 37th Annual Scientific Meeting Committee on Problems of Drug Dependence. Washington, D.C., May 19–21, 1975.
13. Bell, D. S. The precipitants of amphetamine addiction. *Br. J. Psychiatr.* 119:171–77, 1971.
14. Gay, G. R., Sheppard, C. W. Sex in the "drug culture." *Med. Aspects Hum. Sex.* 6:28–50 (Oct) 1972.
15. Dahlberg, C. C. Sexual behavior in the drug culture. *Med. Aspects Hum. Sex.* 5:64–71 (Apr) 1971.
16. Crowley, A. *Diary of a Drug Fiend.* New York: E. P. Dutton and Co., 1922.
17. Cohen, H. *The Amphetamine Manifesto.* New York: Olympia Press, 1972.
18. *High Times Encyclopedia of Recreational Drugs.* New York: Stonehill, 1978.
19. Lowry, T. P. The volatile nitrites as sexual drugs: a user survey. *J. Sex. Educ. Therap.* 1:8–10, 1979.
20. Lowry, T. P. Amyl nitrite: an old high comes back to visit. *Behavioral Med.* 6:19–21, 1979.
21. Everett, G. Amyl nitrite ("poppers") as an aphrodisiac. In Sandler, M., and Gessa, G. L. (eds) *Sexual Behavior—Pharmacology and Biochemistry.* New York: Raven Press, 1975.
22. Brecher, E. M. et al. *Licit and Illicit Drugs: The Consumers Union Report on Narcotics, Stimulants, Depressants, Inhalants, Hallucinogens, and Marijuana—Including Caffeine, Nicotine and Alcohol.* Boston: Little, Brown and Co., 1972.

Chapter 12

1. Brecher, E. M. et al. *Licit and Illicit Drugs: The Consumers Union Report on Narcotics, Stimulants, Depressants, Inhalants, Hallucinogens, and Marijuana—Including Caffeine, Nicotine and Alcohol.* Boston: Little, Brown and Co., 1972.
2. Kramer, S. (Letter) Methaqualone as aphrodisiac. *Amer. J. Psychiatr.* 130:1044, 1973.
3. Cohen, S. Hearings Before the Subcommittee to Investigate Juvenile Delinquency of the Committee on the Judiciary, U.S. Senate, 91st Congress, Sept. 17, 1969. Washington, D.C.: U.S. Government Printing Office, p. 293.
4. Nail, R. L., Gunderson, E. F., Kolb, D. Motives for drug use among light and heavy users. *J. Nerv. Ment. Dis.* 159:131–36, 1974.
5. Freedman, A. M. Drugs and sexual behavior. *Med. Aspect Hum. Sex.* 1(3):25–31 (Nov) 1967.
6. Parr, D. Sexual aspects of drug abuse in narcotic addicts. *Brit. J. Addict.* 71:261–68, 1976.
7. Gay, G. R., Newmeyer, J. A., Elion, R. A. et al. Drug/sex practice in the Haight-Ashbury or "the sensuous hippie." Proc. 37th Annual Scientific Meeting Committee on Problems of Drug Dependence. Washington, D.C. May 19–21, 1975, pp. 1080–1101.

8. Whitlock, F. A. The syndrome of barbiturate dependence. *Med. J. Aust.* 2:391–96, 1970.
9. Ungerer, J. C., Harford, R. J., Brown, F. L. et al. Sex guilt and preferences for illegal drugs among drug abusers. *J. Clin. Psychol.* 32:891–95, 1976.
10. Gay, G. R., Sheppard, C. W. Sex in the "drug culture." *Med. Aspects Hum. Sex.* 6:28–50 (Oct) 1972.
11. Inaba, D. S., Gay, G. R. et al. Methaqualone abuse? "luding out." *J. Amer. Med. Assoc.* 224:1505–9, 1973.
12. *High Times Encyclopedia of Recreational Drugs.* New York: Stonehill, 1978.
13. Piemme, T. E. Sex and illicit drugs. *Med. Aspects. Hum. Sex.* 10:85–86 (Jan) 1976.
14. Uyeno, E. T. Effects of Δ^9-tetrahydrocannabinol and 2,5 dimethoxy—4-methylamphetamine on rat sexual dominance behavior. *Proc. West. Pharmacol. Soc.* 19:369–72, 1976.
15. Kochansky, G. E., Hemenway, T. S., Salzman, C. et al. Methaqualone abusers: a preliminary survey of college students. *Dis. Nerv. Syst.* 36:348–51, 1975.
16. Hollister, L. E. Drugs and sexual behavior in man. *Life Sci.* 17:661–67, 1975.
17. Cocteau, J. *Opium: The Diary of a Cure.* London: New English Library, 1972.
18. DeLeon, G., Wexler, H. K. Heroin addiction: its relation to sexual behavior and sexual experience. *J. Abnormal Psychol.* 81:36–38, 1973.
19. Cicero, T. J., Bell, R. D., Wiest, W. G. et al. The effects of heroin and methadone use on male sexual function. Proc. 37th Annual Scientific Meeting Committee on Problems of Drug Dependence. Washington, D.C., May 19–21, 1975, pp. 361–72.
20. Mills, L. C. Drug-induced impotence. *Amer. Fam. Phys.* 12:104–6 (Aug) 1975.
21. Gossop, M. R. Addiction to narcotics: a brief review of the "junkie" literature. *Brit. J. Addict.* 71:192–95, 1976.
22. Weir, J. G. The pregnant narcotic addict: a psychiatrist's impression. *Proc. R. Soc. Med.* 65:869–70, 1972.
23. Burroughs, W. *Junkie.* New York: Ace Books, 1953.
24. Cushman, P., Jr. Sexual behavior in heroin addiction and methadone maintenance. Correlation with plasma lutenizing hormone. *N.Y. State J. Med.* 72:1261–65, 1972.
25. Mintz, J., O'Hara, K., O'Brien, C. P. et al. Sexual problems of heroin addicts. *Arch. Gen. Psychiatr.* 31:700–3, 1974.
26. Cocteau, J. *Opium: Diary of a Cure.* London: New English Library, 1972.

Chapter 13

1. Fort, J. Youth: drugs, sex and life. *Curr. Prob. Pediatr.* 6(11):1–42 1976.
2. Wells, B. *Psychedelic Drugs.* Baltimore: Penguin Books, 1974.
3. Leary, T. 1966 Playboy Interview, HMH Publishing Co. Reprinted in Leary, *Politics of Ecstasy.* New York: Putnam, 1970.
4. Dahlberg, C. C. Sexual behavior in the drug culture. *Med. Aspects Hum. Sex.* 5:64–71 (Apr) 1971.

5. Gay, G. R., Sheppard, C. W. Sex in the "drug culture." *Med. Aspects Hum. Sex.* 6:28–50 (Oct) 1972.
6. Gay, G. R., Newmeyer, J. A., Elion, R. A. et al. Drug/sex practice in the Haight-Ashbury or "the sensuous hippie." Proc. 37th Annual Scientific Meeting Committee on Problems of Drug Dependence. Washington, D.C., May 19–21, 1975, pp. 1080–1101.
7. Freedman, A. M. Drugs and sexual behavior. *Med. Aspects Hum. Sex.* 1:25–31 (Nov) 1967.
8. Canadian Government Commission of Inquiry. *The Non-Medical Use of Drugs: Interim Report.* Baltimore: Penguin Books, 1971.
9. Stafford, P. G., Golightly, B. H. *LSD: The Problem-Solving Psychedelic.* Award Books, 1967.
10. Gioscia, V. LSD subcultures: acidoxy versus orthodoxy. *Amer. J. Orthopsychiatr.* 39:428–29, 1969.
11. Aronson, B., Osmond, H. *Psychedelics.* Garden City, N.Y.: Doubleday, 1970.
12. Fort, J. *The Pleasure Seekers.* N.Y.: Bobbs-Merrill, 1969.
13. Brecher, E. M. et al. *Licit and Illicit Drugs: The Consumers Union Report on Narcotics, Stimulants, Depressants, Inhalants, Hallucinogens, and Marijuana—Including Caffeine, Nicotine, and Alcohol.* Boston: Little, Brown and Co., 1972.
14. Cohen, S. Lysergic acid diethylamide: side effects and complications. *J. Nerv. Ment. Dis.* 130:30–40, 1960.
15. Chessick, R., Haertzen, C., Wikler, H. Tolerance to LSD-25 in schizophrenic subjects. *Arch. Gen. Psychiatr.* 10:653, 1964.
16. Piemme, T. E. Sex and illicit drugs. *Med. Aspects Hum. Sex.* 10:85–86 (Jan) 1976.
17. *High Times Encyclopedia of Recreational Drugs.* N.Y.: Stonehill, 1978.
18. Gawin, F. H. Pharmacologic enhancement of the erotic: implications of an expanded definition of aphrodisiacs. *J. Sex. Res.* 14(2):107–17, 1978.

Chapter 14

1. Udry, J. R., Morris, N. M., Waller, L. Effect of contraceptive pills on sexual activity in the luteal phase of the human menstrual cycle. *Arch. Sex. Behav.* 2:205–14, 1973.
2. Ellis, A. *The Essence of Beauty—A History of Scent.* London: Secker and Warburg, 1960.
3. Fisher, A. A. Allergic reaction to feminine hygiene sprays. *Arch. Dermatol.* 108:801–2, 1973.
4. Crowley, S., Murphy, C. T., White, P. M. et al. The flora of the perivaginal area: the normal flora and the effect of a deodorant spray. *J. Appl. Bacteriol.* 37:385–92, 1974.
5. Noble, W. C. The aerobic flora of the perivaginal area: its relation to contraception and deodorant sprays. *J. Appl. Bacteriol.* 41:137–42, 1976.
6. Doty, R. L., Ford, M., Preti, G. et al. Changes in the intensity and pleasantness of human vaginal odors during the menstrual cycle. *Science* 190:1316–18, 1975.
7. Freed, D. I. J., Banks, A. J., Longson, D., Burley, D. M. Anabolic steroids in

athletics: crossover double-blind trial on weightlifters. *Br. Med. J.* 2(5959):-471–73, 1975.

8. Ward, P. The effect of an anabolic steroid on strength and lean body mass. *Med. Sci. Sports* 5(4):277–32, 1973.
9. McDonough, P. G. Sexual precocity. *Clin. Obstet. Gynecol.* 14:1037–56, 1971.
10. Bryan, G. T. Normal and abnormal sexual maturation. *Amer. Fam. Physician* 9(6):123–35, 1974.
11. Zachmann, M., Prader, A. Anabolic and androgenic effect of testosterone in sexually immature boys and its dependency on growth hormone. *J. Clin. Endocrinol. Metab.* 30:85–95, 1970.
12. Kligman, A., Leyden, J. Acne vulgaris a treatable disease. *Postgrad. Med.* 55:99–105, 1974.
13. Rigg, L. A., Hermann, H. Absorption of estrogens from vaginal creams. *New Engl. J. Med.* 298:195–97, 1978.
14. Quigley, M. M., Hammond, C. B. Estrogen-replacement therapy—help or hazard? *New Engl. J. Med.* 301:646–48, 1979.
15. Tyson, J. E., Zacur, H. A. Diagnosis and treatment of abnormal lactation. *Clin. Obstet. Gynecol.* 18:65–93, 1975.

Chapter 15

1. Berman, A., Francke, D. E. Medicines and drug use tomorrow, some biological and social considerations. In Wertheimer, A. I. and Bush, P. J. (eds) *Perspectives on Medicines in Society.* Hamilton, Ill.: Drug Intelligence Publications, 1977.
2. Bell, D. S. The precipitants of amphetamine addiction. *Br. J. Psychiatr.* 119:171–77, 1971.
3. Kent, S. On the trail of an authentic aphrodisiac. *Geriatrics* 30: 96–99 (Dec) 1975.
4. Lamy, P. P. Influence of gender on drug therapy. *Prof. Pharm.* 4(4):3, 1977.

Index